A Sequence for Academic Writing

A Sequence for Academic Writing

THIRD EDITION

Laurence Behrens
University of California, Santa Barbara

Leonard J. Rosen
Bentley College

PEARSON
Longman

New York • San Francisco • Boston
London • Toronto • Sydney • Tokyo • Singapore • Madrid
Mexico City • Munich • Paris • Cape Town • Hong Kong • Montreal

Executive Editor: Lynn M. Huddon
Senior Supplements Editor: Donna Campion
Media Supplements Editor: Jenna Egan
Senior Marketing Manager: Sandra McGuire
Production Manager: Eric Jorgensen
Project Coordination, Text Design, and Electronic Page Makeup: Pre-Press Co., Inc.
Cover Design Manager: Wendy Ann Fredericks
Cover Designer: Nancy Sacks
Cover Art: Getty Images/The Bridgeman Art Library
Photo Researcher: Chrissy McIntyre
Manufacturing Manager: Mary Fischer
Printer and Binder: RR Donnelley & Sons Company
Cover Printer: Coral Graphic Services

For permission to use copyrighted material, grateful acknowledgment is made
to the copyright holders on pages 357–62, which are hereby made part of this
copyright page.

Library of Congress Cataloging-in-Publication Data

Behrens, Laurence.
    A sequence for academic writing / Laurence Behrens, Leonard J. Rosen. -- 3rd ed.
      p. cm.
    Includes bibliographical references and index.
    ISBN 0-321-45681-5
      1. English language--Rhetoric. 2. Academic writing. I. Rosen, Leonard J. II. Title.
  PE1408.B46926 2007
  808'.042--dc22

                                                                        2006048471

Please visit us at www.ablongman.com

ISBN 0-321-45681-5

2 3 4 5 6 7 8 9 10 — DOC — 09 08 07

DETAILED CONTENTS

Chapter 2—Critical Reading and Critique   53

Chapter 5—Analysis   **183**

A Sequence for Academic Writing evolved out of our other text, *Writing and Reading Across the Curriculum (WRAC)*. Through nine editions over the last 25 years, *WRAC* has helped hundreds of thousands of students prepare for the writing done well beyond the freshman composition course. *WRAC* features a rhetoric in which students are introduced to the core skills of summary, critique, synthesis, and analysis, and a reader that presents readings in the disciplines to which students can apply the skills learned in the earlier chapters. Because the skills of summary, critique, synthesis, and analysis are so central to academic thinking and writing, many instructors—both those teaching writing across the curriculum and those using other approaches to composition instruction—have found *WRAC* a highly useful introduction to college-level writing. We therefore adapted the rhetoric portion of *WRAC*, creating a separate book that instructors can use, apart from any additional reading content they chose to incorporate in their writing courses. *A Sequence for Academic Writing* is both an adaptation of *WRAC* and an expansion: it includes a new "case study" chapter, as well as additional writing assignments not found in the parent text.

We proceed through a sequence from Summary, Paraphrase, and Quotation to Critical Reading and Critique, to Explanatory Synthesis and Argument Synthesis to Analysis. Students will find in Chapter 6 a discussion of the writing process that is reinforced throughout the text. Locating, Mining, and Citing Sources introduces students to the tools and techniques they will need to apply skills learned earlier to sources they gather themselves when conducting research. The book ends with two new chapters, A Case Study in Academic Writing and Practicing Academic Writing (see A Note on the Third Edition). We make a special effort in all chapters to address the issue of plagiarism: We offer techniques for steering well clear of the problem, at the same time encouraging students to live up to the highest ethical standards.

Key features in *A Sequence for Academic Writing* include *boxes,* which sum up important concepts in each chapter; brief writing *exercises,* which prompt individual and group activities; *writing assignments,* which encourage students to practice the skills they learn in each chapter; and *model papers,* which provide example responses to writing assignments discussed in the text. An Instructor's Manual and Companion Web site provide further resources for teaching with this text.

While we are keenly aware of the overlapping nature of the skills on which we focus, and while we could endlessly debate an appropriate order in which to cover these skills, a book is necessarily linear. We have chosen the sequence that makes the most sense to us, though individual instructors may choose to cover these skills in their own sequence. Teachers should feel perfectly free to use these chapters in whatever order they feel is most useful to their individual aims and philosophies. Understanding the material in a later chapter does not, in most cases, depend on students having read material in the earlier chapters.

A NOTE ON THE THIRD EDITION

The third edition of *Sequence for Academic Writing* represents a significant reorganization and expansion of the previous editions. We now divide the book into three parts: Structures, Strategies, and (new to this edition) Applications. The five structures chapters (1–5) cover summary, critical reading and critique, explanatory synthesis, argument synthesis, and analysis. The two strategies chapters (6–7) cover the writing process and research.

The applications section consists of two new chapters. A Case Study in Academic Writing, Chapter 8, includes a model student paper that combines all of the structures previously discussed: summary, critique, synthesis (explanation, comparison-contrast, and argument), and analysis. The model paper, a comparative analysis of John Singer Sargent's painting *Death and Victory* and Erich Maria Remarque's *All Quiet on the Western Front*, is accompanied by extracts from sources, an outline and discussion of the paper's thesis, a section from a preliminary draft, and a concluding discussion of the final paper. In Chapter 9, Practicing Academic Writing, students are encouraged to practice the skills they have learned in writing summaries, critiques, syntheses, and analysis by working with a set of readings and a series of carefully sequenced assignments that build toward an argument on the controversial practice of "legacy" admissions—the granting of preferential treatment in the admissions process to the sons and daughters of college alumni.

Almost all the chapters in the current edition have been revised, some significantly. Chapter 1 (Summary, Paraphrase, and Quotation) includes a new narrative summary based on Bruce Chatwin's celebrated *In Patagonia* (1977) and a new summary exercise on the political genius of Abraham Lincoln. Chapter 2 (Critical Reading and Critique) features a new model student paper on the issues arising from a mother's charge of discrimination when the San Francisco Ballet School refused admission to her daughter, who (claimed the school) had the wrong "body type." A new practice critique in this same chapter focuses on the advantages of same-sex schools. Chapter 3 (Explanatory Synthesis) also has a new model paper (rough and final drafts) focusing on the advantages of the hydrogen fuel-cell vehicle. A new comparison-contrast synthesis in Chapter 4 (Argument Synthesis) models a possible response to an exam question concerning some key differences between World War I and World War II that students in a modern history course might be asked to write. In addition, we have revised other chapters: Chapter 7 (Locating, Mining, and Citing Sources) now includes citation format for the kind of databases available to most students at their college library. Instruction on proper citation styles reflects the latest editions of the MLA and APA manuals. Throughout the book new boxes, summarizing key text material, have been added and exercises updated.

SUPPLEMENTS

Instructor's Manual

The *Instructor's Manual* provides sample syllabi and assignment ideas for traditional and Web based courses. Each IM chapter opens with summaries of each chapter in the student text, followed by bulleted highlights that outline each chapter. Writing/Critical Thinking Activities offer additional exercises making use of Internet sources and Revision Exercises are also provided for Chapters 1–5. Each IM chapter also provides extensive lists of Web source material for both students and instructors.

MyCompLab

MyCompLab provides multimedia resources for students and teachers on one easy-to-use site. In this site, students will find guided assistance through each step of the writing process; interactive tutorials and videos that illustrate key concepts; over 30 model documents from across the curriculum; *Exchange,* Longman's online peer-review program; the "Avoiding Plagiarism" tutorial; diagnostic grammar tests and thousands of practice questions; and *Research Navigator*™, a database with thousands of magazines and academic journals, the subject-search archive of the *New York Times,* "Link Library," library guides, and more. Learn more about MyCompLab at **http://www.mycomplab.com**.

ACKNOWLEDGMENTS

We would like to thank the following reviewers for their help in the preparation of this text: Patricia Baldwin, Pitt Community College; Sherri Brouillette, Millersville University; Bryce Campbell, Victor Valley College; Wendy Hayden, University of Maryland; Randall McClure, Minnesota State University-Mankato; Jamil Mustafa, Lewis University; Deborah Richey, Owens Community College. We would also like to thank reviewers of previous editions of this text: Cora Agatucci, Central Oregon Community College; Bruce Closser, Andrews University; Clinton R. Gardner, Salt Lake Community College; Margaret Graham, Iowa State University; Susanmarie Harrington, Indiana University and Purdue University Indianapolis; Georgina Hill, Western Michigan University; Jane M. Kinney, Valdosta State University; Susan E. Knutson, University of Minnesota-Twin Cities; Cathy Leaker, North Carolina State University; Lyle W. Morgan, Pittsburg State University; Joan Perkins, University of Hawaii; Catherine Quick, Stephen F. Austin State University; Emily Rogers,

University of Illinois-Urbana Champaign; William Scott Simkins, University of Southern Mississippi; Doug Swartz, Indiana University Northwest; Marcy Taylor, Central Michigan University; Zach Waggoner, Western Illinois University; Heidemarie Z. Weidner, Tennessee Technological University; Betty R. Youngkin, The University of Dayton; and Terry Meyers Zawacki, George Mason University. And we are grateful to UCSB librarian Lucia Snowhill for helping us update the reference sources in Chapter 7.

Thanks to Lynn Huddon, our editor at Longman Publishers, for seeing this project through from conception to completion. We are also grateful to our copyeditor, Elsa van Bergen, and to Patrick Franzen, project manager at Pre-Press Company, for careful and attentive handling of the manuscript throughout the production process. Each has contributed mightily to this effort, and we extend our warmest appreciation.

LAURENCE BEHRENS
LEONARD J. ROSEN

In your sociology class, you are assigned to write a paper on the role of peer groups in influencing attitudes toward smoking. Your professor expects you to read some of the literature on the subject as well as to conduct interviews with members of such groups. For an environmental studies course, you must write a paper on how one or more industrial plants in a particular area have been affecting the local ecosystem. In your film studies class, you must select a contemporary filmmaker—you are trying to decide between Robert Altman and Spike Lee—and examine how at least three of his films demonstrate a distinctive point of view.

These writing assignments are typical of those you will undertake during your college years. In fact, such assignments are also common for those in professional life: for instance, scientists writing environmental impact statements, social scientists writing accounts of their research for professional journals, and film critics showing how the latest effort by a filmmaker fits into the general body of his or her work.

Core Skills

To succeed in such assignments, you will need to develop and hone particular skills in critical reading, thinking, and writing. You must develop—not necessarily in this order—the ability to

- read and accurately *summarize* a selection of material on your subject;
- determine the quality and relevance of your sources through a process of *critical reading* and assessment;
- *synthesize* different sources by discovering the relationships among them and showing how these relationships produce insights about the subject under discussion;
- *analyze* objects or phenomena by applying particular perspectives and theories;
- develop effective techniques for (1) discovering and using pertinent, authoritative information and ideas and (2) presenting the results of your work in generally accepted disciplinary formats.

A Sequence for Academic Writing will help you to meet these goals. In conversations with faculty across the curriculum, time and again we have been struck by a shared desire to see students thinking and writing in subject-appropriate ways. Psychology, biology, and engineering teachers want you to think, talk, and write like psychologists, biologists, and engineers. We set out, therefore, to learn the strategies writers use to enter conversations in their respective disciplines. We discovered that four readily learned strategies—summary, critique, synthesis, and analysis—provided the basis for the great majority of writing in freshman- through senior-level courses, and in courses across disciplines. We therefore made these skills the centerpiece of instruction for this book.

Applications Beyond College

While summary, critique, synthesis, and analysis are primary critical thinking and writing skills practiced throughout the university, these skills are also crucial to the work you will do in your life outside the university. In the professional world, people write letters, memos, and reports in which they must summarize procedures, activities, and the like. Critical reading and critique are important skills for writing legal briefs, business plans, and policy briefs. In addition, these same types of documents—common in the legal, business, and political worlds, respectively—involve synthesis. A business plan, for example, will often include a synthesis of ideas and proposals in one coherent plan. Finally, the ability to analyze complex data, processes, or ideas, to apply theories or perspectives to particular subjects, and then to effectively convey the results of analysis in writing is integral to writing in medicine, law, politics, business—in short, just about any career you might pursue.

Part One ▪ *Structures*

- Chapter 1
Summary, Paraphrase, and Quotation

- Chapter 2
Critical Reading and Critique

- Chapter 3
Explanatory Synthesis

- Chapter 4
Argument Synthesis

- Chapter 5
Analysis

Summary, Paraphrase, and Quotation

■ WHAT IS A SUMMARY?

The best way to demonstrate that you understand the information and the ideas in any piece of writing is to compose an accurate and clearly written summary of that piece. By a *summary* we mean a *brief restatement, in your own words, of the content of a passage* (a group of paragraphs, a chapter, an article, a book). This restatement should focus on the *central idea* of the passage. The briefest of summaries (one or two sentences) will do no more than this. A longer, more complete summary will indicate, in condensed form, the main points in the passage that support or explain the central idea. It will reflect the order in which these points are presented and the emphasis given to them. It may even include some important examples from the passage. But it will not include minor details. It will not repeat points simply for the purpose of emphasis. And it will not contain any of your own opinions or conclusions. A good summary, therefore, has three central qualities: *brevity, completeness,* and *objectivity.*

■ CAN A SUMMARY BE OBJECTIVE?

Of course, the last quality mentioned above, objectivity, might be difficult to achieve in a summary. By definition, writing a summary requires you to select some aspects of the original and leave out others. Since deciding what to select and what to leave out calls for your personal judgment, your summary really is a work of interpretation. And, certainly, your interpretation of a passage may differ from another person's. One factor affecting the nature and quality of your interpretation is your *prior knowledge* of the subject. For example, if you're attempting to summarize an anthropological article and you're a novice in that field, then your summary of the article will likely differ from that of your professor, who has spent 20 years studying this particular area and whose judgment about what is more or less significant is undoubtedly more reliable than your own. By the same token, your personal or professional *frame of reference* may also affect your interpretation. A union representative and a management representative attempting to summarize the latest management offer would probably come up with two very different accounts. Still, we believe that in most cases it's possible to produce a reasonably objective summary of a passage if you make a conscious, good-faith effort to be unbiased and to prevent your own feelings on the subject from distorting your account of the text.

Where Do We Find Written Summaries?

Here are just a few of the types of writing that involve summary:

ACADEMIC WRITING

- **Critique papers.** Summarize material in order to critique it.
- **Synthesis papers.** Summarize to show relationships between sources.
- **Analysis papers.** Summarize theoretical perspectives before applying them.
- **Research papers.** Note-taking and reporting research require summary.
- **Literature reviews.** Overviews of work presented in brief summaries.
- **Argument papers.** Summarize evidence and opposing arguments.
- **Essay exams.** Demonstrate understanding of course materials through summary.

WORKPLACE WRITING

- **Policy briefs.** Condense complex public policy.
- **Business plans.** Summarize costs, relevant environmental impacts, and other important matters.
- **Memos, letters, and reports.** Summarize procedures, meetings, product assessments, expenditures, and more.
- **Medical charts.** Record patient data in summarized form.
- **Legal briefs.** Summarize relevant facts of cases.

■ USING THE SUMMARY

In some quarters, the summary has a bad reputation—and with reason. Summaries often are provided by writers as substitutes for analyses. As students, many of us have summarized books that we were supposed to *review critically.* All the same, the summary does have a place in respectable college work. First, writing a summary is an excellent way to understand what you read. This in itself is an important goal of academic study. If you don't understand your source material, chances are you won't be able to refer to it usefully in an essay or research paper. Summaries help you understand what you read because they force you to put the text into your own words. Practice with writing summaries also develops your general writing habits, since a good summary, like any other piece of good writing, is clear, coherent, and accurate.

Second, summaries are useful to your readers. Let's say you're writing a paper about the McCarthy era in the United States, and in part of that paper you want to discuss Arthur Miller's *Crucible* as a dramatic treatment of the subject. A summary of the plot would be helpful to a reader who hasn't seen or read—or who doesn't remember—the play. Or perhaps you're writing a paper about the politics of recent American military interventions. If your reader isn't likely to be familiar with American actions in Kosovo and Afghanistan, it would be a good idea to summarize these events at some early point in the paper. In many cases (an exam, for instance), you can use a summary to demonstrate your knowledge of what your professor already knows; when writing a paper, you can use a summary to inform your professor about some relatively unfamiliar source.

Third, summaries are required frequently in college-level writing. For example, on a psychology midterm, you may be asked to explain Carl Jung's theory of the collective unconscious and to show how it differs from Sigmund Freud's theory of the personal unconscious. You may have read about this theory in your textbook or in a supplementary article, or your instructor may have outlined it in his or her lecture. You can best demonstrate your understanding of Jung's theory by summarizing it. Then you'll proceed to contrast it with Freud's theory—which, of course, you must also summarize.

■ THE READING PROCESS

It may seem to you that being able to tell (or retell) in summary form exactly what a passage says is a skill that ought to be taken for granted in anyone who can read at high school level. Unfortunately, this is not so: For all kinds of reasons, people don't always read carefully. In fact, it's probably safe to say that usually they don't. Either they read so inattentively that they skip over words, phrases, or even whole sentences, or, if they do see the words in front of them, they see them without registering their significance.

When a reader fails to pick up the meaning and implications of a sentence or two, usually there's no real harm done. (An exception: You could lose credit on an exam or paper because you failed to read or to realize the significance of a crucial direction by your instructor.) But over longer stretches—the paragraph, the section, the article, or the chapter—inattentive or haphazard reading interferes with your goals as a reader: to perceive the shape of the argument, to grasp the central idea, to determine the main points that compose it, to relate the parts of the whole, and to note key examples. This kind of reading takes a lot more energy and determination than casual reading. But, in the long run, it's an energy-saving method because it enables you to retain the content of the material and to use that content as a basis for your own responses. In other words, it allows you to develop an accurate and coherent written discussion that goes beyond summary.

Given the often large quantity of reading they are asked to do in college, many students skim their assignments. Skimming can be a useful way of managing some kinds of course material. For example, textbooks that outline broad concepts that a professor elaborates on in a lecture might be skimmed before the lecture, then read more carefully later to fill in gaps in your understanding. However, for the most part you should carefully read and understand the material you are assigned.

One effective strategy with which to approach course readings is to ask yourself how the reading fits into the course—in terms of both theme and *purpose*. Why is the reading assigned? How do different readings relate to one another? For example, many college courses require you to read chapters from a textbook as well as articles selected from a reader or anthology. Textbooks usually provide general overviews, laying out and defining important concepts. Articles often follow up by narrowing the focus, showing the concepts in action, critiquing them, or providing more in-depth discussion of some key concept or issue. When you understand the purpose of the reading you're doing, you will benefit more from it.

A useful way to approach reading assignments is to think of reading as a process, and try to enjoy it as you're doing it, rather than focusing entirely on the result and just powering through to the end. Try to think of reading as a circular movement through a text rather than a linear movement. In other words, when you start at the beginning of an article or chapter, rather than moving through it in a straight, uninterrupted path to the end of the reading, stop reading periodically to sum up in your mind, flag difficult passages with notes or question marks in the margin, and circle back to reread those passages after you've read further and gained more understanding. Use *paraphrase* (see pp. 32–37) to sum up difficult points in your own words and record them in the margins or in reading notes.

As you read, pay attention to the stages of thought contained in a piece. Some readings are separated into sections with subheadings, which specifically identify the stages of thought. Other readings won't be sectioned off in this way, and you'll have to be alert to the shifts in focus that occur. If you're reading a difficult piece and find yourself confused, ask yourself not only what the author is *saying*, but also what he or she is *doing* in that portion of the reading. In other words, why is the author discussing this now? Is the writer providing examples, discussing opposing arguments, further elaborating an earlier point? By looking at what an author seems to be doing as well as saying, you'll have a better sense of how the parts of a reading make up the whole. Paying close attention to transitional words and phrases such as *on the other hand*, *for example*, *therefore*, and *conversely* will also help you locate the shifts in thought that occur in a piece of writing.

Read actively: Stop and think, question, and (if you own the book or if you're working with a photocopy) write notes of agreement, disagreement, confusion, or identification in the margin. Underline key points, but try not to go crazy with the highlighter as you read. Often the first time you read something, every point strikes you as a potentially key idea. You

Critical Reading for Summary

- *Examine the context.* Note the credentials, occupation, and publications of the author. Identify the source in which the piece originally appeared. This information helps illuminate the author's perspective on the topic he or she is addressing.
- *Note the title and subtitle.* Some titles are straightforward, whereas the meanings of others become clearer as you read. In either case, titles typically identify the topic being addressed, and often reveal the author's attitude toward that topic.
- *Identify the main point.* Whether a piece of writing contains a thesis statement in the first few paragraphs or builds its main point without stating it up front, look at the entire piece to arrive at an understanding of the overall point being made.
- *Identify the subordinate points.* Notice the smaller subpoints that make up the main point, and make sure you understand how they relate to the main point. If a particular subpoint doesn't clearly relate to the main point you've identified, you may need to modify your understanding of the main point.
- *Break the reading into sections.* Notice which paragraph(s) make up a piece's introduction, body, and conclusion. Break up the body paragraphs into sections that address the writer's various subpoints.
- *Distinguish between points, examples, counterarguments.* Critical reading requires careful attention to what a writer is *doing* as well as what he or she is *saying*. When a writer quotes someone else, or relays an example of something, ask yourself why this is being done. What point is the example supporting? Is another source being quoted as support for a point, or as a counterargument that the writer sets out to address?
- *Watch for transitions within and between paragraphs.* In order to follow the logic of a piece of writing, as well as to distinguish between points, examples, and counterarguments, pay attention to the transitional words and phrases writers use. Transitions function like road signs, preparing the reader for what's next.
- *Read actively and recursively.* Don't treat reading as a passive, linear progression through a text. Instead, read as though you are engaged in a dialogue with the writer: Ask questions of the text as you read, make notes in the margin, underline key ideas in pencil, put question or exclamation marks next to passages that confuse or excite you. Go back to earlier points once you finish a reading, stop during your reading to recap what's come so far, and move back and forth through a text.

end up with pages that are almost entirely covered in fluorescent yellow or pink, and this can be distracting later on when you review your reading. (And of course, overmarking defeats the whole purpose of highlighting.) Underlining with a pencil, or making marks in the margin, can be more effective, for several reasons. First, when you underline with a pencil, you have to focus on the words more than you do when you quickly whisk a highlighter over them; therefore, you'll be further comprehending the ideas as you underline them. Second, your first impression of which points are important is likely to be a little off the mark. If you use a pencil, you can erase the underlining of less crucial passages after you've read the entire piece.

These tips are meant to help you get the most out of reading, whether or not your main purpose is to summarize. We've included more suggestions for critical reading and summary in the box on Critical Reading for Summary, on page 7. Now we turn to the next step: how you take what you've read and condense and rephrase it.

■ HOW TO WRITE SUMMARIES

Every article you read will present a unique challenge as you work to summarize it. As you'll discover, saying in a few words what has taken someone else a great many can be difficult. But like any other skill, the ability to summarize improves with practice. Here are a few pointers to get you started. They represent possible stages, or steps, in the process of writing a summary. These pointers are not meant to be ironclad rules; rather, they are designed to encourage habits of thinking that will allow you to vary your technique as the situation demands.

Guidelines for Writing Summaries

- *Read the passage carefully.* Determine its structure. Identify the author's purpose in writing. (This will help you distinguish between more important and less important information.) Make a note in the margin when you get confused or when you think something is important; highlight or underline points sparingly, if at all.
- *Reread.* This time divide the passage into sections or stages of thought. The author's use of paragraphing will often be a useful guide. *Label,* on the passage itself, each section or stage of thought. *Underline* key ideas and terms. Write notes in the margin.
- *Write one-sentence summaries,* on a separate sheet of paper, of each stage of thought.

(continues)

- *Write a thesis—a one- or two-sentence summary of the entire passage.* The thesis should express the central idea of the passage, as you have determined it from the preceding steps. You may find it useful to follow the approach of most newspaper stories—naming the *what, who, why, where, when,* and *how* of the matter. For persuasive passages, summarize in a sentence the author's conclusion. For descriptive passages, indicate the subject of the description and its key feature(s). *Note:* In some cases, *a suitable thesis may already be in the original passage.* If so, you may want to quote it directly in your summary.
- *Write the first draft of your summary* by (1) combining the thesis with your list of one-sentence summaries or (2) combining the thesis with one-sentence summaries *plus* significant details from the passage. In either case, eliminate repetition and less important information. Disregard minor details or generalize them (e.g., George H. W. Bush and Bill Clinton might be generalized as "recent presidents"). Use as few words as possible to convey the main ideas.
- *Check your summary against the original passage* and make whatever adjustments are necessary for accuracy and completeness.
- *Revise your summary,* inserting transitional words and phrases where necessary to ensure coherence. Check for style. *Avoid a series of short, choppy sentences.* Combine sentences for a smooth, logical flow of ideas. Check for grammatical correctness, punctuation, and spelling.

■ DEMONSTRATION: SUMMARY

To demonstrate these points at work, let's go through the process of summarizing a passage of expository material—that is, writing that is meant to inform and/or persuade. Read the following selection carefully. Try to identify its parts and understand how they work together to create an overall point.

THE FUTURE OF LOVE: KISS ROMANCE GOODBYE, IT'S TIME FOR THE REAL THING

Barbara Graham*

Author of the satire Women Who Run With Poodles: Myths and Tips for Honoring Your Mood Swings *(Avon, 1994), Barbara Graham has written articles for* Vogue, Self, Common Boundary, *and other publications. She regularly contributes articles to the* Utne Reader, *from which this essay was taken.*

Freud and his psychoanalytic descendants are no doubt correct in their assessment that the search for ideal love—for that one perfect soulmate—is the futile

———————
*Barbara Graham, "The Future of Love: Kiss Romance Goodbye, It's Time for the Real Thing," Utne Reader *Jan.–Feb. 1997: 20–23.*

wish of not fully developed selves. But it also seems true that the longing for a profound, all-consuming erotic connection (and the heightened state of awareness that goes with it) is in our very wiring. The yearning for fulfillment through love seems to be to our psychic structure what food and water are to our cells.

Just consider the stories and myths that have shaped our consciousness: Beauty and the Beast, Snow White and her handsome prince, Cinderella and Prince Charming, Fred and Ginger, Barbie and Ken. (Note that, with the exception of the last two couples, all of these lovers are said to have lived happily ever after—even though we never get details of their lives after the weddings, after children and gravity and loss have exacted their price.) Still, it's not just these lucky fairy tale characters who have captured our collective imagination. The tragic twosomes we cut our teeth on—Romeo and Juliet, Tristan and Iseult, Launcelot and Guinevere, Heathcliff and Cathy, Rhett and Scarlett—are even more compelling role models. Their love is simply too powerful and anarchic, too shattering and exquisite, to be bound by anything so conventional as marriage or a long-term domestic arrangement.

If recent divorce and remarriage statistics are any indication, we're not as astute as the doomed lovers. Instead of drinking poison and putting an end to our love affairs while the heat is still turned up full blast, we expect our marriages and relationships to be long-running fairy tales. When they're not, instead of examining our expectations, we switch partners and reinvent the fantasy, hoping that this time we'll get it right. It's easy to see why: Despite all the talk of family values, we're constantly bombarded by visions of perfect romance. All you have to do is turn on the radio or TV or open any magazine and check out the perfume and lingerie ads. "Our culture is deeply regressed," says Florence Falk, a New York City psychotherapist. "Everywhere we turn, we're faced with glamorized, idealized versions of love. It's as if the culture wants us to stay trapped in the fantasy and does everything possible to encourage and expand that fantasy." Trying to forge an authentic relationship amidst all the romantic hype, she adds, makes what is already a tough proposition even harder.

What's most unusual about our culture is our feverish devotion to the belief that romantic love and marriage should be synonymous. Starting with George and Martha, continuing through Ozzie and Harriet right up to the present day, we have tirelessly tried to formalize, rationalize, legalize, legitimize, politicize and sanitize rapture. This may have something to do with our puritanical roots, as well as our tendency toward oversimplification. In any event, this attempt to satisfy all of our contradictory desires under the marital umbrella must be put in historical context in order to be properly understood.

5   "Personal intimacy is actually quite a new idea in human history and was never part of the marriage ideal before the 20th century," says John Welwood, a Northern California–based psychologist and author, most recently, of *Love and Awakening.* "Most couples throughout history managed to live together their whole lives without ever having a conversation about what was going on within or between them. As long as family and society prescribed the rules of marriage, individuals never had to develop any consciousness in this area."

In short, marriage was designed to serve the economic and social needs of families, communities, and religious institutions, and had little or nothing to do with love. Nor was it expected to satisfy lust.

In *Myths To Live By,* Joseph Campbell explains how the sages of ancient India viewed the relationship between marriage and passion. They concluded that there are five degrees of love, he writes, "through which a worshiper is increased in the service and knowledge of his God." The first degree has to do with the relationship of the worshiper to the divine. The next three degrees of love, in order of importance, are friendship, the parent/child relationship, and marriage. The fifth and highest form is passionate, illicit love. "In marriage, it is declared, one is still possessed of reason," Campbell adds. "The seizure of passionate love can be, in such a context, only illicit, breaking in upon the order of one's dutiful life in virtue as a devastating storm."

No wonder we're having problems. The pressures we place on our tender unions are unprecedented. Even our biochemistry seems to militate against long-term sexual relationships. Dr. Helen Fisher, an anthropologist at Rutgers University and author of *Anatomy of Love,* believes that human pair-bonds originally evolved according to "the ancient blueprint of serial monogamy and clandestine adultery" and are originally meant to last around four years—at least long enough to raise a single dependent child through toddlerhood. The so-called seven-year-itch may be the remains of a four-year reproductive cycle, Fisher suggests.

Increasingly, Fisher and other researchers are coming to view what we call love as a series of complex biochemical events governed by hormones and enzymes. "People cling to the idea that romantic love is a mystery, but it's also a chemical experience," Fisher says, explaining that there are three distinct mating emotions and each is supported in the brain by the release of different chemicals. Lust, an emotion triggered by changing levels of testosterone in men and women, is associated with our basic sexual drive. Infatuation depends on the changing levels of dopamine, norepinephrine, and phenylethylamine (PEA), also called the "chemicals of love." They are natural—addictive—amphetaminelike chemicals that stimulate euphoria and make us want to stay up all night sharing our secrets. After infatuation and the dizzying highs associated with it have peaked—usually within a year or two—this brain chemistry reduces, and a new chemical system made up of oxytocin, vasopressin, and maybe the endorphins kicks in and supports a steadier, quieter, more nurturing intimacy. In the end, regardless of whether biochemistry accounts for cause or effect in love, it may help to explain why some people—those most responsive to the release of the attachment chemicals—are able to sustain a long-term partnership, while thrillseekers who feel depressed without regular hits of dopamine and PEA are likely to jump from one liaison to the next in order to maintain a buzz.

10   But even if our biochemistry suggests that there should be term limits on love, the heart is a stubborn muscle and, for better or worse, most of us continue to yearn for a relationship that will endure. As a group, Generation Xers—many of whom are children of divorce—are more determined than any other demographic group to have a different kind of marriage than their parents and to avoid divorce, says Howard Markman, author of *Fighting for Your Marriage.* What's more, lesbians and gay men who once opposed marriage and all of its heterosexual, patriarchal implications, now seek to reframe marriage as a more flexible, less repressive arrangement. And, according to the U.S. National Center for Health Statistics, in one out of

an estimated seven weddings, either the bride or the groom—or both—are tying the knot for at least the third time—nearly twice as many as in 1970. There are many reasons for this, from the surge in the divorce rate that began in the '70s, to our ever-increasing life span. Even so, the fact that we're still trying to get love right—knowing all we know about the ephemeral nature of passion, in a time when the stigmas once associated with being divorced or single have all but disappeared—says something about our powerful need to connect.

And, judging from the army of psychologists, therapists, clergy, and other experts who can be found dispensing guidance on the subject, the effort to save—or reinvent, depending on who's doing the talking—love and marriage has become a multimillion dollar industry. The advice spans the spectrum. There's everything from *Rules*, by Ellen Fein and Sherrie Schneider, a popular new book which gives 90's women 50's-style tips on how to catch and keep their man, to Harville Hendrix's *Getting the Love You Want*, and other guides to "conscious love." But regardless of perspective, this much is clear: Never before have our most intimate thoughts and actions been so thoroughly dissected, analyzed, scrutinized and medicalized. Now, people who fall madly in love over and over are called romance addicts. Their disease, modeled on alcoholism and other chemical dependencies, is considered "progressive and fatal."

Not everyone believes the attempt to deconstruct love is a good thing. The late philosopher Christopher Lasch wrote in his final (and newly released) book, *Women and the Common Life:* "The exposure of sexual life to scientific scrutiny contributed to the rationalization, not the liberation, of emotional life." His daughter, Elisabeth Lasch-Quinn, an historian at Syracuse University and the editor of the book, agrees. She contends that the progressive demystification of passionate life since Freud has promoted an asexual, dispassionate and utilitarian form of love. Moreover, like her father, she believes that the national malaise about romance can be attributed to insidious therapeutic modes of social control—a series of mechanisms that have reduced the citizen to a consumer of expertise. "We have fragmented life in such a way," she says, "as to take passion out of our experience."

Admittedly, it's a stretch to picture a lovesick 12th century French troubadour in a 12-step program for romance addicts. Still, we can't overlook the fact that our society's past efforts to fuse together those historically odd bedfellows—passionate love and marriage—have failed miserably. And though it's impossible to know whether all the attention currently being showered on relationships is the last gasp of a dying social order—marriage—or the first glimmer of a new paradigm for relating to one another, it's obvious that something radically different is needed.

Read, Reread, Underline

Let's consider our recommended pointers for writing a summary.

As you reread the passage, note in the margins of the essay important points, shifts in thought, and questions you may have. Consider the essay's significance as a whole and its stages of thought. What does it say? How is it organized? How does each part of the passage fit into the whole? What do all these points add up to?

Here is how the first few paragraphs of Graham's article might look after you had marked the main ideas, by highlighting and by marginal notations.

Freud and his psychoanalytic descendants are no doubt correct in their assessment that the search for ideal love—for that one perfect soulmate—is the futile wish of not fully developed selves. But it also seems true that the longing for a profound, all-consuming erotic connection (and the heightened state of awareness that goes with it) is in our very wiring. The yearning for fulfillment through love seems to be to our psychic structure what food and water are to our cells.

psychic importance of love

Just consider the stories and myths that have shaped our consciousness: Beauty and the Beast, Snow White and her handsome prince, Cinderella and Prince Charming, Fred and Ginger, Barbie and Ken. (Note that, with the exception of the last two couples, all of these lovers are said to have lived happily ever after—even though we never get details of their lives after the weddings, after children and gravity and loss have exacted their price.) Still, it's not just these lucky fairy tale characters who have captured our collective imagination. The tragic twosomes we cut our teeth on—Romeo and Juliet, Tristan and Iseult, Launcelot and Guinevere, Heathcliff and Cathy, Rhett and Scarlett—are even more compelling role models. Their love is simply too powerful and anarchic, too shattering and exquisite, to be bound by anything so conventional as marriage or a long-term domestic arrangement.

fictional, sometimes tragic examples of ideal love

If recent divorce and remarriage statistics are any indication, we're not as astute as the doomed lovers. Instead of drinking poison and putting an end to our love affairs while the heat is still turned up full blast, we expect our marriages and relationships to be long-running fairy tales. When they're not, instead of examining our expectations, we switch partners and reinvent the fantasy, hoping that this time we'll get it right. It's easy to see why: Despite all the talk of family values, we're constantly bombarded by visions of perfect romance. All you have to do is turn on the radio or TV or open any magazine and check out the perfume and lingerie ads. "Our culture is deeply regressed," says Florence Falk, a New York City psychotherapist. "Everywhere we turn, we're faced with glamorized, idealized versions of love. It's as if the culture wants us to stay trapped in the fantasy and does everything possible to encourage and expand that fantasy." Trying to forge an authentic relationship amidst all the romantic hype, she adds, makes what is already a tough proposition even harder.

difficulty of having a real relationship in a culture that glamorizes ideal love

What's most unusual about our culture is our feverish devotion to the belief that romantic love and marriage should be synonymous. Starting with George and Martha, continuing through Ozzie and Harriet right up to the present day, we have tirelessly tried to formalize, rationalize, legalize, legitimize, politicize and sanitize rapture. This may have something to do with our puritanical roots, as well as our tendency toward oversimplification. In any event, this attempt to satisfy all of our contradictory desires under the marital umbrella must be put in historical context in order to be properly understood.

contradictions of ideal love and marriage

"personal intimacy" never considered part of marriage before 20th century

"Personal intimacy is actually quite a new idea in human history and was never part of the marriage ideal before the 20th century," says John Welwood, a Northern California–based psychologist and author, most recently, of *Love and Awakening*. "Most couples throughout history managed to live together their whole lives without ever having a conversation about what was going on within or between them. As long as family and society prescribed the rules of marriage, individuals never had to develop any consciousness in this area."

In short, marriage was designed to serve the economic and social needs of families, communities, and religious institutions, and had little or nothing to do with love. Nor was it expected to satisfy lust.

Divide into Stages of Thought

When a selection doesn't contain sections with thematic headings, as is the case with "The Future of Love," how do you determine where one stage of thought ends and the next one begins? Assuming that what you have read is coherent and unified, this should not be difficult. (When a selection is unified, all of its parts pertain to the main subject; when a selection is coherent, the parts follow one another in logical order.) Look, particularly, for transitional sentences at the beginning of paragraphs. Such sentences generally work in one or both of the following ways: (1) they summarize what has come before; (2) they set the stage for what is to follow.

For example, look at the sentence that opens paragraph 10: "But even if our biochemistry suggests that there should be term limits on love, the heart is a stubborn muscle, and for better or worse, most of us continue to yearn for a relationship that will endure." Notice how the first part of this sentence restates the main idea of the preceding section. The second part of the transitional sentence announces the topic of the upcoming section: three paragraphs devoted to the efforts people make to attain, save, or reinvent romantic relationships.

Each section of an article generally takes several paragraphs to develop. Between paragraphs, and almost certainly between sections of an article, you will usually find transitions that help you understand what you have just read and what you are about to read. For articles that have no subheadings, try writing your own section headings in the margins as you take notes. Then proceed with your summary.

The sections of Graham's article may be described as follows:

Section 1: *Introduction*--a yearning for "fulfillment through love" pervades our culture, and that yearning is shaped by myths and romantic fantasies (paragraphs 1-3).

Section 2: *Marriage and love*--we expect passionate love to lead to happy, lifelong marriage. This is a relatively new and unique practice in human history (paragraphs 4-7).

Section 3: *Biochemistry and love*--love has a biochemical component, which complicates our abilities to sustain long-term relationships (paragraphs 8-9).

Section 4: *Marriage and love revisited*--many people are currently trying to preserve and/or reinvent marriage and love (paragraphs 10-12).

Section 5: *Conclusion*--the fusion of passionate love with the institution of marriage hasn't worked very well, and we need something "radically different" to replace it (paragraph 13).

Write a One- or Two-Sentence Summary of Each Stage of Thought

The purpose of this step is to wean you from the language of the original passage, so that you are not tied to it when writing the summary. Here are one-sentence summaries for each stage of thought in "The Future of Love" article's five sections:

Section 1: Introduction—a yearning for "fulfillment through love" pervades our culture, and that yearning is shaped by myths and romantic fantasies (paragraphs 1–3).

> Most members of American culture crave romantic love, but we have unreal expectations based upon idealized images of love we learn from fantasies and fairy tales.

Section 2: Marriage and love—we expect passionate love to lead to happy, lifelong marriage. This is a relatively new and unique practice in human history (paragraphs 4–7).

> We expect the passionate love of fairy tales to lead to "happily ever after" in the institution of marriage, and when this fails, we move on and try it again. Ironically, the idea that marriage should be based on love--rather than upon social and economic concerns--is a relatively recent practice in Western history.

Section 3: Biochemistry and love—love has a biochemical component, which complicates our abilities to sustain long-term relationships (paragraphs 8–9).

> Biochemists are discovering that love and lust have hormonal causes, and their evidence suggests that our biological makeup predisposes us to seek the excitement of short-term relationships.

Section 4: Marriage and love revisited—many people are currently trying to preserve and/or reinvent marriage and love (paragraphs 10–12).

> Despite all the difficulties, we spend a lot of time analyzing the elements of relationships in order to preserve or perhaps reinvent marriage. We clearly want to make it work.

Section 5: Conclusion—the fusion of passionate love with the institution of marriage hasn't worked very well, and we need something "radically different" to replace it (paragraph 13).

> Because confining passionate love to the institution of marriage hasn't worked very well, we need to revise our model for human relationships.

Write a Thesis: A One- or Two-Sentence Summary of the Entire Passage

The thesis is the most general statement of a summary (or any other type of academic writing—see Chapter 6 for a more complete discussion of thesis statements). It is the statement that announces the paper's subject and the claim that you or—in the case of a summary—another author will be making about that subject. Every paragraph of a paper illuminates the thesis by providing supporting detail or explanation. The relationship of these paragraphs to the thesis is analogous to the relationship of the sentences within a paragraph to the topic sentence. Both the thesis and the topic sentences are general statements (the thesis being the more general) that are followed by systematically arranged details.

To ensure clarity for the reader, *the first sentence of your summary should begin with the author's thesis, regardless of where it appears in the article itself.* Authors may locate their thesis at the beginning of their work, in which case the thesis operates as a general principle from which details of the presentation follow. This is called a *deductive* organization: thesis first, supporting details second. Alternately, an author may locate his or her thesis at the end of the work, in which case the author begins with specific details and builds toward a more general conclusion, or thesis. This is called an *inductive* organization—an example of which you see in "The Future of Love."

A thesis consists of a subject and an assertion about that subject. How can we go about fashioning an adequate thesis for a summary of "The Future of Love"? Probably no two proposed thesis statements for this article would be worded identically, but it is fair to say that any reasonable thesis will indicate that the subject is the current state of love and marriage in American society. How does Graham view the topic? What *is* the current state of love and marriage, in her view? Looking back over our section summaries, Graham's focus on the illusions of fairy tales and myths, the difference between marriage in the present day and its earlier incarnations, and the problems of divorce and "romance addiction" suggest she does not view the current state of affairs in an altogether positive light. Does she make a statement anywhere that pulls all this together? Her conclusion, in paragraph 13, contains her main idea: "our society's past efforts to fuse together those historically odd bedfellows—passionate love and marriage—have failed miserably." Moreover, in the next sentence, she says "it's obvious that something radically different is needed." Further evidence of Graham's main point can be found in the complete title of the essay: "The Future of Love: Kiss Romance Goodbye, It's Time for the Real Thing." Mindful of Graham's subject and the assertion she makes about it, we can write a thesis statement *in our own words* and arrive at the following:

> The contemporary institution of marriage is in trouble, and this may be due to our unrealistic expectations that passionate love leads to lasting union; it may be time to develop a new model for love and relationships.

To clarify for our readers the fact that this idea is Graham's and not ours, we'll qualify the thesis as follows:

> In her article "The Future of Love: Kiss Romance Goodbye--It's Time for the Real Thing," Barbara Graham describes how our unrealistic expectations that passionate love leads to lasting union may be partly causing the troubled state of marriage today; thus she suggests we develop a new model for love and relationships.

The first sentence of a summary is crucially important, for it orients readers by letting them know what to expect in the coming paragraphs. In the example above, the sentence refers directly to an article, its author, and the thesis for the upcoming summary. The author and title reference also could be indicated in the summary's title (if this were a freestanding summary), in which case their mention could be dropped from the thesis. And lest you become frustrated too quickly, keep in mind that writing an acceptable thesis for a summary takes time. In this case, it took three drafts, or roughly seven minutes to compose one sentence and another few minutes of fine-tuning after a draft of the entire summary was completed. The thesis needed revision because the first draft was too vague and incomplete; the second draft was more specific and complete, but left out the author's point about correcting the problem; the third draft was more complete, but was cumbersome.

Draft 1: Barbara Graham argues that our attempts to confine passionate love to the institution of marriage have failed.
(too vague--the problem isn't clear enough)

Draft 2: Barbara Graham ~~argues that our attempts to confine passionate love to the institution of marriage have failed.~~ describes how the contemporary institution of marriage is in trouble, and this may be due, she thinks, to our unrealistic expectations that passionate love will lead to lasting union.
(Incomplete--what about her call for a change?)

Draft 3: In her article "The Future of Love: Kiss Romance Goodbye, It's Time for the Real Thing," Barbara Graham describes how ~~the contemporary institution of marriage is in trouble, and this may be due, she thinks, to~~ our unrealistic expectations that passionate love will lead to lasting union may

be causing the troubles in the contemporary institution of marriage today, so
she argues that perhaps it's time to develop a new model for love and
relationships.
(Wordy)

Final: In her article "The Future of Love: Kiss Romance Goodbye, It's Time for
the Real Thing," Barbara Graham describes how our unrealistic expectations
that passionate love leads to lasting union may be partly causing the
troubled state of ~~in the contemporary institution of~~ marriage today; thus she
suggests we develop a new model for love and relationships.
(Add 'partly.' Cut out wordiness. Replace 'so' with 'thus')

Write the First Draft of the Summary

Let's consider two possible summaries of the example passage: (1) a short
summary, combining a thesis with one-sentence section summaries, and (2)
a longer summary, combining thesis, one-sentence section summaries, and
some carefully chosen details. Again, realize that you are reading final versions; each of the following summaries is the result of at least two full drafts.

Summary 1: Combine Thesis Sentence with One-Sentence Section Summaries

> In her article "The Future of Love: Kiss Romance Goodbye, It's Time for the
> Real Thing," Barbara Graham describes how our unrealistic expectations that
> passionate love leads to lasting union may be partly causing the troubled state
> of marriage today; thus she suggests we develop a new model for love and
> relationships. The existing model, and our craving for romantic love, is based
> heavily upon idealized images of love we learn from fantasies and fairy tales.
>
> We expect the passionate love of fairy tales to lead to "happily ever
> after" in the institution of marriage, and when this fails, we move on and try
> it again. Ironically, the idea that marriage should be based on love--rather
> than upon social and economic concerns--is a relatively recent practice in
> Western history. While the romantic marriage ideal doesn't fit with tradition,
> biological evidence is mounting against it as well. Biochemists are
> discovering that love and lust have hormonal causes, and their evidence
> suggests that our biological makeup predisposes us to seek the excitement of
> short-term relationships.
>
> Nonetheless, despite all the difficulties, we spend a lot of time analyzing
> the elements of relationships in order to preserve or perhaps reinvent
> marriage. We clearly want to make it work. Because confining passionate love
> to the institution of marriage hasn't worked very well, Graham ends by
> suggesting that we ought to revise our model for human relationships.

Discussion   This summary consists essentially of a restatement of Graham's
thesis plus the section summaries, altered or expanded a little for stylistic
purposes. The first sentence encompasses the summary of Section 1 and is

followed by the summaries of Sections 2, 3, 4, and 5. Notice the insertion of a transitional sentence (highlighted) between the summaries of Sections 2 and 3, helping to link the ideas more coherently.

Summary 2: Combine Thesis Sentence, Section Summaries, and Carefully Chosen Details

The thesis and one-sentence section summaries also can be used as the outline for a more detailed summary. However, most of the details in the passage won't be necessary in a summary. It isn't necessary even in a longer summary of this passage to discuss all of Graham's examples—specific romantic fairy tales, ancient Indian views of love and passion, the specific hormones involved with love and lust, or the examples of experts who examine and write about contemporary relationships. It would be appropriate, though, to mention one example of fairy tale romance, to refer to the historical information on marriage as an economic institution, and to explain some of the biological findings about love's chemical basis.

None of these details appeared in the first summary, but in a longer summary, a few carefully selected details might be desirable for clarity. How do you decide which details to include? First, since the idea that love and marriage are not necessarily compatible is the main point of the essay, it makes sense to cite some of the most persuasive evidence supporting this idea. For example, you could mention that for most of Western history, marriage was meant "to serve the economic and social needs of families, communities, and religious institutions," not the emotional and sexual needs of individuals. Further, you might explain the biochemists' argument that serial monogamy based on mutual interests, and clandestine adultery—not lifelong, love-based marriage—are the forms of relationships best serving human evolution.

You won't always know which details to include and which to exclude. Developing good judgment in comprehending and summarizing texts is largely a matter of reading skill and prior knowledge (see page 1). Consider the analogy of the seasoned mechanic who can pinpoint an engine problem by simply listening to a characteristic sound that to a less experienced person is just noise. Or consider the chess player who can plot three separate winning strategies from a board position that to a novice looks like a hopeless jumble. In the same way, the more practiced a reader you are, the more knowledgeable you become about the subject, and the better able you will be to make critical distinctions between elements of greater and lesser importance. In the meantime, read as carefully as you can and use your own best judgment as to how to present your material.

Here's one version of a completed summary, with carefully chosen details. Note that we have highlighted phrases and sentences added to the original, briefer summary.

(Thesis)   In her article "The Future of Love: Kiss Romance Goodbye, It's Time for the Real Thing," Barbara Graham describes how our unrealistic expectations that passionate love leads to lasting union may be partly causing the troubled

state of marriage today; thus she suggests we develop a new model for love and relationships.

Most members of American culture crave romantic love, but we have unreal expectations based upon idealized images of love we learn from fantasies and fairy tales such as "Beauty and the Beast" and "Cinderella." Tragedies such as Romeo and Juliet teach us about the all-consuming nature of "true love," and these stories are tragic precisely because the lovers never *(Section 1,* get to fulfill what we've been taught is the ideal: living happily ever after, in *¶s 1-3)* wedded bliss. The idea that romantic love should be confined to marriage is perhaps the biggest fantasy to which we subscribe. When we are unable to make this fantasy real--and it seems that this is often the case--we end that marriage and move on to the next one. The twentieth century is actually the first century in Western history in which so much was asked of marriage. *(Section 2,* In earlier eras, marriage was designed to meet social and economic purposes, *¶s 4-7)* rather than fulfill individual emotional and sexual desires.

Casting further doubt on the effectiveness of the current model of marriage, biochemists are discovering how hormones and enzymes influence feelings of love and lust. It turns out that the "chemistry" a person newly in love often feels for another has a basis in fact, as those early feelings of excitement and contentment are biochemical in nature. When people jump *(Section 3,* from one relationship to the next, they may be seeking that chemical "rush." *¶s 8-9)* Further, these biochemical discoveries fit with principles of evolutionary survival, because short-term relationships--and even adulterous affairs--help to more quickly propagate the species.

Nonetheless, despite such historical and biological imperatives, we don't seem interested in abandoning the pursuit of love and marriage. In order to preserve or perhaps reinvent marriage, we spend a lot of time scrutinizing and *(Section 4,* dissecting the dynamics of relationships. Self-help books on the subject of *¶s 10-12)* love and relationships fill bookstore shelves and top best-seller lists.

While some argue that such scrutiny ruins rather than reinvigorates love, perhaps our efforts to understand relationships can help us to invent *(Section 5,* some kind of revised model for human relationships--since trying to confine *¶ 13)* passionate love to the institution of marriage clearly hasn't worked very well.

Discussion   The final two of our suggested steps for writing summaries are (1) to check your summary against the original passage, making sure that you have included all the important ideas, and (2) to revise so that the summary reads smoothly and coherently.

The structure of this summary generally reflects the structure of the original—with one notable departure. As we noted earlier, Graham uses an inductive approach, stating her thesis at the end of the essay. The summary, however, states the thesis right away, then proceeds deductively to develop that thesis.

Compared to the first, briefer summary, this effort mentions fairy tales and tragedy, develops the point about traditional versus contemporary versions of marriage, explains the biochemical/evolutionary point, and refers specifically to self-help books and their role in the issue.

How long should a summary be? This depends on the length of the original passage. A good rule of thumb is that a summary should be no longer than one-fourth of the original passage. Of course, if you were summarizing an entire chapter or even an entire book, it would have to be much shorter than that. The summary above is about one-fourth the length of the original passage. Although it shouldn't be very much longer, you have seen (p. 18) that it could be quite a bit shorter.

The length as well as the content of the summary also depends on its *purpose.* Let's suppose you decided to use Graham's piece in a paper that dealt with the biochemical processes of love and lust. In this case, you might summarize *only* Graham's discussion of Fisher's findings, and perhaps the point Graham makes about how biochemical discoveries complicate marriage. If, instead, you were writing a paper in which you argued against attempts to redefine marriage, you would likely give less attention to the material on biochemistry. To help support your view, you might summarize Graham's points in paragraph 10 about the persistent desire for lasting union found among members of Generation X and evidenced in the high numbers of marriages and remarriages. Thus, depending on your purpose, you would summarize either selected portions of a source or an entire source, as we will see more fully in the chapters on syntheses.

Exercise 1.1
Individual and Collaborative Summary Practice

Turn to Chapter 2 and read Christine Flowers's essay "With No Boys to Ogle, We Had Time to Learn" (pp. 79–80). Follow the steps for writing summaries outlined above—read, underline, and divide into stages of thought. Write down a one- or two-sentence summary of each stage of thought in Flowers's essay. Then gather in groups of three or four classmates, and compare your summary sentences. Discuss the differences in your sentences, and come to some consensus about the divisions in Flowers's stages of thought—and the ways in which to best sum these up.

As a group, write a one- or two-sentence thesis statement summing up the entire passage. You could go even further, and, using your individual summary sentences—or the versions of these your group revised—put together a brief summary of Flowers's essay. Model your work on the brief summary of Graham's essay, on page 18.

■ SUMMARIZING A NARRATIVE OR PERSONAL ESSAY

Narratives and personal essays differ from expository essays in that they focus on personal experiences and/or views, they aren't structured around an explicitly stated thesis, and their ideas are developed more through the description of events or ideas than through factual evidence or logical explanation. A *narrative* is a story, a retelling of a person's experiences. That person and those experiences may be imaginary, as is the case with fiction, or they may be real, as in biography. In first-person narratives, you can't assume that the narrator represents the author of the piece, unless you know the narrative is a memoir or biography. In a *personal essay,* on the other hand, the narrator is the author. And while the writer of a personal essay may tell stories about his or her experiences, usually writers of such essays discuss thoughts and ideas as much as or more than telling stories. Personal essays also tend to contain more obvious points than do narratives. Summarizing personal essays or narratives presents certain challenges—challenges that are different from those presented by summarizing expository writing.

You have seen that an author of an *expository* piece (such as Graham's "The Future of Love") follows assertions with examples and statements of support. Narratives, however, usually are less direct. The author relates a story—event follows event—the point of which may never be stated directly. The charm, the force, and the very point of the narrative lie in the telling; generally, narratives do not exhibit the same logical development of expository writing. They do not, therefore, lend themselves to summary in quite the same way. Narratives do have a logic, but that logic may be emotional, imaginative, or plot-bound. The writer who summarizes a narrative is obliged to give an overview—a synopsis—of the story's events and an account of how these events affect the central character(s). The summary must explain the significance or *meaning* of the events.

Similarly, while personal essays sometimes present points more explicitly than do narratives, their focus and structure link them to narratives. Personal essays often contain inexplicit main points, or multiple points; they tend to *explore* ideas and issues, rather than make explicit *assertions* about those ideas. This exploratory character often means that personal essays exhibit a loose structure, and they often contain stories or narratives within them. While summarizing a personal essay may not involve a synopsis of events, an account of the progression of thoughts and ideas is necessary and, as with a narrative, summaries of personal essays must explain the significance of what goes on in the piece being summarized.

The following forms the first chapter of Bruce Chatwin's celebrated *In Patagonia* (1977), his narrative account of a journey to the remotest reaches of South America. Read the chapter, and as you do so consider how you might summarize it. Imagine that you might provide a summary of the opening to Chatwin's *In Patagonia* for a review of the book or for a paper on literature of travel.

DREAMS OF PATAGONIA
*Bruce Chatwin**

Bruce Chatwin (1942–1989) began his career as a specialist in modern art at Sotheby's auction house. He later studied archeology and served as a journalist for the London Sunday Times Magazine, *which sent him on far-flung assignments, whetting his appetite for travel and*

*Bruce Chatwin, In Patagonia, *New York: Penguin Books, 1977. pp.1–3.*

honing his literary skills. After three years, he left the magazine to devote himself full time to travel writing, fiction, and essay writing. In Patagonia won the 1978 Hawthornden Prize and the 1979 E. M. Forster Award of the American Academy of Arts and Letters. Chatwin is equally well-known for his second literary travelogue, The Songlines (1987), an account of aboriginal "walkabouts" in Australia.

In my grandmother's dining-room there was a glass-fronted cabinet and in the cabinet a piece of skin. It was a small piece only, but thick and leathery, with strands of coarse, reddish hair. It was stuck to a card with a rusty pin. On the card was some writing in faded black ink, but I was too young then to read.

"What's that?"

"A piece of brontosaurus."

My mother knew the names of two prehistoric animals, the brontosaurus and the
5   mammoth. She knew it was not a mammoth. Mammoths came from Siberia.

The brontosaurus, I learned, was an animal that had drowned in the Flood, being too big for Noah to ship aboard the Ark. I pictured a shaggy lumbering creature with claws and fangs and a malicious green light in its eyes. Sometimes the brontosaurus would crash through the bedroom wall and wake me from my sleep.

This particular brontosaurus had lived in Patagonia, a country in South America, at the far end of the world. Thousands of years before, it had fallen into a glacier, travelled down a mountain in a prison of blue ice, and arrived in perfect condition at the bottom. Here my grandmother's cousin, Charley Milward the Sailor, found it.

Charley Milward was captain of a merchant ship that sank at the entrance to the Strait of Magellan. He survived the wreck and settled nearby, at Punta Arenas, where he ran a ship-repairing yard. The Charley Milward of my imagination was a god among men—tall, silent and strong, with black mutton-chop whiskers and fierce blue eyes. He wore his sailor's cap at an angle and the tops of his sea-boots turned down.

Directly he saw the brontosaurus poking out of the ice, he knew what to do. He had it jointed, salted, packed in barrels, and shipped to the Natural History Museum in South Kensington. I pictured blood and ice, flesh and salt, gangs of Indian workmen and lines of barrels along a shore—a work of giants and all to no purpose; the brontosaurus went rotten on its voyage through the tropics and arrived in London a putrefied mess; which was why you saw brontosaurus bones in the museum, but no skin.

10   Fortunately cousin Charley had posted a scrap to my grandmother.

My grandmother lived in a red-brick house set behind a screen of yellow-spattered laurels. It had tall chimneys, pointed gables and a garden of blood-coloured roses. Inside it smelled of church.

I do not remember much about my grandmother except her size. I would clamber over her wide bosom or watch, slyly, to see if she'd be able to rise from her chair. Above her hung paintings of Dutch burghers, their fat buttery faces nesting in white ruffs. On the mantelpiece were two Japanese homunculi with red and white ivory eyes that popped out on stalks. I would play with these, or with a German articulated monkey, but always I pestered her: "Please can I have the piece of brontosaurus."

Never in my life have I wanted anything as I wanted that piece of skin. My grandmother said I should have it one day, perhaps. And when she died I said: "Now I *can* have the piece of brontosaurus," but my mother said: "Oh, that thing! I'm afraid we threw it away."

At school they laughed at the story of the brontosaurus. The science master said I'd mixed it up with the Siberian mammoth. He told the class how Russian scientists had dined off deep-frozen mammoth and told me not to tell lies. Besides, he said, brontosauruses were reptiles. They had no hair, but scaly armoured hide. And he showed us an artist's impression of the beast—so different from that of my imagination—grey-green, with a tiny head and gigantic switchback of vertebrae, placidly eating weed in a lake. I was ashamed of my hairy brontosaurus, but I knew it was not a mammoth.

It took some years to sort the story out. Charley Milward's animal was not a brontosaurus, but the mylodon or Giant Sloth. He never found a whole specimen, or even a whole skeleton, but some skin and bones, preserved by the cold, dryness and salt, in a cave on Last Hope Sound in Chilean Patagonia. He sent the collection to England and sold it to the British Museum. This version was less romantic but had the merit of being true.

My interest in Patagonia survived the loss of the skin; for the Cold War woke in 15 me a passion for geography. In the late 1940s the Cannibal of the Kremlin shadowed our lives; you could mistake his moustaches for teeth. We listened to lectures about the war he was planning. We watched the civil defence lecturer ring the cities of Europe to show the zones of total and partial destruction. We saw the zones bump one against the other leaving no space in between. The instructor wore khaki shorts. His knees were white and knobbly, and we saw it was hopeless. The war was coming and there was nothing we could do.

Next, we read about the cobalt bomb, which was worse than the hydrogen bomb and could smother the planet in an endless chain reaction.

I knew the colour cobalt from my great-aunt's paintbox. She had lived on Capri at the time of Maxim Gorky and painted Capriot boys naked. Later her art became almost entirely religious. She did lots of St Sebastians, always against a cobalt-blue background, always the same beautiful young man, stuck through and through with arrows and still on his feet.

So I pictured the cobalt bomb as a dense blue cloudbank, spitting tongues of flame at the edges. And I saw myself, out alone on a green headland, scanning the horizon for the advance of the cloud.

And yet we hoped to survive the blast. We started an Emigration Committee and made plans to settle in some far corner of the earth. We pored over atlases. We learned the direction of prevailing winds and the likely patterns of fall-out. The war would come in the Northern Hemisphere, so we looked to the Southern. We ruled out Pacific Islands for islands are traps. We ruled out Australia and New Zealand, and we fixed on Patagonia as the safest place on earth.

I pictured a low timber house with a shingled roof, caulked against storms, with 20 blazing log fires inside and the walls lined with the best books, somewhere to live when the rest of the world blew up.

Then Stalin died and we sang hymns of praise in chapel, but I continued to hold Patagonia in reserve.

How to Summarize Personal Essays and Narratives

- Your summary will *not* be a narrative, but rather the synopsis of a narrative or personal account. Your summary will likely be a paragraph at most.
- You will want to name and describe the principal character(s) of the narrative and describe the narrative's main actions or events; or, in the case of the personal essay, identify the narrator and his or her relationship to the discussion.
- You should seek to connect the narrative's character(s) and events: describe the significance of events for (or the impact of events on) the character(s), and/or the narrator.

If you have read the book *In Patagonia,* you may have done so because you were interested in the subject or because someone recommended it to you. Or you may have encountered this passage during the process of research or as an assigned reading for a course on the literature of travel, the culture and geography of South America, or social anthropology. In any case, you could draw on this passage for a number of purposes: to demonstrate the interplay of imagination and memory in motivating travel writers to set off on their journeys; to study narrative technique; to understand how an accomplished writer can, within a few pages—even within a few paragraphs—establish a voice; or to investigate how, in storytelling, facts can sometimes conflict with emotional truth. Having established your purpose, you decide to use the events recounted in this passage to support one or more points you intend to make.

When you summarize a narrative or personal essay, bear in mind the principles that follow, as well as those listed in the box above.

To summarize events, reread the narrative and make a marginal note each time you see that an action advances the story from one moment to the next. (In Chatwin, the "actions" are two memories, separate but linked to the same remote, fascinating place: Patagonia.) The key here is to recall that narratives take place *in time.* In your summary, be sure to re-create for your reader a sense of time flowing. Name and describe the character(s) as well. (For our purposes, *character* refers to the person, real or fictional, about whom the narrative is written.) The trickiest part of the summary will be describing the connection between events and characters. Earlier (p. 1) we made the point that summarizing any selection involves a degree of interpretation, and this is especially true of summarizing narratives and personal essays. What, in the case of Chatwin, is the significance of his narrative—or of any particular event he recounts? For example, what is the significance of the fact that the brontosaurus that figured so prominently in his childhood imagination turned out to be a remnant of a Giant Sloth? Or of his equally vivid, but mistaken, conviction that the world was going to end in a nuclear catastrophe and that he had better find the remotest region on earth if he hoped to survive? Such narrative moments—in Chatwin's case recollections—may be used to illustrate a particular point. The events on which you choose to focus while summarizing a narrative will depend entirely on your purpose in using the narrative in the first place.

The general principles of summarizing narratives are similar to those of summarizing expository or persuasive passages. Make sure that you cover the major events, in the order in which they occurred (in line with your overall purpose, of course). Bring in details only to the extent that they support your purpose.

Here is a three-paragraph summary of the first chapter in Bruce Chatwin's *In Patagonia*. (The draft is the result of two prior drafts.)

> In the first chapter of In Patagonia, Bruce Chatwin recounts two childhood memories, one based on a misunderstanding and the other on an unrealized fear, that sparked his desire "to hold Patagonia in reserve" and one day travel there. First, Chatwin recalls a patch of brontosaurus skin (supposedly from Patagonia); later, he recalls the fear of a Soviet-inspired nuclear holocaust and the realization that to survive he would need to travel to a safe, remote location (such as Patagonia).
>
> Growing up, Chatwin coveted a flap of weathered skin his grandmother kept in a glass case and which he understood to be the partial remains of a brontosaurus. To account for the specimen, he constructed an elaborate story centered on an actual but mythologized distant relation, "Charley Milward the Sailor." When Captain Milward's ship sank at the tip of South America and he settled in Patagonia, he discovered, preserved, and shipped back to England a dinosaur that emerged whole from a glacier. The scrap of dinosaur skin found a place of honor in Grandmother's home, alongside "paintings of Dutch burghers . . . and Japanese homunculi." Patagonia later figured into young Chatwin's imagination when, growing up in England at the start of the Cold War, he feared an imminent nuclear holocaust. It was the Stalin era in the Soviet Union, and English school children like Chatwin believed that inhabitants of the Northern Hemisphere would soon be incinerated or die of radiation sickness. Chatwin and others therefore formed "an Emigration Committee [that] made plans to settle in some far corner of the earth" and survive the destruction. That "far corner" was Patagonia.
>
> Both memories were proved unfounded. The brontosaurus skin that prompted in young Chatwin visions of "a shaggy lumbering creature with claws and fangs and a malicious green light in its eyes" turned out to be the remains of a Giant Sloth, part of which (not the whole animal) had been preserved in the dry, cold environment of Patagonia. Nor did Stalin launch the much-feared nuclear war that had prompted Chatwin to investigate a place so remote that the "likely patterns of fallout" would not reach him. Both memories nonetheless prompted in young Chatwin a fascination with

one of the most remote and, to his mind, one of the most exotic places on earth. His fascination would last into adulthood, eventually prompting the trip that would lead to his award-winning travelogue, In Patagonia.

Of course, depending upon how you use Chatwin's passage, you may not need as many details as are provided in the preceding summary. A briefer version would treat only the major events—the two childhood memories, one based on a misunderstanding and the other on a fear, but both contributing to a lifelong fascination. You might in this case preserve only a sentence or two of each of the original summary's three paragraphs, omitting such details as the description of the brontosaurus or of Grandmother's house. (The description of his grandmother and her home that "smelled of church" would be more relevant if you were writing a paper on the economy with which Chatwin describes people. The details you choose for a summary depend on the purpose to which you put the summary.)

Here is a briefer summary of the passage:

> In the first chapter of In Patagonia, Bruce Chatwin recounts two childhood memories, one based on a misunderstanding and the other on an unrealized fear, that sparked his interest in one day traveling to Patagonia. As a child, Chatwin was fascinated by a patch of what he thought was brontosaurus skin on display in his grandmother's home. That specimen was sent by distant relation "Charley Milward the Sailor" from Patagonia. Patagonia again figured into young Chatwin's imagination when, growing up in England at the start of the Cold War, he feared an imminent nuclear disaster and, in response, formed "an Emigration Committee" to scout remote locations that would escape nuclear destruction. Events later blurred these two memories. The brontosaurus skin turned out to be the remains of a Giant Sloth, and the much-feared war never materialized. Still, Chatwin's memories prompted in him a lifelong fascination with one of the most remote and, to his mind, one of the most exotic places on earth. As an adult, he would eventually make the trip that would end in his award-winning travelogue, In Patagonia.

Of course, the passage could be made briefer still: your purpose in your paper might be served by a one-sentence reference to Chatwin's narrative:

> In the first chapter of his award-winning travelogue, Bruce Chatwin recounts two childhood memories that prompted his lifelong fascination with Patagonia.

Here, only the major purpose of Chatwin's opening chapter is treated, with no details offered about the two memories that prompted his later fascination with Patagonia. Brief as it is, this summary conveys how Chatwin traces his motivation to travel in and write about Patagonia to events in his childhood.

■ SUMMARIZING FIGURES AND TABLES

In your reading in the sciences and social sciences, often you will find data and concepts presented in nontext forms—as figures and tables. Such visual devices offer a snapshot, a pictorial overview of material that is more quickly and clearly communicated in graphic form than as a series of (often complicated) sentences. Note that in essence, figures and tables are themselves summaries. The writer uses a graph, which in an article or book is labeled as a numbered "figure," to present the quantitative results of research as points on a line or a bar, or as sections ("slices") of a pie. Pie charts show relative proportions, or percentages. Graphs, especially effective in showing patterns, relate one variable to another: for instance, income to years of education, or a college student's grade point average to hours of studying.

In the following sections, we present a number of figures and tables from two different sources, all related to romance and relationships. Figures 1.1, 1.2, and 1.3 and Table 1.1 come from a study of the criteria used by participants on television dating shows in the United States and Israel to pick dating partners.* The categories are self-explanatory, although we should note that the category "physical appearance" denotes features of height, weight, facial features, and hair, while "sexual anatomy and bedroom behavior" refers to specifically sexual features of physical appearance, as well as to "kissing technique," "foreplay tactics," and the like. Figure 1.1 shows the criteria 266 American and Israeli men chose as most important in selecting a dating partner. Study this pie chart.

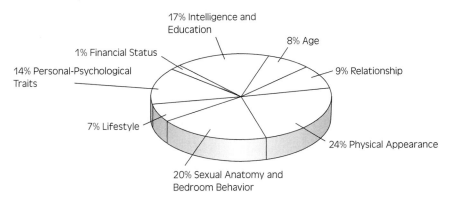

Figure 1.1   Categories Used by American and Israeli Males to Screen Dating Candidates

---

*Amir Hetsroni, "Choosing a Mate in Television Dating Games: The Influence of Setting, Culture, and Gender," Sex Roles 42.1–2 (2000): 90–97.

Here is a summary of the information presented:

> Males rated the categories of "physical appearance" and "sexual anatomy and bedroom behavior" as most important to them. Nearly half the males in the sample, or 44%, rated these two categories, which both center on external rather than internal characteristics, as the most important ones for choosing a dating partner. Internal characteristics represented by the categories of "personal-psychological traits" and "intelligence and education" account for the next most important criteria, with a combined 31%. Males rated "relationship," "lifestyle," and "age" as nearly equal in their priorities; interestingly, a negligible 1% rated "financial status" as an important criterion when selecting a dating candidate.

Figure 1.2 shows, in percentages, how women rate dating criteria.

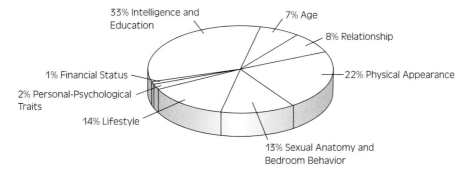

Figure 1.2   Categories Used by American and Israeli Females to Screen Dating Candidates

---

Exercise 1.2

Summarizing Charts

Write a brief summary of the data in Figure 1.2. Use our summary of Figure 1.1 as a model, but structure and word your own summary differently.

Bar graphs are useful for comparing two sets of data. Figure 1.3 illustrates this with a comparison of categories males and females use to select dating partners.

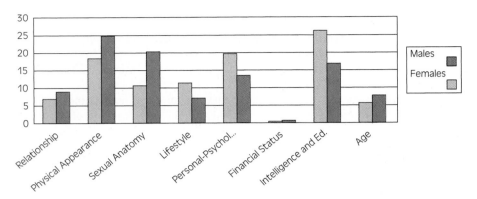

Figure 1.3   Comparison of Categories Used by American and Israeli Males and Females to Screen Dating Candidates

Here is a summary of the information in Figure 1.3:

> Males clearly differ from females in the criteria they use to select dating partners. Males in this sample focused on external characteristics such as "physical appearance" and especially "sexual anatomy and bedroom behavior" at significantly higher rates than did females. Conversely, females selected the internal characteristics of "lifestyle," "personal-psychological traits," and "intelligence and education" at much higher rates than did males. However, less significant differences exist between males and females when rating the importance of "relationship," "financial status," and "age"; both male and female participants rated these three criteria as of lesser importance when selecting a dating partner.

A table presents numerical data in rows and columns for quick reference. If the writer chooses, tabular information can be converted to graphic information. Charts and graphs are preferable when the writer wants to emphasize a pattern or relationship; tables are used when the writer wants to emphasize numbers. While the previous charts and graphs combined the Israeli with the American data collected in the TV dating show study, Table 1.1 breaks down the percentages by sex and nationality, revealing some significant differences between the nationality groups. (Note: *n* refers to the total number of respondents in each category.)

Sometimes a single graph presents information on two or more populations, or data sets, all of which are tracked with the same measurements. Figure 1.4 comes from a study of 261 college students—93 males and 168 females. The students were asked (among other things) to rate the acceptability of a hypothetical instance of sexual betrayal by both a male and a female heterosexual romantic partner who has agreed to be monogamous. The graph plots the ways in which gender of the transgressor played into the acceptability ratings given by male and female respondents. The researchers

Table 1.1 Categories Used by American and Israeli Males and Females to Screen Dating Candidates

Category	American Males (%) (n = 120)	Israeli Males (%) (n = 146)	American Females (%) (n = 156)	Israeli Females (%) (n = 244)
Relationship	9.5	8.0	9.5	5.0
Physical appearance	18.5	30.0	12.0	22.0
Sexual anatomy and bedroom behavior	11.5	27.5	4.5	15.0
Lifestyle	9.0	6.0	11.0	11.5
Personal-psychological traits	20.0	8.0	27.0	15.0
Financial status	1.5	—	—	1.0
Intelligence and education	22.5	12.5	29.0	24.0
Age	7.5	8.0	7.0	6.0
Total	100.0	100.0	100.0	100.0

established mean values of 1 to 4 (indicating ratings of "totally unacceptable" to "totally acceptable"). A *mean* indicates the average of the ratings or scores given by a population or, in numerical terms, the sum of the scores divided by the number of scores. When respondents in the study were asked to assign a numerical rating of acceptability to instances of sexual betrayal, they chose numbers on a scale from 1 to 4, and these choices were averaged

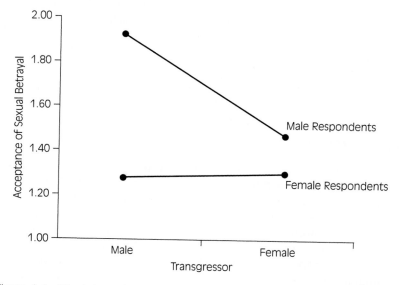

Figure 1.4   The Interaction of Sex of Respondent and Sex of Transgressor on the Acceptance of Sexual Betrayal

into mean acceptability ratings. None of the scores given by respondents in this study surpassed a mean acceptability rating of 2, but differences are evident between male and female ratings. The male respondents were more accepting of betrayal than the females, with an overall mean acceptability score of 1.63, whereas the females' mean score was 1.31.

A complete, scientific understanding of these findings would require more data, and statistical analysis of such data would yield precise information such as the exact amount of difference between male and female ratings. For example, in the original text of this study, the authors note that males were 11.6 times more accepting of sexual betrayal by male transgressors than were females. Even without such details, it is possible to arrive at a basic understanding of the data represented in the graph, and to summarize this information in simple terms. Here is a summary of the information reported in this graph:

> While males and females both rated sexual betrayal as unacceptable, males (with a mean rating of 1.63) were significantly more accepting overall than were females (with a mean rating of 1.31). Even more dramatic, however, is the difference between male and female ratings when the gender of the transgressor is factored in. Males rated male transgression as markedly more acceptable than female transgression, with approximate means of 1.90 for male transgressions and 1.43 for female transgressions. The males' ratings contrast sharply with those of females, who indicated a mean acceptability rating of approximately 1.25 for male transgressors, and 1.30 for female transgressors. Therefore, while both sexes found transgression by members of their own sex more acceptable than transgressions by the opposite sex, men were more accepting overall than women, and men believed male transgressors were significantly more acceptable than female transgressors. On the other hand, women found transgression overall less acceptable than males did, and women indicated far less difference in their ratings of male versus female transgressors than did the male respondents.

■ PARAPHRASE

In certain cases, you may want to *paraphrase* rather than summarize material. Writing a paraphrase is similar to writing a summary: It involves recasting a passage into your own words, so it requires your complete understanding of the material. The difference is that while a summary is a shortened version of the original, the paraphrase is approximately the same length as the original.

Why write a paraphrase when you can quote the original? You may decide to offer a paraphrase of material written in language that is dense, abstract, archaic, or possibly confusing. For example, suppose you were writing a paper on some aspect of human progress and you came across the following passage by the Marquis de Condorcet, a French economist and politician, written in the late eighteenth century:

> If man can, with almost complete assurance, predict phenomena when he knows their laws, and if, even when he does not, he can still, with great expectations of success, forecast the future on the basis of his experience of the past, why, then, should it be regarded as a fantastic undertaking to sketch, with some pretense to truth, the future destiny of man on the basis of his history? The sole foundation for belief in the natural science is this idea, that the general laws directing the phenomena of the universe, known or unknown, are necessary and constant. Why should this principle be any less true for the development of the intellectual and moral faculties of man than for the other operations of nature?

You would like to introduce Condorcet's idea on predicting the future course of human history, but you also don't want to slow down your narrative with this dense and somewhat abstract quotation. You may decide to attempt a paraphrase, as follows:

> The Marquis de Condorcet believed that if we can predict such physical events as eclipses and tides, and if we can use past events as a guide to future ones, we should be able to forecast human destiny on the basis of history. Physical events, he maintained, are determined by natural laws that are knowable and predictable. Since humans are part of nature, why should their intellectual and moral development be any less predictable than other natural events?

Each sentence in the paraphrase corresponds to a sentence in the original. The paraphrase is somewhat shorter, owing to the differences of style between eighteenth- and twenty-first-century prose (we tend to be more brisk and efficient, although not as eloquent). But the main difference is that we have replaced the language of the original with our own language. For example, we have paraphrased Condorcet's "the general laws directing the phenomena of the universe, known or unknown, are necessary and constant" with "Physical events, he maintained, are determined by natural laws that are knowable and predictable." To contemporary readers, "knowable and predictable" might be clearer than "necessary and constant" as a description of natural (i.e., physical) laws. Note that we added the specific examples of eclipses and tides to clarify what might have been a somewhat abstract idea. Note also that we included two attributions to Condorcet within the paraphrase to credit our source properly.

When you come across a passage that you don't understand, the temptation is strong to skip over it. Resist this temptation! Use a paraphrase as a tool for explaining to yourself the main ideas of a difficult passage. By translating another writer's language into your own, you can clarify what you understand and pinpoint what you don't. The paraphrase therefore becomes a tool for learning the subject. The following pointers will help you write paraphrases.

■   **How to Write Paraphrases**

- Make sure that you understand the source passage.
- Substitute your own words for those of the source passage; look for synonyms that carry the same meaning as the original words.
- Rearrange your own sentences so that they read smoothly. Sentence structure, even sentence order, in the paraphrase need not be based on that of the original. A good paraphrase, like a good summary, should stand by itself.

Let's consider some other examples. If you were investigating the ethical concerns relating to the practice of in vitro fertilization, you might conclude that you should read some medical literature. You might reasonably want to hear from the doctors who are themselves developing, performing, and questioning the procedures that you are researching. In professional journals and bulletins, physicians write to one another, not to the general public. They use specialized language. If you wanted to refer to a technically complex selection, you might need to write a paraphrase for the following selection.

In Vitro Fertilization: From Medical Reproduction to Genetic Diagnosis

Dietmar Mieth

[I]t is not only an improvement in the success-rate that participating research scientists hope for but, rather, developments in new fields of research in in-vitro gene diagnosis and in certain circumstances gene therapy. In view of this, the French expert J. F. Mattei has asked the following question: "Are we forced to accept that in vitro fertilization will become one of the most compelling methods of genetic diagnosis?" Evidently, by the introduction of a new law in France and Sweden (1994), this acceptance (albeit with certain restrictions) has already occurred prior to the application of in vitro fertilization reaching a technically mature and clinically applicable phase. This may seem astonishing in view of the question placed by the above-quoted French expert: the idea of embryo production so as to withhold one or two embryos before implantation presupposes a definite "attitude towards eugenics." And to destroy an embryo merely because of its genetic characteristics could signify the reduction of a human life to the sum of its genes. Mattei asks: "In face of a molecular judgment on our lives, is there no possibility for appeal? Will the diagnosis of inherited monogenetic illnesses soon be extended to genetic predisposition for multi-factorial illnesses?"*

---

*Dietmar Mieth, "In Vitro Fertilization: From Medical Reproduction to Genetic Diagnosis," Biomedical Ethics: Newsletter of the European Network for Biomedical Ethics *1.1 (1996): 45.*

Like most literature intended for physicians, the language of this selection is somewhat forbidding to an audience of nonspecialists, who have trouble with phrases such as "predisposition for multi-factorial illnesses." As a courtesy to your readers and in an effort to maintain a consistent tone and level in your essay, you could paraphrase this paragraph of the medical newsletter. First, of course, you must understand the meaning of the passage, perhaps no small task. But, having read the material carefully (and perhaps consulting a dictionary), you might eventually prepare a paraphrase like this one:

> Writing in the Newsletter of the European Network for Biomedical Ethics, Dietmar Mieth reports that fertility specialists today want not only to improve the success rates of their procedures but also to diagnose and repair genetic problems before they implant fertilized eggs. Since the result of the in vitro process is often more fertilized eggs than can be used in a procedure, doctors may examine test-tube embryos for genetic defects and "withhold one or two" before implanting them. The practice of selectively implanting embryos raises concerns about eugenics and the rights of rejected embryos. On what genetic grounds will specialists distinguish flawed from healthy embryos and make a decision whether or not to implant? The appearance of single genes linked directly to specific, or "monogenetic," illnesses could be grounds for destroying an embryo. More complicated would be genes that predispose people to an illness but in no way guarantee the onset of that illness. Would these genes, which are only one factor in "multi-factorial illnesses" also be labeled undesirable and lead to embryo destruction? Advances in fertility science raise difficult questions. Already, even before techniques of genetic diagnosis are fully developed, legislatures are writing laws governing the practices of fertility clinics.

We begin our paraphrase with the same "not only/but also" logic of the original's first sentence, introducing the concepts of genetic diagnosis and therapy. The next four sentences in the original introduce concerns of a "French expert." Rather than quoting Mieth, quoting the expert, and immediately mentioning new laws in France and Sweden, we decided (first) to explain that in vitro fertilization procedures can give rise to more embryos than needed. We reasoned that nonmedical readers would appreciate our making explicit the background knowledge that the author assumes other physicians possess. Then we quote Mieth briefly ("withhold one or two" embryos) to provide some flavor of the original. We maintain focus on the ethical questions and wait until the end of the paraphrase before mentioning the laws to which Mieth refers. Our paraphrase is roughly the same length as the original, and it conveys the author's concerns about eugenics. As you can see, the paraphrase requires a writer to make some decisions about the presentation of material. In many, if not most, cases, you will need to do more than simply "translate" from the original, sentence by sentence, to write your paraphrase.

Finally, let's consider a passage written by a fine writer that may, nonetheless, best be conveyed in paraphrase. In "Identify All Carriers," an article on AIDS, editor and columnist William F. Buckley makes the following statement:

> I have read and listened, and I think now that I can convincingly crystallize the thoughts chasing about in the minds of, first, those whose concern with AIDS victims is based primarily on a concern for them, and for the maintenance of the most rigid standards of civil liberties and personal privacy, and, second, those whose anxiety to protect the public impels them to give subordinate attention to the civil amenities of those who suffer from AIDS and primary attention to the safety of those who do not.

In style, Buckley's passage is more like Condorcet's than the medical newsletter: It is eloquent, balanced, and literate. Still, it is challenging, consisting of another lengthy sentence, perhaps a bit too eloquent for some readers to grasp. For your paper on AIDS, you decide to paraphrase Buckley. You might draft something like this:

> Buckley finds two opposing sides in the AIDS debate: those
> concerned primarily with the civil liberties and the privacy of AIDS
> victims, and those concerned primarily with the safety of the public.

Paraphrases are generally about the same length as (sometimes shorter than) the passages on which they are based. But sometimes clarity requires that a paraphrase be longer than a tightly compacted source passage. For example, suppose you wanted to paraphrase this statement by Sigmund Freud:

> We have found out that the distortion in dreams which hinders our understanding of them is due to the activities of a censorship, directed against the unacceptable, unconscious wish-impulses.

If you were to paraphrase this statement (the first sentence in the Tenth Lecture of his *General Introduction to Psychoanalysis*), you might come up with something like this:

> It is difficult to understand dreams because they contain distortions.
> Freud believed that these distortions arise from our internal censor,
> which attempts to suppress unconscious and forbidden desires.

Essentially, this paraphrase does little more than break up one sentence into two and somewhat rearrange the sentence structure for clarity.

Like summaries, then, paraphrases are useful devices, both in helping you to understand source material and in enabling you to convey the essence of this source material to your readers. When would you choose to write a summary instead of a paraphrase (or vice versa)? The answer to this question depends on your purpose in presenting your source material. As we've said, summaries are generally based on articles (or sections of articles) or books. Paraphrases are generally based on particularly difficult (or important) paragraphs or sentences. You would seldom paraphrase a long passage, or summarize a short one, unless there were particularly good reasons for doing so. (For example, a lawyer might want to paraphrase several pages of legal language so that his or her client, who is not a lawyer, could understand it.) The purpose of a summary is generally to save your reader time by presenting him or her with a brief and quickly readable version of a lengthy source. The purpose of a paraphrase is generally to clarify a short passage that might otherwise be unclear. Whether you summarize or paraphrase may also depend on the importance of your source. A particularly important source—if it is not too long—may rate a paraphrase. If it is less important, or peripheral to your central argument, you may choose to write a summary instead. And, of course, you may choose to summarize only part of your source—the part that is most relevant to the point you are making.

Exercise 1.3

Summarizing and Paraphrasing

The following passage is excerpted from an article written in 1866 by Frederick Douglass, entitled "Reconstruction." In this piece the famed advocate for African-American rights appeals to the Second Session of the Thirty-ninth United States Congress, as it considered issues of state and federal rights in the aftermath of the Civil War. Read this passage and write both a summary and a paraphrase.

> Fortunately, the Constitution of the United States knows no distinction between citizens on account of color. Neither does it know any difference between a citizen of a State and a citizen of the United States. Citizenship evidently includes all the rights of citizens, whether State or national. If the Constitution knows none, it is clearly no part of the duty of a Republican Congress now to institute one. The mistake of the last session was the attempt to do this very thing, by a renunciation of its power to secure political rights to any class of citizens, with the obvious purpose to allow the rebellious States to disfranchise, if they should see fit, their colored citizens. This unfortunate blunder must now be retrieved, and the emasculated citizenship given to the negro supplanted by that contemplated in the Constitution of the United States, which declares that the citizens of each State shall enjoy all the rights and immunities of citizens of the several States,—so that a legal voter in any State shall be a legal voter in all the States.*

Exercise 1.4

More Paraphrasing

Locate and photocopy three relatively complex, but brief, passages from readings currently assigned in your other courses. Paraphrase these passages, making the language more readable and understandable. Attach the photocopies to the paraphrases.

---

*Frederick Douglass, "Reconstruction," The Atlantic Monthly, 18. 1866: 761–65.

■ QUOTATIONS

A *quotation* records the exact language used by someone in speech or writing. A *summary*, in contrast, is a brief restatement in your own words of what someone else has said or written. And a *paraphrase* also is a restatement, although one that is often as long as the original source. Any paper in which you draw upon sources will rely heavily on quotation, summary, and paraphrase. How do you choose among the three?

Remember that the papers you write should be your own—for the most part: your own language and certainly your own thesis, your own inferences, and your own conclusion. It follows that references to your source materials should be written primarily as summaries and paraphrases, both of which are built on restatement, not quotation. You will use summaries when you need a *brief* restatement, and paraphrases, which provide more explicit detail than summaries, when you need to follow the development of a source closely. When you quote too much, you risk losing ownership of your work: more easily than you might think, your voice can be drowned out by the voices of those you've quoted. So *use quotation sparingly*, as you would a pungent spice.

Nevertheless, *quoting just the right source at the right time can significantly improve your papers.* The trick is to know when and how to use quotations.

Choosing Quotations

You'll find that using quotations can be particularly helpful in several situations.

Quoting Memorable Language

Assume you're writing a paper on Napoleon Bonaparte's relationship with the celebrated Josephine. Through research you learn that two days after their marriage, Napoleon, given command of an army, left his bride for what was to be a brilliant military campaign in Italy. How did the young general respond to leaving his wife so soon after their wedding? You come across the following, written by Napoleon from the field of battle on April 3, 1796:

> I have received all your letters, but none has such an impact on me as the last. Do you have any idea, darling, what you are doing, writing to me in those terms? Do you not think my situation cruel enough without intensifying my longing for you, overwhelming my soul? What a style! What emotions you evoke! Written in fire, they burn my poor heart!*

A *summary* of this passage might read as follows:

> On April 3, 1796, Napoleon wrote to Josephine, expressing how sorely he missed her and how passionately he responded to her passionate letters.

*Francis Mossiker, trans. Napoleon and Josephine *(New York: Simon and Schuster, 1964), 437.

When to Quote

- Use quotations when another writer's language is particularly memorable and will add interest and liveliness to your paper.
- Use quotations when another writer's language is so clear and economical that to make the same point in your own words would, by comparison, be ineffective.
- Use quotations when you want the solid reputation of a source to lend authority and credibility to your own writing.

You might write the following as a *paraphrase* of the passage:

> On April 3, 1796, Napoleon wrote to Josephine that he had received her letters and that one among all others had had a special impact, overwhelming his soul with fiery emotions and longing.

How feeble this summary and paraphrase are when compared with the original! Use the vivid language that your sources give you. In this case, quote Napoleon in your paper to make your subject come alive with memorable detail:

> On April 3, 1796, a passionate, lovesick Napoleon responded to a letter from Josephine; she had written longingly to her husband, who, on a military campaign, acutely felt her absence. "Do you have any idea, darling, what you are doing, writing to me in those terms? . . . What emotions you evoke!" he said of her letters. "Written in fire, they burn my poor heart!"

Quotations can be direct or indirect. A *direct* quotation is one in which you record precisely the language of another, as we did with the sentences from Napoleon's letter. An *indirect* quotation is one in which you report what someone has said, although you are not obligated to repeat the words exactly as spoken (or written):

Direct quotation: Franklin D. Roosevelt said, "The only thing we have to fear is fear itself."

Indirect quotation: Franklin D. Roosevelt said that we have nothing to fear but fear itself.

The language in a direct quotation, which is indicated by a pair of quotation marks (" "), must be faithful to the language of the original passage. When using an indirect quotation, you have the liberty of changing words (although not changing meaning). For both direct and indirect quotations, *you must credit your sources,* naming them either in (or close to) the sentence that includes the quotation or in a parenthetical citation. (Note: We haven't included parenthetical citations in our examples here; see Chapter 7, pp. 288–306, for specific rules on citing sources properly.)

Quoting Clear and Concise Language

You should quote a source when its language is particularly clear and economical—when your language, by contrast, would be wordy. Read this passage from a text by Patricia Curtis on biology:

> The honeybee colony, which usually has a population of 30,000 to 40,000 workers, differs from that of the bumblebee and many other social bees or wasps in that it survives the winter. This means that the bees must stay warm despite the cold. Like other bees, the isolated honeybee cannot fly if the temperature falls below 10°C (50°F) and cannot walk if the temperature is below 7°C (45°F). Within the wintering hive, bees maintain their temperature by clustering together in a dense ball; the lower the temperature, the denser the cluster. The clustered bees produce heat by constant muscular movements of their wings, legs, and abdomens. In very cold weather, the bees on the outside of the cluster keep moving toward the center, while those in the core of the cluster move to the colder outside periphery. The entire cluster moves slowly about on the combs, eating the stored honey from the combs as it moves.*

A summary of this paragraph might read as follows:

> Honeybees, unlike many other varieties of bee, are able to live through the winter by "clustering together in a dense ball" for body warmth.

A paraphrase of the same passage would be considerably more detailed:

> Honeybees, unlike many other varieties of bee (such as bumblebees), are able to live through the winter. The 30,000 to 40,000 bees within a honeybee hive could not, individually, move about in cold winter temperatures. But when "clustering together in a dense ball," the bees generate heat by constantly moving their body parts. The cluster also moves slowly about the hive, those on the periphery of the cluster moving into the center, those in the center moving to the periphery, and all eating honey stored in the combs. This nutrition, in addition to the heat generated by the cluster, enables the honeybee to survive the cold winter months.

In both the summary and the paraphrase we've quoted Curtis's "clustering together in a dense ball," a phrase that lies at the heart of her description of wintering honeybees. For us to describe this clustering in any language other than Curtis's would be pointless since her description is admirably brief and precise.

Quoting Authoritative Language

You will also want to use quotations that lend authority to your work. When quoting an expert or some prominent political, artistic, or historical figure, you elevate your own work by placing it in esteemed company. Quote re-

---

*Patricia Curtis, "Winter Organization," Biology, 2nd ed. (New York: Worth, 1976), 822–23.

spected figures to establish background information in a paper, and your readers will tend to perceive that information as reliable. Quote the opinions of respected figures to endorse some statement that you've made, and your statement becomes more credible to your readers. For example, in an essay on the importance of reading well, you could make use of a passage from Thoreau's *Walden:*

> Reading well is hard work and requires great skill and training. It "is a noble exercise," writes Henry David Thoreau in Walden, "and one that will task the reader more than any exercise which the customs of the day esteem. . . . Books must be read as deliberately and reservedly as they were written."

[See below, pp. 44–45, for a discussion of when to use ellipses within quotations.]

By quoting a famous philosopher and essayist on the subject of reading, you add legitimacy to your discussion. Not only do *you* regard reading to be a skill that is both difficult and important, so too does Henry David Thoreau, one of our most influential thinkers. The quotation has elevated the level of your work.

You can also quote to advantage well-respected figures who have written or spoken about the subject of your paper. Here is a discussion of space flight. Author David Chandler refers to a physicist and a physicist-astronaut:

> A few scientists—notably James Van Allen, discoverer of the Earth's radiation belts—have decried the expense of the manned space program and called for an almost exclusive concentration on unmanned scientific exploration instead, saying this would be far more cost-effective.
>
> Other space scientists dispute that idea. Joseph Allen, physicist and former shuttle astronaut, says, "It seems to be argued that one takes away from the other. But before there was a manned space program, the funding on space science was zero. Now it's about $500 million a year."

Note that in the first paragraph Chandler has either summarized or used an indirect quotation to incorporate remarks made by James Van Allen into the discussion on space flight. In the second paragraph, Chandler directly quotes his next source, Joseph Allen. Both quotations, indirect and direct, lend authority and legitimacy to the article, for both James Van Allen and Joseph Allen are experts on the subject of space flight. Note also that Chandler provides brief but effective biographies of his sources, identifying both so that their qualifications to speak on the subject are known to all:

James Van Allen, *discoverer of the Earth's radiation belts . . .*

Joseph Allen, *physicist and former shuttle astronaut . . .*

The phrases in italics are called *appositives.* Their function is to rename the nouns they follow by providing explicit, identifying detail. Any information about a person that can be expressed in the following sentence pattern can be made into an appositive phrase:

> James Van Allen is the *discoverer of the Earth's radiation belts.*
>
> He has decried the expense of the manned space program.

Sentence with an appositive:

> James Van Allen, *discoverer of the Earth's radiation belts,* has decried the expense of the manned space program.

Appositives (in the example above, "discoverer of the Earth's radiation belts") efficiently incorporate identifying information about the authors you quote, while adding variety to the structure of your sentences.

Incorporating Quotations into Your Sentences

Quoting Only the Part of a Sentence or Paragraph That You Need

We've said that a writer selects passages for quotation that are especially *vivid and memorable, concise,* or *authoritative.* Now put these principles into practice. Suppose that while conducting research on college sports, you've come across the following, written by Robert Hutchins, former president of the University of Chicago:

> If athleticism is bad for students, players, alumni, and the public, it is even worse for the colleges and universities themselves. They want to be educational institutions, but they can't. The story of the famous halfback whose only regret, when he bade his coach farewell, was that he hadn't learned to read and write is probably exaggerated. But we must admit that pressure from trustees, graduates, "friends," presidents, and even professors has tended to relax academic standards. These gentry often overlook the fact that a college should not be interested in a fullback who is a half-wit. Recruiting, subsidizing and the double educational standard cannot exist without the knowledge and the tacit approval, at least, of the colleges and universities themselves. Certain institutions encourage susceptible professors to be nice to athletes now admitted by paying them for serving as "faculty representatives" on the college athletic board.*

Suppose that in this entire paragraph you find a gem, a sentence with quotable words that will enliven your discussion. You may want to quote part of the following sentence:

> These gentry often overlook the fact that a college should not be interested in a fullback who is a half-wit.

---

*Robert Hutchins, "Gate Receipts and Glory," The Saturday Evening Post 3 Dec. 1983: 38.

Incorporating the Quotation into the Flow of Your Own Sentence

Once you've selected the passage you want to quote, work the material into your paper in as natural and fluid a manner as possible. Here's how we would quote Hutchins:

> Robert Hutchins, former president of the University of Chicago, asserts that "a college should not be interested in a fullback who is a half-wit."

Note that we've used an appositive to identify Hutchins. And we've used only the part of the paragraph—a single clause—that we thought memorable enough to quote directly.

Avoiding Freestanding Quotations

A quoted sentence should never stand by itself—as in the following example:

> Various people associated with the university admit that the pressures of athleticism have caused a relaxation of standards. "These gentry often overlook the fact that a college should not be interested in a fullback who is a half-wit." But this kind of thinking is bad for the university and even worse for the athletes.

Even if it includes a parenthetical citation, a freestanding quotation would have the problem of being jarring to the reader. Introduce the quotation with a *signal phrase* that attributes the source not in a parenthetical citation, but in some other part of the sentence—beginning, middle, or end. Thus, you could write:

> As Robert Hutchins notes, "These gentry often overlook the fact that a college should not be interested in a fullback who is a half-wit."

Here's a variation with the signal phrase in the middle:

> "These gentry," asserts Robert Hutchins, "often overlook the fact that a college should not be interested in a fullback who is a half-wit."

Another alternative is to introduce a sentence-long quotation with a colon:

> But Robert Hutchins disagrees: "These gentry often overlook the fact that a college should not be interested in a fullback who is a half-wit."

Use colons also to introduce indented quotations (as in the cases when we introduce long quotations in this chapter).

When attributing sources in signal phrases, try to vary the standard *states, writes, says,* and so on. Other, stronger verbs you might consider: *asserts, argues, maintains, insists, asks,* and even *wonders.*

Exercise 1.5

Incorporating Quotations

Return to the passage by Bruce Chatwin, "Dreams of Patagonia," pages 22–24, and find some sentences that you think make interesting points. Imagine you want to use these points in a paper you're writing on travel literature. Write five different sentences that use a variety of the techniques discussed thus far to incorporate whole sentences as well as phrases from the "Patagonia" passage.

Using Ellipses

Using quotations becomes somewhat complicated when you want to quote the beginning and end of a passage but not its middle—as was the case when we quoted Henry David Thoreau. Here's part of the paragraph in *Walden* from which we quoted a few sentences:

> To read well, that is to read true books in a true spirit, is a noble exercise, and one that will task the reader more than any exercise which the customs of the day esteem. It requires a training such as the athletes underwent, the steady intention almost of the whole life to this object. Books must be read as deliberately and reservedly as they were written.*

And here was how we used this material:

> Reading well is hard work, writes Henry David Thoreau in <u>Walden</u>, "that will task the reader more than any exercise which the customs of the day esteem. . . . Books must be read as deliberately and reservedly as they were written."

Whenever you quote a sentence but delete words from it, as we have done, indicate this deletion to the reader with three spaced periods—called an "ellipsis"—in the sentence at the point of deletion. The rationale for using an ellipsis mark is that a direct quotation must be reproduced *exactly* as it was written or spoken. When writers delete or change any part of the quoted material, readers must be alerted so they don't think the changes were part of the original. When deleting an entire sentence or sentences from a quoted paragraph, as in the example above, end the sentence you have quoted with a period, place the ellipsis, and continue the quotation.

If you are deleting the middle of a single sentence, use an ellipsis in place of the deleted words:

> "To read well . . . is a noble exercise, and one that will task the reader more than any exercise which the customs of the day esteem."

If you are deleting material from the end of one sentence through to the beginning of another sentence, add a sentence period before the ellipsis:

> "It requires a training such as the athletes underwent. . . . Books must be read as deliberately and reservedly as they were written."

---

*Henry David Thoreau, Walden (New York: Signet Classic, 1960): 72.

If you begin your quotation of an author in the middle of his or her sentence, you need not indicate deleted words with an ellipsis. Be sure, however, that the syntax of the quotation fits smoothly with the syntax of your sentence:

> Reading "is a noble exercise," writes Henry David Thoreau.

Using Brackets to Add or Substitute Words

Use brackets whenever you need to add or substitute words in a quoted sentence. The brackets indicate to the reader a word or phrase that does not appear in the original passage but that you have inserted to avoid confusion. For example, when a pronoun's antecedent would be unclear to readers, delete the pronoun from the sentences and substitute an identifying word or phrase in brackets. When you make such a substitution, no ellipsis marks are needed. Assume that you wish to quote either of the underlined sentences in the following passage by Jane Yolen:

> Golden Press's *Walt Disney's Cinderella* set the new pattern for America's Cinderella. This book's text is coy and condescending. (Sample: "And her best friends of all were—guess who—the mice!") The illustrations are poor cartoons. And Cinderella herself is a disaster. She cowers as her sisters rip her homemade ball gown to shreds. (Not even homemade by Cinderella, but by the mice and birds.) <u>She answers her stepmother with whines and pleadings. She is a sorry excuse for a heroine, pitiable and useless.</u> She cannot perform even a simple action to save herself, though she is warned by her friends, the mice. She does not hear them because she is "off in a world of dreams." Cinderella begs, she whimpers, and at last has to be rescued by—guess who—the mice!*

In quoting one of these sentences, you would need to identify to whom the pronoun *she* refers. You can do this inside the quotation by using brackets:

> Jane Yolen believes that "[Cinderella] is a sorry excuse for a heroine, pitiable and useless."

If the pronoun begins the sentence to be quoted, you can identify the pronoun outside the quotation and simply begin quoting your source one word later:

> Jane Yolen believes that in the Golden Press version, Cinderella "is a sorry excuse for a heroine, pitiable and useless."

Here's another example of a case where the pronoun needing identification occurs in the middle of the sentence to be quoted. Newspaper reporters

---

*Jane Yolen, "America's 'Cinderella,'" *Children's Literature in Education* 8 (1977): 22.

When to Summarize, Paraphrase, and Quote

SUMMARIZE:

- To present main points of a lengthy passage (article or book)
- To condense peripheral points necessary to discussion

PARAPHRASE:

- To clarify a short passage
- To emphasize main points

QUOTE:

- To capture another writer's particularly memorable language
- To capture another writer's clearly and economically stated language
- To lend authority and credibility to your own writing

must use brackets in these cases frequently when quoting sources, who in interviews might say something like the following:

> After the fire they did not return to the station house for three hours.

If the reporter wants to use this sentence in an article, he or she needs to identify the pronoun:

> An official from City Hall, speaking on the condition that he not be identified, said, "After the fire [the officers] did not return to the station house for three hours."

You also will need to add bracketed information to a quoted sentence when a reference essential to the sentence's meaning is implied but not stated directly. Read the following paragraphs from physicist Robert Jastrow's "Toward an Intelligence Beyond Man's":

> These are amiable qualities for the computer; it imitates life like an electronic monkey. As computers get more complex, the imitation gets better. Finally, the line between the original and the copy becomes blurred. In another 15 years or so—two more generations of computer evolution, in the jargon of the technologists—we will see the computer as an emergent form of life.
>
> The proposition seems ridiculous because, for one thing, computers lack the drives and emotions of living creatures. But when drives are useful, they can be programmed into the computer's brain, just as nature programmed them into our ancestors' brains as a part of the equipment for survival. For example, computers, like people, work better and learn faster when they are motivated. Arthur Samuel made this discovery when he taught two IBM computers how to play checkers. They polished their game by playing each

Incorporating Quotations Into Your Sentences

- **Quote only the part of a sentence or paragraph that you need.** Use no more of the writer's language than you need to make or reinforce your point.

- **Incorporate the quotation into the flow of your own sentence.** The quotation must fit, both syntactically and stylistically, into your surrounding language.

- **Avoid freestanding quotations.** A quoted sentence should never stand by itself. Use a *signal phrase*—at the beginning, the middle, or the end of the sentence—to attribute the source of the quotation.

- **Use ellipsis marks.** Indicate deleted language in the middle of a quoted sentence with ellipsis marks. Deleted language at the beginning or end of a sentence generally does not require ellipsis marks.

- **Use brackets to add or substitute words.** Use brackets to add or substitute words in a quoted sentence when the meaning of the quotation would otherwise be unclear—for example, when the antecedent of a quoted pronoun is ambiguous.

> other, but they learned slowly. Finally, Dr. Samuel programmed in the will to win by forcing the computers to try harder—and to think out more moves in advance—when they were losing. Then the computers learned very quickly. One of them beat Samuel and went on to defeat a champion player who had not lost a game to a human opponent in eight years.*

If you wanted to quote only the underlined sentence above, you would need to provide readers with a bracketed explanation; otherwise, the words *the proposition* would be unclear. Here is how you would manage the quotation:

> According to Robert Jastrow, a physicist and former official at NASA's Goddard Institute, "The proposition [that computers will emerge as a form of life] seems ridiculous because, for one thing, computers lack the drives and emotions of living creatures."

Exercise 1.6

Using Brackets

Write your own sentences incorporating the following quotations. Use brackets to clarify information that isn't clear outside of its original context—and refer to the original sources to remind yourself of this context.

---

*Robert Jastrow, "Toward an Intelligence Beyond Man's," Time 20 Feb. 1978: 35.

From the Robert Jastrow piece on computers and intelligence:

    a.   Arthur Samuel made *this discovery* when he taught two IBM computers how to play checkers.

    b.   *They* polished their game by playing each other, but *they* learned slowly.

From the Jane Yolen excerpt on Cinderella:

    a.   *This book's* text is coy and condescending.

    b.   *She* cannot perform even a simple action to save herself, though she is warned by her friends, the mice.

    c.   She does not hear *them* because she is "off in a world of dreams."

Remember that when you quote the work of another, you are obligated to credit—or cite—the author's work properly; otherwise, you may be guilty of plagiarism. See pages 288–306 for guidance on citing sources.

■ AVOIDING PLAGIARISM

Plagiarism is generally defined as the attempt to pass off the work of another as one's own. Whether born out of calculation or desperation, plagiarism is the least tolerated offense in the academic world. The fact that most plagiarism is unintentional—arising from ignorance of conventions rather than deceitfulness—makes no difference to many professors.

The ease of cutting and pasting whole blocks of text from Web sources into one's own paper makes it tempting for some to take the easy way out and avoid doing their own research and writing. But apart from the serious ethical issues involved, the same technology that makes such acts possible also makes it possible for instructors to detect them. Software marketed to instructors allows them to conduct Web searches, using suspicious phrases as keywords. The results often provide irrefutable evidence of plagiarism.

Of course, plagiarism is not confined to students. Recent years have seen a number of high profile cases—some of them reaching the front pages of newspapers—of well-known scholars who were shown to have copied passages from sources into their own book manuscripts, without proper attribution. In some cases, the scholars maintained that these appropriations were simply a matter of carelessness, and that in the press and volume of work, they had lost track of which words were theirs and which were the words of their sources. But such excuses sounded hollow: These careless acts inevitably embarrassed the scholars professionally, disappointed their many admirers, and tarnished their otherwise fine work and reputations.

You can avoid plagiarism and charges of plagiarism by following the basic rules provided on page 50.

Following is a passage of text, along with several student versions of the ideas represented. (The passage is from Richard Rovere's article on Senator Joseph P. McCarthy, titled "The Most Gifted and Successful Demagogue This Country Has Ever Known.")

> McCarthy never seemed to believe in himself or in anything he had said. He knew that Communists were not in charge of American foreign policy. He knew that they weren't running the United States Army. He knew that he had spent five years looking for Communists in the government and that—although some must certainly have been there, since Communists had turned up in practically every other major government in the world—he hadn't come up with even one.*

One student version of this passage reads as follows:

> McCarthy never believed in himself or in anything he had said. He knew that Communists were not in charge of American foreign policy and weren't running the United States Army. He knew that he had spent five years looking for Communists in the government, and although there must certainly have been some there, since Communists were in practically every other major government in the world, he hadn't come up with even one.

Clearly, this is intentional plagiarism. The student has copied the original passage almost word for word.

Here is another version of the same passage:

> McCarthy knew that Communists were not running foreign policy or the Army. He also knew that although there must have been some Communists in the government, he hadn't found a single one, even though he had spent five years looking.

This student has attempted to put the ideas into her own words, but both the wording and the sentence structure still are so heavily dependent on the original passage that even if it *were* cited, most professors would consider it plagiarism.

In the following version, the student has sufficiently changed the wording and sentence structure, and she uses a signal phrase (a phrase used to introduce a quotation or paraphrase, signaling to the reader that the words to follow come from someone else) to properly credit the information to Rovere, so that there is no question of plagiarism:

> According to Richard Rovere, McCarthy was fully aware that Communists were running neither the government nor the Army. He also knew that he hadn't found a single Communist in government, even after a lengthy search (192).

And although this is not a matter of plagiarism, as noted above, it's essential to quote accurately. You are not permitted to change any part of a quotation or to omit any part of it without using brackets or ellipses (see pp. 44–48).

Richard Rovere, "The Most Gifted and Successful Demagogue This Country Has Ever Known," New York Times Magazine 30 Apr. 1967.

Rules for Avoiding Plagiarism

- Cite *all* quoted material and *all* summarized and paraphrased material, unless the information is common knowledge (e.g., the Civil War was fought from 1861 to 1865).
- Make sure that both the *wording* and the *sentence structure* of your summaries and paraphrases are substantially your own.

 # WRITING ASSIGNMENT: SUMMARY

Read "The Political Genius of Abraham Lincoln" by Doris Kearns Goodwin. (This selection by the Pulitzer Prize–winning historian is from her 2005 book *Team of Rivals: The Political Genius of Abraham Lincoln.*) Write a summary of the passage, following the directions in this chapter for dividing the article into sections, for writing a one-sentence summary of each section, and then for joining section summaries with a thesis. Prepare for the summary by making notes in the margins. You may find it useful to recall that well-written pieces, like Goodwin's, often telegraph clues to their own structure as a device for assisting readers. Such clues can be helpful when preparing a summary. Your finished product should be the result of two or more drafts.

Note: Additional summary assignments will be found in Chapter 9, "Practicing Academic Writing," focusing on merit vs. privilege in college admissions.

THE POLITICAL GENIUS OF ABRAHAM LINCOLN

Doris Kearns Goodwin*

Doris Kearns Goodwin won the Pulitzer Prize in history for No Ordinary Time. *She is the author of* Wait Till Next Year, The Fitzgeralds and the Kennedys, *and* Lyndon Johnson and the American Dream. *This selection is excerpted from her 2005 book* Team of Rivals: The Political Genius of Abraham Lincoln, *published by Simon and Schuster.*

In 1876, the celebrated orator Frederick Douglass dedicated a monument in Washington, D.C., erected by black Americans to honor Abraham Lincoln. The former slave told his audience that "there is little necessity on this occasion to speak at length and critically of this great and good man, and of his high mission in the world. That ground has been fully occupied. . . . The whole field of fact and fancy

---

*Doris Kearns Goodwin. Team of Rivals: The Political Genius of Abraham Lincoln. *NY: Simon and Schuster, 2005, v–viii.*

has been gleaned and garnered. Any man can say things that are true of Abraham Lincoln, but no man can say anything that is new of Abraham Lincoln."

Speaking only eleven years after Lincoln's death, Douglass was too close to assess the fascination that this plain and complex, shrewd and transparent, tender and iron-willed leader would hold for generations of Americans. In the nearly two hundred years since his birth, countless historians and writers have uncovered new documents, provided fresh insights, and developed an ever-deepening understanding of our sixteenth president.

In my own effort to illuminate the character and career of Abraham Lincoln, I have coupled the account of his life with the stories of the remarkable men who were his rivals for the 1860 Republican presidential nomination—New York senator William H. Seward, Ohio governor Salmon P. Chase, and Missouri's distinguished elder statesman Edward Bates.

Taken together, the lives of these four men give us a picture of the path taken by ambitious young men in the North who came of age in the early decades of the nineteenth century. All four studied law, became distinguished orators, entered politics, and opposed the spread of slavery. Their upward climb was one followed by many thousands who left the small towns of their birth to seek opportunity and adventure in the rapidly growing cities of a dynamic, expanding America.

5   Just as a hologram is created through the interference of light from separate sources, so the lives and impressions of those who companioned Lincoln give us a clearer and more dimensional picture of the president himself. Lincoln's barren childhood, his lack of schooling, his relationships with male friends, his complicated marriage, the nature of his ambition, and his ruminations about death can be analyzed more clearly when he is placed side by side with his three contemporaries.

When Lincoln won the nomination, each of his celebrated rivals believed the wrong man had been chosen. Ralph Waldo Emerson recalled his first reception of the news that the "comparatively unknown name of Lincoln" had been selected: "we heard the result coldly and sadly. It seemed too rash, on a purely local reputation, to build so grave a trust in such anxious times."

Lincoln seemed to have come from nowhere—a backwoods lawyer who had served one undistinguished term in the House of Representatives and had lost two consecutive contests for the U.S. Senate. Contemporaries and historians alike have attributed his surprising nomination to chance—the fact that he came from the battleground state of Illinois and stood in the center of his party. The comparative perspective suggests a different interpretation. When viewed against the failed efforts of his rivals, it is clear that Lincoln won the nomination because he was shrewdest and canniest of them all. More accustomed to relying upon himself to shape events, he took the greatest control of the process leading up to the nomination, displaying a fierce ambition, an exceptional political acumen, and a wide range of emotional strengths, forged in the crucible of personal hardship, that took his unsuspecting rivals by surprise.

That Lincoln, after winning the presidency, made the unprecedented decision to incorporate his eminent rivals into his political family, the cabinet, was evidence of a profound self-confidence and a first indication of what would prove to others a most unexpected greatness. Seward became secretary of state, Chase secretary of the treasury, and Bates attorney general. The remaining top posts Lincoln offered to three former Democrats whose stories also inhabit these pages—Gideon Welles, Lincoln's "Neptune," was made secretary of the navy, Montgomery Blair became post-master general, and Edwin M. Stanton, Lincoln's "Mars," eventually became secretary of war. Every member of this administration was better known, better educated, and more experienced in public life than Lincoln. Their presence in the cabinet might have threatened to eclipse the obscure prairie lawyer from Springfield.

It soon became clear, however, that Abraham Lincoln would emerge the undisputed captain of this most unusual cabinet, truly a team of rivals. The powerful competitors who had originally disdained Lincoln became colleagues who helped him steer the country through its darkest days. Seward was the first to appreciate Lincoln's remarkable talents, quickly realizing the futility of his plan to relegate the president to a figurehead role. In the months that followed, Seward would become Lincoln's closest friend and advisor in the administration. Though Bates initially viewed Lincoln as a well-meaning but incompetent administrator, he eventually concluded that the president was an unmatched leader, "very near being a perfect man." Edwin Stanton, who had treated Lincoln with contempt at their initial acquaintance, developed a great respect for the commander in chief and was unable to control his tears for weeks after the president's death. Even Chase, whose restless ambition for the presidency was never realized, at last acknowledged that Lincoln had outmaneuvered him.

10   This, then, is a story of Lincoln's political genius revealed through his extraordinary array of personal qualities that enabled him to form friendships with men who had previously opposed him; to repair injured feelings that, left untended, might have escalated into permanent hostility; to assume responsibility for the failures of subordinates; to share credit with ease; and to learn from mistakes. He possessed an acute understanding of the sources of power inherent in the presidency, an unparalleled ability to keep his governing coalition intact, a tough-minded appreciation of the need to protect his presidential prerogatives, and a masterful sense of timing. His success in dealing with the strong egos of the men in his cabinet suggests that in the hands of a truly great politician the qualities we generally associate with decency and morality—kindness, sensitivity, compassion, honesty, and empathy—can also be impressive political resources.

Critical Reading and Critique 2

■ CRITICAL READING

When writing papers in college, you are often called on to respond critically to source materials. Critical reading requires the abilities to both summarize and evaluate a presentation. As you have seen in Chapter 1, a *summary* is a brief restatement in your own words of the content of a passage. An *evaluation*, however, is a more difficult matter.

In your college work, you read to gain and *use* new information; but as sources are not equally valid or equally useful, you must learn to distinguish critically among them by evaluating them.

There is no ready-made formula for determining validity. Critical reading and its written equivalent—the *critique*—require discernment, sensitivity, imagination, knowledge of the subject, and above all, willingness to become involved in what you read. These skills cannot be taken for granted and are developed only through repeated practice. You must begin somewhere, though, and we recommend that you start by posing two broad categories of questions about passages, articles, and books that you read: (1) To what extent does the author succeed in his or her purpose? (2) To what extent do you agree with the author?

Question 1: To What Extent Does the Author Succeed in His or Her Purpose?

All critical reading *begins with an accurate summary.* Thus before attempting an evaluation, you must be able to locate an author's thesis and identify the selection's content and structure. You must understand the author's *purpose.* Authors write to inform, to persuade, and to entertain. A given piece may be primarily *informative* (a summary of the research on cloning), primarily *persuasive* (an argument on why the government must do something to alleviate homelessness), or primarily *entertaining* (a play about the frustrations of young lovers). Or it may be all three (as in John Steinbeck's novel *The Grapes of Wrath*, about migrant workers during the Great Depression). Sometimes, authors are not fully conscious of their purpose. Sometimes their purpose changes as they write. Also, more than one purpose can overlap: An essay may need to inform the reader about an issue in order to make a persuasive point. But if the finished piece is coherent, it will have a primary reason for having been written, and it should be apparent that the author is attempting primarily to inform, persuade, or entertain a particular audience. To identify this primary reason—this purpose—is your first job as a critical reader. Your next job is to

Where Do We Find Written Critiques?

Here are just a few types of writing that involve critique:

ACADEMIC WRITING

- **Research papers.** Critique sources in order to establish their usefulness.
- **Position papers.** Stake out a position by critiquing other positions.
- **Book reviews.** Combine summary with critique.
- **Essay exams.** Demonstrate understanding of course material by critiquing it.

WORKPLACE WRITING

- **Legal briefs and legal arguments.** Critique previous rulings or arguments made by opposing counsel.
- **Business plans and proposals.** Critique other, less cost-effective approaches.
- **Policy briefs.** Communicate failings of policies and legislation through critique.

determine how successful the author has been. As a critical reader, you bring different criteria, or standards of judgment, to bear when you read pieces intended to inform, persuade, or entertain.

Writing to Inform

A piece intended to inform will provide definitions, describe or report on a process, recount a story, give historical background, and/or provide facts and figures. An informational piece responds to questions such as the following:

What (or who) is _____?
How does _____ work?
What is the controversy or problem about?
What happened?
How and why did it happen?
What were the results?
What are the arguments for and against _____?

To the extent that an author answers these and related questions and the answers are a matter of verifiable record (you could check for accuracy if you had the time and inclination), the selection is intended to inform. Having determined this, you can organize your response by considering three other criteria: accuracy, significance, and fair interpretation of information.

Evaluating Informative Writing

Accuracy of Information   If you are going to use any of the information presented, you must be satisfied that it is trustworthy. One of your responsibilities as a critical reader, then, is to find out if it is accurate. This means you should check facts against other sources. Government publications are often good resources for verifying facts about political legislation, population data, crime statistics, and the like. You can also search key terms in library databases and on the Web. Since material on the Web is essentially "self-published," however, you must be especially vigilant in assessing its legitimacy. In Chapter 7, on research, we provide a more detailed discussion of how you should approach Web sources. A wealth of useful information is now available on the Internet—but there is also a tremendous amount of misinformation, distorted "facts," and unsupported opinion.

Significance of Information   One useful question that you can put to a reading is "So what?" In the case of selections that attempt to inform, you may reasonably wonder whether the information makes a difference. What can the person who is reading gain from this information? How is knowledge advanced by the publication of this material? Is the information of importance to you or to others in a particular audience? Why or why not?

Fair Interpretation of Information   At times you will read reports, the sole function of which is to relate raw data or information. In these cases, you will build your response on the two aspects of Question 1, introduced on page 53: What is the author's purpose in writing? Does he or she succeed in this purpose? More frequently, once an author has presented information, he or she will attempt to evaluate or interpret it—which is only reasonable, since information that has not been evaluated or interpreted is of little use. One of your tasks as a critical reader is to make a distinction between the author's presentation of facts and figures and his or her attempts to evaluate them. Watch for shifts from straightforward descriptions of factual information ("20% of the population") to assertions about what this information means ("*a mere* 20% of the population"), what its implications are, and so on. Pay attention to whether the logic with which the author connects interpretation with facts is sound. You may find that the information is valuable but the interpretation is not. Perhaps the author's conclusions are not justified. Could you offer a contrary explanation for the same facts? Does more information need to be gathered before firm conclusions can be drawn? Why?

Writing to Persuade

Writing is frequently intended to persuade—that is, to influence the reader's thinking. To make a persuasive case, the writer must begin with an assertion that is arguable, some statement about which reasonable people could disagree. Such an assertion, when it serves as the essential organizing principle of the article or book, is called a *thesis*. Here are two examples:

> Because they do not speak English, many children in this affluent land are being denied their fundamental right to equal educational opportunity.

> Bilingual education, which has been stridently promoted by a small group of activists with their own agenda, is detrimental to the very students it is supposed to serve.

Thesis statements such as these—and the subsequent assertions used to help support them—represent conclusions that authors have drawn as a result of researching and thinking about an issue. You go through the same process yourself when you write persuasive papers or critiques. And just as you are entitled to critically evaluate the assertions of authors you read, so your professors—and other students—are entitled to evaluate *your* assertions, whether they be encountered as written arguments or as comments made in class discussion.

Keep in mind that writers organize arguments by arranging evidence to support one conclusion and oppose (or dismiss) another. You can assess the validity of the argument and the conclusion by determining whether the author has (1) clearly defined key terms, (2) used information fairly, (3) argued logically and not fallaciously (see pp. 58–64).

Exercise 2.1

Informative and Persuasive Thesis Statements

With a partner from your class, identify at least one informative and one persuasive thesis statement from two passages of your own choosing. Photocopy these passages and highlight the statements you have selected.

As an alternative, and also working with a partner, write one informative and one persuasive thesis statement for *three* of the topics listed in the last paragraph of this exercise. For example, for the topic of prayer in schools, your informative thesis statement could read this way:

> Both advocates and opponents of school prayer frame their position as a matter of freedom.

Your persuasive thesis statement might be worded as follows:

> As long as schools don't dictate what kinds of prayers students should say, then school prayer should be allowed and even encouraged.

Don't worry about taking a position that you agree with or feel you could support. The exercise doesn't require that you write an essay at this point. The topics:

school prayer

gun control

sex education in schools

grammar instruction in English class

violent lyrics in music

teaching computer skills in primary schools

curfews in college dormitories

course registration procedures

Evaluating Persuasive Writing

Read the argument that follows on the nation's troubled "star" system for producing elite athletes and dancers. We will illustrate our discussion on defining terms, using information fairly, and arguing logically by referring to Joan Ryan's argument. The example critique that follows these illustrations will be based on this same argument.

WE ARE NOT CREATED EQUAL IN EVERY WAY

Joan Ryan

In an opinion piece for The San Francisco Chronicle *(December 12, 2000), columnist and reporter Joan Ryan takes a stand on whether the San Francisco Ballet School did or did not discriminate against 8-year-old Fredrika Keefer when it declined to admit her on the grounds that she had the wrong body type to be a successful ballerina. Keefer's mother subsequently sued the ballet school for discrimination, claiming that the rejection had caused her daughter confusion and humiliation. Ryan examines the question of setting admissions standards and also the problems some parents create by pushing their young children to meet these standards.*

Fredrika Keefer is an 8-year-old girl who likes to dance, just like her mother and grandmother before her. She relishes playing the lead role of Clara in the Pacific Dance Theater's "Petite Nutcracker." So perhaps she is not as shy as many fourth-graders. But I wonder how she feels about her body being a topic of public discussion.

Fredrika and her mother filed suit because, as her mother puts it, she "did not have the right body type to be accepted" by the San Francisco Ballet School. "My daughter is very sophisticated, so she understands why we're doing this," Krissy Keefer said. "And the other kids think she's a celebrity."

There is no question Keefer raises a powerful point in her complaint. The values placed on an unnaturally thin body for female performers drives some dancers to potentially fatal eating disorders. But that isn't exactly the issue here. This is: Does the San Francisco Ballet School have the right to give preference to leaner body types in selecting 300 students from this year's 1,400 applicants?

Yes, for the same reason UC Berkeley can reject students based on mental prowess and a fashion modeling school can reject students based on comeliness. Every institution has standards that weed out those who are less likely to succeed. I know this flies in the face of American ideals. But the reality is that all men and women are not created equal.

5   Like it or not, the ethereal, elongated body that can float on air is part of the look and feel of classical ballet. You and I might think ballet would be just as pleasing with

larger bodies. But most of those who practice the art disagree, which is their right. This doesn't mean that women with different body types cannot become professional dancers. They just have to find a different type of dance—jazz, tap, modern— just as athletes have to find sports that fit certain body types. A tall, blocky man, for example, could not be a jockey but he could play baseball.

Having written extensively about the damaging pressures on young female gymnasts and figure skaters, I understand Keefer's concerns about body type. But for me, the more disturbing issue in this story isn't about weight but age.

The San Francisco Ballet School is very clear and open about the fact it is strictly a training ground for professional dancers. "We are not a recreation department," said a ballet spokeswoman.

In other words, children at age 8 are already training for adult careers. By age 12 or 13, the children are training so much that they either begin homeschooling or attend a school that accommodates the training schedule. The child has thrown all her eggs into this one little basket at an age when most kids can barely decide what to wear to school in the morning. And the child knows the parents are paying lots of money for this great opportunity.

The ballet school usually has a psychologist to counsel the students, but at the moment there is not one on staff. And the parents are given no training by the school on the pitfalls their daughters might encounter as they climb the ballet ladder: weight issues, physical ailments, social isolation, psychological pressure.

10   Just as in elite gymnastics and figure skating, these children are in the netherland of the law. They are neither hobbyists nor professionals. There is no safety net for them, no arm of government that makes sure that the adults in their lives watch out for their best interests.

Keefer said she would drop her lawsuit if the school accepted her daughter. The San Francisco Ballet School offers the best training in the Bay Area, she said. Fredrika, however, has said she is quite happy dancing where she is. Still, the mother gets to decide what's best for her daughter's dancing career. The child is clearly too young to make such a decision. Yet, in the skewed logic of elite athletics and dancing, she is not too young to pay the price for it.

Exercise 2.2

Critical Reading Practice

Look back at the Critical Reading for Summary box on page 7 of Chapter 1. Use each of the guidelines listed there to examine the essay by Ryan. Note in the margins of the selection, or on a separate sheet of paper, the essay's main point, subpoints, and use of examples.

Persuasive Strategies

Clearly Defined Terms   The validity of an argument depends to some degree on how carefully an author has defined key terms. Take the assertion, for example, that American society must be grounded in "family values."

Just what do people who use this phrase mean by it? The validity of their argument depends on whether they and their readers agree on a definition of "family values"—as well as what it means to be "grounded in" family values. If an author writes that in the recent past "America's elites accepted as a matter of course that a free society can sustain itself only through virtue and temperance in the people" (Charles Murray, "The Coming White Underclass," *Wall Street Journal*, October 20, 1993), readers need to know what, exactly, the author means by "elites" and by "virtue and temperance" before they can assess the validity of the argument. In such cases, the success of the argument—its ability to persuade—hinges on the definition of a term. So, in responding to an argument, be sure you (and the author) are clear on what exactly is being argued. Unless you are, no informed response is possible.

Ryan uses several terms important for understanding her argument. The primary one is the "body type" that the San Francisco Ballet School uses as an application standard. Ryan defines this type (paragraph 5) as "the elongated body that can float on air." Leaving other terms undefined, she writes that the ballet school's use of body-type as a standard "flies in the face of American ideals" (paragraph 4). Exactly *which* ideals she leaves for the reader to define: these might include fair play, equality of access, or the belief that decisions ought to be based on talent, not appearance. The reader cannot be sure. When she reports that a spokeswoman for the school stated that "We are not a recreation department," Ryan assumes the reader will understand the reference. The mission of a recreation department is to give *all* participants equal access. In a youth recreation league, children of all abilities would get to play in a baseball game. In a league for elite athletes, in which winning was a priority, coaches would permit only the most talented children to play.

When writing a paper, you will need to decide, like Ryan, which terms to define and which you can assume the reader will define in the same way you do. As the writer of a critique, you should identify and discuss any undefined or ambiguous term that might give rise to confusion.

Fair Use of Information   Information is used as evidence in support of arguments. When you encounter such evidence, ask yourself two questions: (1) "Is the information accurate and up-to-date?" At least a portion of an argument becomes invalid if the information used to support it is inaccurate or out-of-date. (2) "Has the author cited *representative* information?" The evidence used in an argument must be presented in a spirit of fair play. An author is less than ethical when he presents only evidence favoring his views even though he is well aware that contrary evidence exists. For instance, it would be dishonest to argue that an economic recession is imminent and to cite only indicators of economic downturn while ignoring and failing to cite contrary (positive) evidence.

As you have seen, "We Are Not Created Equal in Every Way" is not an information-heavy essay. The success of the piece turns on the author's use of logic, not facts and figures. In this case, the reader has every reason to trust that Ryan has presented the facts accurately: an 8-year-old girl has been denied admission to a prestigious ballet school. The mother of the girl has sued the school.

Logical Argumentation: Avoiding Logical Fallacies

At some point, you will need to respond to the logic of the argument itself. To be convincing, an argument should be governed by principles of *logic*—clear and orderly thinking. This does *not* mean that an argument should not be biased. A biased argument—that is, an argument weighted toward one point of view and against others, which is in fact the nature of argument—may be valid as long as it is logically sound.

Several examples of faulty thinking and logical fallacies to watch for follow.

Emotionally Loaded Terms   Writers sometimes attempt to sway readers by using emotionally charged words—words with positive connotations to sway readers to their own point of view (e.g., "family values") or words with negative connotations to sway readers away from the opposing point of view. The fact that an author uses emotionally loaded terms does not necessarily invalidate the argument. Emotional appeals are perfectly legitimate and time-honored modes of persuasion. But in academic writing, which is grounded in logical argumentation, they should not be the *only* means of persuasion. You should be sensitive to *how* emotionally loaded terms are being used. In particular, are they being used deceptively or to hide the essential facts?

Ryan appeals to our desire to protect children in "We Are Not Created Equal in Every Way." She writes of "disturbing issue[s]," lack of a "safety net for" young people on the star track to elite performance and an absence of adults "watch[ing] out for [the children's] best interests." Ryan understands that no reader wants to see a child abused; and while she does not use the word *abuse* in her essay, she implies that parents who push young children too hard to succeed commit abuse. That implication is enough to engage the sympathies of the reader. As someone evaluating the essay, you should be alert to this appeal to your emotions and then judge if the appeal is fair and convincing. Above all, you should not let an emotional appeal blind you to shortcomings of logic, ambiguously defined terms, or a misuse of facts.

Ad Hominem Argument   In an *ad hominem* argument, the writer rejects opposing views by attacking the person who holds them. By calling opponents names, an author avoids the issue. Consider this excerpt from a political speech:

> I could more easily accept my opponent's plan to increase revenues by collecting on delinquent tax bills if he had paid more than a hundred dollars in state taxes in each of the past three years. But the fact is, he's a millionaire with a millionaire's tax shelters. This man hasn't paid a wooden nickel for the state services he and his family depend on. So I ask you: Is *he* the one to be talking about taxes to *us*?

Tone

Related to "emotionally loaded terms" is *tone*. When we speak of the tone of a piece of writing, we refer to the overall emotional effect produced by the writer's choice of language.

- Were a film reviewer to repeatedly use such terms as *wonderful, adorable, magnificent performance,* when discussing a film and its actors, we might call the tone gushing.
- If a columnist, in referring to a politician's tax proposal, used such language as *obscene, the lackeys of big business fat cats,* and *sleazeball techniques,* we would call the tone angry.
- If another writer were to use language like "That's a great idea. Let's all give three cheers," when he clearly meant just the opposite, we would call the tone sarcastic.

These are extreme examples of tone; but tone can be more muted, particularly if the writer makes a special effort *not* to inject emotion into the writing. Almost any adjective describing human emotion can be attached to *tone* to describe the mood that is conveyed by the writer and the writing: *playful, objective, brutal, dispassionate, sly, apologetic, rueful, cynical, hopeful, gleeful.*

As we've indicated in the section "Emotionally Loaded Terms," the fact that a writer's tone is highly emotional does not necessarily mean that the writer's argument is invalid. Conversely, a neutral tone does not ensure an argument's validity. One who argues passionately is not necessarily wrong, any more than one who comes across as objective and measured is necessarily right. In either case, we have to examine the validity of the argument on its own merits. We should recognize that we may have been manipulated into agreeing or disagreeing largely through an author's tone, rather than through his or her arguments.

Keep in mind, also, that many college instructors are likely to be put off by student writing that projects a highly emotional tone, a quality they will often consider more appropriate for the op-ed page of the student newspaper than for academic or preprofessional work. (One giveaway indicator of inappropriate emotion is the exclamation mark, which should be used very sparingly.)

It could well be that the opponent has paid virtually no state taxes for three years; but this fact has nothing to do with, and is a ploy to divert attention from, the merits of a specific proposal for increasing revenues. The proposal is lost in the attack against the man himself, an attack that violates the principles of logic. Writers (and speakers) must make their points by citing evidence in support of their views and by challenging contrary evidence.

Does Ryan attack Fredrika Keefer's mother in this essay? You be the judge. Here are lines referring directly or indirectly to Krissy Keefer. Is Ryan attacking the mother, directly or indirectly? Point to specific words and phrases to support your conclusion:

> Fredrika and her mother filed suit because, as her mother puts it, she "did not have the right body type to be accepted" by the San Francisco Ballet School. "My daughter is very sophisticated, so she understands why we're doing this," Krissy Keefer said. "And the other kids think she's a celebrity."

> There is no question Keefer raises a powerful point in her complaint.

> Keefer said she would drop her lawsuit if the school accepted her daughter. The San Francisco Ballet School offers the best training in the Bay Area, she said. Fredrika, however, has said she is quite happy dancing where she is. Still, the mother gets to decide what's best for her daughter's dancing career. The child is clearly too young to make such a decision. Yet, in the skewed logic of elite athletics and dancing, she is not too young to pay the price for it.

Faulty Cause and Effect   The fact that one event precedes another in time does not mean that the first event has caused the second. An example: Fish begin dying by the thousands in a lake near your hometown. An environmental group immediately cites chemical dumping by several manufacturing plants as the cause. But other causes are possible: A disease might have affected the fish; the growth of algae might have contributed to the deaths; or acid rain might be a factor. The origins of an event are usually complex and are not always traceable to a single cause. So you must carefully examine cause-and-effect reasoning when you find a writer using it. In Latin, this fallacy is known as *post hoc, ergo propter hoc* ("after this, therefore because of this").

The debate over the San Francisco Ballet School's refusal to admit Fredrika Keefer involves a question of cause and effect. Is Fredrika Keefer's rejection by the ballet school caused by the school's insistence that its students have an "ethereal, elongated body"? Certainly if the school changes that standard, the outcome changes: Fredrika Keefer is admitted. Or is the cause of the rejection, as the school claims, Fredrika's body type? Change her body type (in a few years she may grow), and she may be admitted. The debate is at least partially about cause and effect. The ballet school and the mother are pointing to the same effect—Fredrika's rejection—but disagree, to the point of going to court, over the cause.

Ryan uses cause-and-effect logic in the essay to suggest that Fredrika Keefer's mother, and by extension all parent managers, can cause their children harm by pushing them too hard in their training. At the end of the essay, Ryan writes that Fredrika is too young "to decide what's best for her . . . dancing career" but that "she is not too young to pay the price for" the decisions her mother makes to promote that career. The "price" Fredrika pays will be "caused" by her mother's (poor) decisions.

Either/Or Reasoning   Either/or reasoning also results from an unwillingness to recognize complexity. If an author analyzes a problem and offers only two courses of action, one of which he or she refutes, then you are entitled to object that the other is not thereby true. Usually, several other options (at the very least) are possible. For whatever reason, the author has chosen to overlook them. As an example, suppose you are reading a selection on genetic engineering and the author builds an argument on the basis of the following:

> Research in gene splicing is at a crossroads: Either scientists will be carefully monitored by civil authorities and their efforts limited to acceptable applications, such as disease control; or, lacking regulatory guidelines, scientists will set their own ethical standards and begin programs in embryonic manipulation that, however well intended, exceed the proper limits of human knowledge.

Certainly, other possibilities for genetic engineering exist beyond the two mentioned here. But the author limits debate by establishing an either/or choice. Such limitation is artificial and does not allow for complexity. As a critical reader, be on the alert for either/or reasoning.

Hasty Generalization   Writers are guilty of hasty generalization when they draw their conclusions from too little evidence or from unrepresentative evidence. To argue that scientists should not proceed with the human genome project because a recent editorial urged that the project be abandoned is to make a hasty generalization. This lone editorial may be unrepresentative of the views of most individuals—both scientists and laypeople—who have studied and written about the matter. To argue that one should never obey authority because Stanley Milgram's Yale University experiments in the 1960s show the dangers of obedience is to ignore the fact that Milgram's experiment was concerned primarily with obedience to *immoral* authority. Thus, the experimental situation was unrepresentative of most routine demands for obedience—for example, to obey a parental rule or to comply with a summons for jury duty—and a conclusion about the malevolence of all authority would be a hasty generalization.

False Analogy   Comparing one person, event, or issue to another may be illuminating, but it may also be confusing or misleading. Differences between the two may be more significant than the similarities, and conclusions drawn from one may not necessarily apply to the other. A writer who argues that it is reasonable to quarantine people with AIDS because quarantine has been effective in preventing the spread of smallpox is assuming an analogy between AIDS and smallpox that is not valid (because of the differences between the two diseases).

Ryan compares the San Francisco Ballet School's setting an admissions standard to both a university's and a modeling school's setting standards. Are the analogies apt? Certainly one can draw a parallel between the standards used by the ballet school and a modeling school: Both emphasize a candidate's appearance, among other qualities. Are the admissions standards to a university based on appearance? In principle, no. At least that's not a criterion any college admissions office would post on its Web site. A critical reader might therefore want to object that one of Ryan's analogies is faulty.

Ryan attempts to advance her argument by making another comparison:

> [The rejection of a candidate because she does not have a body suited to classical ballet] doesn't mean that women with different body types cannot become professional dancers. They just have to find a different type of dance—jazz, tap, modern—just as athletes have to find sports that fit certain body types. A tall, blocky man, for example, could not be a jockey but he could play baseball.

The words "just as" signal an attempt to advance the argument by making an analogy. What do you think? Is the analogy sufficiently similar to Fredrika Keefer's situation to persuade you?

Begging the Question   To beg the question is to assume as a proven fact the very thesis being argued. To assert, for example, that America is not in decline because it is as strong and prosperous as ever is not to prove anything: It is merely to repeat the claim in different words. This fallacy is also known as *circular reasoning*.

When Ryan writes that "There is no safety net for [children placed into elite training programs], no arm of government that makes sure that the adults in their lives watch out for their best interests," she assumes that there should be such a safety net. But, as you will read in the sample critique, this is a point that must be argued, not assumed. Is such intervention wise? Under what circumstances, for instance, would authorities intervene in a family? Would authorities have the legal standing to get involved if there were no clear evidence of physical abuse? Ryan is not necessarily wrong in desiring "safety nets" for young, elite athletes and dancers; but she assumes a point that she should be arguing.

Non Sequitur   *Non sequitur* is Latin for "it does not follow"; the term is used to describe a conclusion that does not logically follow from a premise. "Since minorities have made such great strides in the past few decades," a writer may argue, "we no longer need affirmative action programs." Aside from the fact that the premise itself is arguable (*have* minorities made such great strides?), it does not follow that because minorities *may* have made great strides, there is no further need for affirmative action programs.

Oversimplification   Be alert for writers who offer easy solutions to complicated problems. "America's economy will be strong again if we all 'buy American,'" a politician may argue. But the problems of America's economy are complex and cannot be solved by a slogan or a simple change in buying habits. Likewise, a writer who argues that we should ban genetic engineering assumes that simple solutions ("just say 'no'") will be sufficient to deal with the complex moral dilemmas raised by this new technology.

Exercise 2.3

Understanding Logical Fallacies

Make a list of the nine logical fallacies discussed in the last section. Briefly define each one in your own words. Then, in a group of three or four class-mates, review your definitions and the examples we've provided for each logical fallacy. Collaborate with your group to find or invent examples for each of the fallacies. Compare your examples with those generated by the other groups in your class.

Writing to Entertain

Authors write not only to inform and persuade but also to entertain. One response to entertainment is a hearty laugh, but it is possible to entertain without laughter: A good book or play or poem may prompt you to reflect, grow wistful, become elated, get angry. Laughter is only one of many possible reactions. As with a response to an informative piece or an argument, your response to an essay, poem, story, play, novel, or film should be precisely stated and carefully developed. Ask yourself some of the following questions (you won't have space to explore all of them, but try to consider some of the most important): Did I care for the portrayal of a certain character? Did that character (or a group of characters united by occupation, age, ethnicity, etc.) seem overly sentimental, for example, or heroic? Did his adversaries seem too villainous or stupid? Were the situations believable? Was the action interesting or merely formulaic? Was the theme developed subtly or powerfully, or did the work come across as preachy or shrill? Did the action at the end of the work follow plausibly from what had come before? Was the language fresh and incisive or stale and predictable? Explain as specifically as possible what elements of the work seemed effective or ineffective and why. Offer an overall assessment, elaborating on your views.

Question 2: To What Extent Do You Agree with the Author?

When formulating a critical response to a source, try to distinguish your evaluation of the author's purpose and success at achieving that purpose from your agreement or disagreement with the author's views. The distinction allows you to respond to a piece of writing on its merits. As an unbiased, evenhanded critic, you evaluate an author's clarity of presentation, use of evidence, and adherence to principles of logic. To what extent has the author succeeded in achieving his or her purpose? Still withholding judgment, offer your assessment and give the author (in effect) a grade. Significantly, your assessment of the presentation may not coincide with your views of the author's conclusions: You may agree with an author entirely but feel that the presentation is superficial; you may find the author's logic and use of evidence to be rock solid but at the same time may resist certain conclusions. A critical evaluation works well when it is conducted in two parts. After evaluating the author's purpose and design for achieving that purpose, respond to the author's main assertions. In doing so, you'll want to identify points of agreement and disagreement and also evaluate assumptions.

Identify Points of Agreement and Disagreement

Be precise in identifying points of agreement and disagreement with an author. You should state as clearly as possible what *you* believe, and an effective way of doing this is to define your position in relation to that presented in the piece. Whether you agree enthusiastically, disagree, or agree with reservations, you can organize your reactions in two parts: (1) summarize the author's position; and (2) state your own position and elaborate on your reasons for holding it. The elaboration, in effect, becomes an argument itself, and this is true regardless of the position you take. An opinion is effective when you support it by supplying evidence from your reading (which should be properly cited), your observation, or your personal experience. Without such evidence, opinions cannot be authoritative. "I thought the article on inflation was lousy." Or: "It was terrific." Why? "I just thought so, that's all." This opinion is worthless because the criticism is imprecise: The critic has taken neither the time to read the article carefully nor the time to explore his own reactions carefully.

Exercise 2.4

Exploring Your Viewpoints—in Three Paragraphs

Go to a Web site that presents short persuasive essays on current social issues, such as reason.com, opinion-pages.org, drudgereport.com, or Speakout.com. Or go to an Internet search engine and type in a social issue together with the word "articles," "editorials," or "opinion," and see what you find. Locate a selection on a topic of interest that takes a clear, argumentative position. Print out the selection on which you choose to focus. Write one paragraph summarizing the author's key argument. Write two paragraphs articulating your agreement or disagreement with the author. (Devote each paragraph to a *single* point of agreement or disagreement.) Be sure to explain why you think or feel the way you do and, wherever possible, cite relevant evidence— from your reading, experience, or observation.

Explore the Reasons for Agreement and Disagreement: Evaluate Assumptions

One way of elaborating your reactions to a reading is to explore the underlying *reasons* for agreement and disagreement. Your reactions are based largely on assumptions that you hold and how these assumptions compare with the author's. An *assumption* is a fundamental statement about the world and its operations that you take to be true. A writer's assumptions may be explicitly stated; but just as often assumptions are implicit and you will have to "ferret them out," that is, to infer them. Consider an example:

> *In vitro* fertilization and embryo transfer are brought about outside the bodies of the couple through actions of third parties whose competence and technical activity determine the success of the procedure. Such fertilization entrusts the life and identity of the embryo into the power of doctors and biologists and establishes the domination of technology over the origin and destiny of the human person. Such a relationship of domination is in itself contrary to the dignity and equality that must be common to parents and children.*

This paragraph is quoted from the February 1987 Vatican document on artificial procreation. Then Cardinal Joseph Ratzinger (and now Pope Benedict XVI), principal author of the document, makes an implicit assumption in this paragraph: No good can come of the domination of technology over conception. The use of technology to bring about conception is morally wrong. Yet thousands of childless couples, Roman Catholics included, have rejected this assumption in favor of its opposite: Conception technology is an aid to the barren couple; far from creating a relationship of unequals, the technology brings children into the world who will be welcomed with joy and love.

Assumptions provide the foundation on which entire presentations are built. If you find an author's assumptions invalid—that is, not supported by factual evidence—or if you disagree with value-based assumptions underlying an author's positions, you may well disagree with conclusions that follow from these assumptions. The author of a book on developing nations may include a section outlining the resources and time that will be required to industrialize a particular country and so upgrade its general welfare. Her assumption—that industrialization in that particular country will ensure or even affect the general welfare—may or may not be valid. If you do not share the assumption, in your eyes the rationale for the entire book may be undermined.

How do you determine the validity of assumptions once you have identified them? In the absence of more scientific criteria, you may determine validity by how well the author's assumptions stack up against your own experience, observations, reading, and values. A caution, however: The overall value of an article or book may depend only to a small degree on the validity of the author's assumptions. For instance, a sociologist may do a fine job of

From the Vatican document Instruction on Respect for Human Life in Its Origin and on the Dignity of Procreation, *given at Rome, from the Congregation for the Doctrine of the Faith, 22 Feb. 1987, as presented in* Origins: N.C. Documentary Service 16.40 (19 Mar. 1987): 707.

gathering statistical data about the incidence of crime in urban areas along the eastern seaboard. The sociologist also might be a Marxist, and you may disagree with the subsequent analysis of the data. Yet you may still find the data extremely valuable for your own work.

Readers will want to examine two assumptions at the heart of Ryan's essay on Fredrika Keefer and the San Francisco Ballet School's refusal to admit her. First, Ryan assumes that setting a standard for admission based on a candidate's appearance is equivalent to setting a standard based on a candidate's "mental prowess," the admissions standard (presumably) used by universities. An appearance-based standard, Ryan writes, will "weed out those who are less likely to succeed" in professional ballet. The writer of the critique that follows agrees with Ryan's assumption. But you may not. You may assume, by contrast, that standards based on appearance are arbitrary while those based on intellectual ability rest on documented talent (SAT scores or high school transcripts, for instance). Ryan makes a second assumption: that there is an appropriate and inappropriate way to raise children. She does not state these (appropriate) ways explicitly, but that does not keep Ryan from using them to judge Krissy Keefer harshly. You may disagree with Ryan and find a reason to cheer Krissy Keefer's defense of her daughter's rights. That's your decision. What you must do as a critical reader is recognize assumptions whether they are stated openly or not. You should spell them out and then accept or reject them. Ultimately, your agreement or disagreement with an author will rest on your agreement or disagreement with the author's assumptions.

■ CRITIQUE

In Chapter 1 we focused on summary—the condensed presentation of ideas from another source. Summary is key to much of academic writing because it relies so heavily on the works of others for support of claims. It's not going too far to say that summarizing is the critical thinking skill from which a majority of academic writing builds. However, most academic thinking and writing do not stop at summary; usually we use summary to restate our understanding of things we see or read. Then we put that summary to use. In academic writing, one typical use of summary is as a prelude to critique.

A *critique* is a *formalized, critical reading of a passage*. It also is a personal response, but writing a critique is considerably more rigorous than saying that a movie is "great," or a book is "fascinating," or "I didn't like it." These are all responses, and, as such, they're a valid, even essential, part of your understanding of what you see and read. But such responses don't illuminate the subject for anyone—even you—if you haven't explained how you arrived at your conclusions.

Your task in writing a critique is to turn your critical reading of a passage into a systematic evaluation in order to deepen your reader's (and your own) understanding of that passage. Among other things, you're interested in determining what an author says, how well the points are made, what assumptions underlie the argument, what issues are overlooked, and what implications can be drawn from such an analysis. Critiques, positive or negative, should include a fair and accurate summary of the passage; they may draw on and cite information and ideas from other sources (your reading or your personal experience and observations); and they should include a statement of your own assumptions. It is important to remember that you bring to bear an entire set of assumptions about the world. Stated or not, these assumptions underlie every evaluative comment you make; you therefore have an obligation, both to the reader and to yourself, to clarify your standards by making your assumptions explicit. Not only do your readers stand to gain by your forthrightness, but you do as well: In the process of writing a critical assessment, you are forced to examine your own knowledge, beliefs, and assumptions. Ultimately, the critique is a way of learning about yourself—yet another example of the ways in which writing is useful as a tool for critical thinking.

How to Write Critiques

You may find it useful to organize your critiques into five sections: introduction, summary, assessment of the presentation (on its own terms), your response to the presentation, and conclusion.

The accompanying box offers some guidelines for writing critiques. Note that they are guidelines, not a rigid formula. Thousands of authors write critiques that do not follow the structure outlined here. Until you are more confident and practiced in writing critiques, however, we suggest you follow these guidelines. They are meant not to restrict you, but rather to provide a workable sequence for writing critiques.

■ DEMONSTRATION: CRITIQUE

The critique that follows is based on Joan Ryan's "We Are Not Created Equal in Every Way," which appeared in the *San Francisco Chronicle* as an op-ed piece on December 12, 2000 (see pages 57–58) and which we have to some extent already begun to examine. In this formal critique, you will see that it is possible to agree with an author's main point, at least provisionally, but disagree with other elements of the argument. Critiquing a different selection, you could just as easily accept the author's facts and figures but reject the conclusion he draws from them. As long as you carefully articulate the author's assumptions and your own, explaining in some detail your

Guidelines for Writing Critiques

- *Introduce.* Introduce both the passage under analysis and the author. State the author's main argument and the point(s) you intend to make about it.

  Provide background material to help your readers understand the relevance or appeal of the passage. This background material might include one or more of the following: an explanation of why the subject is of current interest; a reference to a possible controversy surrounding the subject of the passage or the passage itself; biographical information about the author; an account of the circumstances under which the passage was written; or a reference to the intended audience of the passage.

- *Summarize.* Summarize the author's main points, making sure to state the author's purpose for writing.

- *Assess the presentation.* Evaluate the validity of the author's presentation, as distinct from your points of agreement or disagreement. Comment on the author's success in achieving his or her purpose by reviewing three or four specific points. You might base your review on one (or more) of the following criteria:

  Is the information accurate?

  Is the information significant?

  Has the author defined terms clearly?

  Has the author used and interpreted information fairly?

  Has the author argued logically?

- *Respond to the presentation.* Now it is your turn to respond to the author's views. With which views do you agree? With which do you disagree? Discuss your reasons for agreement and disagreement, when possible, tying these reasons to assumptions—both the author's and your own. Where necessary, draw upon outside sources to support your ideas.

- *Conclude.* State your conclusions about the overall validity of the piece—your assessment of the author's success at achieving his or her aims and your reactions to the author's views. Remind the reader of the weaknesses and strengths of the passage.

agreement and disagreement, the critique is yours to take in whatever direction you see fit.

Let's summarize the preceding sections by returning to the core questions that guide critical reading. You will see how, when applied to Joan Ryan's argument, they help to set up a critique.

To What Extent Does the Author Succeed in His or Her Purpose?

To answer this question, you will need to know the author's purpose. Joan Ryan's "We Are Not created Equal in Every Way" is an argument—actually, *two* related arguments. She wants readers to accept her view that (1) a school of performing arts has the right to set admissions standards according to criteria it believes will ensure the professional success of its graduates; and (2) parents may damage their children by pushing them too hard to meet the standards set by these schools.

By supporting a ballet school's right to set admission standards based on appearance, Ryan supports the star system that produces our elite athletes and performers. At the same time, she disapproves of parents who risk their children's safety and welfare by pushing them through this system. Ryan both defends the system and attacks it. Her ambivalence on the issue keeps the argument from fully succeeding.

To What Extent Do You Agree or Disagree with the Author? Evaluate Assumptions.

Ryan's views on the debate surrounding Fredrika Keefer's rejection from the San Francisco School of Ballet rests on the assumption that the school has the right to set its own admissions standards—even if we find those standards harsh. All institutions, she claims, have that right. The writer of the critique that follows agrees with Ryan, although you have seen previously how it is possible to disagree.

Ryan's second argument concerns the wisdom of subjecting an 8-year-old to the rigors of professional training. Ryan disapproves. The writer of the critique, while sympathetic to Ryan's concerns, states that as a practical and even as a legal matter it would be nearly impossible to prevent parents such as Krissy Keefer from doing exactly as they pleased in the name of helping their children. In our culture, parents have the right (short of outright abuse) to raise children however they see fit.

Finally, the writer of the critique notes a certain ambivalence in Ryan's essay: her support of the ballet school's admission standards on the one hand and her distaste of parent managers like Krissy Keefer on the other. The writer does not find evidence of a weak argument in Ryan's mixed message but rather a sign of confusion in the broader culture: We love our young stars but we condemn parents for pushing children to the breaking point in the name of stardom.

The selections you will be likely to critique are those, like Ryan's, that argue a specific position. Indeed, every argument you read is an invitation to agreement or disagreement. It remains only for you to speak up and justify your position.

MODEL CRITIQUE*

Ralston 1

Eric Ralston

Professor Reilly

Writing 2

11 January 2007

A Critique of "We Are Not Created Equal in Every Way" by Joan Ryan

Most freshmen know how it feels to apply to a school and be rejected. Each year, college admissions offices mail thousands of thin letters that begin: "Thank you for your application. The competition this year was unusually strong. . . ." We know that we will not get into every college on our list or pass every test or win the starring role after every audition, but we believe that we deserve the chance to try. And we can tolerate rejection if we know that we compete on a level playing field. But when that field seems to arbitrarily favor some candidates over others, we take offense. At least that's when an ambitious mother took offense, bringing to court a suit that claimed her eight-year-old daughter, Fredrika Keefer, was denied admission to the prestigious San Francisco Ballet School because she had the wrong "body type" (57).

In an opinion piece for the San Francisco Chronicle (12 December 2000), Joan Ryan asks: "Does [a ballet school] have the right to give preference to leaner body types?" Her answer is a firm "yes". Ryan argues that institutions have the right to set whatever standards they want to ensure that those they admit meet the physical or intellectual requirements for professional success. But she also believes that some parents push their children too hard to meet those standards. Ryan offers a questionable approach to protecting children from the possible abuses of such parents. Overall, however, she raises timely issues in discussing the star system that produces our world-class athletes and performers. The sometimes conflicting concerns she expresses reflect contradictions and tensions in our larger culture.

The issue Ryan discusses is a particularly sensitive one because the child's mother charged the ballet school with discrimination. As a society we have made great strides over the past few decades in combating some of the more

---

References to Ryan are to her article as reprinted in Sequence for Academic Writing.

Ralston 2

blatant forms of discrimination--racial, ethnic, and sexual. But is it possible, is it desirable, to eliminate <u>all</u> efforts to distinguish one person from another? When is a standard that permits some (but not all) people entry to an institution discriminatory and when is it a necessary part of doing business? Ryan believes that schools discriminate all the time, and rightly so when candidates for admission fail to meet the stated criteria for academic or professional success. That UC Berkeley does not accept every applicant is <u>discriminating</u>, not discriminatory. Ryan recognizes the difference.

4   She maintains, correctly, that the San Francisco Ballet School, like any other institution, has the right to set standards by which it will accept or reject applicants. Rejection is a part of life, she writes, expressing the view that gives her essay its title: "We Are Not Created Equal in Every Way." And because we are not created equal, not everyone will be admitted to his or her number one school or get a turn on stage. That's the inevitable consequence of setting standards: Some people will meet them and gain admission, others won't. Ryan quotes the spokesperson who explained that the San Francisco Ballet School is "'not a recreation department'" (58). In other words, a professional ballet school, like a university, is within its rights to reject applicants with body types unsuited to its view of success in professional ballet. The standard may be cruel and to some even arbitrary, but it is understandable. To put the matter bluntly, candidates with unsuitable body types, however talented or otherwise attractive, are less likely to succeed in professional ballet than those with "classical" proportions. Female dancers, for example, must regularly be lifted and carried, as if effortlessly, by their male counterparts--a feat that is difficult enough even with "leaner body types." Ryan points out that candidates without the ideal body type for ballet are not barred from professional dance: "[t]hey just have to find a different type of dance . . . just as athletes have to find sports that fit certain body types" (58).

5   The San Francisco Ballet School is <u>not</u> saying that people of a certain skin color or religious belief are not welcome. That <u>would</u> be discriminatory and wrong. But the standard concerning body type cuts across <u>all</u> people, rich or poor, black or white, Protestant or Jew, male or female. Such a broad standard

Ralston 3

could be termed an equal opportunity standard: If it can be used to distinguish among all people equally, it is discriminating, not discriminatory.

(6)   Ryan's parallel concern in this essay is the damage done to children by parents who push them at an early age to meet the high standards set by professional training programs. Children placed onto such star tracks attend special schools (or receive home schooling) in order to accommodate intense training schedules that sometimes lead to physical or psychological injuries. In healthy families, we might expect parents to protect children from such dangers. But parents who manage what they view as their children's "careers" may be too single minded to realize that their actions may place Johnny and Susie at risk.

(7)   Ryan disapproves of a star track system that puts children into professional training at a young age. In pursuing a career in dance, for instance, a young "child has thrown all her eggs into this one little basket at an age when most kids can barely decide what to wear to school in the morning" (58). The law makes no provision for protecting such elite performers in training, writes Ryan: "There is no safety net for them, no arm of government that makes sure that the adults in their lives watch out for their best interests" (58).

(8)   Like the rest of us, Ryan assumes there are appropriate and inappropriate ways to raise children. While she does not explicitly share her preferred approach, she is very clear about what does not work: pushing children like Fredrika Keefer into professional ballet school. When Ryan points out that "no arm of government" looks out for children like Keefer, she implies the need for a Department of Youth Services to supervise parent managers. That is not a good idea.

(9)   There is no sure way to tell when a parent's managing of a child's dance or athletic schedule is abusive or constructive. Intense dedication is necessary for would-be elite athletes and performers to succeed, and such dedication often begins in childhood. Since young children are not equipped to organize their lives in pursuit of a single goal, parents step in to help. That's what the parents of Tiger Woods did on recognizing his talents:

Ralston 4

[H]is father . . . [started] him very early. . . . [Tiger] was on the Mike Douglas show hitting golf balls when he was three years old. I mean, this is a prodigy type thing. This is like Mozart writing his first symphony when he was six, that sort of thing, and he did show unique ability right from the beginning. And his life has been channeled into being a pro. His father has devoted his life to bringing him to this point. His father hasn't worked full-time since 1988. That's what it's been all about. (Feinstein)

(10) Ryan would point out, correctly, that for every Tiger Woods or Michele Kwan there are many child-athletes and performing artists who fall short of their goals. They may later regret the single-minded focus that robbed them of their childhood, but there is no way to know before committing a child to years of dedicated practice if he or she will become the next Tiger or an embittered also-ran. We simply do not have the wisdom to intervene in a parent manager's training program for her child. And Joan Ryan is not going to find an "arm of government" to intervene in the child rearing of Fredrika Keefer, however much she may "pay the price for" (58) her mother's enthusiasm.

(11) The tension in Ryan's essay over high standards and the intense preparation to meet them mirrors a tension in the larger culture. On the one hand, Ryan persuasively argues that elite institutions like the San Francisco Ballet School have the right to set standards for admission. At such institutions, high standards give us high levels of achievement--dancers, for instance, who "can float on air" (57). We cheer brilliant performers like Tiger Woods and Michele Kwan who started on their roads to success while still children. The star system produces stars. On the other hand, Ryan condemns parents who buy into the star system by pushing their children into professional training programs that demand a single-minded focus. We are horrified to learn that McCauley Culkin of the <u>Home Alone</u> movies never really had a childhood (Peterson). Of course Culkin and others like him didn't have childhoods: They were too busy practicing their lines or their jumps and spins. If Ryan defends high standards in one breath and criticizes parents in the next for pushing

children to achieve these standards, she is only reflecting a confusion in the larger culture: We love our stars, but we cannot have our stars without a star system that demands total (and often damaging) dedication from our youngest and most vulnerable citizens. That parents can be the agent of this damage is especially troubling.

(12)   Joan Ryan is right to focus on the parents of would-be stars, and she is right to remind us that young children pressured to perform at the highest levels can suffer physically and psychologically. Perhaps it was better for Fredrika Keefer the child (as opposed to Fredrika Keefer the future professional dancer) that she was not admitted to the San Francisco School of Ballet. For Keefer's sake and that of other child performers, we should pay attention to the dangers of the star system and support these children when we can. But without clear evidence of legally actionable neglect or abuse, we cannot interfere with parent managers, however much we may disagree with their decisions. We may be legitimately concerned, as is Ryan, that such a parent is driving her child to become not the next Tiger Woods but the next admission to a psychiatric ward. In a free society, for better or for worse, parents have the right to guide (or misguide) the lives of their children. All the rest of us can do is watch--and hope for the best.

[New Page]

Works Cited

Feinstein, John. "Year of the Tiger." Interview with Jim Lehrer. Online News Hour. 14 Apr. 1997. 28 Jan. 2006 <http://www.pbs.org/newshour/bb/sports/tiger_4-14.html>.

Peterson, Paul. Interview with Gary James. 28 Jan. 2006 <http://www.classicbands.com/PaulPetersonInterview.html>.

Ryan, Joan. "We Are Not Created Equal in Every Way." San Francisco Chronicle 12 Dec. 2000. A29.

Informal Critique of Sample Essay

Before reading the discussion of this model critique, write your own informal response to the critique. What are its strengths and weaknesses? To what extent does the critique follow the general guidelines for writing critiques that we outlined on pages 69–70? To the extent it varies from the guidelines, speculate on why. Jot down some ideas for a critique that take a different approach to Ryan's essay.

Discussion

- Paragraph 1 of the model critique introduces the issue to be reviewed. It provides brief background information and sets a general context that explains why the topic of fair (and unfair) competition is important.

- Paragraph 2 introduces the author and the essay and summarizes the author's main claims. The paragraph ends (see the final three sentences) with the writer's overall assessment of the essay.

- Paragraph 3 sets a specific context for evaluating Ryan's first claim concerning admissions standards. The writer summarizes Ryan's position by making a distinction between the terms *discriminating* and *discriminatory.*

- Paragraph 4 evaluates Ryan's first claim, that the ballet school has the right to set admission standards. The writer supports Ryan's position.

- Paragraph 5 continues the evaluation of Ryan's first claim. Again, the writer of the critique supports Ryan, returning to the distinction between *discriminating* and *discriminatory.*

- Paragraphs 6–7 summarize Ryan's second claim, that parents can damage their children by pushing them too hard through professional training programs at too early an age.

- Paragraphs 8–10 evaluate Ryan's second claim. In Paragraph 8 the writer states that Ryan makes a mistake in implying that a government agency should safeguard the interests of children like Fredrika Keefer. Paragraphs 9–10 present a logic for disagreeing with Ryan on this point.

- Paragraph 11 evaluates the essay as a whole. Ryan defends the right of schools in the star system to set high standards but objects when parents push young children into this system. This "tension" in the essay reflects a confusion in the larger culture.

- Paragraph 12 concludes the critique. The writer offers qualified support of Ryan's position, agreeing that children caught in the star system can suffer. The writer also states that there is not much we can do about the problem, except watch and hope for the best.

Critical Reading for Critique

- *Use the tips from Critical Reading for Summary on page 7.* Remember to examine the context; note the title and subtitle; identify the main point; identify the subpoints; break the reading into sections; distinguish between points, examples, and counterarguments; watch for transitions within and between paragraphs; and read actively.
- *Establish the writer's primary purpose in writing.* Is the piece primarily meant to inform, persuade, or entertain?
- *Evaluate informative writing. Use these criteria (among others):*

   Accuracy of information

   Significance of information

   Fair interpretation of information
- *Evaluate persuasive writing. Use these criteria (among others):*

   Clear definition of terms

   Fair use and interpretation of information

   Logical reasoning
- *Evaluate writing that entertains. Use these criteria (among others):*

   Interesting characters

   Believable action, plot, and situations

   Communication of theme

   Use of language
- *Decide whether you agree or disagree with the writer's ideas, position, or message.* Once you have determined the extent to which an author has achieved his or her purpose, clarify your position in relation to the writer's.

 WRITING ASSIGNMENT: CRITIQUE

Read and write a critique of "With No Boys to Ogle, We Had Time to Learn," in which columnist and attorney Christine Flowers argues for the continued relevance of single-sex education. You might read such an essay in an education course or in the context of a semester-long focus on devising schools for at-risk children. The piece originally appeared in the "My Turn" section of *Newsweek* on October 24, 2005.

Before reading, review the tips presented in the box *Critical Reading for Critique.* When you're ready to write your critique, start by jotting down notes in response to the tips for critical reading and the earlier discussions of evaluating writing in this chapter. What assumptions does Flowers make? Review the logical fallacies on pages 60–64, and identify any that appear in the essay. Work out your ideas on paper, perhaps producing an outline.

Then write a rough draft of your critique. Review the reading and revise your rough draft at least once before considering it finished. You may want to look ahead to Chapter 6, Writing as a Process, to help guide you through writing your critique.

For an additional exercise in writing critiques, see Chapter 8, a practice chapter that assembles ten readings on the topic of merit vs. privilege in college admissions. You will have the opportunity to write a critique that you then place into a larger argument.

WITH NO BOYS TO OGLE, WE HAD TIME TO LEARN

Christine Flowers

My father was not a braggart. He rarely went to the office armed with stories of his offspring's achievements. He was so reticent about his children that many of his colleagues didn't know how many of us there were. So it was a rare sign of pride when he announced to the entire law firm that his daughter had been accepted to Bryn Mawr College. Most of his co-workers, especially the women, were congratulatory. But Dad's puffed-out chest deflated somewhat when a friend in the litigation department said, "Why do you want to send her to a girls' school where they don't shave their armpits and spend all their time dancing around Maypoles and chanting in Greek?"

Despite that co-worker's (inaccurate) views about the hygienic patterns and pastimes of Bryn Mawrtyrs, I was exceedingly happy at college, especially since it gave me the opportunity to extend my 12 years of single-sex education into 16.

I'm one of those people who believe that males and females should mix at parties, at sporting events and in holy matrimony, but that it's far too distracting to have a member of the opposite sex sitting in class beside you. This is a minority position, and I'm aware that most people think it's important for boys and girls to socialize—supposedly so they can deal appropriately with one another when they become men and women. Still, there's something to be said for separating the genders in school.

At Bryn Mawr, the women I encountered were brilliant, independent and focused. Not all of them arrived that way, as this writer can confirm, but all of them exited confident of success in whichever fields they chose to enter. We idolized both Pallas Athena, Greek goddess of wisdom, and our most famous alumna, Katharine Hepburn. Two very independent dames.

5　I immersed myself in French and Italian, history and philosophy, fencing and swimming. I never once worried about whether I was going to have a date on Friday night (I never once did), nor did I hesitate to contribute a comment in class because I felt intimidated by the attractive young man to my left. More likely than not, a glance to the left would have revealed an earnest, sweat-suit-clad woman in a ponytail, unusually alert for 8:10 in the morning and ready to engage in academic battle. And while academics were the raison d'etre of my alma mater, my tuition covered an additional, albeit intangible, fringe benefit. Bryn Mawr helped me to understand that excellence has no gender preference.

But females aren't the only ones to benefit from a single-sex education. I used to teach at a boys' school in suburban Philadelphia, and while I'm certain that my teenage scholars weren't completely unaware of female charms (including those of the three women on the upper-school faculty), they did seem to focus admirably on their schoolwork between the hours of 8 and 3. The fact that they also focused on pushing each other down staircases and into walls in a release of testosterone just underlines the fact that, left in a natural habitat, boys bond bloody.

I'm not against integrating the sexes. The alternative would result in the extinction of the human race. Ever since the Garden of Eden, we've had to learn how to get along. And it's true that some people function better in a coed environment, although the fellows at The Citadel might have something to say about that.

It's simply that schools are designed for academics, not as social clubs. Children and young adults have ample opportunity to interact after class, what with the dozens of extracurricular activities that clutter their afternoons and early evenings. The ability to spend a few hours concentrating on developing their minds and not their social skills should take precedence over some misguided urge to integrate.

That's why I regret that two of the oldest women's schools in the Philadelphia area are becoming coeducational at the undergraduate level. Chestnut Hill College and Immaculata University have joined a host of formerly female institutions that now accept men. Back in 1980, Bryn Mawr's brother school Haverford started accepting women, which, despite what anyone says, destroyed the cooperation between the partners and limited the number of our students on its campus.

10   While the powers that be may tout coeducation as a way to improve the quality of the student body, I have a suspicion that it's money that speaks loudest these days. Few women, and fewer men, are attracted to single-sex institutions, and administrators may believe that there are only two options: integrate, or disappear altogether.

But a school is more than stone, glass and concrete. It is even more than the sum of its enrollment figures. If the spirit of the place is lost, little else remains. Let's hear it for Athena, Kate and Maypoles.

Explanatory Synthesis ■ 3

■ WHAT IS A SYNTHESIS?

A *synthesis* is a written discussion that draws on two or more sources. It follows that your ability to write syntheses depends on your ability to infer relationships among sources—essays, articles, fiction, and also nonwritten sources, such as lectures, interviews, and observations. This process is nothing new for you, since you infer relationships all the time—say, between something you've read in the newspaper and something you've seen for yourself, or between the teaching styles of your favorite and least favorite instructors. In fact, if you've written research papers, you've already written syntheses. In a *synthesis,* you make explicit the relationships that you have inferred among separate sources.

The skills you've already learned and practiced in the previous two chapters will be vital in writing syntheses. Clearly, before you're in a position to draw relationships between two or more sources, you must understand what those sources say; in other words, you must be able to *summarize* these sources. Readers will frequently benefit from at least partial summaries of sources in your synthesis essays. At the same time, you must go beyond summary to make judgments—judgments based, of course, on your *critical reading* of your sources: what conclusions you've drawn about the quality and validity of these sources, whether you agree or disagree with the points made in your sources, and why you agree or disagree.

Further, you must go beyond the critique of individual sources to determine the relationships among them. Is the information in source B, for example, an extended illustration of the generalizations in source A? Would it be useful to compare and contrast source C with source B? Having read and considered sources A, B, and C, can you infer something else—in other words, D (not a source, but your own idea)?

Because a synthesis is based on two or more sources, you will need to be selective when choosing information from each. It would be neither possible nor desirable, for instance, to discuss in a ten-page paper on the American Civil War every point that the authors of two books make about their subject. What you as a writer must do is select from each source the ideas and information that best allow you to achieve your purpose.

> ■ ### Where Do We Find Written Syntheses?
>
> Here are just a few of the types of writing that involve synthesis:
>
> **ACADEMIC WRITING**
>
> - **Analysis papers.** Synthesize and apply several related theoretical approaches.
> - **Research papers.** Synthesize multiple sources.
> - **Argument papers.** Synthesize different points into a coherent claim or position.
> - **Essay exams.** Demonstrate understanding of course material through comparing and contrasting theories, viewpoints, or approaches in a particular field.
>
> **WORKPLACE WRITING**
>
> - **Newspaper and magazine articles.** Synthesize primary and secondary sources.
> - **Position papers and policy briefs.** Compare and contrast solutions for solving problems.
> - **Business plans.** Synthesize ideas and proposals into one coherent plan.
> - **Memos and letters.** Synthesize multiple ideas, events, and proposals into concise form.
> - **Web sites.** Synthesize information from various sources to present in Web pages and related links.

■ PURPOSE

Your purpose in reading source materials and then in drawing on them to write your own material is often reflected in the wording of an assignment. For instance, consider the following assignments on the Civil War:

American History: Evaluate the author's treatment of the origins of the Civil War.

Economics: Argue the following proposition, in light of your readings: "The Civil War was fought not for reasons of moral principle but for reasons of economic necessity."

Government: Prepare a report on the effects of the Civil War on Southern politics at the state level between 1870 and 1917.

Mass Communications: Discuss how the use of photography during the Civil War may have affected the perceptions of the war by Northerners living in industrial cities.

Literature: Select two twentieth-century Southern writers whose work you believe was influenced by the divisive effects of the Civil War. Discuss the ways this influence is apparent in a novel or a group of short stories written by each author. The works should not be *about* the Civil War.

Applied Technology: Compare and contrast the technology of warfare available in the 1860s with the technology available a century earlier.

Each of these assignments creates for you a particular purpose for writing. Having located sources relevant to your topic, you would select, for possible use in a paper, only those parts that helped you in fulfilling this purpose. And how you used those parts—how you related them to other material from other sources—would also depend on your purpose. For instance, if you were working on the government assignment, you might possibly draw on the same source as another student working on the literature assignment by referring to Robert Penn Warren's novel *All the King's Men*, about Louisiana politics in the early part of the twentieth century. But because the purposes of these assignments are different, you and the other student would make different uses of this source. Those same parts or aspects of the novel that you find worthy of detailed analysis might be mentioned only in passing—or not at all—by the other student.

■ USING YOUR SOURCES

Your purpose determines not only what parts of your sources you will use but also how you will relate them to one another. Since the very essence of synthesis is the combining of information and ideas, you must have some basis on which to combine them. *Some relationships among the material in your sources must make them worth synthesizing.* It follows that the better able you are to discover such relationships, the better able you will be to use your sources in writing syntheses. Notice that the mass communications assignment requires you to draw a *cause-and-effect* relationship between photographs of the war and Northerners' perceptions of the war. The applied technology assignment requires you to *compare and contrast* state-of-the-art weapons technology in the eighteenth and nineteenth centuries. The economics assignment requires you to *argue* a proposition. In each case, *your purpose will determine how you relate your source materials to one another.*

Consider some other examples. You may be asked on an exam question or in instructions for a paper to *describe* two or three approaches to prison reform during the past decade. You may be asked to *compare and contrast* one country's approach to imprisonment with another's. You may be asked to *develop an argument* of your own on this subject, based on your reading. Sometimes (when you are not given a specific assignment) you determine your own purpose: You are interested in exploring a particular subject; you are interested in making a case for one approach or another. In any event, your purpose shapes your essay. Your purpose determines which sources you research, which ones you use, which parts of them you use, at which points in your essay you use them, and in what manner you relate them to one another.

■ HOW TO WRITE SYNTHESES

Although writing syntheses can't be reduced to a lockstep method, it should help you to follow the guidelines listed in the box below.

Guidelines for Writing Syntheses

- *Consider your purpose in writing.* What are you trying to accomplish in your paper? How will this purpose shape the way you approach your sources?
- *Select and carefully read your sources,* according to your purpose. Then reread the passages, mentally summarizing each. Identify those aspects or parts of your sources that will help you fulfill your purpose. When rereading, *label* or *underline* the sources for main ideas, key terms, and any details you want to use in the synthesis.
- *Take notes on your reading.* In addition to labeling or underlining key points in the readings, you might write brief one- or two-sentence summaries of each source. This will help you in formulating your thesis statement, and in choosing and organizing your sources later.
- *Formulate a thesis.* Your thesis is the main idea that you want to present in your synthesis. It should be expressed as a complete sentence. You might do some predrafting about the ideas discussed in the readings in order to help you work out a thesis. If you've written one-sentence summaries of the readings, looking these over will help you to brainstorm connections between readings and to devise a thesis.

  When you write your essay drafts, you will need to consider where your thesis fits in your paper. Sometimes the thesis is the first sentence, but more often it is *the final sentence of the first paragraph.* If you are writing an *inductively arranged* synthesis (see p. 7), the thesis sentence may not appear until the final paragraphs. (See Chapter 6 for more information on writing an effective thesis.)
- *Decide how you will use your source material.* How will the information and the ideas in the passages help you fulfill your purpose?
- *Develop an organizational plan,* according to your thesis. How will you arrange your material? It is not necessary to prepare a formal outline. But you should have some plan that will indicate the order in which you will present your material and that will indicate the relationships among your sources.
- *Draft the topic sentences for the main sections.* This is an optional step, but you may find it a helpful transition from organizational plan to first draft.

(continues)

- *Write the first draft* of your synthesis, following your organizational plan. Be flexible with your plan, however. Frequently, you will use an outline to get started. As you write, you may discover new ideas and make room for them by adjusting the outline. When this happens, reread your work frequently, making sure that your thesis still accounts for what follows and that what follows still logically supports your thesis.
- *Document your sources.* You must do this by crediting them within the body of the synthesis—citing the author's last name and page number from which the point was taken and by providing full citation information in a list of "Works Cited" at the end. Don't open yourself to charges of plagiarism! (See pp. 48–50; see also Chapter 7 for more information on documenting sources.)
- *Revise your synthesis,* inserting transitional words and phrases where necessary. Make sure that the synthesis reads smoothly, logically, and clearly from beginning to end. Check for grammatical correctness, punctuation, and spelling.

Note: *The writing of syntheses is a recursive process, and you should accept a certain amount of backtracking and reformulating as inevitable. For instance, in developing an organizational plan (Step 6 of the procedure), you may discover a gap in your presentation that will send you scrambling for another source—back to Step 2. You may find that formulating a thesis and making inferences among sources occur simultaneously; indeed, inferences often are made before a thesis is formulated. Our recommendations for writing syntheses will give you a structure; they will get you started. But be flexible in your approach; expect discontinuity and, if possible, be comforted that through backtracking and reformulating you will eventually produce a coherent, well-crafted essay.*

■ TYPES OF SYNTHESES: EXPLANATORY AND ARGUMENT

In this and the next chapter we categorize syntheses into two main types: *explanatory* and *argument*. The easiest way to recognize the difference between these two types may be to consider the difference between a newspaper article and an editorial on the same subject. Most likely, we'd say that the main purpose of the newspaper article is to convey *information*, and the main purpose of the editorial is to convey *opinion* or *interpretation*. Of course, this distinction is much too simplified: Newspaper articles often convey opinion or bias, sometimes subtly, sometimes openly; and editorials often convey unbiased information, along with opinion. But as a practical matter, we can generally agree on the distinction between a newspaper article that primarily conveys information and an editorial that primarily conveys opinion. You should be able to observe this distinction in the selections shown here as Explanation and Argument.

EXPLANATION: NEWS ARTICLE FROM THE *WASHINGTON POST*

RESERVIST CONVICTED IN ABUSE OF IRAQIS

By Josh White

Tuesday, September 27, 2005

Pfc. Lynndie R. England, the Army reservist who appeared in infamous photographs humiliating detainees at the Abu Ghraib prison in Iraq, was found guilty of six counts of abuse and indecent acts yesterday in the final court-martial for the original group of soldiers who touched off an international furor over U.S. treatment of prisoners.

England, 22, faces as long as 10 years in prison after a jury of five military officers at Fort Hood, Tex., found her guilty in six of seven criminal counts. She was acquitted of one count of conspiracy to abuse.

England is the last of nine military police and military intelligence reservists who have either been found guilty of abuse at courts-martial or accepted plea deals, largely as a result of dozens of photographs and videos showing them mistreating and beating detainees at the prison west of Baghdad in late 2003. . . .

England's conviction marked a milestone in the worldwide controversy over treatment of prisoners by U.S. forces. She was a central figure in several of the most shocking photographs from Abu Ghraib, where the actions of her military police company spurred more than a dozen major military investigations, numerous congressional hearings, and probes of alleged abuse at detention sites across Iraq and Afghanistan.

Gen. Richard B. Myers, outgoing chairman of the Joint Chiefs of Staff, said in an interview with Pentagon reporters yesterday that . . . "We had a problem, and we dealt with the problem and dealt with it in an appropriate way. . . . Pfc. England's conviction is just one more example of holding people accountable, because that's who did it."

ARGUMENT: EDITORIAL FROM THE *BOSTON GLOBE*

MILITARY ABUSE
September 28, 2005

The court-martial conviction Monday of reservist Lynndie England for her role in the abuse of Iraqi prisoners at Abu Ghraib should fool no one that the Pentagon is taking seriously the mistreatment of Iraqis, especially after the release last Friday of a report on torture by members of the 82d Airborne Division stationed near Fallujah. . . .

If the [new] allegations are found credible, they further demolish the contention by officials that the abuse first reported at Abu Ghraib in 2004 was an isolated case of a few bad apples. Pentagon brass also tried to explain away the activities of England's unit as the actions of relatively untrained reservists. It is less easy to dismiss as a fluke such abuse when it occurs at the hands of the 82d Airborne, a thoroughly trained and highly decorated division.

The new charges, along with other accusations of abuse that have emerged since Abu Ghraib, including 28 suspicious detainee deaths, provide strong evidence that both reservist and active duty troops throughout Iraq were confused about their responsibility to treat detainees as prisoners of war under the terms of the Geneva Conventions. . . . Congress should have long since created a special commission, as proposed in a bill by Senator Carl Levin of Michigan, to investigate the issue of prisoner abuse. . . .

A truly independent inquiry, along the lines of the one done by the 9/11 commission, could trace accountability for prisoner abuse through statements and policies by ranking civilian and military officials in the Bush administration. Accountability for the shame of prisoner torture and abuse should not stop with Lynndie England and her cohort.

We'll say, for the sake of convenience, that the newspaper article provides an explanation and that the editorial provides an argument. This is essentially the distinction we make between explanatory and argument syntheses. As an additional example of the distinction, read the following paragraph:

> Researchers now use recombinant DNA technology to analyze genetic changes. With this technology, they cut and splice DNA from different species, then insert the modified molecules into bacteria or other types of cells that engage in rapid replication and cell division. The cells copy the foreign DNA right along with their own. In short order, huge populations produce useful quantities of recombinant DNA molecules. The new technology also is the basis of genetic engineering, by which genes are isolated, modified, and inserted back into the same organism or into a different one.*

Now read this paragraph:

> Many in the life sciences field would have us believe that the new gene splicing technologies are irrepressible and irreversible and that any attempt to oppose their introduction is both futile and retrogressive. They never stop to even consider the possibility that the new genetic science might be used in a wholly different manner than is currently being proposed. The fact is, the corporate agenda is only one of two potential paths into the Biotech Century. It is possible that the growing number of anti-eugenic activists around the world might be able to ignite a global debate around alternative uses of the new science—approaches that are less invasive, more sustainable and humane and that conserve and protect the genetic rights of future generations.†

Both of these passages deal with the topic of biotechnology, but the two take quite different approaches. The first passage came from a biology textbook, while the second appeared in a magazine article. As we might expect from a textbook on the broad subject of biology, the first passage is explanatory and informative; it defines and explains some of the key concepts of biotechnology without taking a position or providing commentary about the implications of the technology. Magazine articles often present information in the same ways; however, many magazine articles take specific positions, as we see in the second passage. This passage is argumentative or persuasive. Its primary purpose is to convey a point of view regarding the topic of biotechnology.

While each of these excerpts presents a clear instance of writing that is either explanatory or argumentative, it is important to note that the sources for these excerpts—the textbook chapter and the magazine article—contain elements of *both* explanation and argument. The textbook writers, while they refrain from taking a particular position, do note the controversies surrounding

---

*Cecie Starr and Ralph Taggart, "Recombinant DNA and Genetic Engineering," Biology: The Unity and Diversity of Life *(New York: Wadsworth: 1998).*

†*Jeremy Rifkin, "The Ultimate Therapy: Commercial Eugenics on the Eve of the Biotech Century,"* Tikkun *May–June 1998: 35.*

biotechnology and genetic engineering. They might even subtly reveal a certain bias in favor of one side of the issue, through their word choice and tone, and perhaps through devoting more space and attention to one point of view. Explanatory and argumentative writing are not mutually exclusive. The overlap in the categories of explanation and argument is also found in the magazine article: In order to make his case against genetic engineering, the writer has to explain certain elements of the issue. Yet, even while these categories overlap to a certain extent, the second passage clearly has argument as its primary purpose, whereas the first passage is primarily explanatory.

In Chapter 2 we noted that the primary purpose in a piece of writing may be informative, persuasive, or entertaining (or some combination of the three). Some scholars of writing argue that all writing is essentially persuasive, and even without entering into that complex argument, we've just seen how the varying purposes in writing do overlap. In order to persuade others of a particular position we typically must also inform them about it; conversely, a primarily informative piece of writing also must work to persuade the reader that its claims are truthful. Both informative and persuasive writing often include entertaining elements, and writing intended primarily to entertain also typically contains information and persuasion. For practical purposes, however, it is possible—and useful—to identify the *primary* purpose in a piece of writing as informative/explanatory, persuasive/argumentative, or entertaining. Entertainment as a primary purpose is the one least often practiced in purely academic writing—perhaps to your disappointment!—but information and persuasion are ubiquitous. Thus, while recognizing the overlap between these categories, we distinguish in this and the following chapter between two types of synthesis writing: explanatory (or informative), and argument (or persuasive). Just as distinguishing the primary purpose in a piece of writing helps you to critically read and evaluate it, distinguishing the primary purpose in your own writing helps you to make the appropriate choices regarding your approach.

In this chapter we'll focus on explanatory syntheses. In the next chapter, we'll discuss the argument synthesis.

■ THE EXPLANATORY SYNTHESIS

Many of the papers you write in college will be more or less explanatory in nature. An explanation helps readers understand a topic. Writers explain when they divide a subject into its component parts and present them to the reader in a clear and orderly fashion. Explanations may entail descriptions that recreate in words some object, place, emotion, event, sequence of events, or state of affairs. As a student reporter, you may need to explain an event—to relate when, where, and how it took place. In a science lab, you would observe the conditions and results of an experiment and record them for review by others. In a political science course, you might review research on a particular subject—say, the complexities underlying the debate over gay marriage—and then present the results of your research to your professor and the members of your class.

Your job in writing an explanatory paper—or in writing the explanatory portion of an argumentative paper—is not to argue a particular point, but rather *to present the facts in a reasonably objective manner*. Of course, explanatory papers, like other academic papers, should be based on a thesis (see 233–39). But the purpose of a thesis in an explanatory paper is less to advance a particular opinion than to focus the various facts contained in the paper.

■ DEMONSTRATION: EXPLANATORY SYNTHESIS—THE HYDROGEN-POWERED AUTOMOBILE

To illustrate how the process of synthesis works, we'll begin with a number of short extracts from several articles on the same subject.

Suppose you were writing a paper on a matter that auto manufacturers, along with many drivers upset with escalating gasoline prices, are discussing: efficient, environmentally sound alternatives to the internal combustion engine. Some writers and thinkers are excited about the possibility that one alternative energy source in particular, hydrogen fuel cells, could both free Americans of reliance on foreign oil and slow the degradation of the earth's atmosphere. Others, recognizing the need for new ways to power automobiles, cite difficulties with the current state-of-the-art fuel cell technology and favor other approaches, including the hybrid (gasoline and electric) engine.

Exercise 3.1

Exploring the Topic

Before reading what others have written on the subject of alternative energy vehicles, write a page or so exploring what you know and what you think about this topic. You might focus your first paragraph on your own experience with alternative energy sources—for instance, water power, steam, solar, wind, or hybrid. If you have no direct experience with the topic, recall what you have read, seen, or heard about levels of petroleum consumption in the United States, the controversies surrounding the search for oil in this country, or the advertising buzz surrounding hybrid cars. What do you imagine are some concerns people have about alternative energy vehicles? What do you think would be of most interest to journalists, politicians, and businesspeople?

Because the topic of hydrogen fuel cells is technical and you may not have the expertise to write knowledgeably on it just yet, and also because you are aware that the hydrogen fuel cell is but one of several technologies being discussed as replacements to the internal combustion engine, you decide to investigate what has been written on the subject, both in print and electronic texts. In the following pages we present several excerpts from the kinds of articles your research might locate.

Note: To save space and for the purpose of demonstration, we offer excerpts from four sources only; the rest are simply listed in the "Works Cited" of the model synthesis on pp. 117–25. In preparing your paper, of course you would draw upon the entire articles from which these extracts were made. (The discussion of how these passages can form the basis of an explanatory synthesis resumes on p. 98)

THE FUEL SUBSIDY WE NEED
Ricardo Bayon

A fellow at the New America Foundation, Ricardo Bayon writes on the intersection of finance, public policy, and environmental studies. The following is excerpted from an article in Atlantic Monthly, *January/February 2003.*

The American economy is, after Canada's, the most energy-dependent in the advanced industrialized world, requiring the equivalent of a quarter ton of oil to produce $1,000 of gross domestic product. We require twice as much energy as Germany—and three times as much as Japan—to produce the same amount of GDP. Overall the United States consumes 25 percent of the oil produced in the world each year. This binds us to the Middle East, which still holds more than 65 percent of the world's proven oil reserves. Even if we were to buy all our oil from Venezuela, Canada, and Russia, or to find more oil here in the United States (which currently holds only 2.9 percent of proven reserves), Persian Gulf producers with excess capacity, such as Saudi Arabia and the United Arab Emirates, would still largely dictate the price we paid for it.

America's economic vulnerability to oil-price fluctuations has led Washington to strike a tacit bargain with Saudi Arabia and other Persian Gulf oil producers. In return for U.S. military protection and silence about the more unsavory aspects of their societies, these countries increase production when prices get too high and cut it when they get too low. In addition, they price their oil in dollars and recycle their petro-profits through U.S. financial institutions. But this has made the United States vulnerable not only to a sustained spike in oil prices but also to the possible fall of the dollar. In part because the dollar has been strong, we have been able to consume more than we produce and then to make up the difference by borrowing from abroad. As a result, our current net international debt has risen to $2.3 trillion, or 22.6 percent of GDP. What would happen if a war in Iraq went badly or if Islamic extremists gained ground in key oil-producing states? Oil prices could rise and the dollar could fall, inflicting a double blow to the U.S. economy from which it could not easily recover.

The way to escape this abiding insecurity is to wean the U.S. economy—and the world economy, too—off oil. And the way to do that is to encourage the commercial development of a technology called the hydrogen fuel cell. Solar power and windmills will surely be important parts of our energy future, but only the fuel cell can address our oil dependency by challenging the primacy of the internal-combustion engine.

Fuel cells are actually a relatively old technology (they were invented in 1839, Jules Verne wrote about them in the 1870s, and they were used by U.S. astronauts in the 1960s), and the concept underlying them is simple: by mixing hydrogen and oxygen, fuel cells generate both water and electricity. Not only do fuel cells turn two of nature's most abundant elements into enough energy to power a car, but they create no toxic emissions (drinkable water is their only by-product). And fuel cells are completely quiet, meaning that it is now realistic to imagine living in a world of silent cars and trucks.

5   The technology is not science fiction: fuel cells are on their way toward commercial viability. Fuel-cell-powered buses are running in Vancouver, Chicago, London, and parts of Germany. BMW has a prototype car powered solely by fuel cells. Honda, Toyota, and DaimlerChrysler announced recently that they would begin shipping fuel-cell cars to retail customers around the world; General Motors and Ford are not far behind. Honda's car was shipped to its first major customer—the city of Los Angeles—at the beginning of December.

Geoffrey Ballard, the founder of the Canadian manufacturer Ballard Power Systems has said, "The internal-combustion engine will go the way of the horse. It will be a curiosity to my grandchildren." Even large oil companies believe that they must embrace hydrogen power.

PUTTING THE HINDENBURG TO REST
Jim Motavalli

Jim Motavalli is editor of the environmentally focused E Magazine *and writes extensively on environmental matters for newspapers and magazines nationally. This interview appeared in the* New York Times *on June 5, 2005.*

Some transportation experts are betting that hydrogen will eventually power most cars, while others see substantial, perhaps insurmountable, hurdles. Here is a primer on the benefits and disadvantages:

Q. *What is hydrogen, and where does it come from?*

A. *It is the lightest gas and the simplest, most abundant element in the universe. Because it is present in so many compounds, including water, supplies cannot be exhausted. But hydrogen is not actually a fuel, and can be used in a vehicle only after it is separated from other elements. This process itself consumes energy.*

Q. *How is hydrogen used to power a car? And what's a fuel cell?*

A. *A fuel cell uses a chemical process, similar to that in a battery, to produce electricity—in this case, from hydrogen that flows into the cell from a storage tank. This electricity drives the fuel-cell car's electric motor; the only byproducts are heat and water.*

Q. *What are the potential advantages?*

A. *Because hydrogen is found everywhere, supplies are not only infinite, they pose no geographic challenges. It can be produced, albeit expensively, from emission-free sources like solar panels, wind turbines or even nuclear plants. Fuel cells can be easily scaled up or down in size, so they could replace small computer batteries or large power plants. A hydrogen car emits no pollution or global warming gases, aside from what might have resulted from producing the hydrogen itself.*

Q. *If it's so great, why aren't we driving hydrogen cars right now?*

A. *Widespread use of fuel-cell cars will have to wait until the cells become cheaper and more efficient, and until storage methods have evolved to give vehicles a travel range of perhaps 300 miles. Hydrogen production will have to be scaled up and standardized, and pumping stations equipped for hydrogen refueling at an affordable price.*

Q. *I've heard about the Hindenburg—is hydrogen safe?*

A. *Hydrogen is very flammable, and poses special challenges: it burns without a visible flame, for instance. But it is arguably no more dangerous than gasoline, and fuel-cell cars are built with leak detectors and very strong crash-resistant tanks. As for the Hindenburg tragedy of 1937, a retired NASA engineer, Addison Bain, theorizes that the dirigible burned not because it contained hydrogen, but because its cloth skin was coated with highly flammable paint. Others disagree with his assessment.*

Q. *How will a car carry hydrogen?*

A. *Hydrogen can be stored as a gas, as a liquid or in metal hydrides, which are chemical sponges, but each form has advantages and disadvantages. Still, much of automakers' current research focuses on pressurized hydrogen gas.*

Q. *When will I have a hydrogen car in my driveway?*

A. *Joseph Romm, a former Department of Energy official and author of "The Hype About Hydrogen" (Island Press, 2004), says, "I doubt that in the next 20 years an affordable, durable and efficient vehicle will be delivered that will be attractive to the public." But a renewable energy advocate, Amory Lovins of the Rocky Mountain Institute, says the nation's car fleet could be converted to hydrogen in less than a decade, and a network of small hydrogen reformers (devices that produce hydrogen from natural gas or other sources) could be quickly installed in 10 to 20 percent of the nation's 180,000 gas stations for $2 billion to $4 billion.*

Q. *Is this just a lot of hype?*

A. *Some overblown claims have already been disproved. But there is also groundbreaking research backed by serious testing programs. Lawrence D. Burns, General Motors' vice president for research and planning, says G.M. aims to have a production-ready fuel-cell vehicle (built on an innovative "skateboard" platform that could support a variety of bodies) by 2010. DaimlerChrysler is running 30 fuel-cell buses in Europe and helping to seed a hydrogen infrastructure in Iceland.*

Fuel-cell Toyota Highlanders are being tested at two California universities; both the City of Los Angeles and the State of New York are using Honda FCX's. Nissan will reportedly lease a few X-Trail fuel-cell S.U.V.'s to American businesses in 2007.

Q. *Will fuel-cell cars be cheap to operate? Where will I fill up?*

A. *Hydrogen's current price is three to four times that of gasoline. The Department of Energy has issued optimistic cost estimates, but they assume widespread commercial acceptance of hydrogen fuel—which is at least a decade away. There are only a few hydrogen stations scattered around the country, though California envisions a 170-station "hydrogen highway" by 2010; Florida has announced a similar plan.*

Q. *How long will fuel cells last?*

A. *The journal of the American Institute of Chemical Engineers says the life of fuel cells may be only a fifth as long as that of a typical gasoline engine—about 30,000 miles versus 150,000. Ben Knight, vice president for automotive engineering at Honda, agrees that the durability of fuel-cell stacks is "a work in progress," but promises "a significantly longer life" from newer designs.*

Q. *Can you run a regular engine with hydrogen, without fuel cells?*

A. *Yes. A hydrogen Cadillac was featured at President Jimmy Carter's inauguration in 1977. A Mini with a hydrogen-powered internal combustion engine was displayed at the Frankfurt auto show in 2001, and Ford has shown prototypes. BMW plans to offer a "dual fuel" 7 Series sedan, which could run on either gasoline or hydrogen, by 2008. That V-12 car would have a range of 125 miles on hydrogen and 185 on gasoline.*

USING FOSSIL FUELS IN ENERGY PROCESS GETS US NOWHERE

Jeremy Rifkin

Jeremy Rifkin, a prolific author well known for his cautionary views on technology (especially genetic technologies), is the author of The Hydrogen Economy: The Creation of the World Wide Energy Web and the Redistribution of Power on Earth *(2002). This selection is excerpted from a longer piece in the* Los Angeles Times, *November 9, 2003.*

Hydrogen—the lightest and most abundant element of the universe—is the next great energy revolution. Scientists call it the "forever fuel" because it never runs out. And when hydrogen is used to produce power, the only byproducts are pure water and heat.

The shift to fuel cells and hydrogen energy—when it happens—will be as significant and far-reaching in its effect on the American and global economy as the steam engine and coal in the 19th century and the internal combustion engine and oil in the 20th century.

Hydrogen has the potential to end the world's reliance on oil from the Persian Gulf. It will dramatically cut down on carbon dioxide emissions and mitigate the effects of global warming. And because hydrogen is so plentiful, people who have never before had access to electricity will be able to generate it.

The environmental community is up in arms over the Bush hydrogen agenda. Why? Hydrogen has a Janus face. Though it is found everywhere on Earth, it rarely exists free-floating in nature. Hydrogen has to be extracted from fossil fuels or water or biomass.

5   In other words, there is "black" hydrogen and "green" hydrogen. And it is this critical difference that separates Bush's vision of a hydrogen future from the vision many of us hold in the environmental movement.

Bush and Secretary of Energy Spencer Abraham say hydrogen can free us from dependence on foreign oil. What they leave unsaid is that their plan calls for extracting hydrogen from all of the old energy sources—oil, natural gas and coal—and by harnessing nuclear power. Bush would like to take us into a hydrogen future without ever leaving the fossil fuels and nuclear past.

Today, most commercial hydrogen is extracted from natural gas via a steam re-forming process. Although natural gas emits less carbon dioxide than other fossil fuels in producing hydrogen, it is a finite resource and in relatively short supply.

Hydrogen can also be extracted from coal, and enthusiasts point out that the U.S. enjoys ample coal reserves. The problem is that coal produces twice as much carbon dioxide as natural gas, which means a dramatic increase in global warming.

The coal industry counters that it might be possible to safely store the carbon dioxide emissions underground or in the ocean depths for thousands of years and has convinced the White House to subsidize further research into this. For many environmentalists, the issue of storing carbon dioxide seems eerily reminiscent of the arguments used by the nuclear industry about nuclear waste.

10 The nuclear industry would like to produce hydrogen, but there are still unre-solved issues surrounding the safe storage of nuclear waste, the skyrocketing costs of building new reactors and the vulnerability of nuclear power plants to ter-rorist attacks.

There is another way to produce hydrogen—the green way—that uses no fossil fu-els or nuclear power. Renewable sources of energy—wind, hydro- and geothermal power and photovoltaic cells—are increasingly being used to produce electricity. That electricity, in turn, can be used, in a process called electrolysis, to split water into hydrogen and oxygen.

Hydrogen could also be extracted from sustainable energy crops and agricultural waste in a process called gasification. There would be no increase in carbon diox-ide emissions because the carbon taken from the atmosphere by the plants is re-leased back during hydrogen production.

The White House proposal calls for large subsidies to the coal and nuclear indus-tries to extract hydrogen. The Secretary of Energy claims that the administration is equally committed to research and development of renewable sources of energy to extract hydrogen.

However, the White House and the Republican Party have systematically blocked efforts in Congress to establish target dates for the phasing in of renewable sources of energy in the generation of electricity and for transport.

15 If the U.S. is successful in steering the International Partnership for the Hydrogen Economy toward a black hydrogen future, it could lock the global economy into the old energy regime for much of the 21st century, with dire environmental and eco-nomic consequences.

The real benefits of a hydrogen future can be realized only if renewable sources of energy are phased in and eventually become the primary source for extracting hy-drogen. In the interim, the U.S. government should be supporting much tougher automobile fuel standards, hybrid cars, the overhaul of the nation's power grid with emphasis on smart technology, the Kyoto Protocol on global warming and bench-marks for renewable energy adoption.

All of these other initiatives should be carried on concurrently with an ambitious national effort to subsidize and underwrite the research and development of renewable energy technology, hydrogen and fuel cells.

The goal should be a fully integrated green hydrogen economy by the end of the first half of the 21st century.

LOTS OF HOT AIR ABOUT HYDROGEN

Joseph J. Romm

Joseph Romm is a former acting Assistant Secretary of Energy and author of the book The Hype About Hydrogen: Fact and Fiction in the Race to Save the Climate. *The selection originally appeared in the* Los Angeles Times, *Opinion section, March 29, 2004.*

WASHINGTON—Earlier this month, the South Coast Air Quality Management District approved a $4-million program to put a mustache on the Mona Lisa—at least that's how it seems to me. What the agency actually did was approve spending millions to take 35 or so of the greenest, most energy-efficient sedans ever made—the hybrid gasoline-electric Toyota Prius—and turn them all into dirty energy guzzlers.

It is going to achieve this giant leap backward by converting the hybrids to run on hydrogen, the most overhyped alternative fuel since methyl tertiary-butyl ether, or MTBE.

Hybrids are already extremely efficient. The Prius, for example, generates only about 210 grams of carbon dioxide—the principal heat-trapping gas that causes global warming—per mile. The car is also a partial zero-emission vehicle, which means that when it uses California's low-sulfur gasoline, it produces very little of the smog-forming pollutants, like nitrogen oxides.

Hydrogen is not a primary fuel, like oil, that we can drill for. It is bound up tightly in molecules of water, or hydrocarbons like natural gas. A great deal of energy must be used to unbind it—something the AQMD plans to do by electrolyzing water into its constituents: hydrogen and oxygen. And because the resulting hydrogen is a gas, additional energy must be used to compress it to very high pressures to put it in the tank of your car.

5   With all the energy needed to create and compress that hydrogen—even with the relatively clean electric grid of California—a Prius running on hydrogen would result in twice as much greenhouse gas emissions per mile as an unmodified car. It would result in more than four times as much nitrogen oxides per mile.

I own a Prius, so that's the hybrid I am most familiar with. But Honda also makes a hybrid vehicle, and thanks to California's leadership in vehicle emissions regulations, many other car companies plan to introduce them soon. These cars will get even greener over time as technology improves.

Sadly, two of the features I love most about my car would be wiped out by the AQMD's expensive "upgrade." First, the hybrid has cut my annual fuel bill by half. Hydrogen is so expensive to make that even with California's high gasoline prices, the hydrogen hybrid will have more than four times the annual fuel bill of a gasoline hybrid. Second, my car can go twice as far on a tank of gas as my old Saturn, so I have to make those unpleasant trips to the gas station only half as often. The hydrogen hybrid would have less than half the range of my car. With hydrogen fueling stations so scarce, hydrogen hybrid drivers will constantly be scampering back to the fueling stations before the tanks get too low.

Why is the AQMD spending millions of dollars to increase pollution and destroy all the desirable features of one of the greenest, most efficient cars ever made? It has bought into the hype about hydrogen, the myth that this miracle fuel will somehow solve all of our energy and environmental problems.

When I was helping to oversee clean-energy programs at the U.S. Department of Energy in the mid-1990s, I too was intrigued by hydrogen, mainly because of recent advances in fuel cells. Fuel cells are electrochemical devices that take in hydrogen and oxygen and generate electricity and heat with high efficiency. The only "emission" is water. They have been an elusive technological goal since the first fuel cell was invented in 1839. During the 1990s, we increased funding for hydrogen tenfold and for transportation fuel cells threefold.

10   I began to change my mind about hydrogen while researching a book over the last 12 months. After speaking to dozens of experts and reviewing the extensive literature, I came to realize that hydrogen cars still needed several major breakthroughs and a clean-energy revolution to be both practical and desirable.

A recent Energy Department report noted that transportation fuel cells were 100 times more expensive than internal combustion engines. Historically, even the most aggressively promoted energy technologies, such as wind and solar power, have taken 20 years just to see a tenfold decline in prices.

The most mature onboard hydrogen storage systems—using ultrahigh pressure— contain 10 times less energy per unit volume than gasoline, in addition to requiring a significant amount of compression energy. A National Academy of Sciences panel concluded in February that such storage had "little promise of long-term practicality for light-duty vehicles" and urged the Department of Energy to halt research in this area. Yet this kind of storage is precisely what the AQMD plans to put in its hydrogen hybrids.

Another problem with hydrogen is in how it is made. Although people seem to view hydrogen as a pollution-free elixir, hydrogen is just an energy carrier, like electricity. And, like electricity, it is no cleaner than the fuels used to make it. For the next several decades, the National Academy panel concluded, "it is highly likely that fossil fuels will be the principal sources of hydrogen." Making hydrogen from fossil fuels won't solve our major environmental problems.

It's possible, of course, to make hydrogen with renewable electricity, such as solar and wind power, but that is a lousy use for renewables, since they can directly displace more than four times as much carbon dioxide from coal power compared with using that renewable power to make hydrogen for vehicles. And these savings can all be achieved without spending hundreds of billions of dollars on a new hydrogen infrastructure and hydrogen vehicles.

15   As one 2002 British study concluded, "Until there is a surplus of renewable electricity, it is not beneficial in terms of carbon reduction to use renewable electricity to produce hydrogen—for use in vehicles, or elsewhere." That surplus is, sadly, a long way off, given that Congress hasn't been willing to pass legislation requiring that even 10% of U.S. electricity in 2020 be from renewables like wind and solar.

Finally, delivering renewable hydrogen to a car in usable form is prohibitively expensive today—equal to gasoline at $7 to $10 a gallon—and likely to remain so for decades in the absence of major technology advances.

For at least several decades, hydrogen cars are exceedingly unlikely to be a cost-effective solution for global warming. Until we achieve major breakthroughs in vehicle technology, hydrogen storage, hydrogen infrastructure and renewable hydrogen production, hydrogen cars will remain inferior to the best hybrids in cost, range, annual fueling bill, convenience, roominess, safety and greenhouse gas emissions.

While we wait, California should continue to lead the way in building renewable-power generation and in advancing the most environmentally responsible cars in the world—hybrid partial zero-emission vehicles.

Consider Your Purpose

The student writing the explanatory paper beginning on page 117 drew on more than these brief selections on hydrogen fuel cell technology to write her paper. But these will do here for purposes of demonstration. How did she, how do you, go about synthesizing the sources?

First, remember that before considering the *how*, you must consider the *why*. In other words, what is your *purpose* in synthesizing these sources? You might use them for a paper dealing with a broader issue: "green," or environmentally friendly technologies, for instance. If this were your purpose, these sources would be used for perhaps two sections of your discussion, on the problems associated with petroleum-based technologies and on the eco-neutral potential of fuel cells. Because such a broader paper would consider power sources other than fuel cells (for instance, wind, solar, and geothermal), it would also need to draw on additional sources. For a marketing course, you might consider strategies for encouraging public acceptance of fuel cells, the challenge being that on first introduction they may be more expensive or less convenient than gasoline engines. The sources would clarify for you how fuel cells work, their potential, and the technical challenges that must be overcome in order for them to become a reasonable energy source. For a paper on the challenges of promoting acceptance of fuel cells, you would (again) need to consult more sources than we've gathered here in order to write an effective synthesis. Moving out of the academic world and into the commercial one, you might be an engineer preparing a brochure for your company's new fuel cell design. In this brochure, you might want to address the challenges of conventional designs and the advantages that your company's product offers.

But for now let's keep it simple: You want to write a paper, or a section of a paper, that simply explains the potential of fuel cell technology to alleviate our dependence on foreign oil and to provide a power source for cars that does not degrade the environment. Your job, then, is to write an *explanatory synthesis*—one that presents information but does not advance your own opinion on the *subject*.

Exercise 3.2

Critical Reading for Synthesis

Look over the preceding readings and make a list of the ways they address the problems associated with petroleum-based technology and the potential of alternate technologies, especially fuel cells. Make your list as specific and detailed as you can. Assign a source to each item on the list.

We asked one of our students, Janice Hunte, to read these passages and to use them (and others) as sources in a paper on fuel cell technology. We also asked her to write some additional comments describing the process of developing her ideas into a draft. We'll draw upon some of these comments in the following discussion.

Formulate a Thesis

The difference between a purpose and a thesis is a difference primarily of focus. Your purpose provides direction to your research and focus to your paper. Your thesis sharpens this focus by narrowing it and formulating it in the words of a single declarative statement. (Refer to Chapter 6 for additional discussion on formulating thesis statements.)

Since Hunte's purpose in this case was to synthesize source material with little or no comment, her thesis would be the most obvious statement she could make about the relationship among these passages. By "obvious" we mean a statement that is broad enough to encompass the main points of all these readings. Taken as a whole, what do they *mean*? Here Hunte describes the process she followed in coming up with a preliminary thesis for her explanatory synthesis:

> I began my writing process by looking over all the readings and noting the main point of each reading in a sentence on a piece of paper.
>
> Then I reviewed all of these points and identified the patterns in the readings. These I listed underneath my list of main points:--All the readings focus on the energy needed to power cars and, more generally, the American economy. The readings explain America's dependence on foreign oil, the wisdom of that dependence, technologies that could free us of this dependence, and the plusses and minuses of two technologies in particular, hydrogen fuel cell and gasoline/electric hybrids.
>
> Looking over these points, I drafted a preliminary thesis. This thesis summed up the different issues in the sources and stated how these were interrelated.
>
>> America's dependence on dwindling foreign oil reserves has spurred research into alternate technologies for powering cars.
>
> This was a true statement, but it sounded too vague and too obvious. I didn't feel it adequately represented the readings' points, especially since several experts hotly debate the advantages of fuel cells vs. hybrids. I wanted my thesis to more fully reflect the complexity of people's concerns regarding how these technologies are evolving as auto manufacturers search for ever more efficient designs. My next version followed:
>
>> Many people believe hybrids will solve our energy needs, but since hybrids still depend on gasoline, others insist that another technology will take its place: fuel cells.
>
> This thesis reflected the disagreement among experts concerning the two technologies, but I didn't feel I said enough about what makes fuel cells so attractive--namely, that they are powered by hydrogen, which is a

clean-burning fuel with a virtually inexhaustible supply (unlike petroleum). In my next attempt, I tried to be more specific and a little more emphatic:

> Although many see hybrids as merely transitional vehicles, since they require gasoline, others believe that fuel-cell vehicles powered by hydrogen, a clean-burning and abundant energy source, will become the norm for roadway and highway travel.

Although this sentence was too long and sounded awkward to me, I thought it could be a good working thesis because it would help to define important parts of my paper: for instance, what are hybrids, why would they be transitional, what are fuel cells, what are their advantages over hybrids? Now I proceeded to the next step in writing--organizing my material.

Decide How You Will Use Your Source Material

The easiest way to deal with sources is to summarize them. But because you are synthesizing *ideas* rather than sources, you will have to be more selective than if you were writing a simple summary. You don't have to treat *all* the ideas in your sources, only the ones related to your thesis. Some sources might be summarized in their entirety; others, only in part. Look over your earlier notes or sentences discussing the topics covered in the readings, and refer back to the readings themselves. Focusing on some of the more subtle elements of the issues addressed by the authors, expand your earlier summary sentences. Write brief phrases in the margin of the sources, underline key phrases or sentences, or take notes on a separate sheet of paper or in a word processing file or electronic data filing program. Decide how your sources can help you achieve your purpose and support your thesis. For example, how might you use a diagram explaining the basics of fuel cell technology? How would you present disagreements over the perceived problems with and the potential of fuel cell technology? How much would you discuss gasoline/electric hybrids?

Develop an Organizational Plan

An organizational plan is your map for presenting material to the reader. What material will you present? To find out, examine your thesis. Do the content and structure of the thesis (that is, the number and order of assertions) suggest an organizational plan for the paper? Expect to devote at least one paragraph of your paper to developing each section of this plan. Having identified likely sections, think through the possibilities of arrangement. Ask yourself: What information does the reader need to understand first? How do I build on this first section—what block of information will follow? Think of each section in relation to others until you have placed them all and have worked your way through to a plan for the whole paper.

Study your thesis, and let it help suggest an organization. Bear in mind that any one paper can be written—successfully—according to a variety of plans. Your job before beginning your first draft is to explore possibilities. Sketch a series of rough outlines: Arrange and rearrange your paper's likely sections until you develop a plan that both facilitates the reader's understanding and achieves your objectives as a writer. Think carefully about the logical order of your points: Does one idea or point lead to the next? If not, can you find a more logical place for the point, or are you just not clearly articulating the connections between the ideas?

Your final paper may well deviate from your final sketch, since in the act of writing you may discover the need to explore new material, to omit planned material, to refocus or to reorder your entire presentation. Just the same, a well-conceived organizational plan will encourage you to begin writing a draft.

Hunte describes the process of organizing the material as follows.

Summary Statements

In these notes, Hunte refers to all the sources she used, not just to the four excerpted in this chapter.

In reviewing my sources and writing summary statements, I noted the most important aspects of problems associated with reliance on petroleum and the promise and problems of fuel cells and other alternative technologies:

- Saudi Arabia is running out of oil, and when it does the "Petroleum Age" will end with catastrophic results, unless economies prepare by changing their patterns of energy consumption (Klare).
- America is dangerously dependent on foreign oil. We can "wean" our economy off oil by developing hydrogen fuel cell technology (Bayon).
- Hydrogen fuel cells work by combining hydrogen and oxygen. Because "free hydrogen" does not exist in nature, hydrogen must be separated from the substance to which it has bonded. This process requires energy (Ministry).
- There are eco-friendly (green) ways to isolate hydrogen and unfriendly (black) ways. Unless we focus on the green approaches, the environmental costs of producing hydrogen for fuel cells will be unacceptably high (Rifkin).
- The energy required to isolate hydrogen is "prohibitively expensive" and the much dreamed of "hydrogen economy" creates more problems than it solves (Anthrop).
- High gasoline prices have sparked interest in gasoline/electric hybrid cars such as Toyota's Prius. Though hybrids may not be the technology that ultimately replaces the gasoline engine, hybrids are selling "briskly" today (Mackinnon and Scott).
- Because of the energy needed to isolate hydrogen, the technical problems of storing hydrogen once it is isolated, and the cost of hydrogen to the consumer, hydrogen fuel cell technology should not replace hybrid technology (Romm).

I tried to group some of these topics into categories that would have a logical order. The first thing that I wanted to communicate was the growing awareness that our dependence on petroleum is an increasing problem, both because of the dwindling reserves of the world's oil and because of the greenhouse emissions that result from burning oil.

Next, I thought I should explain what technologies are being developed to replace the gasoline engine: chiefly hybrids and fuel cells.

I also wanted to explain the problems people find with each of these technologies. Because the emphasis of my paper is on hydrogen fuel cells, this is the technology that should receive most of my attention. Still, because hybrid cars are gaining in popularity, I thought I should devote some attention to them--both to their potential and to their limitations.

Finally, I intended to present the serious doubts people have about hydrogen as the fuel of the future. With all the optimism, there are still reasons to be cautious.

I returned to my thesis, converting it to two sentences to make it less awkward and adding a phrase or two:

> Many see hybrids, which use gasoline, as merely transitional vehicles. In the future, they believe, fuel-cell vehicles powered by hydrogen, a clean-burning and abundant energy source, will become the norm for roadway and highway transportation.

Based on her thesis, Hunte developed an outline for a thirteen-paragraph paper, including introduction and conclusion:

A. Set a context. Introduce the problem of global warming.
B. Review the history of alternatives to gasoline-powered internal combustion engines, including compressed natural gas, hybrids, and flexible-fuel hybrids.
C. Present hydrogen as an alternative fuel, including its history. Explain how a hydrogen fuel cell works.
D. Explain the problems that limit widespread use of hydrogen fuel at present. Provide examples of current (limited) use.
E. Report on U.S. government backing for hydrogen fuel cell technology.
F. Conclude.

Write the Topic Sentences

This is an optional step, but writing draft versions of topic sentences will get you started on each main idea of your synthesis and will help give you the sense of direction you need to proceed. Here are Hunte's draft topic sentences for sections based on the thesis and organizational plan she developed. Note that when read in sequence following the thesis, these sentences give an idea of the logical progression of the essay as a whole.

- In recent years, the major automakers have been exploring alternatives to the gasoline-powered internal combustion engine.
- Over the years, many alternative fuel technologies have been proposed, but all have shown limited practicality or appeal.

- The most popular alternative energy vehicle in this country is the hybrid, which combines an electric motor with a standard gasoline engine.
- Hybrids may not be a long-term solution.
- A variation on the standard hybrid is the plug-in, flexible fuel-tank hybrid.
- There are two advantages that make hydrogen stand out from other alternative energy sources.
- The fuel cell was first proposed by a British physicist.
- At present, widespread use of hydrogen technology is not practical.
- Some major automakers recognize the inevitable end of the petroleum era. They have committed themselves to developing and producing fuel-cell vehicles.
- The federal government is supporting the new technology.
- Successful development of hydrogen fuel-cell vehicles faces significant roadblocks.
- There is also the problem of hydrogen leakage from large numbers of fuel-cell vehicles.
- Hydrogen fuel cells use platinum, which is a precious and expensive metal in limited supply.
- Taking these concerns into account, many experts believe that evolving technology will eventually solve the major problems and obstacles.

Organize a Synthesis by Idea, *Not* by Source

A synthesis is a blending of sources organized by *ideas*. The following rough sketches suggest how to organize and how *not* to organize a synthesis. The sketches assume you have read seven sources on a topic, Sources A–G.

INCORRECT: *AVOID* ORGANIZING BY SOURCE + SUMMARY

The following is *not* a synthesis because it does not blend sources. Each source stands alone as an independent summary. No dialogue among sources is possible:

Thesis

Summary of source A in support of the thesis.

Summary of source B in support of the thesis.

Summary of source C in support of the thesis.

Etc.

Conclusion

(continues)

CORRECT: *DO* ORGANIZE BY IDEA

The following *is* a synthesis because the writer blends and creates a dialogue among sources in support of an idea. Each organizing idea, which can be a paragraph or group of related paragraphs, in turn supports the thesis:

Thesis

First idea: Refer to and discuss *parts* of sources (perhaps A, C, F) in support of the thesis.

Second idea: Refer to and discuss *parts* of sources (perhaps B, D) in support of the thesis.

Third idea: Refer to and discuss *parts* of sources (perhaps A, E, G) in support of the thesis.

Etc.

Conclusion

Write Your Synthesis

Here is the first draft of Hunte's explanatory synthesis. Thesis and topic sentences are highlighted. Modern Language Association (MLA) documentation style, explained in Chapter 7, is used throughout.

Written as margin comments on the first draft, we have included comments and suggestions for revision from Hunte's instructor.

■ DISCUSSION AND SUGGESTIONS FOR REVISION

The following section summarizes the key points and suggestions for revision made during the student's conference with her instructor. (For purposes of demonstration, these comments are likely to be more comprehensive than the selective comments provided by most instructors.)

Hunte 1

Janice Hunte

Professor Case

English 101

22 January 2007

The Hydrogen Fuel-Cell Car

One of the most serious problems facing the world today is global warming. According to Michael D. Mastrandrea and Stephen H. Schneider, in their article "Global Warming," "Global warming is an increase in the average temperature of the Earth's surface. Since the Industrial Revolution, that temperature has gone up by 0.7 to 1.4 °F." The authors point out that Americans are responsible for almost 25% of the greenhouse gas pollution that causes global warming, even though they make up only 5% of the world's population. The authors also note that global warming is caused primarily by the burning of fossil fuels, such as coal, natural gas, and oil, and that much of this burning occurs in the gasoline engines that power automobiles, as well as "in factories, and in electric power plants that provide energy for houses and office buildings (47)." It is clear, then, that gasoline-powered cars are a major cause of the greenhouse gas pollution that is responsible for global warming. In the future, some believe, this problem may be solved by vehicles powered by hydrogen, a clean-burning and abundant energy source, which will become the norm for roadway and highway transportation.

Title and Paragraph 1

Your title could be more interesting and imaginative. The first paragraph gets off on the wrong foot because it provides a misleading impression of what the synthesis is going to be about. A reader might reasonably conclude from this paragraph that the paper was going to deal with global warming, rather than with alternative energy vehicles, and particularly with the hydrogen fuel-cell car. By the end of the first paragraph you do get to a thesis that more accurately reflects the actual subject of the paper, but this thesis seems awkwardly tacked on to the end of a paragraph about something else.

Suggestions for Revision

Make the title more interesting. Rewrite the first paragraph so that it provides a clear indication of the subject of the synthesis as a whole. You could begin with an anecdote that illustrates the subject, a provocative quotation, a set of questions, or a historical review of attempts to develop alternatives to the internal combustion engine.

Hunte 2

(2)   In recent years, the major automakers have been exploring alternatives to the gasoline-powered internal combustion engine. A few years ago, the electric car was widely seen as one viable alternative. Between 1996 and 2003, the Big Three U.S. automakers produced prototype electric vehicles, among them G.M.'s EVI, that were leased to a limited number of consumers. But these battery-powered, zero-emission cars proved problematic. Most had to be recharged every 100 miles or so, considerably limiting their range; and drivers found relatively few recharging stations. Manufacturers could never figure out how to reduce the batteries to manageable size or how to produce them at reasonable cost. In the end, the automakers reclaimed all but a few of the leased electric vehicles and destroyed them (Ortiz D1).

(3)   Over the years, many alternative fuel technologies have been proposed, but all have shown limited practicality or appeal. Compressed natural gas (CNG), which powers the Honda Civic GX is a reliable, clean-burning, renewable (though fossil) fuel, in plentiful supply. But because of their limited range (about 200 miles) and the absence of a significant CNG infrastructure, natural gas vehicles are employed primarily in fleets that have relatively short routes and access to their own filling stations (Neil). A third alternative-fuel vehicle, powered by compressed air, is being developed by a French company, Moteur Developpement International. A prototype car can achieve a speed of 70 miles an hour and has a range of 120 miles. It takes about four hours to

Paragraph 2

This paragraph does make the transition to the true subject of the synthesis: alternative energy vehicles, particularly the hydrogen fuel-cell car. But it could be more fully developed: consider discussing other reasons (besides the need to reduce greenhouse gas pollution) for the inevitable end of the internal combustion engine era. For example, we are rapidly exhausting our supplies of petroleum, a fact that may be more significant to automobile manufacturers—as well as to consumers—than the dangers of global warming.

Suggestions for Revision

Devise a clearer thesis and place it at the end of the first or second paragraph (depending upon how you introduce the synthesis). Expand your discussion of why gasoline will soon become impractical as the primary means of powering automobiles.

Hunte 3

recharge the onboard air tanks, using a compressor that can be plugged into a wall outlet. So far, the company's U.S. representative has not sold any manufacturing franchises in this country and has had trouble attracting investment capital (Weikel B2). Another alternative energy source, biodiesel fuel, was promoted in mid-2005 by President Bush. Biodiesel fuel can be made from soybeans (which can be produced domestically). "Biodiesel burns more completely and produces less air pollution than gasoline or regular diesel," declared the president. "And every time we used homegrown diesel, we support American farmers, not foreign oil producers." Critics point out, however, that biodiesel fuel can be as much as 20 cents a gallon more expensive than gasoline (Chen 15). And diesel-powered cars have never caught on in the United States, as they have in Europe.

(4) The most popular alternative energy vehicle in this country is the hybrid, which combines an electric motor with a standard gasoline engine. The battery is used to accelerate the car from a standing position to 30 to 35 miles an hour; then the gasoline engine takes over. Unlike all-electric vehicles, hybrid cars are self-charging; they don't need to be regularly plugged in (Mackinnon and Scott D1). Priuses have been so much in demand that there is an average waiting period of 6 months for new purchasers (McDonald 1). In 2004 Toyota announced that it would step up production of the vehicles and double the number for sale in the U.S. (Ohnsman E3). In 2006 the automaker plans to introduce a hybrid version of its popular Camry.

Paragraph 3
Since this paper is largely about the hydrogen fuel-cell car, you devote too much space to discussing vehicles powered by other energy sources. While you could mention natural gas, compressed air, and biodiesel vehicles in passing, your extensive discussion of them here tends to blur what should be a sharp focus on hydrogen fuel cell vehicles.

Suggestions for Revision
Reduce the information in this paragraph to just two or three sentences. Consider appending these sentences to the paragraph discussing electric cars. This paragraph, then, would concern the least practical, appealing, or marketable alternative fuel technologies. Fix mechanics errors: titles of publications like *Consumer Reports* should be underlined or italicized, not placed within quotation marks.

Paragraphs 4, 5, and 6
These paragraphs cover the subject of hybrids well, but this section is still too long, given that the real subject of the paper is the hydrogen fuel cell car.

Suggestions for Revision
Consider combining these three paragraphs into one shorter paragraph, cutting the discussion by at least one third. Perhaps reduce the block quotation from *Consumer Reports* to a summary sentence.

Hunte 4

Other automakers have also been getting into the act: Honda is currently producing Civic, Insight, and Accord hybrids; Ford has introduced the hybrid Mercury Mariner and the Ford Escape (Mackinnon and Scott D1). Hybrids win praise from both consumers and critics. One satisfied customer, Wendy Brown of Akron, Ohio, said that she went "from Akron to Virginia Beach on one tank of gas. It was awesome" (qtd. in Mackinnon and Scott D1). In its April 2005 Auto Issue, Consumer Reports had this to say about the Prius:

> Toyota's second-generation Prius is unbeatable for its economy, acceleration and interior room. It couples a 1.5 liter gasoline engine with an electric motor, and it automatically switches between them or runs on both as needed. The car shuts the engine off at idle. We got an excellent 44 mpg overall in our tests. . . . Reliability has been outstanding. (77)

(5) But hybrids may not be a long-term solution. Most Americans remain wary of the new technology, perhaps some thinking that with their gasoline engines, they may remain transitional vehicles. From 1999 to mid-2005, 340,000 hybrids have been sold worldwide. But in 2004 alone, Americans bought 900,000 gas-hungry SUVs (McDonald 1). Hybrids may use less gasoline than standard cars, but they still use gasoline, and therefore rely on a rapidly depleting resource. And hybrids aren't cheap: consumers pay a premium of

Hunte 5

about $3,000 over similarly-sized cars: "The higher initial purchase price, coupled with higher insurance premiums and related expenses, offset the gasoline savings, the recent Edmunds study concluded. Edmunds said a typical hybrid might actually cost its owner $5,283 more over five years than its nonhybrid counterpart" (qtd. in Mackinnon and Scott D1).

6   A variation of the standard hybrid is the plug-in, flexible-fuel tank hybrid. According to Newsweek columnist Fareed Zakaria, a standard hybrid that gets 50 miles to the gallon could get 75 if the electric motor could be recharged by plugging in to a 120-volt outlet. And "[r]eplace the conventional fuel tank with a flexible-fuel tank that can run on a combination of 15 percent petroleum and 85 percent ethanol or methanol, and you get between 400 and 500 miles per gallon of gasoline" (Zakaria 27). According to Max Boot, "[t]hat's not science fiction; that's achievable right now." Other advantages of plug-in, flexible-fuel hybrids: such technology would reduce U.S. dependence on foreign (i.e., Middle East) oil, reduce toxic emissions, and give a boost to U.S. carmakers, who could manufacture such vehicles, and sell them not only domestically, but also in Europe and Asia (Boot B5).

7   There are two advantages that make hydrogen stand out from other alternative energy sources. First, it is clean burning (the only by-products from the combining of hydrogen and oxygen are water and electricity), and secondly, it is an inexhaustible

Hunte 7

and widely available element. The principle behind the fuel-cell vehicle is simple. Essentially, an electric current is used to separate hydrogen from other elements with which it is bonded, such as oxygen. When the hydrogen is recombined with oxygen in a fuel cell, the reverse process occurs and electricity is generated. As reporter Elizabeth Kolbert notes, "[t]he elegance of hydrogen technology is hard to resist"(40). She describes a visit to the office of Bragi Aronson. Aronson is a chemistry professor whose office is in Reykjavik, Iceland, a country that relies heavily on clean energy sources:

> On the counter was a device with a photovoltaic cell on one end and a little fan on the other. In between was a cylinder of water, some clear plastic tubes, and a fuel cell, which looked like two sheets of cellophane stretched over some wire mesh. When Aronson turned on a desk lamp, the photovoltaic cell began to produce electricity, which electrolyzed the water. Hydrogen and oxygen ran through the tubes to the fuel cell, where they recombined to produce more water, in the process turning the fan. It was an impressive display. (Kolbert 40)

The fuel cell was first proposed in 1839 by a British physicist (and justice of the high court) William Grove. Jules Verne wrote about hydrogen fuel cells in his 1875 novel The Mysterious Island. And fuel cells have been used by American

Paragraph 7
This paragraph provides a clear description of hydrogen fuel-cell technology, with good use of block quotation. But the transition from other alternative energy vehicles to hydrogen fuel-cell cars, by means of the topic (first) sentence, is overly abrupt. The writing is occasionally wordy and overly passive.

Suggestions for Revision
Develop an introductory sentence that more smoothly and effectively makes the transition between what has come before (a discussion of various alternative energy-source vehicles) to what is to follow (a discussion of hydrogen fuel-cell vehicles). For emphasis, consider making this paragraph a short one and leaving the discussion of the mechanics of the fuel cell to the next paragraph. Rewrite the *weak* "There are" sentence opening ("There are two advantages . . ."), making the sentence more *active* ("Two advantages combine . . ."). Fix surface problems, like the inconsistency of "First" followed by "secondly." Toward the end of the paragraph, the repetition of "Aronson" is awkward. Rewrite, perhaps converting the sentence beginning "Aronson is a chemistry professor" into an appositive phrase ("a chemistry professor") and combining this phrase with the previous sentence. You could also create a stronger transition, after the block quotation, to the historical development of the hydrogen fuel cell.

Hunte 8

astronauts since the 1960s (Bayon 117). It is only in recent years that hydrogen fuel-cells have been proposed and tested for use in automobiles and other vehicles. The fuel-cell vehicle operates on the same principle as the fan in Aronson's office. Pressurized or supercooled liquid hydrogen from a storage cannister in the vehicle flows into a stack of fuel cells, where it is combined with oxygen. This chemical process generates electricity (and water), which impels the electric motor, which turns the vehicle's wheels (Kolbert 38; Motavalli 12.1). The process is clean, cool, and virtually silent (Kolbert 39–40).

(8)   At present, widespread use of hydrogen technology (corresponding to widespread use of hybrid cars) is not practical. For one thing, fuel cells are expensive. It costs more to generate a kilowatt of electricity from a fuel cell than it does to generate a corresponding quantity of power from an internal combustion engine. Second, the nation has no hydrogen infrastructure through which hydrogen can be extracted from water or natural gas and then delivered to customers through a network of hydrogen stations (Bayon 118). But this situation is likely to change, if not over the next few years, then over the next few decades. Hydrogen fuel cells are more promising than that of other alternative fuel technologies, such as electric cars or natural gas or compressed air vehicles. This is because some of the major automakers recognize the inevitable end of the petroleum era. Accordingly, they have to a significant degree committed themselves to developing and producing

Paragraph 8
This paragraph does a nice job of presenting some of the advantages of hydrogen fuel-cell vehicles, but it gets off on the wrong foot by focusing initially on the problems with the technology. Since you deal at some length with these problems later in the synthesis, it would be better to move the opening sentences of the paragraph to a later point. And while the examples of hydrogen prototype vehicles are fine, they may be more than you need to establish the fact that auto manufacturers are interested in developing the new technology.

Suggestions for Revision
Move the first few sentences of this paragraph to a later paragraph where you begin focusing on the problems with and drawbacks of hydrogen fuel technology. Cut some of the repetitive examples of prototype hydrogen fuel-cell vehicles in operation around the world. Fix occasionally awkward phrases ("are more promising than that of other alternative fuel technologies"), choppy sentence structure ("This is because . . ."), and illogical series.

Hunte 9

fuel-cell vehicles. In 2003 General Motors developed an early fuel-cell prototype vehicle, the Hy-Wire, which it proudly showed off to reporters and National Highway Traffic Safety Administration officials (Kolbert 38). GM's vice president for research and planning, Lawrence D. Burns, says that the company "aims to have a production-ready fuel-cell vehicle . . . by 2010" (Motavalli 12.1). In January 2005, GM introduced its hydrogen fuel-cell prototype, the Sequel. This is the first hydrogen fuel-cell vehicle with a range of 300 miles, the minimum necessary to render it marketable. The Ford Motor Company will provide hydrogen-powered buses for passengers at Dallas-Fort Worth International Airport (Schneider A.01). BMW, Honda, Toyota, and DaimlerChrysler are all developing vehicles using the new technology. As Bayon reports, "[f]uel cell-powered buses are running in Vancouver, Chicago, London, and parts of Germany" (Bayon 117). Hydrogen fuel-cell buses are also undergoing trials in other cities, including Perth, Stockholm, Barcelona, Amsterdam, and Madrid ("Buses" 12). Nissan plans to lease fuel-cell SUVs to selected American businesses in 2007 (Motavalli 12.1). And in November 2004, "a Shell station in Washington, D.C. became the first in the nation to provide a hydrogen-fuel dispenser alongside its gasoline pumps" to service the six HydroGen3 minivans that GM uses to demonstrate hydrogen technology to members of Congress (Solheim).

9   The federal government is also supporting the new technology. In 2003 President Bush, who has

Hunte 10

long been identified with the oil industry,
proposed, in his State of the Union address, a $1.2
billion research program for the development of
hydrogen cars (Kolbert 36). The following year he
recommended spending $227 million for fuel cell
research and development in 2005. The ultimate
goal is to make hydrogen fuel-cell vehicles "road
ready by 2020" (Durbin).

(10)   In spite of these promising steps, successful
development of hydrogen fuel-cell vehicles faces
significant roadblocks. As indicated above,
hydrogen fuel cells are expensive to produce and
the nation has no hydrogen infrastructure. But
there may be more fundamental problems.
According to Peter Eisenberger, chairman of the
American Physical Society, "major scientific
breakthroughs are needed for the hydrogen
economy to succeed" (qtd. in Durbin). Though
hydrogen is the most abundant element in the
universe (Motavalli 12.1), it rarely occurs in free
form in nature: it is typically bound up with other
elements, such as oxygen or carbon. Significant
quantities of energy must be employed to unbind
it. Donald F. Anthrop, who is a professor of
environmental science at San Jose State University,
points out that the energy required to operate fuel
cells will exceed the energy that they produce. He
further argues that "[t]he cost of this energy will
be prohibitively expensive" (Anthrop 10). Joseph
Romm, who is a former acting assistant Secretary
of Energy, believes that hybrids are a proven
vehicle technology, and that they are preferable to

Paragraph 9
This paragraph is fine as a means of illustrating federal government support of hydrogen fuel-cell technology.

Suggestions for Revision
Only minor tinkering needed here: perhaps combine the first two and the last two sentences.

Paragraph 10
Since, in this generally well-developed paragraph, you begin discussing the drawbacks of hydrogen fuel-cell technology, you can move some of the material in the opening sentences of paragraph 8 here (as discussed in the comments above) and combine them with the opening sentences of the present paragraph. Otherwise, fix wordy sentences and awkward constructions.

Suggestions for Revision
Combine opening sentences of paragraph 8 and paragraph 10 here. Fix wordiness later in the paragraph by replacing "who is" constructions with appositive phrases. Make "a proven vehicle technology" into another appositive.

Hunte 11

hydrogen fuel-cell vehicles. He argues that it is likely that fossil fuels such as coal and natural gas are likely to be our major sources of hydrogen, and that the process of extracting hydrogen from these sources and then compressing the gas for storage in tanks will not only consume large quantities of energy, it will also generate significant quantities of carbon dioxide. Thus, "[m]aking hydrogen . . . won't solve our major environmental problems" (Romm M3).

(11)   There is also the problem of hydrogen leakage from large numbers of fuel cell vehicles. Over time this process could increase the level of greenhouse gases and affect the world's climate. "Hydrogen is not necessarily more benign," maintains Werner Zittel, a German energy consultant, "It depends on how you produce it" (qtd. in Ananthaswamy 6). Jeremy Rifkin, who is a supporter of hydrogen fuel cell development, cautions that we should focus on the development of "green hydrogen," rather than "black hydrogen." The latter, extracted from such fossil fuels as oil, coal, and natural gas, or derived from nuclear power, generates large quantities of carbon dioxide and other toxic emissions. "Green hydrogen," on the other hand, derives from renewable energy sources such as wind, water, geothermal power, energy crops, and agricultural waste (Rifkin M5).

(12)   Plus, hydrogen fuel cells use platinum, which is a precious and expensive metal in limited supply. There is not enough platinum in the world to replace all the existing internal combustion engines

Paragraph 11
This paragraph works well to establish the potential environmental drawbacks of hydrogen fuel cell technology. It begins awkwardly, however, with a "There is" topic sentence.

Suggestions for Revision
Make the first sentence more active and perhaps combine it with the second sentence. Eliminate the "who is" construction after "Jeremy Rifkin"; create an appositive phrase here.

Hunte 12

with fuel cells--at least not with fuel cells built on existing technology (Mackintosh and Morrison 22). Some people are concerned about the safety of hydrogen. These people remember the Hindenburg disaster in 1937 in which the hydrogen-filled transatlantic German airship burst into flames shortly before landing in Lakehurst, New Jersey, killing 36 persons (Motavalli 12.1). But others downplay both concerns. Alternatives to platinum may be found and future hydrogen fuel cells will use considerably less of the metal (Mackintosh and Morrison 22). Safety measures can prevent another Hindenburg-type disaster (Motavalli 12.1).

(13) Taking these concerns into account, many experts believe that evolving technology will eventually solve the major problems and obstacles. But whether the car of the future is powered by hydrogen fuel cells or by some other form of energy, it is clear that gasoline-powered cars are going the way of the dinosaurs. We must take steps, as soon as possible, to reduce our dependence upon the internal combustion engine. Hopefully, human ingenuity will prevail in solving this critical problem.

Paragraph 12
This paragraph needs a better topic sentence to introduce a paragraph that deals both with shortage and safety issues.

Suggestions for Revision
Write a topic sentence that covers both the platinum supply and safety concerns. Eliminate the awkward repetition of "people" ("Some people . . . These people") later in the paragraph. Provide a transitional word or term before the final sentence of the paragraph.

Paragraph 13
The conclusion is overgeneralized. While the first sentence provides the beginning of an effective transition to the closing, what follows merely summarizes what has come before ("We must take steps . . . to reduce our dependence upon the internal combustion engine"). The final sentence is vague and anticlimactic.

Suggestions for Revision
Develop a conclusion more rooted in specific facts and quotations by those who believe the problems described in the preceding paragraphs will be overcome. Appeal to reader interest in the subject as a way of closing strongly.

Revise Your Synthesis: Global, Local, and Surface Revisions

Many writers find it helpful to plan for three types of revision: global, local, and surface. Global revisions affect the entire paper: the thesis, the type and pattern of evidence employed, the overall organization, the tone. A global revision may also emerge from a change in purpose. For example, the writer of this paper might decide to rewrite, focusing not on a broad introduction to and explanation of fuel-cell technology but on plans to create a national hydrogen infrastructure, similar to the existing network of gas stations, that would enable drivers to re-fuel their hydrogen-powered vehicles at their convenience.

Local revisions affect paragraphs: topic and transitional sentences; the type of evidence presented within a paragraph; evidence added, modified, or dropped within a paragraph; logical connections from one sentence or set of sentences within a paragraph to another.

Surface revisions deal with sentence style and construction, word choice, and errors of grammar, mechanics, spelling, and citation form.

Revising the Example First Draft: Highlights

Global

- Refocus the paper so that it emphasizes hydrogen fuel-cell vehicles and de-emphasizes (while still briefly covering) such other alternative-energy vehicles as hybrids and electrics.
- Sharpen the *thesis* so that it focuses on hydrogen fuel-cell vehicles.
- In the body of the paper (e.g., paragraphs 3–6), cut back on references to alternative energy vehicles other than hydrogen fuel-cell cars.

Local

- More fully develop paragraph 2, providing additional reasons for the inevitable end of the internal combustion engine era.
- Combine information in paragraphs 4, 5, and 6 into one shorter paragraph, cutting the discussion by at least one third.
- Improve topic and transitional sentences in paragraphs 7, 8, and 12.
- Move the opening sentences of paragraph 8 to a corresponding position in paragraph 10 to improve coherence and logic.
- In paragraph 8, cut some of the repetitive examples of prototype hydrogen fuel-cell vehicles around the world.
- Improve the conclusion, making it more specific and appealing more strongly to reader interest.

Surface

- Avoid passive phrases, such as "is used."
- Avoid phrases such as "there is" and "there are."
- Fix mechanics errors, such as placing titles of articles within quotation marks, rather than italicizing or underlining them.
- Follow principle of parallelism for items in series: "First" should be followed by "Second," not "Secondly."
- Reduce wordiness throughout.
- Fix awkward phrases (e.g., "are more promising than that of other alternative fuel technologies").

Revising the Sample Synthesis

Try your hand at creating a final draft of the paper on pages 105–15 by following the revision suggestions above, together with using your own best judgment about how to improve the first draft. Make global, local, and surface changes. After trying your own version of the paper, compare it to the revised version of our student-produced paper below.

REVISED MODEL PAPER

Hunte 1

Janice Hunte

Professor Case

English 101

31 January 2007

The Car of the Future?

(1) In July 2005 a California family, the Spallinos, took proud possession of a new silver and blue Honda FCX. Never heard of the FCX? That's because this particular model is not a part of Honda's standard product line. It's a prototype powered by hydrogen fuel cells. Although companies like Honda, Toyota, GM, and Daimler Chrysler have been experimenting with hydrogen-powered vehicles for some years, the Spallinos' car is the first to be placed in private hands for road testing. The family was selected by Honda because they already own a Civic powered by natural gas and so are used to the inconveniences of driving a vehicle that needs the kind of fuel available only in a limited number of commercial outlets. Mr. Spallino is excited at the prospect of test driving the FCX: "Maybe this is the technology of the future. Maybe it isn't," says Spallino, who commutes 77 miles a day. "But if I can be part of the evolution of this technology, that would be a lot of fun" (Molloy 18).

(2) Are hydrogen fuel-cell cars the wave of the future? In recent years, the major automakers, with some financial incentives from the federal government, have been exploring alternatives to the gasoline-powered internal combustion engine. We've seen vehicles powered by electricity, natural gas, even compressed air. Diesel engines have been popular in Europe for decades,

Hunte 2

though they have a much smaller customer base in the United States. Currently, the most popular alternative energy vehicles are the hybrids, such as the Toyota Prius, vehicles that run on both gasoline engines and electric motors. But many see hybrids, which use gasoline, as merely transitional vehicles. In the future, they believe, fuel-cell vehicles powered by hydrogen, a clean-burning and abundant energy source, will become the norm for roadway and highway transportation.

3   But why not continue to rely indefinitely on gasoline? The answer is that the days of the gasoline-powered internal combustion engine are numbered. First, gasoline is an environmentally dirty fuel that, when burned, creates the toxic greenhouse gas pollution that contributes to global warming. Second, oil is a rapidly depleting resource. As energy expert Paul Roberts points out, "the more you produce, the less remains in the ground, and the harder it is to bring up that remainder"(M1). Today, we import most of our oil from Saudi Arabia, a country previously thought to have virtually inexhaustible supplies of oil. But many experts believe that the Saudi fields are in decline, or have at least "matured," with most of their easily extractable petroleum already gone. In the near future, the Saudis may no longer be able to meet world demand (Klare B9). Roberts notes that the demand for oil today stands at 29 billion barrels of oil a year. Currently, the supply matches the demand; but by 2020, with increasing demands for oil by emerging industrial countries like India and China, the demand will far outstrip the supply, and prices, currently around $60 a barrel, may soar to $100. If the U.S. does not reduce its demand for oil, a future shortage could mean that "the global economy is likely to slip into a recession so severe that the Great Depression will look like a dress rehearsal" (Roberts M1).

4   Over the years, many alternative fuel technologies have been proposed, but all have shown limited practicality or appeal. Fifteen to twenty years ago, electric cars looked attractive. But these battery-powered, zero-emission cars proved problematic: most had to be recharged every 100 miles or so, considerably limiting their range. Manufacturers could never figure out how

Hunte 3

to reduce the batteries to manageable size or how to produce them at reasonable cost. Other alternative fuel sources include compressed natural gas (CNG), compressed air, and biodiesel fuel. While prototype vehicles using these various technologies have been built, none appears likely to succeed in the American mass market.

5   Currently, the most popular alternative energy vehicle in this country is the hybrid, which combines an electric motor with a standard gasoline engine. The battery is used to accelerate the car from a standing position to 30 to 35 miles an hour; then the gasoline engine takes over. Unlike all-electric vehicles, hybrid cars are self-charging; they don't need to be regularly plugged in (Mackinnon and Scott D1). The most popular hybrid, the Toyota Prius, is in so much demand that new purchasers must typically wait six months to get one. Other manufacturers, including Honda, Ford, and General Motors, also sell or soon plan to offer hybrid vehicles. Consumer Reports called the Prius "unbeatable for its economy, acceleration and interior room" and in 2005 declared the Honda Accord hybrid its highest scoring family sedan ("Best" 76-77). Despite their advantages, however, hybrids may still be transitional vehicles. They may use less gasoline than standard cars, but they still use gasoline and therefore rely on a rapidly depleting resource. And hybrids aren't cheap: consumers pay a premium of about $3,000 over similarly sized cars, an amount that could easily offset for years any savings in gasoline expenses. A variation of the standard hybrid, the plug-in, flexible-fuel tank hybrid, offers greatly improved fuel economy. In these vehicles, gasoline could be mixed with cheaper fuels like ethanol or methanol. Of course, consumers may find plugging in their cars inconvenient or (if they are on the road) impractical; and flexible-fuel hybrids would be reliant on a national ethanol/methanol infrastructure, which doesn't yet exist.

6   With these alternatives to the standard gasoline-powered internal combustion engine, what is the special appeal of the hydrogen fuel-cell vehicle? Two advantages combine to make hydrogen stand out from the rest: it is clean burning (the only by-products from the combining of hydrogen and

oxygen are water and electricity), and it is an inexhaustible and widely available element.

(7)   The principle behind the fuel-cell vehicle is simplicity itself. Essentially, an electric current is used to separate hydrogen from other elements with which it is bonded, such as oxygen. When the hydrogen is recombined with oxygen in a fuel cell, the reverse process occurs and electricity is generated. As reporter Elizabeth Kolbert notes, "[t]he elegance of hydrogen technology is hard to resist"(40). She describes a visit to the office of Bragi Aronson, a chemistry professor in his office in Reykjavik, Iceland, a country that relies heavily on clean energy sources:

> On the counter was a device with a photovoltaic cell on one end and a little fan on the other. In between was a cylinder of water, some clear plastic tubes, and a fuel cell, which looked like two sheets of cellophane stretched over some wire mesh. When Aronson turned on a desk lamp, the photovoltaic cell began to produce electricity, which electrolyzed the water. Hydrogen and oxygen ran through the tubes to the fuel cell, where they recombined to produce more water, in the process turning the fan. It was an impressive display. (40)

(8)   The fuel cell is not exactly cutting-edge technology: the concept itself was first proposed in 1839 by British physicist (and justice of the high court) William Grove. Jules Verne wrote about hydrogen fuel cells in his 1875 novel The Mysterious Island. And fuel cells have been used by American astronauts since the 1960s (Bayon 117). It is only in recent years, however, that hydrogen fuel cells have been proposed and tested for use in automobiles and other vehicles. The fuel-cell vehicle operates on the same principle as the fan in Aronson's office. Pressurized or supercooled liquid hydrogen from a storage cannister in the vehicle flows into a stack of fuel cells, where it is combined with oxygen. This chemical process generates electricity (and water), which impels the electric motor, which turns the vehicle's wheels (Kolbert 38; Motavalli 12.1). (See Figure 1.) The process is clean, cool, and virtually silent (Kolbert 39–40).

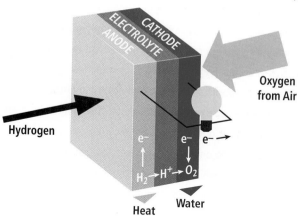

Figure 1 How a hydrogen fuel cell works

(9) What makes the successful development of hydrogen fuel cells more promising than that of other alternative fuel technologies, such as electric cars or natural gas or compressed air vehicles, is that a number of major automakers, recognizing the inevitable end of the petroleum era, have to a significant degree committed themselves to developing and producing fuel-cell vehicles. In 2003 General Motors developed an early fuel-cell prototype vehicle, the Hy-Wire (Kolbert 38). In January 2005, GM introduced the Sequel, a hydrogen vehicle with a range of 300 miles--the minimum necessary to render it marketable. The company "aims to have a production-ready fuel-cell vehicle . . . by 2010" (Motavalli 12.1). The Ford Motor Company plans to provide hydrogen-powered buses for passengers at Dallas-Fort Worth International Airport (Schneider). BMW, Honda, Toyota, and DaimlerChrysler are all developing vehicles using the new technology. As Bayon reports, "[f]uel cell-powered buses are running in Vancouver, Chicago, London, and parts of Germany" (118), and they are undergoing trials elsewhere. Nissan plans to lease fuel cell SUVs to selected American businesses in 2007 (Motavalli 12.1).

(10) The federal government is also supporting the new technology: in 2003 President Bush, long identified with the oil industry, proposed in his State of the Union address a $1.2 billion research program for the development

of hydrogen cars (Kolbert 36). The following year he recommended spending $227 million for fuel-cell research and development in 2005, with the ultimate goal of making hydrogen fuel-cell vehicles "road ready by 2020" (Durbin).

⑪   At present, widespread use of hydrogen technology (corresponding to widespread use of hybrid cars) is not practical (Committee 116–17). For one thing, fuel cells are expensive. It costs more to generate a kilowatt of electricity from a fuel cell than it does to generate a corresponding quantity of power from an internal combustion engine. For another, the nation has no hydrogen infrastructure through which hydrogen can be extracted from water or natural gas and then delivered to customers through a network of hydrogen stations (Bayon 118). This situation is likely to change, however, if not over the next few years, then over the next few decades. But there may be more fundamental problems with hydrogen fuel cell technology. According to Peter Eisenberger, chairman of the American Physical Society, "major scientific breakthroughs are needed for the hydrogen economy to succeed" (qtd. in Durbin). Though hydrogen is the most abundant element in the universe (Motavalli 12.1), it rarely occurs in free form in nature: it is typically bound up with other elements, such as oxygen or carbon. Significant quantities of energy must be employed to unbind it. Donald F. Anthrop, a professor of environmental science at San Jose State University, points out that the energy required to operate fuel cells will exceed the energy that they produce. He further argues that "[t]he cost of this energy will be prohibitively expensive" (10). Joseph Romm, a former acting assistant Secretary of Energy, believes that hybrids, a proven vehicle technology, are preferable to hydrogen fuel-cell vehicles. He argues fossil fuels such as coal and natural gas are likely to be our major sources of hydrogen and that the process of extracting hydrogen from these sources and then compressing the gas for storage in tanks will not only consume large quantities of energy but will also generate significant quantities of carbon dioxide. Thus, "[m]aking hydrogen . . . won't solve our major environmental problems" (Romm M3).

⑫   Others worry about hydrogen leakage from large numbers of fuel-cell vehicles, which could, over time, increase the level of greenhouse gases and affect the world's climate. "Hydrogen is not necessarily more benign," maintains Werner Zittel, a German energy consultant. "[Its ecological impact] depends on how you produce it" (qtd. in Ananthaswamy 6). Jeremy Rifkin, a supporter of hydrogen fuel cell development, cautions that we should focus on the development of "green hydrogen," rather than "black hydrogen." The latter, extracted from such fossil fuels as oil, coal, and natural gas, or derived from nuclear power, generates large quantities of carbon dioxide and other toxic emissions. "Green hydrogen," on the other hand, derives from renewable energy sources such as wind, water, geothermal power, energy crops, and agricultural waste (Rifkin M5).

(13)   Other problems confront hydrogen advocates. Hydrogen fuel cells use platinum, a precious and expensive metal in limited supply. There is not enough platinum in the world to replace all the existing internal combustion engines with fuel cells--at least not with fuel cells built on existing technology (Mackintosh and Morrison 22). Some are concerned about the safety of hydrogen--mindful of the Hindenburg disaster in 1937 in which the hydrogen-filled transatlantic German airship burst into flames shortly before landing in Lakehurst, New Jersey, killing 36 persons (Motavalli 12.1). But others downplay both concerns: alternatives to platinum may be found and future hydrogen fuel cells will use considerably less of the metal (Mackintosh and Morrison 22). And safety measures can prevent another Hindenburg-type disaster (Motavalli 12.1).

(14)   Taking these concerns into account, many experts believe that evolving technology will eventually solve the major problems and obstacles. To critics like Max Boot, widespread use of hydrogen fuel-cell cars is "science fiction" (B5). But it's worth remembering that in 1870 the telephone was science fiction, as was the airplane in 1900, home television in 1920, the desktop computer in 1970, and the World Wide Web in 1990. In none of those years was the know-how and technology yet available for the corresponding scientific develop-ment. Such developments were made possible--and, in later years, both affordable and indispensable to modern life--because of the commitment and

Hunte 8

hard work of one or more individuals. One reader of Joseph Romm's article ("Lots of Hot Air about Hydrogen") responded, "Had bureaucrats like Romm discouraged James Watt in the eighteenth century regarding the harnessing of steam energy, our economic engines would still be powered by horses" (Hoffman B4). It may indeed turn out that the problems of developing affordable and practical hydrogen vehicles on a large scale prove insurmountable. But many believe that the promise of hydrogen fuel cells as a provider of clean and virtually inexhaustible energy makes further research and development vital for the transportation needs of the twenty-first century. As for the internal combustion engine--according to Geoffrey Ballard, founder of Ballard Power Systems, it "will go the way of the horse. It will be a curiosity to my grandchildren" (qtd. in Bayon 118).

[new page]

Hunte 9

Works Cited

Ananthaswamy, Anil. "Reality Bites for the Dream of a Hydrogen Economy." New Scientist 15 Nov. 2003: 6+.

Anthrop, Donald F. Letter. "Renewable Energy and Fuel Cells." Oil and Gas Journal 10 Oct. 2004: 10.

Bayon, Ricardo. "The Fuel Subsidy We Need." Atlantic Monthly Jan./Feb. 2003: 117-18.

"Best 2005 Cars." Consumer Reports Apr. 2005: 76 (Toyota Prius); 77 (Honda Accord).

Boot, Max. "The 500-Mile-Per-Gallon Solution." Los Angeles Times 24 Mar. 2005: B5.

Committee on Alternatives and Strategies for Future Hydrogen Production and Use, Board on Energy and Environmental Systems. The Hydrogen Economy: Opportunities, Costs, Barriers, and RD Needs. Washington: National Academies Press, 2004.

Hunte 10

Durbin, Dee-Ann. "Official Defends Fuel Cell Study Funds." Associated Press 8
    Mar. 2004.

Hoffman, Robert D. Letter. Los Angeles Times 3 Apr. 2004: B4.

"How a Hydrogen Fuel Cell Works." Creating a Sustainable Energy System for
    New Zealand. Ministry of Economic Development, New Zealand. Oct.
    2004. 18 Jan. 2006 <http://www.med.govt.nz/templates/
    MultipageDocumentPage_10138.aspx>.

Klare, Michael T. "The Vanishing Mirage of Saudi Oil: Dwindling Reserves May
    End the Petroleum Age." Los Angeles Times 2 June 2005: B9.

Kolbert, Elizabeth. "The Car of Tomorrow." The New Yorker 11 Aug. 2003:
    36-40.

Mackinnon, Jim, and Dave Scott. "Prices Fueling Hybrid Interest." Akron
    Beacon Journal 24 July 2005: D1+.

Mackintosh, James, and Kevin Morrison. "Car Makers Gear Up for the Next
    Shortage--Platinum." Financial Times [London] 6 July 2005: 22.

Molloy, Tim. "Tomorrow's Car: It's a Gas to Drive." The Courier Mail
    [Queensland, Australia] 2 July 2005: 18.

Motavalli, Jim. "Putting the Hindenberg to Rest." New York Times 5 June
    2005: 12.1.

Rifkin, Jeremy. "Using Fossil Fuels in Energy Process Gets Us Nowhere." Los
    Angeles Times 9 Nov. 2003: M5.

Roberts, Paul. "Running Out of Oil--and Time." Los Angeles Times 7 Mar.
    2004: M1.

Romm, Joseph J. "Lots of Hot Air About Hydrogen." Los Angeles Times 28 Mar.
    2004: M3.

Schneider, Greg. "Automakers Put Hydrogen Power on the Fast Track."
    Washington Post 9 Jan. 2005: A.01.

Critical Reading for Synthesis

- *Use the tips from Critical Reading for Summary on page 7.* Remember to examine the context; note the title and subtitle; identify the main point; identify the subpoints; break the reading into sections; distinguish between points, examples, and counterarguments; watch for transitions within and between paragraphs; and read actively and recursively.
- *Establish the writer's primary purpose.* Use some of the guidelines discussed in Chapter 2; is the piece primarily informative, persuasive, or entertaining? Assess whether the piece achieves its purpose.
- *Read to identify a key idea.* If you begin reading your source materials with a key idea or topic already in mind, read to identify what your sources have to say about the idea.
- *Read to discover a key idea.* If you begin the reading process without a key idea in mind yet, read to discover a key idea that your sources address.
- *Read for relationships.* Regardless of whether you already have a key idea, or whether you are attempting to discover one, your emphasis in reading should be on noting the ways in which the readings relate to each other, to a key idea, and to your purpose in writing the synthesis.

 WRITING ASSIGNMENT: THE "LEGACY" QUESTION IN COLLEGE ADMISSIONS

Now we'll give you an opportunity to practice your skills in planning and writing an explanatory synthesis. See Chapter 9, pages 329–56, where we provide ten sources on the controversial issue of "legacy" status in the college admissions process. At certain schools, the admissions staff gives preferential consideration to the sons and daughters of alumni. Should they? In the synthesis, your task will be to understand and present to others less knowledgeable than you the practice, history, and extent of legacy admissions. You will also explain the debate sparked by legacy admissions.

Note that your instructor may assign related assignments for summary and paraphrase in Chapter 9 to help you prepare for writing an explanatory synthesis.

Exploring Online Sources

The electronic databases to which you have access through your school's library, as well as Internet search engines such as Google.com, will yield many sources beyond the ones gathered on the topic of "Legacy Admissions" in Chapter 9. Read the articles on pages 336–56. Then use one or more of your library's databases or conduct an Internet search to locate articles and discussions on the influence of legacy status in college admissions. You may find more recent pieces than those we've collected here. If you end up using any of the sources you find on the Internet for the explanatory synthesis assignment, please review our cautionary discussion of using Web-based sources in Chapter 7 on Evaluating Sources (pages 270–73).

4 Argument Synthesis

■ WHAT IS AN ARGUMENT SYNTHESIS?

An argument is an attempt to persuade a reader or listener that a particular and debatable claim is true. Writers argue in order to establish facts, to make statements of value, and to recommend policies. For instance, answering the question *Why do soldiers sometimes commit atrocities in wartime?* would involve making an argument. To develop this argument, researchers might conduct experiments, collect historical evidence, and examine and interpret data. The researchers might then present their findings at professional conferences and in journals and books. The extent to which readers (or listeners) accept these findings depends upon the quality of the supporting evidence and upon the care with which the researchers have argued their case. What we are calling an argument *synthesis* draws upon evidence from a variety of sources in an attempt to persuade others of the truth or validity of a debatable claim.

By contrast, the explanatory synthesis, as we have seen, is fairly modest in purpose. It emphasizes the sources themselves, not the writer's use of sources to persuade others. The writer of an explanatory synthesis aims to inform, not persuade. Here, for example, is a thesis devised for an explanatory synthesis on the subject computer-mediated communication (or CMC)—the use of the computer (e-mail, instant messaging, etc.) to form serious online relationships:

> While many praise CMC's potential to bridge barriers and promote meaningful dialogue, others caution that CMC is fraught with dangers.

This thesis summarizes the viewpoints people espouse in regard to CMC, neither arguing for or against any one viewpoint.

In contrast, an argumentative thesis is *persuasive* in purpose. Writers working with the same source material might conceive of and support opposing theses. An example:

> CMC threatens to undermine human intimacy, connection, and ultimately community.

So the thesis for an argument synthesis is a claim about which reasonable people could disagree. It is a claim with which—given the right arguments—your audience might be persuaded to agree. The strategy of your argument synthesis is therefore to find and use convincing *support* for your *claim*.

The Elements of Argument: Claim, Support, and Assumption

Let's consider the terminology we've just used. One way of looking at an argument is to see it as an interplay of three essential elements: claim, support, and assumption.

A *claim* is a proposition or conclusion that you are trying to prove. You prove this claim by using *support* in the form of fact or expert opinion. Linking your supporting evidence to your claim is your *assumption* about the subject. This assumption, also called a *warrant*, is—as we've discussed in Chapter 2—an underlying belief or principle about some aspect of the world and how it operates. By nature, assumptions (which are often unstated) tend to be more general than either claims or supporting evidence.

For example, here are the essential elements of an argument advocating parental restriction of television viewing for their high school children:

Claim

> High school students should be restricted to no more than two hours of TV viewing per day.

Support

> An important new study and the testimony of educational specialists reveal that students who watch more than two hours of TV a night have, on average, lower grades than those who watch less TV.

Assumption

> Excessive TV viewing adversely affects academic performance.

Here are the elements of our CMC argument:

Support

> While the Internet presents us with increased opportunities to meet people, these meetings are limited by geographical distance.

> People are spending increasing amounts of time in cyberspace: In 1998, the average Internet user spent over four hours per week online, a figure that has nearly doubled recently.

> College health officials report that excessive Internet usage threatens many college students' academic and psychological well-being.

> New kinds of relationships fostered on the Internet often pose challenges to pre-existing relationships.

Assumptions

> The communication skills used and the connections formed during Internet contact fundamentally differ from those used and formed during face-to-face contact.

> "Real" connection and a sense of community are sustained by face-to-face contact, not by Internet interactions.

For the most part, arguments should be constructed logically so that assumptions link evidence (supporting facts and expert opinions) to claims. As we'll see, however, logic is only one component of effective arguments.

Practicing Claim, Support, and Assumption

Devise two sets of claims with support and assumptions for each. First, in response to the example immediately above on computer-mediated communication and relationships, devise a one-sentence claim addressing the positive impact (or potentially positive impact) of CMC on relationships—whether you personally agree with the claim or not. Then list the support on which such a claim might rest, and the assumption that underlies these. Second, write a claim that states your own position on any debatable topic you choose. Again, devise statements of support and relevant assumptions.

The Three Appeals of Argument: *Logos, Ethos, Pathos*

Speakers and writers have never relied on logic alone in advancing and supporting their claims. More than 2,000 years ago, the Athenian philosopher and rhetorician Aristotle explained how speakers attempting to persuade others to their point of view could achieve their purpose by relying on one or more *appeals*, which he called *logos, ethos*, and *pathos*.

Since we frequently find these three appeals employed in political argument, we'll use political examples in the following discussion. But keep in mind that these appeals are also used extensively in advertising, legal cases, business documents, and many other types of argument.

Logos

Logos is the rational appeal, the appeal to reason. If speakers expect to persuade their audiences, they must argue logically and must supply appropriate evidence to support their case. Logical arguments are commonly of two types (often combined): deductive and inductive. The *deductive* argument begins with a generalization, then cites a specific case related to that generalization, from which follows a conclusion. A familiar example of deductive reasoning, used by Aristotle himself, is the following:

All men are mortal. (*generalization*)

Socrates is a man. (*specific case*)

Socrates is mortal. (*conclusion about the specific case*)

In the terms we've just been discussing, this deduction may be restated as follows:

Socrates is mortal. (*claim*)

Socrates is a man. (*support*)

All men are mortal. (*assumption*)

An example of a deductive argument may be seen in President John F. Kennedy's address to the nation in June 1963 on the need for sweeping civil rights legislation. Kennedy begins with the generalizations that it "ought to be possible . . . for American students of any color to attend any public institution they select without having to be backed up by troops" and that "it ought to be possible for American citizens of any color to register and vote in a free election without interference or fear of reprisal." Kennedy then provides several specific examples (primarily recent events in Birmingham, Alabama) and statistics to show that this was not the case. He concludes:

> We face, therefore, a moral crisis as a country and a people. It cannot be met by repressive police action. It cannot be left to increased demonstrations in the streets. It cannot be quieted by token moves or talk. It is time to act in the Congress, in your state and local legislative body, and, above all, in all of our daily lives.

Underlying Kennedy's argument is the following reasoning:

All Americans should enjoy certain rights. (*assumption*)

Some Americans do not enjoy these rights. (*support*)

We must take action to ensure that all Americans enjoy these rights. (*claim*)

Another form of logical argumentation is *inductive* reasoning. A speaker or writer who argues inductively begins not with a generalization, but with several pieces of specific evidence. The speaker then draws a conclusion from this evidence. For example, in a 1990 debate on gun control, Senator Robert C. Byrd (D-VA) cites specific examples of rampant crime involving guns: "I read of young men being viciously murdered for a pair of sneakers, a leather jacket, or $20." He also offers statistical evidence of the increasing crime rate: "in 1951, there were 3.2 policemen for every felony committed in the United States; this year [1990] nearly 3.2 felonies will be committed per every police officer." He concludes, "Something has to change. We have to stop the crimes that are distorting and disrupting the way of life for so many innocent, law-respecting Americans. The bill that we are debating today attempts to do just that."

Senator Edward M. Kennedy (D-MA) also used statistical evidence in arguing for passage of the Racial Justice Act of 1990, designed to ensure that minorities were not disproportionately singled out for the death penalty. Kennedy points out that between 1973 and 1980, 17 defendants in Fulton County, Georgia, were charged with killing police officers, but the only defendant who received the death sentence was a black man. Kennedy also cites statistics to show that "those who killed whites were 4.3 times more likely to receive the death penalty than were killers of blacks," and that "in Georgia, blacks who killed whites received the death penalty 16.7 percent of the time, while whites who killed received the death penalty only 4.2 percent of the time."

Of course, the mere piling up of evidence does not in itself make the speaker's case. As Donna Cross explains in "Politics: The Art of Bamboozling,"* politicians are very adept at "card-stacking." And statistics can be selected and manipulated to prove anything, as demonstrated in Darrell Huff's landmark book *How to Lie with Statistics* (1954). Moreover, what appears to be a logical argument may, in fact, be fundamentally flawed. (See Chapter 2 for a discussion of logical fallacies and faulty reasoning strategies.) On the other hand, the fact that evidence can be distorted, statistics misused, and logic fractured does not mean that these tools of reason can be dispensed with or should be dismissed. It means only that audiences have to listen and read critically—perceptively, knowledgeably, and skeptically (though not necessarily cynically).

Sometimes, politicians can turn their opponents' false logic against them. Major R. Owens (D-NY), attempted to counter what he took to be the reasoning on welfare adopted by his opponents:

Welfare programs create dependency and so should be reformed or abolished. (*assumption*)

Aid to Families with Dependent Children (AFDC) is a welfare program. (*support*)

AFDC should be reformed or abolished. (*claim*)

In his speech opposing the Republican welfare reform measure of 1995, Owens simply changes the specific (middle) term, pointing out that federal subsidies for electric power in the West and Midwest and farmers' low-rate home loan mortgages are, in effect, welfare programs. ("We are spoiling America's farmers by smothering them with socialism.") The logical conclusion—that we should reform or eliminate farmers' home loan mortgages—would clearly be unacceptable to many of those pushing for reform of AFDC. Owens thus suggests that opposition to AFDC is based less on reason than on lack of sympathy for its recipients.

Exercise 4.2

Using Deductive and Inductive Logic

Choose an issue currently being debated at your school, or a college-related issue about which you are concerned. Write down a claim about this issue. Then write two paragraphs addressing your claim—one in which you organize your points deductively, and one in which you organize them inductively. Some sample issues might include college admissions policies, classroom crowding, or grade inflation. Alternatively, you could base your paragraphs on a claim generated in Exercise 4.1.

Ethos

Ethos, or the ethical appeal, is based not on the ethical rationale for the subject under discussion, but rather on the ethical nature of the person making

---

Donna Cross, Word Abuse: How the Words We Use Use Us *(New York: Coward, 1979).*

the appeal. A person making an argument must have a certain degree of credibility: That person must be of good character, have sound sense, and be qualified to hold the office or recommend policy.

For example, Elizabeth Cervantes Barrón, running for senator as the peace and freedom candidate, begins her statement with "I was born and raised in central Los Angeles. I grew up in a multiethnic, multicultural environment where I learned to respect those who were different from me. . . . I am a teacher and am aware of how cutbacks in education have affected our children and our communities."

On the other end of the political spectrum, American Independent gubernatorial candidate Jerry McCready also begins with an ethical appeal: "As a self-employed businessman, I have learned firsthand what it is like to try to make ends meet in an unstable economy being manipulated by out-of-touch politicians." Both candidates are making an appeal to *ethos*, based on the strength of their personal qualities for the office they seek.

L. A. Kauffman is not running for office but rather writing an article arguing against socialism as a viable ideology for the future ("Socialism: No." *Progressive*, April 1, 1993). To defuse objections that he is simply a tool of capitalism, Kauffman begins with an appeal to *ethos*: "Until recently, I was executive editor of the journal *Socialist Review*. Before that I worked for the Marxist magazine, *Monthly Review*. My bookshelves are filled with books of Marxist theory, and I even have a picture of Karl Marx up on my wall." Thus, Kauffman establishes his credentials to argue knowledgeably about Marxist ideology.

Conservative commentator Rush Limbaugh frequently makes use of the ethical appeal by linking himself with the kind of Americans he assumes his audiences to be (what author Donna Cross calls "glory by association"):

> In their attacks [on me], my critics misjudge and insult the American people. If I were really what liberals claim—racist, hatemonger, blowhard—I would years ago have deservedly gone into oblivion. The truth is, I provide information and analysis the media refuses to disseminate, information and analysis the public craves. People listen to me for one reason: I am effective. And my credibility is judged in the marketplace every day. . . . I represent America's rejection of liberal elites. . . . I validate the convictions of ordinary people.*

Exercise 4.3

Using Ethos

Return to the claim you used for Exercise 4.2, and write a paragraph in which you use an appeal to *ethos* to make a case for that claim.

Rush Limbaugh, "Why I Am a Threat to the Left," Los Angeles Times, 9 Oct. 1994.

Pathos

Finally, speakers and writers appeal to their audiences by use of *pathos*, the appeal to the emotions. Nothing is inherently wrong with using an emotional appeal. Indeed, since emotions often move people far more powerfully than reason alone, speakers and writers would be foolish not to use emotion. And it would be a drab, humorless world if human beings were not subject to the sway of feeling, as well as reason. The emotional appeal becomes problematic only if it is the *sole* or *primary* basis of the argument. This imbalance of emotion over logic is the kind of situation that led, for example, to the internment of Japanese Americans during World War II or that leads to periodic political spasms to enact anti-flag-burning legislation.

President Reagan was a master of emotional appeal. He closed his first inaugural address with a reference to the view from the Capitol to the Arlington National Cemetery, where lie thousands of markers of "heroes":

> Under one such marker lies a young man, Martin Treptow, who left his job in a small-town barbershop in 1917 to go to France with the famed Rainbow Division. There, on the western front, he was killed trying to carry a message between battalions under heavy artillery fire. We're told that on his body was found a diary. On the flyleaf under the heading, "My Pledge," he had written these words: "America must win this war. Therefore, I will work, I will save, I will sacrifice, I will endure, I will fight cheerfully and do my utmost, as if the issue of the whole struggle depended on me alone." The crisis we are facing today does not require of us the kind of sacrifice that Martin Treptow and so many thousands of others were called upon to make. It does require, however, our best effort and our willingness to believe in ourselves and to believe in our capacity to perform great deeds, to believe that together with God's help we can and will resolve the problems which now confront us.

Surely, Reagan implies, if Martin Treptow can act so courageously and so selflessly, we can do the same. The logic is somewhat unclear, since the connection between Martin Treptow and ordinary Americans of 1981 is rather tenuous (as Reagan concedes); but the emotional power of Martin Treptow, whom reporters were sent scurrying to research, carries the argument.

A more recent president, Bill Clinton, also used *pathos*. Addressing an audience of the nation's governors about his welfare plan, Clinton closed his remarks by referring to a conversation he had held with a welfare mother who had gone through the kind of training program Clinton was advocating. Asked by Clinton whether she thought that such training programs should be mandatory, the mother said, "I sure do." Clinton in his remarks explained what she said when he asked her why:

> "Well, because if it wasn't, there would be a lot of people like me home watching the soaps because we don't believe we can make anything of ourselves anymore. So you've got to make it mandatory." And I said, "What's the best thing about having a job?" She said,

"When my boy goes to school, and they say, 'What does your mama do for a living?' he can give an answer."

Clinton uses the emotional power he counts on in that anecdote to set up his conclusion: "We must end poverty for Americans who want to work. And we must do it on terms that dignify all of the rest of us, as well as help our country to work better. I need your help, and I think we can do it."

Exercise 4.4

Using Pathos

Return to the claim you used for Exercises 4.2 and 4.3, and write a paragraph in which you use an appeal to *pathos* to argue for that claim.

■ DEMONSTRATION: DEVELOPING AN ARGUMENT SYNTHESIS — VOLUNTEERING IN AMERICA

To demonstrate how to plan and draft an argument synthesis, let's consider another subject. If you were taking an economics or sociology course, you might at some point consider the phenomenon of volunteerism, the extent to which Americans volunteer—that is, give away their time freely—for causes they deem worthy. In a market economy, why would people agree to forgo wages in exchange for their labor? Are there other kinds of compensation for people who volunteer? Is peer pressure involved? Can a spirit of volunteerism be taught or encouraged? And, in light of the articles that follow and the example argument based on them, can the government—which has the constitutional right to compel military service—*compel* citizens to serve their communities (rendering their service something other than an act of volunteering)?

Suppose, in preparing to write a short paper on volunteering, you located the following sources:

"A New Start for National Service," John McCain and Evan Bayh

"A Time to Heed the Call," David Gergen

"Volunteering in the United States," U.S. Department of Labor

"National Service, Political Socialization, and Citizenship," Eric B. Gorham

"Calls for National Service," Landrum, Eberly, and Sherraden

"Rumsfeld: No Need for Draft; 'Disadvantages Notable,'" Kathleen T. Rhem

"Politics and National Service: A Virus Attacks the Volunteer Sector," Bruce Chapman

Read these sources (which follow) carefully, noting as you do the kinds of information and ideas you could draw upon to develop an *argument synthesis*.

Note: To save space and for the purpose of demonstration, several of the passages are excerpts only. In preparing your paper, naturally you would draw upon entire articles and book chapters from which the extracts were made. And you would probably draw upon more sources than these in your search for materials in support of your argument (as the writer of the example paper has done on pp. 156–65). But the sources included here set the poles of the debate.

A NEW START FOR NATIONAL SERVICE

John McCain and Evan Bayh

John McCain (R-AZ) and Evan Bayh (D-IN) are United States senators. This Op-ed piece appeared in the New York Times *on November 6, 2001, a few weeks after the terrorist attack of September 11th.*

Since Sept. 11, Americans have found a new spirit of national unity and purpose. Forty years ago, at the height of the cold war, President John F. Kennedy challenged Americans to enter into public service. Today, confronted with a challenge no less daunting than the cold war, Americans again are eager for ways to serve at home and abroad. Government should make it easier for them to do so.

That is why we are introducing legislation to revamp national service programs and dramatically expand opportunities for public service.

Many tasks lie ahead, both new and old. On the home front, there are new security and civil defense requirements, like increased police and border patrol needs. We will charge the Corporation for National Service, the federal office that oversees national volunteer programs, with the task of assembling a plan that would put civilians to work to assist the Office of Homeland Security. The military will need new recruits to confront the challenges abroad, so our bill will also improve benefits for our servicemembers.

At the same time, because the society we defend needs increased services, from promoting literacy to caring for the elderly, we expand AmeriCorps and senior service programs to enlarge our national army of volunteers.

5   AmeriCorps' achievements have been impressive: thousands of homes have been built, hundreds of thousands of seniors given the care they need to live independently and millions of children tutored.

Since its inception in 1993, nearly 250,000 Americans have served stints of one or two years in AmeriCorps. But for all its concrete achievements, AmeriCorps has been too small to rouse the nation's imagination. Under our bill, 250,000 volunteers each year would be able to answer the call—with half of them assisting in civil defense needs and half continuing the good work of AmeriCorps.

We must also ask our nation's colleges to promote service more aggressively. Currently, many colleges devote only a small fraction of federal work-study funds to community service, while the majority of federal resources are used to fill low-skill positions. This was not Congress's vision when it passed the Higher Education Act of 1965. Under our bill, universities will be required to promote student involvement in community activities more vigorously.

And for those who might consider serving their country in the armed forces, the benefits must keep pace with the times. While the volunteer military has been successful, our armed forces continue to suffer from significant recruitment challenges.

Our legislation encourages more young Americans to serve in the military by allowing the Defense Department to create a new, shorter-term enlistment option. This "18-18-18" plan would offer an $18,000 bonus—in addition to regular pay—for 18 months of active duty and 18 months of reserve duty. And we would significantly improve education payments made to service members under current law.

10   Public service is a virtue, and national service should one day be a rite of passage for young Americans. This is the right moment to issue a new call to service and give a new generation a way to claim the rewards and responsibilities of active citizenship.

A TIME TO HEED THE CALL
David Gergen

David Gergen is an editor-at-large for U.S. News & World Report, *in which this essay appeared on December 24, 2001. He has served as an advisor to Presidents Nixon, Ford, Reagan, and Clinton and currently directs the Center for Public Leadership at the John F. Kennedy School of Government.*

Leaving church on a Sunday several weeks ago, Seth Moulton posed a haunting question. Moulton is a clean-cut, good-looking young guy who graduated from Harvard last spring and represented his class as commencement speaker. "I have been planning to go to Wall Street for a while," he said, "Now with what's happened, I think I should give some time to the country. But tell me: Where should I sign up?"

Since September 11, a surge in patriotic sentiment has prompted thousands of others to ask themselves similar questions. People want to help and are trying to figure out how. Some 81 percent recently told surveyors from the firm Penn, Schoen & Berland Associates they would like the federal government to encourage increased community and national service. They strongly support college scholarships, similar to the GI Bill, for young people who serve as police officers, firefighters, or civil-defense workers, and they favor a dramatic expansion of the national service program.

So far, our political leaders have rightly focused on battling terrorists overseas, giving only scant attention to creating a new culture of service at home. But their very successes against Osama bin Laden are opening a second phase in this struggle. We now have a chance to step back and think longer term. How do we transform this new love of nation into a lasting mission? How do we keep the flame alive? With imagination, we could do just that if we boldly call millions of young Americans to give at least a year of service to the nation. Remember FDR's Civilian

Conservation Corps and the magnificent parks all those young people built in the wilderness? There are many parallel responsibilities today. Beefing up border operations, teaching kids in poor schools, helping out in hospitals—those are just a few. Add three months of physical training, with kids from Brooklyn mixing in with kids from Berkeley, and the results would be eye popping.

Giving something back. Voluntary service when young often changes people for life. They learn to give their fair share. Some 60 percent of alumni from Teach for America, a marvelous program, now work full time in education, and many others remain deeply involved in social change. Mark Levine, for example, has started two community-owned credit unions in Washington Heights, N.Y., for recent immigrants. Alumni of City Year, another terrific program, vote at twice the rates of their peers. Or think of the Peace Corps alumni. Six now serve in the House of Representatives, one (Christopher Dodd) in the Senate.

5   A culture of service might also help reverse the trend among many young people to shun politics and public affairs. Presidential voting among 18-to-29-year-olds has fallen over the past three decades from half to less than a third. In a famous poll of a year ago, some 47 percent said their regular source of political news was the late-night comedy shows. If the young were to sign up for national service, as scholar Bill Galston argues, that could lead to greater civic engagement.

President Bush clearly supports the idea. What is lacking, though, is a clarion call, a "certain trumpet" that breaks through, along with a sweeping plan for action. The best plan on offer today is one advanced by Sens. John McCain of Arizona, a Republican, and Democrat Evan Bayh of Indiana and given strong support by the Democratic Leadership Council. It would build on AmeriCorps, the volunteer program started by President Clinton, at first opposed and now embraced by many Republicans. AmeriCorps has achieved significant results but remains modest in size with about 50,000 volunteers. It has never enjoyed the panache of the Peace Corps—as many as 2 out of 3 Americans say they have never heard of the program. McCain and Bayh would expand AmeriCorps fivefold, to 250,000 volunteers a year, and channel half the new recruits into homeland-security efforts. The program would also open up more chances for seniors to serve—another important contribution.

With support from the president, this bill would become one of the first major accomplishments of Congress next year. Interest has been spiraling upward in recent weeks. Some oppose it because they would like all volunteer service to be directed to homeland security. That is a mistake. Our schools are as important to our future as are border patrols. Others dismiss voluntary service as patriotism on the cheap; they would like to see a full-scale restoration of the draft, providing manpower for both military and civilian purposes. There are powerful arguments for a universal draft, but the public isn't ready for that yet. It would be wiser to start here . . . and now.

September 11 was a seminal moment for America. Everyone who lived through it will remember exactly where he or she was when the terrible news came. But the moment will pass unless we seize it and give it more permanent meaning. Fortunately, some already hear the call. Leaving church on Sunday last, Seth Moulton said he had made his choice: He has volunteered for four years in the United States Marines. Now, let the trumpet sound for the rest of his generation.

VOLUNTEERING IN THE UNITED STATES, 2003
Bureau of Labor Statistics, U.S. Department of Labor

Every year, the Bureau of Labor Statistics collects and analyzes patterns of volunteering in the United States. Following is a summary of data collected from September 2002 to September 2003. Tables A and 1 from the BLS report are included in this selection. Other cited tables are omitted for reasons of space.

Both the number of volunteers and the volunteer rate rose over the year ended in September 2003, the Bureau of Labor Statistics of the U.S. Department of Labor reported today. About 63.8 million people did volunteer work at some point from September 2002 to September 2003, up from 59.8 million for the similar period ended in September 2002. The volunteer rate grew to 28.8 percent, up from 27.4 percent.

These data on volunteering were collected through a supplement to the September 2003 Current Population Survey (CPS). Volunteers are defined as persons who did unpaid work (except for expenses) through or for an organization. The CPS is a monthly survey of about 60,000 households that obtains information on employment and unemployment among the nation's civilian noninstitutional population age 16 and over. . . .

Changes in Volunteer Rates

About 25.1 percent of men and 32.2 percent of women did volunteer work in the year ended in September 2003, increases of 1.5 and 1.2 percentage points from 2002, respectively. For teenagers, the volunteer rate jumped by 2.6 percentage points to 29.5 percent. In contrast, the volunteer rate for the group most likely to volunteer, 35- to 44-year olds, was little changed at 34.7 percent. (See Tables A and 1.)

The volunteer rate for whites rose from 29.2 percent for the year ended in September 2002 to 30.6 percent for the year ended in September 2003, while the rates for blacks and Hispanics were little changed. About 18.7 percent of Asians performed some sort of volunteer work through or for an organization over the year ended in September 2003. (Data for Asians were not tabulated in 2002.)

5   Among persons 25 years of age and over, the volunteer rates for those with at least some college education or a bachelor's degree or better rose over the year, while the rates for those whose education had not gone beyond high school graduation remained about the same.

Volunteering Among Demographic Groups

Almost 64 million persons, or 28.8 percent of the civilian noninstitutional population age 16 and over, volunteered through or for organizations at some point from September 2002 to September 2003. Women volunteered at a higher rate than did men, a relationship that held across age groups, education levels, and other major characteristics. (See Table 1.)

By age, 35- to 44-year olds were the most likely to volunteer, closely followed by 45- to 54-year olds. Their volunteer rates were 34.7 percent and 32.7 percent, respectively. Teenagers also had a relatively high volunteer rate, 29.5 percent, perhaps reflecting an emphasis on volunteer activities in schools. Volunteer rates were lowest among persons age 65 years and over (23.7 percent) and among

Table A.   Volunteers by selected characteristics, September 2002 and 2003

(Numbers in thousands)

Characteristic	September 2002r			September 2003		
	Number	Percent of population	Median annual hours	Number	Percent of population	Median annual hours
Sex						
Total, both sexes	59,783	27.4	52	63,791	28.8	52
Men	24,706	23.6	52	26,805	25.1	52
Women.	35,076	31.0	50	36,987	32.2	52
Age						
Total, 16 years and over.	59,783	27.4	52	63,791	28.8	52
16 to 24 years	7,742	21.9	40	8,671	24.1	40
25 to 34 years	9,574	24.8	33	10,337	26.5	36
35 to 44 years	14,971	34.1	52	15,165	34.7	50
45 to 54 years	12,477	31.3	52	13,302	32.7	52
55 to 64 years	7,331	27.5	60	8,170	29.2	60
65 years and over	7,687	22.7	96	8,146	23.7	88
Race and Hispanic or Latino ethnicity						
White (1)	52,591	29.2	52	55,572	30.6	52
Black or African American (1)	4,896	19.1	52	5,145	20.0	52
Asian (1).	(2)	(2)	(2)	1,735	18.7	40
Hispanic or Latino Ethnicity.	4,059	15.5	40	4,364	15.7	40

Educational attainment (3)

Less than a high school diploma.	2,806	10.1	48	2,793	9.9	48
High school graduate, no college (4)	12,542	21.2	49	12,882	21.7	48
Less than a bachelor's degree (5)	15,066	32.8	52	15,966	34.1	52
College graduates	21,627	43.3	60	23,481	45.6	60
Employment status						
Civilian labor force	42,773	29.3	48	45,499	30.9	48
Employed	40,742	29.5	48	43,138	31.2	48
Full time (6)	32,210	28.3	46	33,599	29.6	48
Part time (7)	8,532	35.4	52	9,539	38.4	52
Unemployed	2,031	25.1	50	2,361	26.7	48
Not in the labor force	17,010	23.7	72	18,293	24.6	66

(1) Beginning in 2003, persons who selected this race group only; persons who selected more than one race group are not included. Prior to 2003, persons who reported more than one race group were included in the group they identified as the main race.

(2) Data for Asians were not tabulated in 2002.

(3) Data refer to persons 25 years and over.

(4) Includes high school diploma or equivalent.

(5) Includes the categories: some college, no degree, and associate degree.

(6) Usually work 35 hours or more a week at all jobs.

(7) Usually work less than 35 hours a week at all jobs.

r = revised. Estimates for 2002 have been revised to reflect the use of Census 2000-based population controls.

NOTE: Estimates for the above race groups (white, black or African American, and Asian) do not sum to totals because data are not presented for all races. In addition, persons whose ethnicity is identified as Hispanic or Latino may be of any race and, therefore, are classified by ethnicity as well as by race.

those in their early twenties (19.7 percent). Within the 65 years and over group, volunteer rates decreased as age increased.

Parents with children under age 18 were more likely to volunteer than persons with no children of that age, with volunteer rates of 37.5 percent and 25.0 percent, respectively. Volunteer rates were higher among married persons (34.0 percent) than among never-married persons (22.8 percent) and persons of other marital statuses (22.5 percent).

Whites volunteered at a higher rate (30.6 percent) than did blacks (20.0 percent) and Asians (18.7 percent). Among individuals of Hispanic or Latino ethnicity, 15.7 percent volunteered.

10   Overall, 31.2 percent of all employed persons had volunteered during the year ended in September 2003. By comparison, the volunteer rates of persons who were unemployed (26.7 percent) or not in the labor force (24.6 percent) were lower. Among the employed, part-time workers were more likely than full-time workers to have participated in volunteer activities—38.4 percent and 29.6 percent, respectively.

Total Annual Hours Spent Volunteering

Volunteers spent a median of 52 hours on volunteer activities during the period from September 2002 to September 2003, unchanged from the previous survey period. The median number of hours men and women spent volunteering was the same (52 hours). (Table 2.)

Among the age groups, volunteers age 65 and over devoted the most time—a median of 88 hours—to volunteer activities. Those age 25 to 34 years spent the least time, volunteering a median of 36 hours during the year.

Number and Type of Organizations

Most volunteers were involved with one or two organizations—69.2 percent and 19.2 percent, respectively. Individuals with higher educational attainment were more likely to volunteer for multiple organizations than were individuals with less education. (Table 3.)

The main organization—the organization for which the volunteer worked the most hours during the year—was either religious (34.6 percent of all volunteers) or educational/youth-service related (27.4 percent). Another 11.8 percent of volunteers performed activities mainly for social or community service organizations, and 8.2 percent volunteered the most hours for hospitals or other health organizations. This distribution is largely the same as in the prior year. (Table 4.)

15   Older volunteers were more likely to work mainly for religious organizations than were their younger counterparts. For example, 46.5 percent of volunteers age 65 and over performed volunteer activities mainly through or for a religious organization, compared with 29.1 percent of volunteers age 16 to 24 years. Younger individuals were more likely to volunteer for educational or youth service organizations.

Among volunteers with children under 18 years, 47.2 percent of mothers and 36.1 percent of fathers volunteered mainly for an educational/youth-service related organization, such as a school or little league. Parents were more than twice as likely to volunteer for such organizations as persons with no children of that age. Conversely, volunteers with no children under 18 were about twice as likely as parents to volunteer for some other types of organizations, such as social or community service organizations.

Volunteer Activities for Main Organization

The activities of volunteers varied. Among the more commonly reported (volunteers could report more than one activity) were fundraising or selling items to raise money (28.8 percent); coaching, refereeing, tutoring, or teaching (28.6 percent); collecting, preparing, distributing, or serving food (24.9 percent); providing information, which would include being an usher, greeter, or minister (22.0 percent); and engaging in general labor (21.8 percent). (Table 5.)

Some demographic groups were more likely to engage in certain activities than were others. For example, parents of children under 18 were much more likely to coach, referee, tutor, or teach than were persons with no children of that age. College graduates were more than four times as likely as those with less than a high school diploma to provide professional or management assistance.

The volunteer activity categories were redesigned for 2003 to be more consistent conceptually and to provide better information about the types of volunteer activities performed. The redesign eliminated a "catch-all" category used in 2002 that received over two-fifths of all responses to the question on the type of volunteer activities performed. As a result of the redesign, the 2003 data on volunteer activities performed are not comparable with the data for 2002.

How Volunteers Became Involved with Main Organization

20 Two in five volunteers became involved with the main organization for which they did volunteer work on their own initiative; that is, they approached the organization. Almost 44 percent were asked to become a volunteer, most often by someone in the organization. (Table 6.)

Reasons for Not Volunteering

Among those who had volunteered at some point in the past, the most common reason given for not volunteering in the year ended September 2003 was lack of time (44.7 percent), followed by health or medical problems (14.7 percent) and family responsibilities or childcare problems (9.5 percent). Lack of time was the most common reason for all groups except those age 65 and over and for those with less than a high school diploma, or who were not in the labor force—both of which contained a relatively high proportion of older persons. For each of these three groups, health or medical problems was the primary reason for not volunteering.

Changes in Volunteer Estimates

Estimates shown in this release for the years ended September 2002 and September 2003 are based on Census 2000 population controls. For this reason, the estimates for the year ended September 2002 appearing in this release may differ from those published earlier, which were based on population controls derived from the 1990 census.

Table 1. Volunteers by selected characteristics, September 2003

(Numbers in thousands)

Characteristics in September 2003	Total, both sexes			Men			Women		
	Civilian noninstitutional population	Volunteers Number	Volunteers Percent of population	Civilian noninstitutional population	Volunteers Number	Volunteers Percent of population	Civilian noninstitutional population	Volunteers Number	Volunteers Percent of population
Age									
Total, 16 years and over	221,779	63,791	28.8	106,744	26,805	25.1	115,035	36,987	32.2
16 to 24 years	35,979	8,671	24.1	18,079	3,782	20.9	17,900	4,888	27.3
16 to 19 years	16,131	4,758	29.5	8,176	2,098	25.7	7,955	2,661	33.4
20 to 24 years	19,848	3,912	19.7	9,903	1,685	17.0	9,945	2,228	22.4
25 years and over	185,800	55,121	29.7	88,665	23,022	26.0	97,135	32,098	33.0
25 to 34 years	39,072	10,337	26.5	19,375	3,976	20.5	19,697	6,360	32.3
35 to 44 years	43,691	15,165	34.7	21,440	6,308	29.4	22,251	8,857	39.8
45 to 54 years	40,692	13,302	32.7	19,863	5,829	29.3	20,828	7,474	35.9
55 to 64 years	28,003	8,170	29.2	13,437	3,569	26.6	14,566	4,602	31.6
65 years and over	34,342	8,146	23.7	14,550	3,341	23.0	19,792	4,806	24.3
Race and Hispanic or Latino ethnicity									
White	181,696	55,572	30.6	88,462	23,507	26.6	93,234	32,065	34.4
Black or African American	25,784	5,145	20.0	11,501	1,975	17.2	14,283	3,170	22.2
Asian	9,278	1,735	18.7	4,362	774	17.7	4,916	961	19.5
Hispanic or Latino ethnicity	27,808	4,364	15.7	14,233	1,702	12.0	13,575	2,662	19.6
Educational attainment (1)									
Less than a high school diploma	28,243	2,793	9.9	13,659	1,141	8.4	14,584	1,652	11.3
High school graduate, no college (2)	59,241	12,882	21.7	27,666	4,985	18.0	31,575	7,896	25.0
Less than a bachelor's degree (3)	46,786	15,966	34.1	21,341	6,146	28.8	25,444	9,819	38.6
College graduates	51,530	23,481	45.6	25,999	10,750	41.3	25,531	12,731	49.9

Marital status									
Single, never married	60,017	13,670	22.8	31,962	5,953	18.6	28,055	7,718	27.5
Married, spouse present..........	118,986	40,486	34.0	59,925	18,155	30.3	59,061	22,331	37.8
Other marital status (4)	42,775	9,635	22.5	14,856	2,697	18.2	27,919	6,938	24.9
Presence of own children under 18 years (5)									
Without own children under 18....	155,359	38,907	25.0	77,121	16,969	22.0	78,238	21,938	28.0
With own children under 18	66,420	24,884	37.5	29,623	9,836	33.2	36,797	15,049	40.9
Employment status									
Civilian labor force	147,322	45,499	30.9	78,854	21,231	26.9	68,468	24,268	35.4
Employed	138,477	43,138	31.2	74,155	20,247	27.3	64,322	22,890	35.6
Full time (6)	113,636	33,599	29.6	65,952	17,741	26.9	47,684	15,857	33.3
Part time (7)	24,841	9,539	38.4	8,203	2,506	30.5	16,638	7,033	42.3
Unemployed	8,844	2,361	26.7	4,699	983	20.9	4,146	1,378	33.2
Not in the labor force	74,457	18,293	24.6	27,890	5,574	20.0	46,567	12,719	27.3

(1) Data refer to persons 25 years and over.
(2) Includes high school diploma or equivalent.
(3) Includes the categories: some college, no degree, and associate degree.
(4) Includes divorced, separated, and widowed persons.
(5) Own children include sons, daughters, stepchildren, and adopted children. Not included are nieces, nephews, grandchildren, and other related and unrelated children.
(6) Usually work 35 hours or more a week at all jobs.
(7) Usually work less than 35 hours a week at all jobs.

NOTE: Data on volunteers relate to persons who performed unpaid volunteer activities for an organization at any point from September 1, 2002, through the survey period in September 2003. Estimates for the above race groups (white, black or African American, and Asian) do not sum to totals because data are not presented for all races. In addition, persons whose ethnicity is identified as Hispanic or Latino may be of any race and, therefore, are classified by ethnicity as well as by race.

NATIONAL SERVICE, POLITICAL SOCIALIZATION, AND CITIZENSHIP

Eric B. Gorham

This passage from the first chapter of Eric B. Gorham's National Service, Citizenship, and Political Education *(1992) provides a definition and brief overview of the history of national service in the United States. In the book, Gorham argues that the language government uses to promote programs for national service betrays an effort to "reproduce a postindustrial, capitalist economy in the name of good citizenship." Eric Gorham is associate professor of political science at Loyola University, New Orleans.*

Many politicians, academics, and planners define national service as a nation-wide program of community work that citizens, mostly young people, enter for one or two years. It is either voluntary or coercive, and employs participants in public sector or "voluntary" sector jobs at subminimum wages. In the process, participants serve the needs of the nation, acquire job and life skills, and learn the essentials of American citizenship.

This definition has evolved from William James's conception of national service in the early part of this century. James argued that the "gilded youth" of America ought to be required to serve the nation in order to "toughen" their spirit, and help them recognize the poverty which afflicts their country. James proposed a "moral equivalent of war" in order that Americans may become more concerned with their communities, and in order that a "peaceful" alternative to the military be offered to the public.[1] Individuals could then view their country from different perspectives and not merely conform their behavior to certain nonmilitary standards.

After James, a number of other prominent Americans accepted his idea on principle, but offered competing proposals for a service program. Franklin Delano Roosevelt proposed that programs were needed to put young people to work during the depression. On March 21, 1933, he announced his intention to create the Civilian Conservation Corps (CCC):

> We can take a vast army of these unemployed into healthful surroundings. We can eliminate, to some extent, at least, the threat that enforced idleness brings to spiritual and moral stability.[2]

For Roosevelt, the CCC was necessary to employ underprivileged youth, not James's "gilded youth," and to provide them with certain physical and moral standards by which they could improve their lot.

After World War II, James's theme of educating youth returned in the form of John F. Kennedy's Peace Corps proposal. An international "moral equivalent of war," the Peace Corps offered thousands of privileged youth the opportunity to work selflessly for their country and for others. A domestic program, Volunteers in Service to America (VISTA), was established to provide similar opportunities for work in the poorer regions of America. More recently, there have also been a number of university programs that promote service—like Campus Compact and the Campus Outreach Opportunity League (COOL).

5 At the same time, various administrations have experimented with employment programs for youth. The Johnson Administration instituted a National Job Corps program, and that program has had various incarnations throughout the past twenty-five years. Regional conservation programs were created; among the most

prominent have been the California and Wisconsin conservation corps. Finally, cities have developed service programs for their young citizens—for example, the New York City Service Corps or Seattle's Program for Local Service. These programs are aimed at giving young people job skills while teaching them the values they will need to prosper as adults.

The apparent success of such programs has recently sparked interest in a national program of voluntary service. These programs would create a new institution—generally in the form of a national service foundation—to oversee a comprehensive program of citizen service for young people. The arguments for this program are generally threefold: (1) the nation has needs that remain unfulfilled, like environmental conservation, day care, health care, etc.; (2) young people need to develop themselves morally, and national service can help (here supporters commonly cite such problems as drug dependency, crime, idleness, and teenage pregnancy); and (3) Americans, especially young people, need to develop a stronger sense of citizenship. Proponents of national service believe that the program can enhance the well-being of the nation and restore a sense of community to American public life.

Since the late 1970s, national service has become a very important issue. Numerous bills have been introduced in Congress promoting versions of this proposal, new books have emerged on the subject almost every year, national politicians have endorsed the idea, and public and private conferences and commissions have been held every few years on the matter. The most publicized proposal has been the Sam Nunn–Dave McCurdy national service bill (SR3-1989), which ties federal education aid to service programs. On a smaller, less systematic scale, the [first] Bush administration has introduced the Youth Entering Service (YES) program, which earmarks twenty-five million dollars for voluntary service work for young people.

On November 16, 1990, President Bush [senior] signed into law the National and Community Service Act of 1990 (PL 101-610). This national service law differs from previous efforts in one very important way—it attempts to merge service programs for both "gilded" and underprivileged youth, in order to provide the youth of America with a common set of norms and opportunities. It is a comprehensive law which includes a variety of youth service schemes, and it is designed to test the feasibility of national service for a number of different socioeconomic groups.

All service programs, whether for rich or poor, have had one component in common. Proponents maintain that young people must learn citizenship, and either they argue that such programs inculcate this generally, or they have attached particular programs designed to increase the civic competence of young adults.[3] Indeed, the rhetoric of citizenship justifies the program ideologically; that is, it defends national service on moral and political grounds, rather than instrumental ones.

Notes

1. William James, "The Moral Equivalent of War," *International Conciliation*, no. 27 (Washington, D.C.: Carnegie Endowment for International Peace, 1910), pp. 8–20.
2. Quoted in John A. Salmond, *The Civilian Conservation Corps, 1933–1942: A New Deal Case Study* (Durham, N.C.: Duke University Press, 1967), p. 13.
3. The National and Community Service Act of 1990 states that its *primary* purpose is "to renew the ethic of civic responsibility in the United States" (section 2[1]). This

purpose is also the primary justification given by Senator Edward Kennedy, its chief sponsor, in arguing for its passage. Press Release, on the Conference Report on the National and Community Service Act of 1990, Office of Senator Edward M. Kennedy, October 12, 1990.

CALLS FOR NATIONAL SERVICE
Roger Landrum, Donald J. Eberly, and Michael W. Sherraden

The passage that follows introduces the work of William James (mentioned prominently in the Gorham selection), a Harvard philosopher whose speech "The Moral Equivalent of War" (1906) helped set an agenda for the national service movement. The essay appears in a collection of scholarly commentaries on national service, edited by Sherraden and Eberly.

The first major call for a national service in the United States was by the social philosopher and psychologist William James. James' seminal essay "The Moral Equivalent of War," was given as a major address at Stanford University in 1906 and first published in 1910. The essay proposed national service as a pragmatic means by which a democratic nation could maintain social cohesiveness apart from the external threat of war. In his extraordinarily vivid language, James attacked a view he considered ingrained in Western civilization from Alexander the Great through Theodore Roosevelt: that war's "dreadful hammer is the welder of men into cohesive states, and nowhere but in such states can human nature adequately develop its capacity." James wasn't any easier on pacifists, suggesting that the "duties, penalties, and sanctions pictured in the utopias they paint are all too weak and tame to substitute for war's disciplinary function." The most promising line of conciliation between militarists and pacifists, James thought, was some "moral equivalent of war."

> Men now are proud of belonging to a conquering nation, and without a murmur they lay down their persons and their wealth, if by so doing they may fight off subjugation. But who can be sure that other aspects of one's country may not, with time and education and suggestion enough, come to be regarded with similarly effective feelings of pride and shame? Why should men not someday feel that it is worth a blood-tax to belong to a collectivity superior in any ideal respect? Why should they not blush with indignant shame if the community that owns them is vile in any way whatsoever?
>
> Individuals, daily more numerous, now feel this civic passion. It is only a question of blowing on the spark till the whole population gets incandescent, and on the ruins of the old morals of military honor, until a stable system of morals of civic honor builds itself up. What the whole community comes to believe in grasps the individual as in a vise. The war function has grasped us so far; but constructive interests may someday seem no less imperative, and impose on the individual a hardly lighter burden.
>
> If now—and this is my idea—there were, instead of military conscription, a conscription of the whole youthful population to form for a certain number of years a part of the army enlisted against *Nature*, the injustice would tend to be evened out, and numerous other goods to the commonwealth would follow. . . .
>
> Such a conscription, with the state of public opinion that would have required it, and the many moral fruits it would bear, would preserve in the midst of a pacific

civilization the manly virtues which the military party is so afraid of seeing disappear in peace.[1]

James argued that a permanently successful peace economy cannot be a simple pleasure economy. He proposed a conscription of the youthful population of the United States into national service to provide a new sense of "civic discipline" outside the context of war. James also believed that national service would benefit young people. They would experience "self-forgetfulness" rather than "self-seeking." No one would be "flung out of employment to degenerate because there is no immediate work for them to do." None would "remain blind, as the luxurious classes now are blind, to man's relations to the globe he lives on." The childishness would be "knocked out of them." The moral equivalent of war would cultivate in youth "toughness without callousness, healthier sympathies and soberer ideas, ideals of hardihood and discipline, and civic temper."

The logic and rhetoric of James' call for national service have an antique ring today. James was clearly thinking only of young men and the image of Ivy League undergraduates seemed to be at the center of his thinking. He didn't consider the issue of constitutional limits on involuntary servitude. His recommendation of conscription was softened only by the concepts of collectivity and social sanctions: "What the whole community comes to believe in grasps the individual as in a vise." He said nothing of cost and organization. Of course, there were half as many young people in those days, only 15 percent of them in high school, and a vastly different organization of the work force. Still, James succeeded in embedding a phrase, "the moral equivalent of war," in the national consciousness; he raised the fundamental issue of proper socialization of youth in the context of a democracy at peace; and he planted the idea of national service.

Note

1. William James, "The Moral Equivalent of War," *International Conciliation*, no. 27 (Washington, D.C.: Carnegie Endowment for International Peace, 1910), pp. 8–20.

RUMSFELD: NO NEED FOR DRAFT; 'DISADVANTAGES NOTABLE'

Kathleen T. Rhem

Kathleen Rhem is a reporter for the American Forces Press Service. This article was posted on the DefenseLINK Web site on January 7, 2003.

WASHINGTON, Jan. 7, 2003—The United States is not going to implement a military draft, because there is no need for it, Defense Secretary Donald Rumsfeld said today.

Rep. Charles Rangel said last week he was planning to introduce such legislation in the New Year. Rep. John Conyers Jr. has since expressed support.

"I believe that if those calling for war knew their children were more likely to be required to serve—and to be placed in harm's way—there would be more caution and a greater willingness to work with the international community in dealing with Iraq," Rangel wrote in a recent commentary in the *New York Times*.

Rumsfeld dismissed the notion out of hand during a Pentagon press briefing. "I don't know of anyone in this building or in the administration who thinks that anyone ought to go to war lightly," he said. "I know the president doesn't, and I know I don't."

5   The country doesn't need a draft because the all-volunteer force works—in fact, the United States has the most effective military in the world precisely because it is all-volunteer, Joint Chiefs Chairman Air Force Gen. Richard B. Myers said.

"[The all-volunteer force is] efficient; it's effective; it's given the United States of America, the citizens of this great country, a military that is second to none," Myers said.

"The people that are in the armed services today . . . are there because they want to be there and are ready and willing and, without any question, capable of doing whatever the president may ask," Rumsfeld added.

The secretary described "notable disadvantages" to having a conscripted force. He said people are involuntarily forced to serve, some for less than they could earn on the outside. There are many exemptions, which change all the time, thus providing for unfair situations. Troops are "churned" through training, serve the minimum amount of time and leave—thus causing more money to be spent to churn more draftees through the system.

He also dismissed the notion that the all-volunteer force leads to a disproportionate number of blacks and other minorities being killed in battle.

10   "I do not know that that's historically correct," Rumsfeld said. "And I do not know that, even if it were historically correct, that it's correct today."

He and Myers kept coming back to their bottom line: America is better off for the force it has today.

"We have people serving today—God bless 'em—because they volunteered," Rumsfeld said. "They want to be doing what it is they're doing. And we're just lucky as a country that there are so many wonderfully talented young men and young women who each year step up and say, 'I'm ready; let me do that.'"

POLITICS AND NATIONAL SERVICE: A VIRUS ATTACKS THE VOLUNTEER SECTOR

Bruce Chapman

Bruce Chapman, former U.S. Ambassador to the UN organizations in Vienna and former senior fellow at the Hudson Institute, currently serves as president of the Discovery Institute of Seattle, Washington, a public policy center for studying national and international affairs. An early proponent of the all-volunteer army who dedicated many years to public service (as secretary of state for the State of Washington, former director of the U.S. Census Bureau, and as aide to President Reagan), Chapman argues that volunteerism, "true service," is "corrupted" when it is in any way coerced or induced—through government programs, for instance, that pay stipends. The excerpted selection that follows appears in a collection of essays, National Service: Pro & Con *(1990).*

Proposals for government-operated national service, like influenza, flare up from time to time, depress the resistance of the body politic, run their course, and seem to disappear, only to mutate and afflict public life anew. Unfortunately, another epi-

demic may be on the way. The disease metaphor comes to mind not as an asper-
sion on the advocates of national service because, with good-natured patience,
persistence, and seemingly relentless political invention, they mean well, but from
the frustration of constantly combating the changing strains of a statist idea that
one thought had been eliminated in the early 1970s, along with smallpox.

Why does the national service virus keep coming back? Perhaps because its romance is so easy to catch, commanding a nostalgic imagination and evoking times
when Americans were eager to sacrifice for their country. Claiming to derive inspiration from both military experience and the social gospel—if we could only get
America's wastrel youth into at least a psychic uniform we might be able to teach
self-discipline again and revive the spirit of giving—it hearkens back to William
James's call for a "moral equivalent of war." But at the end of the twentieth century
should we be looking to war for moral guidance?

True service is one of the glories of our civilization in the West, especially in the
great independent (or volunteer) sector of American society. Inspiration for service
in the West comes from the Bible in parable and admonition and is constantly restated in the long historical tradition of Judeo-Christian faith. Personal service is a
freewill offering to God. This is very different from performance of an obligation to
government, which is a tax on time or money.

True service, then, has a spiritual basis, even for some outside the Judeo-Christian
tradition per se. Fulfillment of an obligation to government, in contrast, has a contractual basis unless it is founded on an outright commitment to a coercive utopianism. Either way, it is not true service. Nor can enrollment in a government-funded
self-improvement project or acceptance of a government job be called true service.
Indeed, when coercion or inducements are provided, as in the various national service schemes, the spirit of service is to that degree corrupted.

5   In practice the service in a federal program of national service would be con-
taminated by governmental determination of goals, bureaucratization of procedures, and, inevitably, government insistence on further regulating the independent
sector with which it contracted. National service would tend to demoralize those
citizens who volunteer without expectation of financial reward and stigmatize the
honest labor of people whose fields were invaded by stipened and vouchered
volunteers.

Government intervention is always a potential threat to the voluntary sector. When
totalitarians have come to power in other Western countries, they have sought to ab-
sorb this sector, conferring official sponsorship on certain organizations and scorning
others, thereby inculcating in the citizenry the government's valuation even on use of
free time. Although in the United States totalitarianism is not a current danger to our
liberal democracy, coercive utopianism is always a legitimate concern.

Alexis de Tocqueville saw in our own early history that the genius of voluntary association was America's superior answer to the leadership energy provided in other societies by aristocracies. But government, he warned, may seek to direct the voluntary
sector in the same way it erroneously seeks to control industrial undertakings:

> Once it leaves the sphere of politics to launch out on this new task, it will, even
> without intending this, exercise an intolerable tyranny. For a government can only
> dictate precise rules. It imposes the sentiments and ideas which it favors, and it is
> never easy to tell the difference between its advice and its commands.[1]

Note
  1. Alexis de Tocqueville, *Democracy in America*, vol. 2, book 2, chap. 5, J. P. Mayer (New York: Doubleday, 1969).

Exercise 4.5

Critical Reading for Synthesis

Having read the selections relating to national service, pages 136–52, take a sheet and write a one-sentence summary of each. On the same sheet, list two or three topics that you think are common to several of the selections. Beneath each topic, list the authors who have something to say and briefly note what they have to say. Finally, for each topic, jot down what *you* have to say. Now regard your effort. With each topic you have created a discussion point suitable for inclusion in a paper. (Of course, until you know the claim of such a paper, you would not know to what end you would put the discussion.) Write a paragraph or two in which you introduce the topic and then conduct a brief conversation among the interested parties (including yourself).

Consider Your Purpose

As with the explanatory synthesis, your specific purpose in writing an argument synthesis is crucial. What, exactly, you want to do will affect your claim, the evidence you select to support your claim, and the way you organize the evidence. Your purpose may be clear to you before you begin research, may emerge during the course of research, or may not emerge until after you have completed your research. Of course, the sooner your purpose is clear to you, the fewer wasted motions you will make. On the other hand, the more you approach research as an exploratory process, the likelier that your conclusions will emerge from the sources themselves, rather than from preconceived ideas. For a discussion on locating and evaluating sources, see Chapter 7.

Let's say that while reading these sources, your own encounters with a service organization (perhaps you help school children improve their literacy skills) have influenced your thinking on the subject. You find yourself impressed that so many people at the literacy center volunteer without being compelled to do so. You observe that giving time freely adds to the pleasures of volunteering, and to its significance as well. Meanwhile, perhaps your school is considering a service "requirement"—that is, a mandate that all students perform a given number of community service hours in order to graduate. The juxtaposition of "compelled" service with freely given service sparks in you an idea for a source-based paper.

On the one hand, you can understand and even sympathize with the viewpoints of educators who believe that while they have students in their clutches (so to speak), they have an opportunity to pass on an ethic of service. To students who would not volunteer time on their own, setting a graduation requirement makes sense. On the other hand, it seems to you that forced volunteerism, a contradiction in terms if ever there was one, defeats the essential quality of volunteering: that it is time given freely. The donation of time to meet the needs of others is an act of selflessness that brings you profound satisfaction. Your purpose in writing, then, emerges from these kinds of responses to the source material.

Making a Claim: Formulate a Thesis

As we indicated in the introduction to this chapter, one useful way of approaching an argument is to see it as making a *claim*. A claim is a proposition, a conclusion that you are trying to prove or demonstrate. If your purpose is to demonstrate that the state should not compel people to serve their communities, then that is the claim at the heart of your argument. The claim is generally expressed in one-sentence form as a *thesis*. You draw *support* from your sources as you argue logically for your claim. At times, you may also argue by making appeals to *ethos* and *pathos* (see pp. 132–35).

Of course, not every piece of information in a source is useful for supporting a claim. By the same token, you may draw support for your claim from sources that make entirely different claims. You may use as support for your own claim, for example, a sentiment expressed in William James's "On the Moral Equivalent of War," that values such as selfless concern for the common good, learned through service, "are absolute and permanent human goods." Yet while James called for "a conscription of the whole youthful population" to nonmilitary service projects, you may believe that service should be voluntary. Still, you could cite James and comment, where you think appropriate, on where you and he diverge.

Similarly, you might use one source as part of a *counterargument*—an argument opposite to your own—so that you can demonstrate its weaknesses and, in the process, strengthen your own claim. On the other hand, the author of one of your sources may be so convincing in supporting a claim that you adopt it yourself, either partially or entirely. The point is that *the argument is in your hands:* You must devise it yourself and use your sources in ways that will support the claim expressed in your thesis.

You may not want to divulge your thesis until the end of the paper, to draw the reader along toward your conclusion, allowing the thesis to flow naturally out of the argument and the evidence on which it is based. If you do this, you are working *inductively*. Or you may wish to be more direct and *begin* with your thesis, following the thesis statement with evidence to support it. If you do this, you are working *deductively*. In academic papers, deductive arguments are far more common than inductive arguments.

Based on your own experience and reactions to reading sources, you find yourself agreeing with Bruce Chapman's argument that compelled or monetarily induced service "corrupts" the experience of service. At the same time, you find yourself unwilling to take Chapman's extreme stance that even modest stipends such as the ones earned while working for AmeriCorps and other government programs constitute "corruption." While you believe that government programs encouraging service are beneficial, you certainly don't want to see the federal government create a nonmilitary version of compulsory national service. After a few tries, you develop the following thesis:

The impulse to expand service through volunteer programs like AmeriCorps, VISTA, and the Peace Corps is understandable, even praiseworthy. But as volunteerism grows and gains public support, we should resist letting its successes become an argument for <u>compulsory</u> national service.

Decide How You Will Use Your Source Material

Your claim commits you to (1) discussing the benefits of service in government-sponsored programs like AmeriCorps and VISTA, and (2) arguing that, benefits notwithstanding, there are compelling reasons not to make national service compulsory. The sources provide plenty of information and ideas—that is, evidence—that will allow you to support your claim. (You might draw on one universally available source, the U.S. Constitution, not included in the materials here.) The statistics generated by the Department of Labor offer current, accurate information on volunteerism in America. The selections by David Gergen and Senators McCain and Bayh provide pro-service arguments, while the essay by Chapman provides a negative one. Eric Gorham and Roger Landrum, Donald Eberly, and Michael Sherraden provide a philosophical and historical foundation for the synthesis. (Note that other sources not included in this chapter will be cited in the example paper.)

Develop an Organizational Plan

Having established your overall purpose and your claim, having developed a thesis (which may change as you write and revise the essay), and having decided how to use your source materials, how do you logically organize your essay? In many cases, including this one, a well-written thesis will suggest an overall organization. Thus, the first part of your argument synthesis will define volunteerism and set a broad context regarding its pervasiveness and history, along with mention of a possible early attempt to make national service compulsory. The second part will argue that national service should *not* be made compulsory. Sorting through your material and categorizing it by topic and subtopic, you might arrive at the following outline:

I.   Introduction. Pervasiveness of volunteerism in America. Use Bureau of Labor Statistics data.
II. The desire to "make more of a good thing." The McCain/Bayh "Call to Service Act." Thesis.
III. Intellectual history of service:
     A.   Recent history. Refer to William James. State that service need not be military.
     B.   Ancient history. Refer to Plato. State that citizens owe the State an obligation.
IV. Can the U.S. government compel citizens to service?
     A.   Military service. Yes. Right granted by U.S. Constitution.
     B.   Transition: military vs. civilian.

   C. Civilian service: No.
      1. Logical reason: public service is not analogous to military service.
      2. Legal reason: U.S. Constitution (Amendment XIII) forbids involuntary servitude.
      3. Moral reason: compelled or induced service (that is, with money) "corrupts" spirit of service.
         a. Concede point that "less pure" forms of service that pay stipends, such as AmeriCorps and VISTA, are beneficial.
         b. But state forcefully that compulsory (as opposed to minimally compensated) service does corrupt the spirit of service.
   V. Conclusion:
      A. Government should expand opportunities to serve <u>voluntarily</u> (even with pay).
      B. It should resist the impulse to compel young people to serve.

Argument Strategy

The argument represented by this outline will build not only on evidence drawn from sources but also on the writer's assumptions. Consider the bare-bones logic of the argument:

   Voluntary service, paid or unpaid, promotes good citizenship and benefits the community. (*assumption*)

   People who have worked in volunteer programs have made significant contributions to community and public life. (*support*)

   We should support programs that foster volunteerism. (*claim*)

The crucial point about which reasonable people will disagree is the *assumption* that unpaid *and* paid volunteer service promote good citizenship. One source author, Bruce Chapman, makes a partial and extreme form of this assumption when he writes that financially rewarded service is "corrupted" (see p. 151). A less-extreme assumption—the one guiding the model paper— is possible: Citizenship can be learned in a minimally paid environment such as AmeriCorps. The writer of the model paper agrees with Chapman, however, about another assumption: that service should never be compelled.

   Writers can accept or partially accept an opposing assumption by making a *concession*, in the process establishing themselves as reasonable and willing to compromise (see pp. 171–72). In our example, the writer does exactly this (see ¶ 10 in the sample synthesis that follows) and then uses as *supporting evidence* facts from David Gergen's report that many paid veterans of government-sponsored teaching programs learn about citizenship and continue to teach after their contracted time is up. By raising potential objections and making concessions, the writer blunts the effectiveness of *counterarguments*.

   The *claim* of the example argument about service is primarily a claim about *policy*, about actions that should (or should not) be taken. An argument can also concern a claim about *facts* (Does X exist? Does X lead to Y? How can we define X?) or a claim about *value* (What is X worth?). You have seen that the present argument rests on an assumed definition of "service." Depending on how you define the term, you will agree—or not—with the writer. Among the source authors, Bruce Chapman defines service one way (it is neither rewarded with money nor compelled), while David Gergen and Senators McCain and Bayh define it another (as work done with or without minimal pay to help others and re-enforce core values). As you read the following paper, watch how these opposing views are woven into the argument.

A well-reasoned argument will involve a claim primarily about fact, value, *or* policy. Secondary arguments are sometimes needed, as in the present example, to help make a case.

Draft and Revise Your Synthesis

The final draft of a completed synthesis, based on the above outline, follows. Thesis, transitions, and topic sentences are highlighted; Modern Language Association (MLA) documentation style, explained in Chapter 7, is used throughout. Note that for the sake of clarity, references in the following synthesis are to pages in *A Sequence for Academic Writing*. For sources not reproduced in *Sequence*, page references are to the sources as originally published.

A cautionary note: When writing syntheses, it is all too easy to become careless in properly crediting your sources. Before drafting your paper, please review the section on "Avoiding Plagiarism" in Chapter 1 (pp. 48–50) as well as the relevant sections on "Citing Sources" in Chapter 7 (pp. 288–306).

MODEL SYNTHESIS

Kikuchi 1

Michael Kikuchi

Professor Carcich

English 3

31 January 2007

Keeping Volunteerism Voluntary

The spirit of volunteerism flourishes in America. In 2002-2003, 28.8 percent of Americans, 16 and older, some 63.8 million, freely gave time to their communities (Bureau, "Volunteering" 139). Prompted by a desire to serve others without thought of personal gain, more than one-quarter of us donate 52 hours a year, more than one full work-week, to building shelters, coaching Little League, caring for the elderly, teaching literacy, and countless other community minded pursuits (Bureau, "Volunteering" 139; "Table 1" 144). Not included in these numbers are the many tens of thousands who donate time

Kikuchi 2

through less "pure" volunteer programs run by the government, such as AmeriCorps, VISTA (Volunteers in Service to America), and the Peace Corps, all of which pay recruits a small stipend. Volunteerism is so pervasive that it seems bred into the American character. A former director of the U.S. Census Bureau observes that "Alexis de Tocqueville saw in [America's] early history that the genius of voluntary association was [the country's] superior answer to the leadership energy provided in other societies by aristocracies" (Chapman 151).

Advocates claim that volunteerism builds character, teaches citizenship, and addresses unfulfilled national needs (Gorham 147). But if only one American in four volunteers, a percentage that surely could be improved, and if volunteerism is such a boon to communities, it is little wonder that from time to time politicians propose to make more of a good thing. In this spirit, in November 2001 Senators John McCain (R-AZ) and Evan Bayh (D-IN) introduced Bill S1274, the "Call to Service Act," which would dramatically increase the opportunities to serve in government-sponsored volunteer programs. "Public service is a virtue," write the senators in a New York Times op-ed piece not quite two months after the horrors of September 11, 2001. "[N]ational service should one day be a rite of passage for young Americans." The senators believe that this "is the right moment to issue a new call to service and give a new generation a way to claim the rewards and responsibilities of active citizenship" (137). The impulse to expand service through volunteer programs like AmeriCorps, VISTA, and the Peace Corps is understandable, even praiseworthy. But as volunteerism grows and gains public support, we should resist letting its successes become an argument for compulsory national service.

Senators McCain and Bayh do not call for compulsory service. Nonetheless, one can hear an echo of the word "compulsory" in their claim that "national service should one day be a rite of passage for young Americans." The word "should" suggests nothing if not obligation, and the word "all" is clearly implied. It's not a stretch to imagine the senators and others at some point endorsing a program of compulsory service, an idea that has been around for nearly a century. In 1906, the philosopher William James called for "a conscription of the whole youthful population" to non-military projects that would improve character (148). James, whom many consider the intellectual father of national service, admired the discipline and sacrifice of soldiers but thought it absurd that such "[m]artial virtues" as "intrepidity, contempt of softness, surrender of private interest, [and] obedience to command" should be developed only in the service of war. He imagined a "reign of peace" in which these qualities would "remain the rock upon which" peaceful states might be built (16). In a famous passage of his talk at Stanford University, which he titled "The Moral Equivalent of War," James urges on youth a hard (but non-military) service:

> To coal and iron mines, to freight trains, to fishing fleets in December, to dishwashing, clothes-washing, and window washing, to road-building and tunnel-making, to foundries and stoke-holes, and to the frames of skyscrapers, would our gilded youths be drafted off, according to their choice, to get the childishness knocked out of them, and to come back into society with healthier sympathies and soberer ideas. They would have paid their blood-tax, done their own part in the immemorial human warfare against nature; they would tread the earth more proudly, the women would value them more highly, they would be better fathers and teachers of the following generation. (17)

James's "gilded youths" were the (male) students of elite colleges. In the early twentieth century, there were not nearly as many young people as today, both in absolute terms and in college (Landrum, Eberly, and Sherraden 149), and so the logistics of compulsory national service may have seemed manageable. A century later we might regard his proposal as impractical or even illegal, but at the time he struck an important chord. His vision of learning the virtues and disciplines of citizenship through a non-military regimen in peace time (a "moral equivalent of war") entered our national vocabulary and remains a part of it today (Landrum, Eberly, and Sherraden 149).

The question of what sort of service, or obligation, citizens owe a country is as old as the first gathering of peoples into a collective for mutual safety and comfort. In one of his famous dialogues, Plato records a conversation between

Kikuchi 4

Socrates, whom Athens had imprisoned and condemned to death for corrupting the city's youth with his teachings, and a friend who urges that he escape and save himself. Socrates argues that if he has accepted and enjoyed the privileges of citizenship, then he must also accept the judgment of the State, even if that judgment calls for his execution:

> [A]fter having brought you into the world, and nurtured and educated you, and given you and every other citizen a share in every good that we [that is, the State] had to give, we further proclaim and give the right to every Athenian, that if he does not like us when he has come of age and has seen the ways of the city, and made our acquaintance, he may go where he pleases and take his goods with him; and none of us laws will forbid him or interfere with him. Any of you who does not like us and the city, and who wants to go to a colony or to any other city, may go where he likes, and take his goods with him. But he who has experience of the manner in which we order justice and administer the State, and still remains, has entered into an implied contract that he will do as we command him. (qtd. in Plato)

Citizens obligate themselves to the State when they accept its bounties and protections. But how is that obligation to be paid? Some twenty-four hundred years after Socrates accepted his fate and drank his cup of hemlock, Americans pay their obligations to the government through taxes, jury duty, and obedience to laws passed by elected representatives.

⑤ Can the government compel us to do more? Can it compel us, for instance, to military or non-military service? The U.S. Constitution grants Congress the right to raise armies (Article 1, Section 8, Clause 14). The way Congress chooses to do this, however, reflects the needs of a particular time. During World War II and the Vietnam War, the government implemented a military draft. Today, for reasons of professionalism and morale, the Department of Defense prefers an all-volunteer army to an army of conscripts. The Chairman of the Joint Chiefs of Staff was recently reported to have said that the "country

Kikuchi 5

doesn't need a draft because the all-volunteer force works--in fact, the United States has the most effective military in the world precisely because it is all-volunteer" (Rehm 150). Defense Secretary Rumsfeld sees distinct disadvantages to the draft: "[P]eople are involuntarily forced to serve, some for less than they could earn on the outside. . . . Troops are 'churned' through training, serve the minimum amount of time and leave--thus causing more money to be spent to churn more draftees through the system" (qtd. in Rehm 150).

(6) Clearly the State has a constitutional right to compel young people into military service in times of military need, whether it chooses to exercise that right through an all-volunteer or a conscripted army. Does the State have an equivalent right to press citizens into non-military service? For example, because our libraries are understaffed, our parks ill-kept, and our youth reading below grade level, should the State compel citizens into service for the common good? No--for logical, legal, and moral reasons.

(7) Military need is not logically equivalent to non-military need, primarily because non-military needs are typically met through the normal operations of representative government and the market economy. When the State identifies work to be done for the common good, it taxes citizens and directs its employees to perform that work. Alternately, it may put out bids and pay contractors to perform the work. This is how highways and libraries get built. If the State does not adequately perform these basic functions, it fails in its responsibilities. The remedy to this failure should not be the drafting of America's youth into national service for one or two years. The State could not honestly or reasonably call for universal service as a means of upgrading the moral character of youth when its real need is to plug holes in its own leaky ship. Such disingenuous arguments would only call attention to the State's failures. If the State lacks the money or competence to do its work, then citizens should overhaul the system by electing a new, more efficient administration. If necessary, the legislature could raise taxes. But it should not make a bogus public "need" into an occasion to compel public service.

Kikuchi 6

8 Nor does the State have a legal basis on which to press its citizens into national service. While the Constitution grants Congress the authority to raise armies, it expressly forbids forced service: "Neither slavery nor involuntary servitude, except as a punishment for crime whereof the party shall have been duly convicted, shall exist within the United States, or any place subject to their jurisdiction" (Amendment XIII). A program for compulsory national service, however noble its aims, would never withstand a legal challenge.

9 But even if advocates could circumvent the logical and legal obstacles to compulsory national service, they could not on moral grounds compel youth to serve against their will. Advocates argue, persuasively, that volunteerism builds character and promotes citizenship (Gorham 147). And, in fact, volunteer service does foster selflessness, a concern for community, and an appreciation of country (McCain and Bayh; Gergen; James; Patterson). Still, the essential quality of volunteerism is that it is time given freely. "True service," writes Bruce Chapman, "has a spiritual basis [rooted in the Judeo-Christian tradition]. . . . Fulfillment of an obligation to government, in contrast, has a contractual basis." Chapman argues that "performance of an obligation to government . . . is a tax on time and money." The spirit of service is "corrupted" when it is compelled or encouraged with stipends (151).

10 One need not agree, however, that volunteer programs that pay youth in room and board, health care, and tuition vouchers "corrupt" the spirit of giving. Chapman makes an extreme argument that ignores the financial realities of many young people. Were they to get no compensation, many would forgo volunteering and the possibility of learning from programs that encourage civic participation and patriotism. That would be a shame, for the members of AmeriCorps, the Peace Corps, and VISTA, all of whom are paid a small stipend, grow as individuals and as citizens, learning life-long lessons. David Gergen vividly makes this point:

> Voluntary service when young often changes people for life. They
> learn to give their fair share. Some 60 percent of alumni from

Teach for America, a marvelous program, now work full
time in education, and many others remain deeply involved
in social change. Mark Levine, for example, has started two
community-owned credit unions in Washington Heights, NY,
for recent immigrants. Alumni of City Year, another terrific
program, vote at twice the rates of their peers. Or think of
the Peace Corps alumni. Six now serve in the House of
Representatives, one (Christopher Dodd) in the Senate.

(138)

Unquestionably, national programs for volunteers can benefit both the
individuals serving and the communities served. For example, AmeriCorps sets
goals lofty enough to ensure that all involved will benefit. The Corps helps
communities when it places members in projects designed to have a positive
educational, social, and environmental impact. Communities are also
strengthened when culturally and racially diverse people work side by side to
achieve project goals. Additionally, AmeriCorps seeks through its
programming and its job- and educational benefits to improve the lives of
members (Corporation). Both communities and individuals gain from
AmeriCorps' efforts.

⑪   Still, as Chapman points out, volunteerism that is compelled in any
way, that turns the impulse to serve into an obligation, would be a
corruption. If the State instituted obligatory non-military service for
the "good" of the individual (and recall that it could not reasonably or
honestly do so for the social "needs" of the State), the act of service
would no longer be rooted in generosity. And it is the spirit of generosity,
of one person's freely giving to another, that underlies all the good that
volunteering achieves. Convert the essential generous impulse to an
obligation, and the very logic for compelling service--to teach civic values--
disappears. The State could no more expect the veterans of obligatory
service to have learned the values of good citizenship or to feel special
affection for the country than we could expect a child whose parents

Kikuchi 8

order him to "make friends with Johnny" to have learned anything useful about friendship or to feel a special kinship with Johnny. Affection, citizenship, and patriotism don't work that way. They are freely given, or they are coerced. And if coerced, they are corrupt. Compelled allegiance is a form of bullying that teaches nothing so much as resentment.

(12)   Without any inducement other than the good it would do their communities and their own hearts, 63.8 million Americans--more than one quarter of the country--volunteer. Could more people volunteer, specifically more young people? Yes, especially in light of the finding that young people in their early twenties volunteer the least, relative to all other age groups (Bureau, "Table 1" 144). The McCain/Bayh "Call to Service Act" deserves enthusiastic support, as does any government effort to encourage service by people younger than 25. Those who learn to serve while young turn out to be more involved with their communities over the course of their lives (Gergen; AmeriCorps), and such involvement can only benefit us all. Reasonable inducements such as tuition vouchers, minimal pay, health care, and room and board can give young people the safety net they need to experiment with serving others and in that way discover their own wellsprings of generosity.

(13)   So let's support McCain/Bayh and every such effort to encourage service. Ideally, enough programs will be in place one day to offer all high school and college graduates the option of serving their communities. "[T]oo often," writes Richard North Patterson, "we offer young people a vision of community which extends to the nearest shopping mall." Government-sponsored programs for service can make us better than that, and we should promote volunteerism wherever and whenever we can. But we must guard against using the success of these programs as a pretext for establishing mandatory national or community service. Such a mandate would fail legal and logical tests and, most importantly, a moral test: Volunteerism is built on choice. To command someone to do good works, to make good works obligatory, is to poison the very essence of service.

Kikuchi 9
Works Cited

Bureau of Labor Statistics. "Table 1: Volunteers by Selected Characteristics, September 2003." 17 Dec. 2003. 17 Jan. 2004 <http://www.bls.gov/news.release/volun.t01.htm>.

---. "Volunteering in the United States, 2003." 18 Dec. 2003. 17 Jan. 2004 <http://www.bls.gov/news.release/volun.nr0.htm>.

Chapman, Bruce. "Politics and National Service: A Virus Attacks the Volunteer Sector." National Service: Pro & Con. Ed. Williamson M. Evers. Stanford, CA: Hoover Institution P, 1990. 133-44.

"Constitution of the United States of America." The New York Public Library Desk Reference. New York: Webster's New World, 1989.

Corporation for National and Community Service. "AmeriCorps Mission." AmeriCorps: Getting Things Done. Program Directory, Spring/Summer 1995. Microfiche Y2N.21/29 10AM3. Washington, DC: GPO, 1995.

Gergen, David. "A Time to Heed the Call." U.S. News & World Report 24 Dec. 2001: 60.

Gorham, Eric B. "National Service, Political Socialization, and Citizenship." National Service, Citizenship, and Political Education. Albany: SUNY P, 1992. 5-30.

James, William. "The Moral Equivalent of War." International Conciliation 27 (Washington, DC: Carnegie Endowment for International Peace, 1910): 8-20.

Landrum, Roger, Donald J. Eberly, and Michael W. Sherraden. "Calls for National Service." National Service: Social, Economic and Military Impacts. Ed. Michael W. Sherraden and Donald J. Eberly. New York: Pergamon, 1982. 21-38.

McCain, John, and Evan Bayh. "A New Start for National Service." New York Times 6 Nov. 2001: Op-ed.

Patterson, Richard North. "Keeping Alive the Spirit of National Service." Boston Globe 1 Aug. 1999: Op-ed.

Plato. "Crito." Classic Literature Online Library. Trans. Benjamin Jowett. 17 July 2004 <http://www.greece.com/library/plato/crito_04.html>.

Kikuchi 10

Rhem, Kathleen T. "Rumsfeld: No Need for Draft." American Forces Information Service 7 Jan. 2003. 17 July 2004 <http://www.dod.gov/news/Jan2003/n01072003_200301074.html>.

Discussion

The writer of this argument synthesis on compulsory national service attempts to support a *claim*—one that favors national service but that insists on keeping it voluntary—by offering *support* in the form of facts (rates of volunteerism from the Bureau of Labor Statistics) and opinions (testimony of experts). However, since the writer's claim rests on a definition of "true service," its effectiveness depends partially upon the extent to which we, as readers, agree with the *assumptions* underlying that definition. (See our discussion of assumptions in Chapter 2, pages 66–68.) An assumption (sometimes called a *warrant*) is a generalization or principle about how the world works or should work—a fundamental statement of belief about facts or values. In this particular case, the underlying assumption is that "true service" to a community must be voluntary, never required. The writer makes this assumption explicit. Though you are under no obligation to do so, stating assumptions explicitly will clarify your arguments to readers.

Assumptions often are deeply rooted in people's psyches, sometimes deriving from lifelong experiences and observations and not easily changed, even by the most logical of arguments. People who learned the spirit of volunteerism early in life, perhaps through "required" activities in religious or public school, might not accept the support offered for the claim that required service would be illogical, illegal, and "corrupted." But others might well be persuaded and might agree that programs to expand opportunities for national service should be supported, though service itself should never be compelled. A discussion of the model argument's paragraphs, along with the argument strategy for each, follows. Note that the paper devotes one paragraph to developing every section of the outline on pages 154–55. Note also that the writer avoids plagiarism by careful attribution and quotation of sources.

- **Paragraph 1:** The writer uses statistics to establish that a culture of volunteerism is and has been alive and well in America from its earliest days.

    Argument strategy: In this opening paragraph, the writer sets up the general topic—volunteerism in America—and establishes that Americans volunteer in impressive numbers. The writer uses information from the Bureau of Labor Statistics, as well as the reference to volunteerism in early America, to anticipate and deflect possible criticism from those who might say: "So few of us volunteer that we should require national service in order to promote citizenship and to build character."

- **Paragraph 2:** Here the writer sets a context for and introduces the McCain/Bayh proposal to expand national service. The writer then presents the thesis.

    Argument strategy: This paragraph moves in one direction with an inspiring call to service by Senators McCain and Bayh and then takes a sharp, contrasting turn to the thesis. The first part of the thesis, "as volunteerism grows and gains public support," clearly follows from (and summarizes) the first part of paragraph 2. The transition "But" signals the contrast, which sets up the warning. A contrast generates interest by creating tension, in this case prompting readers to wonder: "Why *should* we resist compulsory service?"

- **Paragraphs 3 and 4:** In these paragraphs, the writer discusses the intellectual history of service: first, the writing of William James in the early years of the past century, and next, Plato's account of a dialogue between Socrates and a student. The writer quotes both authors at length and then discusses their relevance to the issue at the center of this essay: service to the greater community.

    Argument strategy: At this point, the writer is *preparing* to offer reasons for accepting the claim that we must resist compulsory service. The goal of paragraphs 3 and 4 is to set a deep historical context for the essay by establishing service as a significant cultural norm in America and, more broadly, by showing that the notion of obligation to the State is fundamental to civil societies. The end of paragraph 4 makes a transition to modern-day America and begins to move from the preparation for argument to argument.

- **Paragraph 5:** This paragraph opens with a question and sets up a key distinction in the essay between military and non-military service. After raising the distinction, the writer devotes the paragraph to establishing the right of the American government to draft citizens into the army. High-ranking military administrators are quoted to the effect that the all-volunteer army is a better fighting force than earlier, conscripted armies.

    Argument strategy: This paragraph begins moving the reader into the argument by introducing and discussing the first part of the distinction just presented: military service. The writer establishes that compelled military service is constitutional and in keeping with the historical obligations that citizens owe the State. But even here, in a case in which the State has the clear authority to conscript people, the writer quotes military officials to the effect that voluntary service is superior to compulsory service. The reader will find this strong preference for volunteerism continued in the second part of the essay devoted to non-military service.

- **Paragraph 6:** This transitional paragraph raises the core question on which the argument hangs: Does the State have the right, as it does in military matters, to press citizens into non-military, national service? The writer answers the question in the final sentence of this paragraph and, in so doing, forecasts the discussion to follow.

  Argument strategy: Here the writer sets up the second part of the essay, where reasons for accepting the claim will be presented. Up to this point, the writer has established that (1) volunteers can build character through service, (2) citizens owe a debt to the State, and (3) the State can legally collect on that debt by drafting citizens into the army in time of war. In this transition paragraph, the writer poses the question that will take the rest of the paper to answer. The question becomes an invitation to read.

- **Paragraphs 7–9:** In each of these three paragraphs, the writer answers—in the negative—the question posed in paragraph 6. The State does *not* have the right to press citizens into national service. Paragraph 7 offers a logical reason: that military and non-military service are not equivalent. Paragraph 8 offers a legal reason: that the Constitution prohibits "involuntary servitude." Paragraph 9 offers a moral reason: that coerced or compelled service is "corrupted."

  Argument strategy: These paragraphs lay out the main reasons for accepting the claim that we should resist letting the successes of volunteerism become an argument for compulsory national service. The writer argues on multiple grounds—logical, legal, and moral—in an effort to build a strong case.

- **Paragraph 10:** Here the writer concedes a problem with the view (expressed by Chapman) in paragraph 9 that service that is either compelled or financially rewarded is corrupted. Allowing that this extreme position does not take into account the financial needs of young people, the writer endorses an alternate view, that minimal payment for service is legitimate. To support this more moderate position, the writer quotes David Gergen at length and also refers to the AmeriCorps mission statement.

  Argument strategy: With this concession, the writer backs off an extreme view. The tactic makes the writer look both reasonable and realistic just prior to arguing very firmly, in the next paragraph, against compulsory service.

- **Paragraph 11:** Here the writer endorses one of Chapman's strongly held positions: Forced service is not service at all and corrupts the spirit of volunteerism.

Argument strategy: Here is the emotional core of the argument. The writer has previously argued that for logical (paragraph 7) and legal (paragraph 8) reasons compulsory service must be rejected. The writer devotes three paragraphs to developing moral reasons. In paragraph 11, the writer uses an analogy for the first time: Compelling service is equivalent to compelling a child to like someone. Neither works. The value of service rests on the offering of oneself freely to those in need.

- **Paragraphs 12–13:** The writer concludes by restating the claim—in two paragraphs.

  Argument strategy: These concluding paragraphs parallel the two-part structure of the thesis: Part 1 (paragraph 12), that volunteerism has many benefits and deserves support; Part 2 (paragraph 13), that we must resist any effort to make service compulsory.

Other approaches to an argument synthesis would be possible, based on the sources provided here. One could agree with Bruce Chapman and adopt the extreme view against both compulsory and paid service. Such an argument would make no concessions of the sort found in paragraph 10 of the model synthesis. Another approach would be to argue that young people must be taught the value of service before they take these values on themselves, and that the best way to teach an ethic of service is to require a year or two of "compulsory volunteering." That which is required, goes the logic of this argument, eventually becomes second nature. We might make a parallel case about teaching kids to read. Kids may not enjoy practicing thirty minutes every night, but eventually they come to realize the joys and benefits of reading, which last a lifetime. Still another argument might be to focus on the extent to which Americans meet (or fail to meet) their obligations to the larger community. This would be a glass-half-full/half-empty argument, beginning with the statistic that one-quarter of Americans regularly volunteer. The half-full argument would praise current efforts and, perhaps, suggest policies for ensuring continued success. The half-empty argument would cite the statistic with alarm, claim that we have a problem of shockingly low volunteer rates, and then propose a solution. Whatever your approach to the subject, in first *critically examining* the various sources and then *synthesizing* them to support a position about which you feel strongly, you are engaging in the kind of critical thinking that is essential to success in a good deal of academic and professional work.

■ DEVELOPING AND ORGANIZING THE SUPPORT FOR YOUR ARGUMENTS

Experienced writers seem to have an intuitive sense of how to develop and present supporting evidence for their claims; this sense is developed through much hard work and practice. Less experienced writers wonder what to say first, and having decided on that, wonder what to say next. There is no single

Developing and Organizing Support for Your Arguments

- *Summarize, paraphrase, and quote supporting evidence.* Draw upon the facts, ideas, and language in your sources.
- *Provide various types of evidence and motivational appeal.* Appeal to *logos*, *ethos*, and *pathos*. The appeal to *logos* is based on evidence from facts, statistics, and expert testimony.
- *Use climactic order.* Save the most important evidence in support of your argument for the *end* where it will have the most impact. Use the next most important evidence *first*.
- *Use logical or conventional order.* Use a form of organization appropriate to the topic, such as problem/solution; sides of a controversy; comparison/contrast; or a form of organization appropriate to the academic or professional discipline, such as a report of an experiment or a business plan.
- *Present and respond to counterarguments.* Anticipate and respond to arguments against your position.
- *Use concession.* Concede that one or more arguments against your position have some validity; re-assert, nonetheless, that your argument is the stronger one.

method of presentation. But the techniques of even the most experienced writers often boil down to a few tried and tested arrangements.

As we've seen in the model synthesis in this chapter, the key to devising effective arguments is to find and use those kinds of support that most persuasively strengthen your claim. Some writers categorize support into two broad types: *evidence* and *motivational appeals*. Evidence, in the form of facts, statistics, and expert testimony, helps make the appeal to *logos* or reason. Motivational appeals—appeals to *pathos* and *ethos*—are employed to get people to change their minds, to agree with the writer or speaker, or to decide upon a plan of activity.

Following are some of the most common principles for using and organizing support for your claims.

Summarize, Paraphrase, and Quote Supporting Evidence

In most of the papers and reports you will write in college and the professional world, evidence and motivational appeals derive from summarizing, paraphrasing, and quoting material in the sources that either have been provided to you or that you have independently researched. (See Chapter 1 on when to summarize, paraphrase, and quote material from sources.) For example, in paragraph 10 of the model argument synthesis you will find a block quotation from David Gergen used to make the point that minimally paid volunteer programs can provide lifelong lessons. You will find two other block quotations in the argument and a number of brief quotations woven into sentences throughout. In addition, you will find summaries and a paraphrase. In each case, the writer is careful to cite sources.

Provide Various Types of Evidence and Motivational Appeals

Keep in mind the appeals to both *logos* and *pathos*. As we've discussed, the appeal to *logos* is based on evidence that consists of a combination of *facts*, *statistics*, and *expert testimony*. In the model synthesis, the writer uses all of these varieties of evidence: facts (from David Gergen's article on how "[v]oluntary service . . . often changes people for life"); statistics (the incidence of volunteering in the United States); and testimony (from Eric Gorham, Bruce Chapman, David Gergen, Roger Landrum, Donald Rumsfeld, and William James). The model synthesis makes an appeal to *pathos* by engaging the reader's self interest: Certainly if the federal government were to institute compulsory national service, the lives of readers would be touched. More explicitly, paragraph 11 makes a moral argument against compulsory service. Through analogy (compelling citizens to service is equivalent to ordering a child to like someone), the writer attempts to claim the reader's sympathy and respect for common sense. In effect, the writer says, responsible parents would never do such a thing; responsible governments shouldn't either. (Of course, readers could reject the analogy and the assumption about good parenting on which it rests. Some parents might very well push their children into friendships and believe themselves justified for doing so.)

Use Climactic Order

Climactic order is an arrangement of examples or evidence in order of anticipated impact on the reader, least to greatest. Organize by climactic order when you plan to offer a number of categories or elements of support for your claim. Recognize that some elements will be more important—and likely more persuasive—than others. The basic principle here is that you should *save the most important evidence for the end*, since whatever you have said last is what readers are likely to most remember. A secondary principle is that whatever you say first is what they are *next* most likely to remember. Therefore, when you have several reasons to support your claim, an effective argument strategy is to present the second most important, then one or more additional reasons, and finally, the most important reason. Paragraphs 7–11 of the model synthesis do exactly this.

Use Logical or Conventional Order

Using logical or conventional order means that you use as a template a pre-established pattern or plan for arguing your case.

- One common pattern is describing or arguing a *problem/solution*. Using this pattern, you begin with an introduction in which you typically define the problem, then perhaps explain its origins, then offer one or more solutions, then conclude.

- Another common pattern is presenting *two sides of a controversy*. Using this pattern, you introduce the controversy and (if an argument synthesis) your own point of view or claim, then explain the other side's arguments, providing reasons why your point of view should prevail.

- A third common pattern is *comparison-contrast*. In fact, this pattern is so important that we will discuss it separately in the next section.

- The order in which you present elements of an argument is sometimes dictated by the conventions of the discipline in which you are writing. For example, lab reports and experiments in the sciences and social sciences often follow this pattern: *Opening* or *Introduction, Methods and Materials* [of the experiment or study], *Results, Discussion*. Legal arguments often follow the so-called IRAC format: *Issue, Rule, Application, Conclusion*.

Present and Respond to Counterarguments

When developing arguments on a controversial topic, you can effectively use *counterargument* to help support your claims. When you use counterargument, you present an argument *against* your claim, but then show that this argument is weak or flawed. The advantage of this technique is that you demonstrate that you are aware of the other side of the argument and that you are prepared to answer it.

Here is how a counterargument typically is developed:

   I. Introduction and claim
  II. Main opposing argument
 III. Refutation of opposing argument
 IV. Main positive argument

Use Concession

Concession is a variation of counterargument. As in counterargument, you present the opposing (or otherwise objectionable) viewpoint, but instead of demolishing that argument, you *concede* that it does have some validity and even some appeal, although your own argument is the stronger one. This concession bolsters your own standing—your own ethos—as a fair-minded person who is not blind to the virtues of the other side. See paragraphs 9 and 10 of the model synthesis for one version of the concession argument. You'll find that instead of making an opposing argument, the writer produces a supporting argument but views one part of it as flawed. The writer rejects that section (the extreme position that *any* form of compensation corrupts the spirit of volunteerism) and endorses the remaining sections. In terms of overall argument strategy, the result—the reader sees the writer as being reasonable—is the same as it would be if the writer used the more standard concession in which an opposing argument is viewed as having some merit. Here is an outline for a more typical concession argument:

I. Introduction and claim
II. Important opposing argument
III. Concession that this argument has some validity
IV. Positive argument(s)

Sometimes, when you are developing a counterargument or concession argument, you may become convinced of the validity of the opposing point of view and change your own views. Don't be afraid of this happening. Writing is a tool for learning. To change your mind because of new evidence is a sign of flexibility and maturity, and your writing can only be the better for it.

Avoid Common Fallacies in Developing and Using Support

In Chapter 2, in the section Critical Reading, we considered some of the criteria that, as a reader, you may use for evaluating informative and persuasive writing (see pp. 60–64). We discussed how you can assess the accuracy, the significance, and the author's interpretation of the information presented. We also considered the importance in good argument of clearly defined key terms and the pitfalls of emotionally loaded language. Finally, we saw how to recognize such logical fallacies as either/or reasoning, faulty cause-and-effect reasoning, hasty generalization, and false analogy. As a writer, no less than as a critical reader, be aware of these common problems and try to avoid them.

Be aware, also, of your responsibility to cite source materials appropriately. When you quote a source, double and triple check that you have done so accurately. When you summarize or paraphrase, take care to use your own language and sentence structures (though you can, of course, also quote within these forms). When you refer to someone else's idea—even if you are not quoting, summarizing, or paraphrasing—give the source credit. By maintaining an ethical stance with regard to the use of sources, you take your place in and perpetuate the highest traditions of the academic community.

Practicing Arguments

Read the articles in Chapter 9 on legacy admissions in the college application process. To practice your skills in writing arguments, you will argue for or against the practice of giving sons and daughters of alumni an advantage in the college application process; or you will argue that the practice should or should not be made public. Chapter 9 provides a series of sequenced assignments that will help to prepare you for writing your argument. As you read the selections on pages 336–56, you will need to decide what types of evidence—facts, statistics, and expert opinions—would best support your claim. What motivational appeals would be appropriate? Which counterarguments would you address, and how would you address them? Finally, what concessions would you make (if any)?

■ THE COMPARISON-AND-CONTRAST SYNTHESIS

A particularly important type of argument synthesis is built on patterns of comparison and contrast. Techniques of comparison and contrast enable you to examine two subjects (or sources) in terms of one another. When you compare, you consider *similarities*. When you contrast, you consider *differences*. By comparing and contrasting, you perform a multifaceted analysis that often suggests subtleties that otherwise might not have come to your (or the reader's) attention.

To organize a comparison-and-contrast argument, you must carefully read sources in order to discover *significant criteria for analysis*. A *criterion* is a specific point to which both of your authors refer and about which they may agree or disagree. (For example, in a comparative report on compact cars, criteria for *comparison and contrast* might be road handling, fuel economy, and comfort of ride.) The best criteria are those that allow you not only to account for obvious similarities and differences—those concerning the main aspects of your sources or subjects—but also to plumb deeper, exploring subtle yet significant comparisons and contrasts among details or subcomponents, which you can then relate to your overall thesis.

Note that comparison-contrast is frequently not an end in itself, but serves some larger purpose. Thus, a comparison-contrast synthesis may be a component of a longer paper that is essentially a critique, an explanatory synthesis, an argument synthesis, or an analysis.

Organizing Comparison-and-Contrast Syntheses

Two basic approaches to organizing a comparison-and-contrast synthesis are available: organization by *source* and organization by *criteria*.

Organizing by Source or Subject

You can organize a comparative synthesis by first summarizing each of your sources or subjects, and then discussing significant similarities and differences between them. Having read the summaries and become familiar with the distinguishing features of each source, your readers will most likely be able to appreciate the more obvious similarities and differences. In the discussion, your task is to focus on both the obvious and subtle comparisons and contrasts, focusing on the most significant—that is, on those that most clearly support your thesis.

Organization by source or subject is best saved for passages that can be briefly summarized. If the summary of your source or subject becomes too long, your readers might forget the points you made in the first summary as they are reading the second. A comparison-and-contrast synthesis organized by source or subject might proceed like this:

I.   Introduce the paper; lead to thesis.

II. Summarize source/subject A by discussing its significant features.

III. Summarize source/subject B by discussing its significant features.

IV. Write a paragraph (or two) in which you discuss the significant points of comparison and contrast between sources or subjects A and B. Alternatively, begin comparison-contrast in section III upon introducing source or subject B.

End with a conclusion in which you summarize your points and, perhaps, raise and respond to pertinent questions.

Organizing by Criteria

Instead of summarizing entire sources one at a time with the intention of comparing them later, you could discuss two sources simultaneously, examining the views of each author point by point (criterion by criterion), comparing and contrasting these views in the process. The criterion approach is best used when you have a number of points to discuss or when passages or subjects are long and/or complex. A comparison-and-contrast synthesis organized by criteria might look like this:

I.   Introduce the paper; lead to thesis.

II. Criterion 1

   A. Discuss what author #1 says about this point. Or present situation #1 in light of this point.

   B. Discuss what author #2 says about this point, comparing and contrasting #2's treatment of the point with #1's. Or present situation #2 in light of this point and explain its differences from situation #1.

III. Criterion 2

   A. Discuss what author #1 says about this point. Or present situation #1 in light of this point.

   B. Discuss what author #2 says about this point, comparing and contrasting #2's treatment of the point with #1's. Or present situation #2 in light of this point and explain its differences from situation #1.

And so on. Proceed criterion by criterion until you have completed your discussion. Be sure to arrange criteria with a clear method; knowing how the discussion of one criterion leads to the next will ensure smooth transitions throughout your paper. End by summarizing your key points and, perhaps, raising and responding to pertinent questions.

However you organize your comparison-and-contrast synthesis, keep in mind that comparing and contrasting are not ends in themselves. Your discussion should point somewhere: to a conclusion, an answer to "So what—why bother to compare and contrast in the first place?" If your discussion is part of a larger synthesis, point to and support the larger claim. If you write a stand-alone comparison-and-contrast, though, you must by the final paragraph answer the "why bother?" question. The model comparison-and-contrast synthesis that follows does exactly this.

Exercise 4.7

Comparing and Contrasting

Refer back to the readings on the compulsory national service controversy. Select two that take opposing sides, such as Bruce Chapman's "Politics and National Service: A Virus Attacks the Volunteer Sector" (pp. 150–52) and David Gergen's "A Time to Heed the Call" (pp. 137–38). Identify at least two significant criteria that you can use for a comparative analysis—two specific points to which both authors refer, and about which they agree or disagree. Then imagine you are preparing to write a short comparison-and-contrast paper and devise two outlines: the first organized by source, and the second organized by criteria.

A Case for Comparison-Contrast: World War I and World War II

We'll see how these principles can be applied to a response to a final examination question in a course on modern history. Imagine that having attended classes involving lecture and discussion, and having read excerpts from such texts as John Keegan's *The First World War* and Tony Judt's *Postwar: A History of Europe Since 1945*, students were presented with the following examination question:

> *Based on your reading to date, compare-and-contrast the two World Wars in light of any four or five criteria you think significant. Once you have called careful attention to both similarities and differences, conclude with an observation. What have you learned? What can your comparative analysis teach us?*

Comparison-Contrast (Organized by Criteria)

Here is a plan for a response, essentially a comparison-contrast synthesis, organized by *criteria*. (For an example of a comparison-contrast synthesis organized by source, see the sample paper in Chapter 8, pages 320–26.) The thesis—and the *claim*—follows:

> <u>Thesis</u>: In terms of the impact on cities and civilian populations, the military aspects of the two wars in Europe, and their aftermaths, the differences between World War I and World War II considerably outweigh the similarities.

    I.   Introduction. World Wars I and II were the most devastating conflicts in history. <u>Thesis</u>

   II.   Summary of main similarities: causes, countries involved, battlegrounds, global scope.

  III.   First major difference: Physical impact of war.
      A. WWI was fought mainly in rural battlegrounds.
      B. In WWII cities were destroyed.

  IV.   Second major difference: Effect on civilians.
      A. WWI fighting primarily involved soldiers.
      B. WWII involved not only military but also massive non-combatant casualties: civilian populations were displaced, forced into slave labor, and exterminated.

   V.   Third major difference: Combat operations
      A. World War I, in its long middle phase, was characterized by trench warfare.
      B. During the middle phase of World War II, there was no major military action in Nazi-occupied Western Europe.

  VI.   Fourth major difference: Aftermath.
      A. Harsh war terms imposed on defeated Germany contributed significantly to the rise of Hitler and World War II.
      B. Victorious allies helped rebuild West Germany after World War II, but allowed Soviets to take over Eastern Europe.

 VII. Conclusion. Since the end of World War II, wars have been far smaller in scope and destructiveness, and warfare has expanded to involve stateless combatants committed to acts of terror.

Following is a comparison-contrast synthesis by criteria, written according to the preceding plan. (Thesis and topic sentences are highlighted.)

MODEL EXAM RESPONSE

1   World War I (1914-18) and World War II (1939-45) were the most catastrophic and destructive conflicts in human history. For those who believed in the steady but inevitable progress of civilization, it was impossible to imagine that two wars in the first half of the twentieth century could reach levels of barbarity and horror that would outstrip those of any previous era. Historians estimate that more than 22 million people, soldiers and civilians, died in World War I; they estimate that between 40 and 50 million died in World War II. In many ways, these two conflicts were similar: they were fought on many of the same European and Russian battlegrounds, with more or less

the same countries on opposing sides. Even many of the same people were involved: Winston Churchill and Adolf Hitler figured in both wars. And the main outcome in each case was the same: total defeat for Germany. However, in terms of the impact on cities and civilian populations, the military aspects of the two wars in Europe, and their aftermaths, the differences between World Wars I and II considerably outweigh the similarities.

The similarities are clear enough. In fact, many historians regard World War II as a continuation--after an intermission of about twenty years--of World War I. One of the main causes of each war was Germany's dissatisfaction and frustration with what it perceived as its diminished place in the world. Hitler launched World War II partly out of revenge for Germany's humiliating defeat in World War I. In each conflict Germany and its allies (the Central Powers in WWI, the Axis in WWII) went to war against France, Great Britain, Russia (the Soviet Union in WWII), and eventually, the United States. Though neither conflict literally included the entire world, the participation of countries not only in Europe, but also in the Middle East, the Far East, and the Western hemisphere made both of these conflicts global in scope. And as indicated earlier, the number of casualties in each war was unprecedented in history, partly because modern technology had enabled the creation of deadlier weapons--including tanks, heavy artillery, and aircraft--than had ever been used in warfare.

Despite these similarities, the differences between the two world wars are considerably more significant. One of the most noticeable differences was the physical impact of each war in Europe and Russia--the western and eastern fronts. The physical destruction of World War I was confined largely to the battlefield. The combat took place almost entirely in the rural areas of Europe and Russia. No major cities were destroyed in the first war; cathedrals, museums, government buildings, urban houses and apartments were left untouched. During the second war, in contrast, almost no city or town of any size emerged unscathed. Rotterdam, Warsaw, London, Minsk, and--when the Allies began their counterattack--almost every major city in Germany and Japan, including Berlin and Tokyo, were flattened. Of course, the physical devastation of the cities created millions of refugees, a phenomenon never experienced in World War I.

(4) The fact that World War II was fought in the cities as well as on the battlefields meant that the second war had a much greater impact on civilians than did the first war. With few exceptions, the civilians in Europe during WWI were not driven from their homes, forced into slave labor, starved, tortured, or systematically exterminated. But all of these crimes happened routinely during WWII. The Nazi occupation of Europe meant that the civilian population of France, Belgium, Norway, the Netherlands and other conquered lands, along with the industries, railroads, and farms of these countries, were put into the service of the Third Reich. Millions of people from conquered Europe--those who were not sent directly to the death camps--were forcibly transported to Germany and put to work in support of the war effort.

(5) During both wars, the Germans were fighting on two fronts--the western front in Europe and the eastern front in Russia. But while both wars were characterized by intense military activity during their initial and final phases, the middle and longest phases--at least in Europe--differed considerably. The middle phase of the First World War was characterized by trench warfare, a relatively static form of military activity in which fronts seldom moved, or moved only a few hundred yards at a time, even after major battles. By contrast, in the years between the German conquest of most of Europe by early 1941 and the Allied invasion of Normandy in mid-1944, there was no major fighting in Nazi-occupied Western Europe. (The land battles then shifted to North Africa and the Soviet Union.)

(6) And of course, the two world wars differed in their aftermaths. The most significant consequence of World War I was that the humiliating and costly war reparations imposed on the defeated Germany by the terms of the 1919 Treaty of Versailles made possible the rise of Hitler and thus led directly to World War II. In contrast, after the end of the Second World War in 1945, the Allies helped rebuild West Germany (the portion of a divided Germany which it controlled), transformed the new country into a democracy, and helped make it into one of the most thriving economies of the world. But perhaps the most

significant difference in the aftermath of each war involved Russia. That country, in a considerably weakened state, pulled out of World War I a year before hostilities ended so that it could consolidate its 1917 Revolution. Russia then withdrew into itself and took no significant part in European affairs until the Nazi invasion of the Soviet Union in 1941. In contrast, it was the Red Army in World War II that was most responsible for the crushing defeat of Germany. In recognition of its efforts and of its enormous sacrifices, the Allies allowed the Soviet Union to take control of the countries of Eastern Europe after the war, leading to fifty years of totalitarian rule--and the Cold War.

(7)   While the two world wars that devastated much of Europe were similar in that, at least according to some historians, they were the same war interrupted by two decades, and similar in that combatants killed more efficiently than armies throughout history ever had, the differences between the wars were significant. In terms of the physical impact of the fighting, the impact on civilians, the action on the battlefield at mid-war, and the aftermaths, World Wars I and II differed in ways that matter to us decades later. Recently, the Iraq, Afghanistan, and Bosnia wars have involved an alliance of nations pitted against single nations; but we have not seen, since the two world wars, grand alliances moving vast armies across continents. The destruction implied by such action is almost unthinkable today. Warfare is changing, and "stateless" combatants like Hamas and Al Qaeda wreak destruction of their own. But we may never see, one hopes, the devastation that follows when multiple nations on opposing sides of a conflict throw millions of soldiers--and civilians--into harm's way.

Discussion

The general strategy of this argument is an organization by *criteria*. The writer argues that although the two world wars of the first part of the twentieth century evinced some similarities, the differences between the two conflicts were more significant. Note that the writer's thesis doesn't merely establish these significant differences; it enumerates them in a way that anticipates both the content and the structure of the response to follow.

In argument terms, the *claim* the writer makes is the conclusion that the two global conflicts were significantly different, if superficially similar. The *assumption* is that careful attention to the impact of the wars upon cities and civilian populations and to the consequences of the Allied victories are keys to understanding the differences between them. The *support* comes in the form of particular historical facts regarding the level of casualties, the scope of destruction, the theaters of conflict, the events following the conclusions of the wars, and so on.

- **Paragraph 1:** The writer begins by commenting on the unprecedented level of destruction of World Wars I and II and concludes with the thesis summarizing the key similarities and differences.

- **Paragraph 2:** The writer summarizes the key similarities in the two wars: the wars' causes, their combatants, their global scope, the level of destructiveness made possible by modern weaponry.

- **Paragraph 3:** The writer discusses the first of the key differences: the fact that the battlegrounds of World War I were largely rural, but in World War II cities were targeted and destroyed.

- **Paragraph 4:** The writer discusses the second of the key differences: the impact on civilians. In World War I, civilians were generally spared from the direct effects of combat; in World War II, civilians were targeted by the Nazis for systematic displacement and destruction.

- **Paragraph 5:** The writer discusses the third key difference: combat operations during the middle phase of World War I were characterized by static trench warfare. During World War II, in contrast, there were no major combat operations in Nazi-occupied Western Europe during the middle phase of the conflict.

- **Paragraph 6:** The writer focuses on the fourth key difference: the aftermath of the two wars. After World War I, the victors imposed harsh conditions on defeated Germany, leading to the rise of Hitler and the Second World War. After World War II, the Allies helped Germany rebuild and thrive. However, the Soviet victory in 1945 led to its postwar domination of Eastern Europe.

- **Paragraph 7:** In the conclusion, the writer sums up the key similarities and differences just covered, but makes some additional comments about the course of more recent wars since World War II. In this way the writer responds to the question posed in the latter part of the assignment: "What have you learned? What can your comparative analysis teach us?"

■ SUMMARY OF SYNTHESIS CHAPTERS

In this chapter and Chapter 3 preceding it, we've considered three main types of synthesis: the *explanatory synthesis*, the *argument synthesis*, and the *comparison-contrast synthesis*. Although for ease of comprehension we've placed them into separate categories, these types are not, of course, mutually exclusive. Both explanatory syntheses and argument syntheses often involve elements of one another, and comparison-contrast syntheses can fall into either of the previous categories. Which approach you choose will depend upon your *purpose* and the method that you decide is best suited to achieve this purpose.

If your main purpose is to help your audience understand a particular subject, and in particular to help them understand the essential elements or significance of this subject, then you will be composing an explanatory synthesis. If your main purpose, on the other hand, is to persuade your audience to agree with your viewpoint on a subject, or to change their minds, or to decide upon a particular course of action, then you will be composing an argument synthesis. If one effective technique of making your case is to establish similarities or differences between your subject and another one, then you will compose a comparison-contrast synthesis—which may well be just *part* of a larger synthesis.

In planning and drafting these syntheses, you can draw on a variety of strategies: supporting your claims by summarizing, paraphrasing, and quoting from your sources; using appeals to *logos*, *pathos*, and *ethos*; and choosing from among strategies such as climactic or conventional order, counterargument, and concession that will best help you to achieve your purpose.

The strategies of synthesis you've practiced in these last two chapters will be dealt with again in Chapter 7, on research, where we'll consider a category of synthesis commonly known as the research paper. The research paper involves all of the skills in summary, critique, and synthesis that we've discussed so far, the main difference being, of course, that you won't find the sources you need in this particular text. We'll discuss approaches to locating and critically evaluating sources, selecting material from among them to provide support for your claims, and, finally, documenting your sources in standard professional formats.

We turn, now, to analysis, which is another important strategy for academic thinking and writing. Chapter 5, Analysis, will introduce you to a strategy that, like synthesis, draws upon all the strategies you've been practicing as you move through *A Sequence for Academic Writing*.

WRITING ASSIGNMENT: THE "LEGACY" QUESTION IN COLLEGE

Now we'll give you an opportunity to practice your skills in planning and writing an argument synthesis. See Chapter 9, pages 329–56, where we provide ten sources on the controversial issue of "legacy" status in the college admissions process. At certain schools, the admissions staff gives preferential consideration to the sons and daughters of alumni. Should they? In the synthesis, you will take a stand in response to this question and then defend your response to readers.

Analysis ■ 5

■ WHAT IS AN ANALYSIS?

An *analysis* is an argument in which you study the parts of something to understand how it works, what it means, or why it might be significant. The writer of an analysis uses an analytical tool: a *principle* or *definition* on the basis of which an object, an event, or a behavior can be divided into parts and examined. Here are excerpts from two analyses of L. Frank Baum's *The Wizard of Oz:*

> At the dawn of adolescence, the very time she should start to distance herself from Aunt Em and Uncle Henry, the surrogate parents who raised her on their Kansas farm, Dorothy Gale experiences a hurtful reawakening of her fear that these loved ones will be rudely ripped from her, especially her Aunt (Em—M for Mother!). [Harvey Greenberg, *The Movies on Your Mind* (New York: Dutton, 1975)]

> [*The Wizard of Oz*] was originally written as a political allegory about grass-roots protest. It may seem harder to believe than Emerald City, but the Tin Woodsman is the industrial worker, the Scarecrow [is] the struggling farmer, and the Wizard is the president, who is powerful only as long as he succeeds in deceiving the people. [Peter Dreier, "Oz Was Almost Reality," *Cleveland Plain Dealer* 3 Sept. 1989.]

As these paragraphs suggest, what you discover through an analysis depends entirely on the principle or definition you use to make your insights. Is *The Wizard of Oz* the story of a girl's psychological development, or is it a story about politics? The answer is *both*. In the first example, psychiatrist Harvey Greenberg applies the principles of his profession and, not surprisingly, sees *The Wizard of Oz* in psychological terms. In the second example, a newspaper reporter applies the political theories of Karl Marx and, again not surprisingly, discovers a story about politics.

Different as they are, these analyses share an important quality: Each is the result of a specific principle or definition used as a tool to divide an object into parts to see what it means and how it works. The writer's choice of analytical tool simultaneously creates and limits the possibilities for analysis. Thus, working with the principles of Freud, Harvey Greenberg sees *The Wizard of Oz* in psychological, not political, terms; working with the theories of Karl Marx, Peter Dreier understands the movie in terms of the economic relationships among characters. It's as if the writer of an analysis who adopts one analytical tool puts on a pair of glasses and sees an object in a specific way. Another writer, using a different tool (and a different pair of glasses), sees the object differently.

Where Do We Find Written Analyses?

Here are just a few types of writing that involve analysis:

ACADEMIC WRITING

- **Experimental and lab reports.** Analyze the meaning or implications of study results in the Discussion section.
- **Research papers.** Analyze information in sources; apply theories to material being reported.
- **Process analysis.** Break down the steps or stages involved in completing a process.
- **Literary analysis.** Analyze characterization, plot, imagery, or other elements in works of literature.
- **Essay exams.** Demonstrate understanding of course material by analyzing data using course concepts.

WORKPLACE WRITING

- **Grant proposals.** Analyze the issues you seek funding for in order to address them.
- **Reviews of the arts.** Employ dramatic or literary analysis to assess artistic works.
- **Business plans.** Break down and analyze capital outlays, expenditures, profits, materials, and the like.
- **Medical charts.** Perform analytical thinking and writing in relation to patient symptoms and possible treatment options.
- **Legal briefs.** Break down and analyze facts of cases and elements of legal precedents; apply legal rulings and precedents to new situations.
- **Case studies.** Describe and analyze the particulars of a specific medical, social service, advertising, or business case.

You might protest: Are there as many analyses of *The Wizard of Oz* as there are people to read it? Yes, or at least as many analyses as there are analytical tools. This does not mean that all analyses are equally valid or useful. The writer must convince the reader. In creating an essay of analysis, the writer must organize a series of related insights, using the analytical tool to examine first one part and then another of the object being studied. To read Harvey Greenberg's essay on *The Wizard of Oz* is to find paragraph after paragraph of related insights—first about Aunt Em, then the Wicked Witch, then Toto, and then the Wizard. All these insights point to Greenberg's single conclusion: that "Dorothy's 'trip' is a marvelous metaphor for the psychological journey every adolescent must make."* Without Greenberg's analysis, we probably would not have thought about the movie as a psychological journey. This is precisely the power of an analysis: its ability to reveal objects or events in ways we would not otherwise have considered.

The writer's challenge is to convince readers that (1) the analytical tool being applied is legitimate and well matched to the object being studied; and (2) the analytical tool is being used systematically to divide the object into parts and to make a coherent, meaningful statement about these parts and the object as a whole.

■ DEMONSTRATION: ANALYSIS

Two examples of analyses follow. The first is written by a professional writer. The second is written by a student, in response to an assignment in his sociology class. Each analysis illustrates the two defining features of analysis just discussed: a statement of an analytical principle or definition, and the use of that principle or definition in closely examining an object, behavior, or event. As you read, try to identify these features. An exercise with questions for discussion follows each example.

THE PLUG-IN DRUG
Marie Winn

The following analysis of television viewing as an addictive behavior appeared originally in Marie Winn's 2002 book, The Plug-In Drug: Television, Computers, and Family Life. *A writer and media critic, Winn has been interested in the effect of television on both individuals and the larger culture. In this passage, she carefully defines the term* addiction *and then applies it systematically to the behavior under study.*

The word "addiction" is often used loosely and wryly in conversation. People will refer to themselves as "mystery-book addicts" or "cookie addicts." E. B. White wrote of his annual surge of interest in gardening: "We are hooked and are making an attempt to kick the habit." Yet nobody really believes that reading mysteries or ordering seeds by catalogue is serious enough to be compared with addictions to heroin or alcohol. In these cases the word "addiction" is used jokingly to denote a tendency to overindulge in some pleasurable activity.

People often refer to being "hooked on TV." Does this, too, fall into the light-hearted category of cookie eating and other pleasures that people pursue with unusual intensity? Or is there a kind of television viewing that falls into the more serious category of destructive addiction?

Not unlike drugs or alcohol, the television experience allows the participant to blot out the real world and enter into a pleasurable and passive mental state. To be sure, other experiences, notably reading, also provide a temporary respite from

---

*See Harvey Greenberg, Movies on Your Mind *(New York: Dutton, 1975).*

reality. But it's much easier to stop reading and return to reality than to stop watching television. The entry into another world offered by reading includes an easily accessible return ticket. The entry via television does not. In this way television viewing, for those vulnerable to addiction, is more like drinking or taking drugs—once you start it's hard to stop.

Just as alcoholics are only vaguely aware of their addiction, feeling that they control their drinking more than they really do ("I can cut it out any time I want—I just like to have three or four drinks before dinner"), many people overestimate their control over television watching. Even as they put off other activities to spend hour after hour watching television, they feel they could easily resume living in a different, less passive style. But somehow or other while the television set is present in their homes, it just stays on. With television's easy gratifications available, those other activities seem to take too much effort.

5   A heavy viewer (a college instructor) observes:

> I find television almost irresistible. When the set is on, I cannot ignore it. I can't turn it off. I feel sapped, will-less, enervated. As I reach out to turn off the set, the strength goes out of my arms. So I sit there for hours and hours.

Self-confessed television addicts often feel they "ought" to do other things—but the fact that they don't read and don't plant their garden or sew or crochet or play games or have conversations means that those activities are no longer as desirable as television viewing. In a way, the lives of heavy viewers are as unbalanced by their television "habit" as drug addicts' or alcoholics' lives. They are living in a holding pattern, as it were, passing up the activities that lead to growth or development or a sense of accomplishment. This is one reason people talk about their television viewing so ruefully, so apologetically. They are aware that it is an unproductive experience, that by any human measure almost any other endeavor is more worthwhile.

It is the adverse effect of television viewing on the lives of so many people that makes it feel like a serious addiction. The television habit distorts the sense of time. It renders other experiences vague and curiously unreal while taking on a greater reality for itself. It weakens relationships by reducing and sometimes eliminating normal opportunities for talking, for communicating.

And yet television does not satisfy, else why would the viewer continue to watch hour after hour, day after day? "The measure of health," wrote the psychiatrist Lawrence Kubie, "is flexibility . . . and especially the freedom to cease when sated." But heavy television viewers can never be sated with their television experiences. These do not provide the true nourishment that satiation requires, and thus they find that they cannot stop watching.

Exercise 5.1

Reading Critically: Winn

In analyses, an author typically first presents the analytical principle in full and then systematically applies parts of the principle to the object or phenomenon under study. In her brief analysis of television viewing, Marie Winn pursues an alternate, though equally effective, strategy by *distributing* parts of her analytical principle across the essay. Locate where Winn defines key elements of addition. Locate where she uses each element as an analytical lens to examine television viewing as a form of addiction.

What function does paragraph 4 play in the analysis?

In the first two paragraphs, how does Winn create a funnel-like effect that draws readers into the heart of her analysis?

Recall a few television programs that genuinely moved you, educated you, humored you, or stirred you to worthwhile reflection or action. To what extent does Winn's analysis describe your positive experiences as a television viewer? (Consider how Winn might argue that from within an addicted state, a person may feel "humored, moved or educated" but is in fact—from a sober outsider's point of view—deluded.) If Winn's analysis of television viewing as an addiction does *not* account for your experience, does it follow that her analysis is flawed? Explain.

Edward Peselman wrote the following paper as a first-semester sophomore, in response to the following assignment from his sociology professor:

> *Read Chapter 3, "The Paradoxes of Power," in Randall Collins's* Sociological Insights: An Introduction to Non-Obvious Sociology *(2nd ed., 1992). Use any of Collins's observations to examine the sociology of power in a group with which you are familiar. Write for readers much like yourself: freshmen or sophomores who have taken one course in sociology. Your object in this paper is to use Collins as a way of learning something "nonobvious" about a group to which you belong or have belonged.*

Note: The citations are in APA format. (See Chapter 7.)

MODEL PAPER

Coming Apart 1

The Coming Apart of a Dorm Society

Edward Peselman

Sociology of Everyday Life

Murray State University

Murray, Kentucky

23 March 2007

Center information horizontally and vertically.

The Coming Apart of a Dorm Society

(1) During my first year of college, I lived in a dormitory, like most freshmen on campus. We inhabitants of the dorm came from different cultural and economic backgrounds. Not surprisingly, we brought with us many of the traits found in people outside of college. Like many on the outside, we in the dorm sought personal power at the expense of others. The gaining and maintaining of power can be an ugly business, and I saw people hurt and in turn hurt others all for the sake of securing a place in the dorm's prized social order. Not until one of us challenged that order did I realize how fragile it was.

(2) Randall Collins, a sociologist at the University of California, Riverside, defines the exercise of power as the attempt "to make something happen in society" (1992, p. 61). A society can be understood as something as large and complex as "American society"; something more sharply defined—such as a corporate or organizational society; or something smaller still—a dorm society like my own, consisting of six 18-year-old men who lived at one end of a dormitory floor in an all male dorm.

(3) In my freshman year, my society was a tiny but distinctive social group in which people exercised power. I lived with two roommates, Dozer and Reggie. Dozer was an emotionally unstable, excitable individual who vented his energy through anger. His insecurity and moodiness contributed to his difficulty in making friends. Reggie was a friendly, happy-go-lucky sort who seldom displayed emotions other than contentedness. He was shy when encountering new people, but when placed in a socially comfortable situation he would talk for hours.

(4) Eric and Marc lived across the hall from us and therefore spent a considerable amount of time in our room. Eric could be cynical and was often blunt: He seldom hesitated when sharing his frank and sometimes unflattering opinions. He commanded a grudging respect in the dorm. Marc could be very moody and, sometimes, was violent. His temper and stubborn streak made him particularly susceptible to conflict. The final member of our miniature society was Benjamin, cheerful yet insecure. Benjamin had certain characteristics

Coming Apart 3

which many considered effeminate, and he was often teased about his sexuality—which in turn made him insecure. He was naturally friendly but, because of the abuse he took, he largely kept to himself. He would join us occasionally for a pizza or late-night television.

Together, we formed an independent social structure. Going out to parties together, playing cards, watching television, playing ball: these were the activities through which we got to know each other and through which we established the basic pecking order of our community. Much like a colony of baboons, we established a hierarchy based on power relationships. According to Collins, what a powerful person wishes to happen must be achieved by controlling others. Collins's observation can help to define who had how much power in our social group. In the dorm, Marc and Eric clearly had the most power. Everyone feared them and agreed to do pretty much what they wanted. Through violent words or threats of violence, they got their way. I was next in line: I wouldn't dare to manipulate Marc or Eric, but the others I could manage through occasional quips. Reggie, then Dozer, and finally Benjamin.

Up and down the pecking order, we exercised control through macho taunts and challenges. Collins writes that "individuals who manage to be powerful and get their own way must do so by going along with the laws of social organization, not by contradicting them" (p. 61). Until mid year, our dorm motto could have read: "You win through rudeness and intimidation." Eric gained power with his frequent and brutal assessments of everyone's behavior. Marc gained power with his temper—which, when lost, made everyone run for cover. Those who were not rude and intimidating drifted to the bottom of our social world. Reggie was quiet and unemotional, which allowed us to take advantage of him because we knew he would back down if pressed in an argument. Yet Reggie understood that on a "power scale" he stood above Dozer and often shared in the group's tactics to get Dozer's food (his parents were forever sending him care packages). Dozer, in turn, seldom missed opportunities to take swipes at Benjamin, with references to his sexuality. From the very first week of school, Benjamin could never—and never

Coming Apart 4

wanted to—compete against Eric's bluntness or Marc's temper. Still, Benjamin hung out with us. He lived in our corner of the dorm, and he wanted to be friendly. But everyone, including Benjamin, understood that he occupied the lowest spot in the order.

⑦ That is, until he left mid-semester. According to Collins, "any social arrangement works because people avoid questioning it most of the time" (p. 74). The inverse of this principle is as follows: When a social arrangement is questioned, that arrangement can fall apart. The more fragile the arrangement (the flimsier the values on which it is based), the more quickly it will crumble. For the entire first semester, no one questioned our rude, macho rules and because of them we pigeon-holed Benjamin as a wimp. In our dorm society, gentle men had no power. To say the least, ours was not a compassionate community. From a distance of one year, I am shocked to have been a member of it. Nonetheless, we had created a mini-society that somehow served our needs.

⑧ At the beginning of the second semester, we found Benjamin packing up his room. Marc, who was walking down the hall, stopped by and said something like: "Hey buddy, the kitchen get too hot for you?" I was there, and I saw Benjamin turn around and say: "Do you practice at being such a

_____, or does it come naturally? I've never met anybody who felt so good about making other people feel lousy. You'd better get yourself a job in the army or in the prison system, because no one else is going to put up with your

_____." Marc said something in a raised voice. I stepped between them, and Benjamin said: "Get out." I was cheering.

⑨ Benjamin moved into an off-campus apartment with his girlfriend. This astonished us, first because of his effeminate manner (we didn't know he had a girlfriend) and second because none of the rest of us had been seeing girls much (though we talked about it constantly). Here was Benjamin, the gentlest among us, and he blew a hole in our macho society. Our social order never really recovered, which suggests its flimsy values. People in the dorm mostly went their own ways during the second semester. I'm not surprised, and I was more than a little grateful. Like most people in the dorm, save for Eric and Marc, I both got my lumps and I gave them, and I never felt good about either. Like Benjamin, I wanted to fit in with my new social surroundings. Unlike him, I didn't have the courage to challenge the unfairness of what I saw.

⑩ By chance, six of us were thrown together into a dorm and were expected, on the basis of proximity alone, to develop a friendship. What we did was sink to the lowest possible denominator. Lacking any real basis for friendship, we allowed the forceful, macho personalities of Marc and Eric to set the rules, which for one semester we all subscribed to—even those who suffered.

⑪ The macho rudeness couldn't last, and I'm glad it was Benjamin who brought us down. By leaving, he showed a different and a superior kind of power. I doubt he was reading Randall Collins at the time, but he somehow had come to Collins's same insight: As long as he played by the rules of our group, he suffered because those rules placed him far down in the dorm's pecking order. Even by participating in pleasant activities, like going out for pizza, Benjamin supported a social system that ridiculed him. Some systems are so oppressive and small minded that they can't be changed from the inside. They've got to be torn down. Benjamin had to move, and in moving he made me (at least) question the basis of my dorm friendships.

[new page]

Reference

Collins, R. (1992). *Sociological insight: An introduction to non-obvious sociology* (2nd ed.). New York: Oxford University Press.

What is the function of ¶1? Though Peselman does not use the word *sociology*, what signals does he give that this will be a paper that examines the social interactions of a group? Peselman introduces Collins in ¶2. Why? What does Peselman accomplish in ¶s3–4? How does his use of Collins in ¶5 logically follow the presentation in ¶s3–4? The actual analysis in this paper takes place in ¶s5–11. Point to where Peselman draws on the work of Randall Collins, and explain how he uses Collins to gain insight into dorm life.

■ HOW TO WRITE ANALYSES

Consider Your Purpose

Whether you are assigned a topic to write on or are left to your own devices, you inevitably face this question: What is my idea? Like every paper, an analysis has at its heart an idea you want to convey. For Edward Peselman, it was the idea that a social order based on flimsy values is not strong enough to sustain a direct challenge to its power, and thus will fall apart eventually. From beginning to end, Peselman advances this one idea: first, by introducing readers to the dorm society he will analyze; next, by introducing principles of analysis (from Randall Collins); and finally, by examining his dorm relationships in light of these principles. The entire set of analytical insights coheres as a paper because the insights are *related* and point to Peselman's single idea.

Guidelines for Writing Analyses

Unless you are asked to follow a specialized format, especially in the sciences or the social sciences, you can present your analysis as a paper by following the guidelines below. As you move from one class to another, from discipline to discipline, the principles and definitions you use as the basis for your analyses will change, but the following basic components of analysis will remain the same:

• *Create a context for your analysis.* Introduce and summarize for readers the object, event, or behavior to be analyzed. Present a strong case about why an analysis is needed: Give yourself a motivation to write, and give readers a motivation to read. Consider setting out a problem, puzzle, or question to be investigated.

• *Introduce and summarize the key definition or principle* that will form the basis of your analysis. Plan to devote the first part of your analysis to arguing for the validity of this principle or definition *if* your audience is not likely to understand it or if they are likely to think that the principle or definition is *not* valuable.

(continues)

> - *Analyze your topic.* Systematically apply elements of this definition or principle to parts of the activity or object under study. You can do this by posing specific questions, based on your analytic principle or definition, about the object. Discuss what you find part by part (organized, perhaps, by question), in clearly defined sections of the essay.
> - *Conclude by stating clearly what is significant about your analysis.* When considering your essay as a whole, what new or interesting insights have you made concerning the object under study? To what extent has your application of the definition or principle helped you to explain how the object works, what it might mean, or why it is significant?

Peselman's paper offers a good example of the personal uses to which analysis can be put. Notice that he gravitated toward events in his life that confused him and about which he wanted some clarity. Such topics can be especially fruitful for analysis because you know the particulars well and can provide readers with details; you view the topic with some puzzlement; and, through the application of your analytical tool, you may come to understand it. When you select topics to analyze from your experience, you provide yourself with a motivation to write and learn. When you are motivated in this way, you spark the interest of readers.

Using Randall Collins as a guide, Edward Peselman returns again and again to the events of his freshman year in the dormitory. We sense that Peselman himself wants to know what happened in that dorm. He writes, "I saw people hurt and in turn hurt others all for the sake of securing a place in the dorm's prized social order." Peselman does not approve of what happened, and the analysis he launches is meant to help him understand.

Locate an Analytical Principle

When you are given an assignment that asks for analysis, use two specific reading strategies to identify principles and definitions in source materials.

- **Look for a sentence that makes a general statement about the way something works.** The statement may strike you as a rule or a law. The line that Edward Peselman quotes from Randall Collins has this quality: "[A]ny social arrangement works because people avoid questioning it most of the time." Such statements are generalizations—conclusions to sometimes complicated and extensive arguments. You can use these conclusions to guide your own analyses as long as you are aware that for some audiences, you will need to re-create and defend the arguments that resulted in these conclusions.

- **Look for statements that take this form: "X" can be defined as (or "X" consists of) the following: A, B, and C.** The specific elements of the definition—A, B, and C—are what you use to identify and analyze parts of the object being studied. You've seen an example of this approach in Marie Winn's multipart definition of addiction, which she uses to analyze television viewing. As a reader looking for definitions suitable for conducting an analysis, you might come across Winn's definition of addiction and then use it for your own purposes, perhaps to analyze the playing of video games as an addiction.

Essential to any analysis is the validity of the principle or definition being applied, the analytical tool. Make yourself aware, both as writer and reader, of a tool's strengths and limitations. Pose these questions of the analytical principles and definitions you use: Are they accurate? Are they well accepted? Do *you* accept them? What are the arguments against them? What are their limitations? Since every principle or definition used in an analysis is the end product of an argument, you are entitled—even obligated—to challenge it. If the analytical tool is flawed, then the analysis that follows from it will be flawed also.

Following is a page from Collins's *Sociological Insight;* Edward Peselman uses a key sentence from this extract as an analytical tool in his essay on power relations in his dorm (see p. 190). Notice that Peselman underlines the sentence he will use in his essay.

SOCIOLOGICAL INSIGHTS

Randall Collins

Try this experiment some time. When you are talking to someone, make them explain everything they say that isn't completely clear. The result, you will discover, is a series of uninterrupted interruptions:

A: Hi, how are you doing?

B: What do you mean when you say "how"?

A: You know. What's happening with you?

B: What do you mean, "happening"?

A: Happening, you know, what's going on.

B: I'm sorry. Could you explain what you mean by "what"?

A: What do you mean, what do I mean? Do you want to talk to me or not?

It is obvious that this sort of questioning could go on endlessly, at any rate if the listener doesn't get very angry and punch you in the mouth. But it illustrates two important points. First, virtually everything can be called into question. We are able to get along with other people not because everything is clearly spelled out, but because we are willing to take most things people say without explanation. Harold Garfinkel, who actually performed this sort of experiment, points out that there is an infinite regress of assumptions that go into any act of social communication. Moreover, some expressions are simply not explainable in words at all. A word like "you," or "here," or "now" is what Garfinkel calls "indexical." You have to know what it means already; it can't be explained.

"What do you mean by 'you'?"

"I mean *you, you!*" About all that can be done here is point your finger.

5   The second point is that people get mad when they are pressed to explain things that they ordinarily take for granted. This is because they very quickly see that explanations could go on forever and the questions will never be answered. If you really demanded a full explanation of everything you hear, you could stop the conversation from ever getting past its first sentence. The real significance of this for a sociological understanding of the way the world is put together is not the anger, however. It is the fact that people try to avoid these sorts of situations. They tacitly recognize that we have to avoid these endless lines of questioning. Sometimes small children will start asking an endless series of "whys," but adults discourage this.

In sum, any social arrangement works because people avoid questioning it most of the time. That does not mean that people do not get into arguments or dispute about just what ought to be done from time to time. But to have a dispute already implies there is a considerable area of agreement. An office manager may dispute with a clerk over just how to take care of some business letter, but they at any rate know more or less what they are disputing about. They do not get off into a . . . series of questions over just what is meant by everything that is said. You could very quickly dissolve the organization into nothingness if you followed that route: there would be no communication at all, even about what the disagreement is over.

Social organization is possible because people maintain a certain level of focus. If they focus on one thing, even if only to disagree about it, they are taking many other things for granted, thereby reinforcing their social reality.

The statement that Peselman has underlined—"any social arrangement works because people avoid questioning it most of the time"—is the end result of an argument that takes Collins several paragraphs to develop. Peselman agrees with the conclusion and uses it in ¶7 of his essay. Observe that for his own purposes Peselman does *not* reconstruct Collins's argument. He selects *only* Collins's conclusion and then imports that into his essay. Once he identifies in Collins a principle he can use in his analysis, he converts the principle into questions that he then directs to his topic: life in his freshman dorm. Two questions follow directly from Collins's insight:

1. What was the social arrangement in the dorm?
2. How was this social arrangement questioned?

Peselman clearly defines his dormitory's social arrangement in ¶s3–6 (with the help of another principle borrowed from Collins). Beginning with ¶7, he explores how one member of his dorm questioned that arrangement:

> That is, until he left mid-semester. According to Collins, "any social arrangement works because people avoid questioning it most of the time" (p. 74). The inverse of this principle is as follows: When a social arrangement is questioned, that arrangement can fall apart. The more fragile the arrangement (the flimsier the values on which it

is based), the more quickly it will crumble. For the entire first semester, no one questioned our rude, macho rules and because of them we pigeon-holed Benjamin as a wimp. In our dorm society, gentle men had no power. To say the least, ours was not a compassionate community. From a distance of one year, I am shocked to have been a member of it. Nonetheless, we had created a mini-society that somehow served our needs.

Formulate a Thesis

An analysis is a two-part argument. The first part states and establishes the writer's agreement with a certain principle or definition.

Part One of the Argument

This first argument essentially takes this form:

> **Claim #1:** Principle "X" (or definition "X") is valuable.

Principle "X" can be a theory as encompassing and abstract as the statement that *myths are the enemy of truth*. Principle "X" can be as modest as the definition of a term—for instance, "addiction" or "comfort." As you move from one subject area to another, the principles and definitions you use for analysis will change, as these assignments illustrate:

> **Sociology:** *Write a paper in which you place yourself in American society by locating both your absolute position and relative rank on each single criterion of social stratification used by Lenski & Lenski. For each criterion, state whether you have attained your social position by yourself or if you have "inherited" that status from your parents.*

> **Literature:** *Apply principles of Jungian psychology to Hawthorne's "Young Goodman Brown." In your reading of the story, apply Jung's principles of the* shadow, persona, *and* anima.

> **Physics:** *Use Newton's second law* (F = ma) *to analyze the acceleration of a fixed pulley, from which two weights hang:* m_1 *(.45 kg) and* m_2 *(.90 kg). Explain in a paragraph the principle of Newton's law and your method of applying it to solve the problem. Assume your reader is not comfortable with mathematical explanations: do not use equations in your paragraph.*

> **Finance:** *Using Guidford C. Babcock's "Concept of Sustainable Growth" [Financial Analysis 26 (May–June 1970): 108–14], analyze the stock price appreciation of the XYZ Corporation, figures for which are attached.*

The analytical tools to be applied in these assignments change from discipline to discipline. Writing in response to the sociology assignment, you would use sociological principles developed by Lenski and Lenski. In your literature class, you would use principles of Jungian psychology; in physics, Newton's second law; and in finance, a particular writer's concept of "sustainable growth." But whatever discipline you are working in, the first part of your analysis will clearly state which (and whose) principles and definitions you are applying. For audiences unfamiliar with these principles, you will need to explain them; if you anticipate objections, you will need to argue that they are legitimate principles capable of helping you as you conduct an analysis.

Part Two of the Argument

In the second part of an analysis, you *apply* specific parts of your principle or definition to the topic at hand. Regardless of how it is worded, this second argument in an analysis can be rephrased to take this form:

> **Claim #2:** By applying Principle (or definition) "X," we can understand *(topic)* as *(conclusion based on analysis)*.

This is your thesis, the main idea of your analytical essay. Fill in the first blank with the specific object, event, or behavior you are examining. Fill in the second blank with your conclusion about the meaning or significance of this object, based on the insights made during your analysis. Marie Winn completes the second claim of her analysis this way:

> By applying my multipart definition, we can understand *television viewing* as *an addiction*.

Develop an Organizational Plan

You will benefit enormously in the writing of a first draft if you plan out the logic of your analysis. You will want to turn key elements of your analytical principle or definition into questions and then develop the paragraph-by-paragraph logic of the paper.

Turning Key Elements of a Principle or Definition into Questions

Prepare for an analysis by developing questions based on the definition or principle you are going to apply, and then by directing these questions to the activity or object to be studied. The method is straightforward: State as clearly as possible the principle or definition to be applied. Divide the principle or definition into its parts and, using each part, develop a question. For example, Marie Winn develops a multipart definition of addiction, each part of which is readily turned into a question that she directs at a specific behavior: television viewing. Her analysis of television viewing can be understood as *responses* to each of her analytical questions. Note that in her brief analysis, Winn does not first define addiction and then analyze television viewing. Rather, *as* she defines aspects of addiction, she analyzes television viewing.

Developing the Paragraph-by-Paragraph Logic of Your Paper

The following paragraph from Edward Peselman's essay illustrates the typical logic of a paragraph in an analytical essay:

> Up and down the pecking order, we exercised control through macho taunts and challenges. Collins writes that "individuals who manage to be powerful and get their own way must do so by going

along with the laws of social organization, not by contradicting them" (p. 61). Until mid year, our dorm motto could have read: "You win through rudeness and intimidation." Eric gained power with his frequent and brutal assessments of everyone's behavior. Marc gained power with his temper—which, when lost, made everyone run for cover. Those who were not rude and intimidating drifted to the bottom of our social world. Reggie was quiet and unemotional, which allowed us to take advantage of him because we knew he would back down if pressed in an argument. Yet Reggie understood that on a "power scale" he stood above Dozer and often shared in the group's tactics to get Dozer's food (his parents were forever sending him care packages). Dozer, in turn, seldom missed opportunities to take swipes at Benjamin, with references to his sexuality. From the very first week of school, Benjamin could never—and never wanted to—compete against Eric's bluntness or Marc's temper. Still, Benjamin hung out with us. He lived in our corner of the dorm, and he wanted to be friendly. But everyone, including Benjamin, understood that he occupied the lowest spot in the order.

We see in this example paragraph the typical logic of analysis.

The writer introduces a specific analytical tool. Peselman quotes a line from Randall Collins:

> "[I]ndividuals who manage to be powerful and get their own way must do so by going along with the laws of social organization, not by contradicting them."

The writer applies this analytical tool to the object being examined. Peselman states his dorm's law of social organization:

> Until mid year, our dorm motto could have read: "You win through rudeness and intimidation."

The writer uses the tool to identify and then examine the meaning of parts of the object. Peselman shows how each member (the "parts") of his dorm society conforms to the laws of "social organization":

> Eric gained power with his frequent and brutal assessments of every-one's behavior. Marc gained power with his temper—which, when lost, made everyone run for cover. Those who were not rude and in-timidating drifted to the bottom of our social world. . . .

An analytical paper takes shape when a writer creates a series of such paragraphs and then links them with an overall logic. Here is the logical organization of Edward Peselman's paper:

¶1: Introduction states a problem—provides a motivation to write and to read.

¶2: Randall Collins is introduced—the author whose work will provide principles for analysis.

¶s3–4: Background information is provided—the cast of characters in the dorm.

¶s5–9: The analysis proceeds—specific parts of dorm life are identified and found significant, using principles from Collins.

¶s10–11: Summary and conclusion are provided—the freshman dorm society disintegrated for reasons set out in the analysis. A larger point is made: Some oppressive systems must be torn down.

Draft and Revise Your Analysis

You will usually need at least two drafts to produce a paper that presents your idea clearly. The biggest changes in your paper will typically come between your first and second drafts. No paper that you write, including an analysis, will be complete until you revise and refine your single compelling idea: your analytical conclusion about what the object, event, or behavior being examined means or how it is significant. You revise and refine by evaluating your first draft, bringing to it many of the same questions you pose when evaluating any piece of writing, including these:

- Are the facts accurate?
- Are my opinions supported by evidence?
- Are the opinions of others authoritative?
- Are my assumptions clearly stated?
- Are key terms clearly defined?
- Is the presentation logical?
- Are all parts of the presentation well developed?
- Are dissenting points of view presented?

Address these same questions to the first draft of your analysis, and you will have solid information to guide your revision.

Write an Analysis, Not a Summary

The most common error made in writing analyses—which is *fatal* to the form— is to present readers with a summary only. For analyses to succeed, you must *apply* a principle or definition and reach a conclusion about the object, event, or behavior you are examining. By definition, a summary (see Chapter 1) includes none of your own conclusions. Summary is naturally a part of analysis; you will need to summarize the object or activity being examined and, depending on the audience's needs, summarize the principle or definition being applied. But in an analysis, you must take the next step and share insights that suggest the meaning or significance of some object, event, or behavior.

Make Your Analysis Systematic

Analyses should give the reader the sense of a systematic, purposeful examination. Marie Winn's analysis illustrates the point: She sets out specific elements of addictive behavior in separate paragraphs and then uses each, within its paragraph, to analyze television viewing. Winn is systematic in her method, and we are never in doubt about her purpose.

Imagine another analysis in which a writer lays out four elements of a definition but then applies only two, without explaining the logic for omitting the others. Or imagine an analysis in which the writer offers a principle for analysis but directs it to only a half or a third of the object being discussed, without providing a rationale for doing so. In both cases, the writer would be failing to deliver on a promise basic to analyses: Once a principle or definition is presented, it should be thoroughly and systematically applied.

Answer the "So What" Question

An analysis should make readers *want* to read. It should give readers a sense of getting to the heart of the matter, that what is important in the object or activity under analysis is being laid bare and discussed in revealing ways. If when rereading the first draft of your essay, you cannot imagine readers saying, "I never thought of _____ this way," then something may be seriously wrong. Reread closely to determine why the paper might leave readers flat and exhausted, as opposed to feeling that they have gained new and important insights. Closely reexamine your own motivations for writing. Have *you* learned anything significant through the analysis? If not, neither will readers, and they will turn away. If you have gained important insights through your analysis, communicate them clearly. At some point, pull together your related insights and say, in effect: "Here's how it all adds up."

Attribute Sources Appropriately

By nature of the form, in an analysis you work with one or two sources and apply insights from those to some object or phenomenon you want to understand more thoroughly. Because you are not synthesizing a great many sources, and because the strength of an analysis derives mostly from *your* application of a principle or definition, the opportunities for not appropriately citing sources are diminished. Take special care to cite and quote, as necessary, the one or two sources you use throughout the analysis.

For an additional opportunity to hone your skills in writing analyses, see Chapter 9. Using principles of ethical decision making, you will analyze the ethics of "legacy admissions," the practice of granting special consideration to the sons and daughters of alumni in the college application process.

Critical Reading for Analysis

- *Read to get a sense of the whole in relation to its parts.* Whether you are clarifying for yourself a principle or definition to be used in an analysis, or are reading a text that you will analyze, understand

(continues)

how parts function to create the whole. If a definition or principle consists of parts, use these to organize sections of your analysis. If your goal is to analyze a text, be aware of its structure: Note the title and subtitle; identify the main point and subordinate points and where they are located; break the material into sections.

- *Read to discover relationships within the object being analyzed.* Watch for patterns. When you find them, be alert—for you create an occasion to analyze, to use a principle or definition as a guide in discussing what the pattern may mean.

   In fiction, a pattern might involve responses of characters to events or to each other, recurrence of certain words or phrasings, images, themes, or turns of plot, to name a few.

   In poetry, a pattern might involve rhyme schemes, rhythm, imagery, figurative or literal language, and more.

Your challenge as a reader is first to see a pattern (perhaps using a guiding principle or definition to do so) and then to locate other instances of that pattern. By reading carefully in this way, you prepare yourself to conduct an analysis.

WRITING ASSIGNMENT: ANALYSIS

Read the following passage, "A Theory of Human Motivation" by Abraham Maslow. Then write a paper using Maslow's theory as an analytical tool, applying what he says about human motivation to some element of your own reading, knowledge, or personal experience. You may wish to use Edward Peselman's analysis of Randall Collins's theories as a model for your own paper. (More specific suggestions follow the passage.)

A THEORY OF HUMAN MOTIVATION
Abraham H. Maslow

Abraham Maslow (1908–1970) was one of the most influential humanistic psychologists of the twentieth century. He earned his PhD at the University of Wisconsin and spent most of his academic career at Brandeis University in Waltham, Massachusetts. Maslow's theories have been widely applied in business, the military, and academia. His books include Motivation and Psychology *(1954) and* Toward a Psychology of Being *(1962). This selection is excerpted from an article that first appeared in* Psychological Review 50 *(1943): 371–96.*

The Basic Needs

The "physiological" needs   The needs that are usually taken as the starting point for motivation theory are the so-called physiological drives. . . .

[A]ny of the physiological needs . . . serve as channels for all sorts of other needs as well. That is to say, the person who thinks he is hungry may actually be seeking more for comfort, or dependence, than for vitamins or proteins. Conversely, it is possible to satisfy the hunger need in part by other activities such as drinking water or smoking cigarettes. . . .

Undoubtedly these physiological needs . . . exceed all others in power. What this means specifically is, that in the human being who is missing everything in life in an extreme fashion, it is most likely that the major motivation would be the physiological needs rather than any others. A person who is lacking food, safety, love, and esteem would most probably hunger for food more strongly than for anything else.

Obviously a good way to obscure the "higher" motivations, and to get a lopsided view of human capacities and human nature, is to make the organism extremely and chronically hungry or thirsty. Anyone who attempts to make an emergency picture into a typical one, and who will measure all of man's goals and desires by his behavior during extreme physiological deprivation is certainly being blind to many things. It is quite true that man lives by bread alone—when there is no bread. But what happens to man's desires when there is plenty of bread and when his belly is chronically filled?

5   At once other (and "higher") needs emerge and these, rather than physiological hungers, dominate the organism. And when these in turn are satisfied, again new (and still "higher") needs emerge and so on. This is what we mean by saying that the basic human needs are organized into a hierarchy of relative prepotency.

One main implication of this phrasing is that gratification becomes as important a concept as deprivation in motivation theory, for it releases the organism from the domination of a relatively more physiological need, permitting thereby the emergence of other more social goals. The physiological needs, along with their partial goals, when chronically gratified cease to exist as active determinants or organizers of behavior. They now exist only in a potential fashion in the sense that they may emerge again to dominate the organism if they are thwarted. But a want that is satisfied is no longer a want. The organism is dominated and its behavior organized only by unsatisfied needs. If hunger is satisfied, it becomes unimportant in the current dynamics of the individual.

The safety needs   If the physiological needs are relatively well gratified, there then emerges a new set of needs, which we may categorize roughly as the safety needs. All that has been said of the physiological needs is equally true, although in lesser degree, of these desires. The organism may equally well be wholly dominated by them. They may serve as the almost exclusive organizers of behavior, recruiting all the capacities of the organism in their service, and we may then fairly describe the whole organism as a safety-seeking mechanism. Again we may say of the receptors, the effectors, of the intellect and the other capacities that they are primarily safety-seeking tools. Again, as in the hungry man, we find that the dominating goal [strongly determines] not only of his current world-outlook and philosophy but also of his philosophy of the future. Practically everything looks less important than safety (even sometimes the physiological needs which being satisfied, are now underestimated). A man, in this state, if it is extreme enough and chronic enough, may be characterized as living almost for safety alone. . . .

The healthy, normal, fortunate adult in our culture is largely satisfied in his safety needs. The peaceful, smoothly running, 'good' society ordinarily makes its members feel safe enough from wild animals, extremes of temperature, criminals, assault and murder, tyranny, etc. Therefore, in a very real sense, he no longer has any safety needs as active motivators. Just as a sated man no longer feels hungry a safe man no longer feels endangered. If we wish to see these needs directly and clearly we must turn to neurotic or near-neurotic individuals, and to the economic and social underdogs. In between these extremes, we can perceive the expressions of safety needs only in such phenomena as, for instance, the common preference for a job with tenure and protection, the desire for a savings account, and for insurance of various kinds (medical, dental, unemployment, disability, old age).

Other broader aspects of the attempt to seek safety and stability in the world are seen in the very common preference for familiar rather than unfamiliar things, or for the known rather than the unknown. The tendency to have some religion or world-philosophy that organizes the universe and the men in it into some sort of satisfactorily coherent, meaningful whole is also in part motivated by safety-seeking. Here too we may list science and philosophy in general as partially motivated by the safety needs.

10 *The love needs*   If both the physiological and the safety needs are fairly well gratified, then there will emerge the love and affection and belongingness needs, and the whole cycle already described will repeat itself with this new center. Now the person will feel keenly, as never before, the absence of friends, or a sweetheart, or a wife, or children. He will hunger for affectionate relations with people in general, namely, for a place in his group, and he will strive with great intensity to achieve this goal. He will want to attain such a place more than anything else in the world and may even forget that once, when he was hungry he sneered at love. . . .

One thing that must be stressed at this point is that love is not synonymous with sex. Sex may be studied as a purely physiological need. Ordinarily sexual behavior is multi-determined, that is to say, determined not only by sexual but also by other needs, chief among which are the love and affection needs. Also not to be overlooked is the fact that the love needs involve both giving and receiving love.

The esteem needs   All people in our society (with a few pathological exceptions) have a need or desire for a stable, firmly based, (usually) high evaluation of themselves, for self-respect, or self-esteem, and for the esteem of others. By firmly based self-esteem, we mean that which is soundly based upon . . . achievement and respect from others. These needs may be classified into two subsidiary sets. These are, first, the desire for strength, for achievement, for adequacy, for confidence in the face of the world, and for independence and freedom. Secondly, we have what we may call the desire for reputation or prestige (defining it as respect or esteem from other people), recognition, attention, importance or appreciation. . . .

Satisfaction of the self-esteem need leads to feelings of self-confidence, worth, strength, capability and adequacy of being useful and necessary in the world. But thwarting of these needs produces feelings of inferiority, of weakness and of helplessness. These feelings in turn give rise to either basic discouragement or else compensatory or neurotic trends. An appreciation of the necessity of basic self-confidence and an understanding of how helpless people are without it, can be easily gained from a study of severe traumatic neurosis.

The need for self-actualization Even if all these needs are satisfied, we may still often (if not always) expect that a new discontent and restlessness will soon develop, unless the individual is doing what he is fitted for. A musician must make music, an artist must paint, a poet must write, if he is to be ultimately happy. What a man can be, he must be. This need we may call self-actualization.

15   This term . . . refers to the desire for self-fulfillment, namely, to the tendency for him to become actualized in what he is potentially. This tendency might be phrased as the desire to become more and more what one is, to become everything that one is capable of becoming.

The specific form that these needs will take will of course vary greatly from person to person. In one individual it may take the form of the desire to be an ideal mother, in another it may be expressed athletically, and in still another it may be expressed in painting pictures or in inventions. It is not necessarily a creative urge although in people who have any capacities for creation it will take this form.*

The clear emergence of these needs rests upon prior satisfaction of the physiological, safety, love and esteem needs. We shall call people who are satisfied in these needs, basically satisfied people, and it is from these that we may expect the fullest (and healthiest) creativeness. Since, in our society, basically satisfied people are the exception, we do not know much about self-actualization, either experimentally or clinically. It remains a challenging problem for research. . . .

Further Characteristics of the Basic Needs

The degree of fixity of the hierarchy of basic needs We have spoken so far as if this hierarchy were a fixed order but actually it is not nearly as rigid as we may have implied. It is true that most of the people with whom we have worked have seemed to have these basic needs in about the order that has been indicated. However, there have been a number of exceptions.

Degrees of relative satisfaction So far, our theoretical discussion may have given the impression that these five sets of needs are somehow in a step-wise, all-or-none relationships to each other. We have spoken in such terms as the following: "If one need is satisfied, then another emerges." This statement might give the false impression that a need must be satisfied 100 percent before the next need emerges. In actual fact, most members of our society who are normal, are partially satisfied in all their basic needs and partially unsatisfied in all their basic needs at the same time. A more realistic description of the hierarchy would be in terms of decreasing percentages of satisfaction as we go up the hierarchy of prepotency. For instance, if I may assign arbitrary figures for the sake of illustration, it is as if the average citizen is satisfied perhaps 85 percent in his physiological needs, 70 percent in his safety needs, 50 percent in his love needs, 40 percent in his self-esteem needs, and 10 percent in his self-actualization needs.

20   As for the concept of emergence of a new need after satisfaction of the prepotent need, this emergence is not a sudden salutatory phenomenon but rather a gradual

---

In another section of his article Maslow considers the human "desires to know and to understand" as "in part, techniques for the achievement of basic safety in the world," and in part, "expressions of self-actualization." Maslow also indicates that "freedom of inquiry and expression" are "preconditions of satisfactions of the basic needs." [Eds.]

emergence by slow degrees from nothingness. For instance, if . . . need A is satisfied only 10 percent then need B may not be visible at all. However, as this need A becomes satisfied 25 percent, need B may emerge 5 percent, as need A becomes satisfied 75 percent need B may emerge 90 percent, and so on.

Unconscious character of needs   These needs are neither necessarily conscious nor unconscious. On the whole, however, in the average person, they are more often unconscious rather than conscious. It is not necessary at this point to overhaul the tremendous mass of evidence which indicates the crucial importance of unconscious motivation. It would by now be expected . . . that unconscious motivations would on the whole be rather more important than the conscious motivations. What we have called the basic needs are very often largely unconscious although they may, with suitable techniques, and with sophisticated people, become conscious. . . .

Multiple motivations of behavior   These needs must be understood not to be exclusive or single determiners of certain kinds of behavior. An example may be found in any behavior that seems to be physiologically motivated, such as eating, or sexual play or the like. The clinical psychologists have long since found that any behavior may be a channel through which flow various determinants. Or to say it in another way, most behavior is multi-motivated. Within the sphere of motivational determinants any behavior tends to be determined by several or all of the basic needs simultaneously rather than by only one of them. The latter would be more an exception than the former. Eating may be partially for the sake of filling the stomach, and partially for the sake of comfort and amelioration of other needs. One may make love not only for pure sexual release, but also to convince one's self of one's masculinity: or to make a conquest, to feel powerful, or to win more basic affection. As an illustration, I may point out that it would be possible (theoretically if not practically) to analyze a single act of an individual and see in it the expression of his physiological needs, his safety needs, his love needs, his esteem needs and self-actualization.

References
Cannon, W. B. (1932). *Wisdom of the body*. New York: Norton.
Kardiner, A. (1941). *The traumatic neuroses of war*. New York: Hoeber.
Young, P. (1936). *Motivation of behavior*. New York: Wiley.
———. (1941). The experimental analysis of appetite. *Psychology Bulletin*, 38, 129–164.

In his final sentence, Maslow himself points the way to a potentially productive analysis using his hierarchy of needs: "I may point out that it would be possible (theoretically if not practically) to analyze a single act of an individual and see in it the expression of his physiological needs, his safety needs, his love needs, his esteem needs and self-actualization." One way, then, of conceiving your analysis is as follows: Choose a single act—yours or anyone's—and analyze it according to Maslow's system. You might begin by introducing the person and setting a context for the act; introducing Maslow's hierarchy, and then proceeding with the analysis itself as you apply one element of the hierarchy at a time. Use each element as a lens through which you look and see the act in a new or revealing way. As you conduct your analysis, recall Maslow's caution: that single acts will typically have "multiple motivations."

■ ANALYZING VISUAL MEDIA

Some people believe that *visual literacy*—that is, the ability to read and understand visual artifacts, such as painting, architecture, film, and graphic arts (including Web design)—will be as important in the twenty-first century as textual literacy was in earlier times. While this may be an extreme view, there's no denying that in this multimedia age, interpreting visual media is a vital skill. And of the various forms of visual media, advertising is perhaps the most omnipresent.

Scholars in the humanities and social sciences study advertising from a number of angles: In the fields of cultural studies, literary studies, and American studies, scholars interpret the messages of advertisements much as they do the messages and meanings of artifacts from "high culture," such as literature and art. In opposition to high culture, advertisements (along with television shows, films, and the like) are considered examples of "popular culture" (or "pop culture"), and in the past 20 years or so, the study of these highly pervasive and influential works has attracted academic attention. Scholars in the fields of sociology, communications, and anthropology are also interested in studying pop cultural artifacts, since they exert such powerful influences on our lives.

Analysis of advertisements has therefore become a fairly common practice in academia. Let's now take the analytical thinking skills we used in analysis of a social situation (the subject of the Peselman paper), and apply them to print advertisements. In this case, rather than lead you through the analytical process, we will show you several advertisements, along with two critical approaches to analyzing advertisements, and then ask you to perform your own analysis of the ads' features, thereby arriving at a sense of their overall meaning or significance.

WRITING ASSIGNMENT: ANALYZING VISUAL MEDIA

Following are three advertisements. The first was created to promote Fancy Feast cat food; the second was created to promote Ikea products; and the third advertises G.E. Monogram kitchen appliances. Study the illustrations and the text in the ads. Then read the two selections following. The first, Roland Marchand's "The Appeal of the Democracy of Goods," from his 1985 book *Advertising the American Dream*, describes a common theme underlying many advertisements. The second, Dorothy Cohen's "Elements of an Effective Layout," offers a number of guiding principles for assessing the layout of visual elements in print advertising.

"You know, I don't ask for much. I'll settle for a pair of jeans that fit, a man who can surprise me occasionally with a gift (no, honey, I didn't mean a lawnmower…), kids who don't drink too much soda, friends who don't drink too much wine, a red carpet hairdo… and a new kitchen.

So, how am I supposed to make it happen? Dress up my husband as a handyman? Or dress up myself? Or do you expect me to mortgage the house for a million dollars to get a beautiful kitchen that doesn't make my turkey any tastier than before? That's not happening. Huh? What about IKEA? They don't have kitchens do they?"

Is it possible to get great kitchen at IKEA?

90th FL 10 RMS W VU. NEW YORK AT YOUR FEET. $17 MILLION.

SO WHAT'S COOKING IN THE KITCHEN ?

In this unoccupied 90th floor penthouse, there's a
GE Monogram kitchen.
Every other apartment in this, the tallest residential
building in the world, has a GE Monogram kitchen, too.
Interested parties, please contact Mr. Trump personally.

GE Monogram
Visit monogram.com

imagination at work

In addition to Cohen's principles, consider some of the following questions as you study each ad.

- What is depicted in the ad's images?
- What is the ad's text?
- How do text and images relate to each other in creating the ad's meaning?
- How are shading/font styles used?
- How are words and various images in the ad placed in relation to one another, and how do these spatial relationships create meaning?
- What is the mood—that is, the emotional output—of the ad? How does this mood help create the ad's meaning?
- How does the ad allude to images/ideas/events/trends from our knowledge of the contemporary world?

Choose one of these advertisements and the passage by *either* Cohen *or* Marchand. Use the principles presented in the passage you have selected to analyze the ad or ads of your choice. Apply the principles of analytical reasoning demonstrated in the analysis by Edward Peselman in the first part of this chapter. That is, apply one or more of the principles explained in the article to the subject of study—in this case, one or more advertisements. Develop your analysis in a well-organized, well-developed paper. (*Note:* Before attempting this assignment, you may want to "limber up" by completing Exercise 5.3 on page below.)

For a more ambitious version of this paper, you might consider using *two* or even *three* ads as the subject of your paper. Review the principles of comparison and contrast in Chapter 4 (pp. 173–75). And for an even more ambitious assignment, you could perform a complex analysis, applying both Marchand's *and* Cohen's principles to one or more ads. That is, show how (a) the graphic elements of the ad and (b) its underlying message work to create a unified effect on readers, influencing them to want to buy the product(s) being advertised.

Exercise 5.3

Analyzing an Advertisement

As a preliminary exercise prior to writing the paper, work through the questions listed above, answering them in as much detail as you can. Then use your answers, along with some of the analytical principles described by Cohen or Marchand, to write a paragraph proposing an overall interpretation of the ad's message.

An alternate exercise: Look through a popular magazine and find an ad that interests you—for whatever reason—and analyze the ad's features, using the questions above and some of the principles discussed by Cohen. Remember to be critical and detailed as you take apart the ad's elements and ultimately put them back together to arrive at an interpretation of the ad's message. Describe both its explicit message (usually just "buy this product") as well as any implicit or covert messages about what kind of person the product might help you become, or what kinds of values the ad is portraying as desirable.

THE APPEAL OF THE DEMOCRACY OF GOODS

Roland Marchand

Roland Marchand is a professor of history at the University of California, Davis. The following selection originally appeared in Marchand's 1985 book Advertising the American Dream: Making Way for Modernity 1920–1940.

As they opened their September 1929 issue, readers of the *Ladies Home Journal* were treated to an account of the care and feeding of young Livingston Ludlow Biddle III, son and heir of the wealthy Biddles of Philadelphia, whose family coat-of-arms graced the upper right-hand corner of the page. Young Master Biddle, mounted on his tricycle, fixed a serious, slightly pouting gaze upon the reader, while the Cream of Wheat Corporation rapturously explained his constant care, his carefully regulated play and exercise, and the diet prescribed for him by "famous specialists." As master of Sunny Ridge Farm, the Biddle's winter estate in North Carolina, young Livingston III had "enjoyed every luxury of social position and wealth, since the day he was born." Yet, by the grace of a . . . modern providence, it happened that Livingston's health was protected by "a simple plan every mother can use." Mrs. Biddle gave Cream of Wheat to the young heir for both breakfast and supper. The world's foremost child experts knew of no better diet; great wealth could procure no finer nourishment. Cream of Wheat summarized the central point of the advertisement by claiming that "every mother can give her youngsters the fun and benefits of a Cream of Wheat breakfast just as do the parents of these boys and girls who have the best that wealth can command."

While enjoying this glimpse of childrearing among the socially distinguished, *Ladies Home Journal* readers found themselves drawn in by one of the most pervasive of all advertising strategies of the 1920's—the concept of the Democracy of Goods. According to this idea, the wonders of modern mass production and distribution enabled everyone to enjoy society's most desirable pleasures, conveniences, or benefits. The particular pleasure, benefit, or convenience varied, of course, with each advertiser who used the formula. But the cumulative effect of the constant reminders that "any woman can . . ." and "every home can afford . . ." was to publicize an image of American society in which concentrated wealth at the top of a hierarchy of social classes restricted no family's opportunity to acquire the most desirable products. By implicitly defining "democracy" in terms of equal access to consumer products, these advertisements offered Americans an inviting vision of their society as one of incontestable equality.

In its most common advertising formula, the concept of the Democracy of Goods asserted that although the rich enjoyed a great variety of luxuries, the acquisition of their *one* most precious luxury would provide anyone with the ultimate in satisfaction. For instance, a Chase and Sanborn's Coffee advertisement, with an elegant butler serving a family in a dining room with a sixteen-foot ceiling, reminded Chicago families that although "compared with the riches of the more fortunate, your way of life may seem modest indeed," yet no one—"king, prince, statesman, or capitalist"—could enjoy better coffee. The Association of Soap and Glycerine Producers proclaimed that the charm of cleanliness was as readily available to the poor as to the rich, and Ivory Soap reassuringly related how one young housewife, who couldn't afford a $780-a-year maid like her neighbor, still maintained "nice hands" by using Ivory. The C. F. Church Manufacturing Company epitomized this feature of the Democracy of Goods technique in an ad entitled "a bathroom luxury everyone can afford": "If you lived in one of those palatial apartments on Park Avenue, in New York City, where you have to pay $2,000 to $7,000 a year rent, you still couldn't have a better toilet seat in your bathroom than they have—the Church Sani-white Toilet Seat, which you can afford to have right now."

   Thus, according to the concept of the Democracy of Goods, no differences in wealth could prevent the humblest citizens, provided they chose their purchases wisely, from coming home to a setting in which they could contemplate their essential equality, through possession of a particular product, with the nation's millionaires. In 1929, Howard Dickinson, a contributor to *Printers' Ink,* concisely expressed the social psychology behind Democracy of Goods advertisements: "'With whom do the mass of people think they want to foregather?' asks the psychologist in advertising. 'Why, with the wealthy and socially distinguished, of course!' If we can't get an invitation to tea for our millions of customers, we can at least present the fellowship of using the same brand of merchandise. And it works."

ELEMENTS OF AN EFFECTIVE LAYOUT
Dorothy Cohen

This selection originally appeared in Dorothy Cohen's textbook Advertising *(1988).*

Fundamentally a good layout should attract attention and interest and should provide some control over the manner in which the advertisement is read. The message to be communicated may be sincere, relevant, and important to the consumer, but because of the competitive "noise" in the communication channel, the opportunity to be heard may depend on the effectiveness of the layout. In addition to attracting attention, the most important requisites for an effective layout are balance, proportion, movement, utility, clarity, and emphasis.

Balance

Balance is a fundamental law in nature and its application to layout design formulates one of the basic principles of this process. Balance is a matter of weight distribution; in layout it is keyed to the *optical center* of an advertisement, the point which the reader's eye designates as the center of an area. In an advertisement a vertical line which divides the area into right and left halves contains the center; however the optical center is between one-tenth and one-third the distance above the mathematical horizontal center line. . . .

In order to provide good artistic composition, the elements in the layout must be in equilibrium. Equilibrium can be achieved through balance, and this process may be likened to the balancing of a seesaw. The optical center of the advertisement serves as the fulcrum or balancing point, and the elements may be balanced on both sides of this fulcrum through considerations of their size and tonal quality.

The simplest way to ensure formal balance between the elements to the right and left of the vertical line is to have all masses in the left duplicated on the right in size, weight, and distance from the center. . . . Formal balance imparts feelings of dignity, solidity, refinement, and reserve. It has been used for institutional advertising and suggests conservatism on the part of the advertiser. Its major deficiency is that it may present a static and somewhat unexciting appearance; however, formal balance presents material in an easy-to-follow order and works well for many ads.

5   To understand informal balance, think of children of unequal weight balanced on a seesaw; to ensure equilibrium it is necessary to place the smaller child far from the center and the larger child closer to the fulcrum. In informal balance the elements are balanced, but not evenly, because of different sizes and color contrast. This type of a symmetric balance requires care so that the various elements do not create a lopsided or top-heavy appearance. A knowledge or a sense of the composition can help create the feeling of symmetry in what is essentially asymmetric balance.

Informal balance presents a fresh, untraditional approach. It creates excitement, a sense of originality, forcefulness, and, to some extent, the element of surprise. Whereas formal balance may depend on the high interest value of the illustration to attract the reader, informal balance may attract attention through the design of the layout. . . .

Proportion

Proportion helps develop order and creates a pleasing impression. It is related to balance but is concerned primarily with the division of the space and the emphasis to be accorded each element. Proportion, to the advertising designer, is the relationship between the size of one element in the ad to another, the amount of space between elements, as well as the width of the total ad to its depth. Proportion also involves the tone of the ad: the amount of light area in relation to dark area and the amount of color and noncolor.*

As a general rule unequal dimensions and distances make the most lively design in advertising. The designer also places the elements on the page so that each element is given space and position in proportion to its importance in the total advertisement and does not look like it stands alone.

---

*Roy Paul Nelson, The Design of Advertising, *4th ed. (Dubuque, IA: Wm. C. Brown Co., 1981), 18.*

Movement

If an advertisement is to appear dynamic rather than static, it must contain some movement. *Movement* (also called *sequence*) provides the directional flow for the advertisement, gives it its follow-through, and provides coherence. It guides the reader's eye from one element to another and makes sure he or she does not miss anything.

10   Motion in layout is generally from left to right and from top to bottom—the direction established through the reading habits of speakers of Western language. The directional impetus should not disturb the natural visual flow but should favor the elements to be stressed, while care should be taken not to direct the reader's eye out of the advertisement. This can be done by the following:

- *Gaze motion* directs the reader's attention by directing the looks of the people or animals in an ad. If a subject is gazing at a unit in the layout, the natural tendency is for the reader to follow the direction of that gaze; if someone is looking directly out of the advertisement, the reader may stop to see who's staring.

- *Structural motion* incorporates the lines of direction and patterns of movement by mechanical means. An obvious way is to use an arrow or a pointed finger. . . .

Unity

Another important design principle is the unification of the layout. Although an advertisement is made up of many elements, all of these should be welded into a compact composition. Unity is achieved when the elements tie into one another by using the same basic shapes, sizes, textures, colors, and mood. In addition, the type should have the same character as the art.

A *border* surrounding an ad provides a method of achieving unity. Sets of borders may occur within an ad, and, when they are similar in thickness and tone, they provide a sense of unity.

Effective use of white space can help to establish unity. . . . *White space* is defined as that part of the advertising space which is not occupied by any other elements; in this definition, white space is not always white in color. White space may be used to feature an important element by setting it off, or to imply luxury and prestige by preventing a crowded appearance. It may be used to direct and control the reader's attention by tying elements together. If white space is used incorrectly, it may cause separation of the elements and create difficulty in viewing the advertisement as a whole.

Clarity and Simplicity

The good art director does not permit a layout to become too complicated or tricky. An advertisement should retain its clarity and be easy to read and easy to understand. The reader tends to see the total image of an advertisement; thus it should not appear fussy, contrived, or confusing. Color contrasts, including tones of gray, should be strong enough to be easily deciphered, and the various units should be clear and easy to understand. Type size and design should be selected for ease of reading, and lines of type should be a comfortable reading length. Too many units in an advertisement are distracting; therefore, any elements that can be eliminated without destroying the message should be. One way in which clarity can be achieved is by combining the logo, trademark, tag line, and company name into one compact group.

Emphasis

15 Although varying degrees of emphasis may be given to different elements, one unit should dominate. It is the designer's responsibility to determine how much emphasis is necessary, as well as how it is to be achieved. The important element may be placed in the optical center or removed from the clutter of other elements. Emphasis may also be achieved by contrasts in size, shape, and color, or the use of white space.

■ ANALYSIS: A TOOL FOR UNDERSTANDING

As this chapter has demonstrated, analysis involves applying principles as a way to probe and understand. With incisive principles guiding your analysis, you will be able to pose questions, observe patterns and relationships, and derive meaning. Do not forget that this meaning will be one of several possible meanings. Someone else, possibly you, using different analytical tools could observe the same phenomena and arrive at very different conclusions regarding meaning or significance. We end the chapter, therefore, as we began it: with the two brief analyses of *The Wizard of Oz*. The conclusions expressed in one look nothing like the conclusions expressed in the other, save for the fact that both seek to interpret the same movie. And yet we can say that both are useful. Both reveal meaning:

> At the dawn of adolescence, the very time she should start to distance herself from Aunt Em and Uncle Henry, the surrogate parents who raised her on their Kansas farm, Dorothy Gale experiences a hurtful reawakening of her fear that these loved ones will be rudely ripped from her, especially her Aunt (Em—M for Mother!). [Harvey Greenberg, *The Movies on Your Mind* (New York: Dutton, 1975)]

> [*The Wizard of Oz*] was originally written as a political allegory about grass-roots protest. It may seem harder to believe than Emerald City, but the Tin Woodsman is the industrial worker, the Scarecrow [is] the struggling farmer, and the Wizard is the president, who is powerful only as long as he succeeds in deceiving the people. [Peter Dreier, "Oz Was Almost Reality," *Cleveland Plain Dealer* 3 Sept. 1989]

You have seen in this chapter how it is possible for two writers, analyzing the same object or phenomenon but applying different analytical principles, to reach vastly different conclusions about what the object or phenomenon may mean or why it is significant. *The Wizard of Oz* is both an inquiry into the psychology of adolescence and a political allegory. What else the classic film may be awaits revealing with the systematic application of other analytical tools. The insights you gain as a writer of analyses depend entirely on your choice of tool and the subtlety with which you apply it.

Note: Additional analysis assignments will be found in Chapter 9, the Practice Chapter.

Part Two • *Strategies*

Writing as a Process 6

■ WRITING AS THINKING

Most of us regard writing as an activity that culminates in a product: a paper, a letter to a friend, study notes, and the like. We tend to focus on the result rather than on the process of getting there. But how *do* we produce that paper or letter? Does the thought that you write down not exist until it appears on the page? Does thought precede writing? If so, is writing merely a translation of prior thought? The relationship between thinking and writing is complex and not entirely understood. But it is worth reflecting on, especially as you embark on your writing-intensive career as a college student. Every time you take up a pen or sit down to a computer to write, you engage in a thinking process—and what and how and when you think both affects and is affected by your writing in a variety of ways. Consider the possibilities as you complete the following brief exercises:

> **A:** You find yourself enrolled in a composition class at a particular school. Why are you attending this school and not another? Write for 5 minutes on the question.

> **B:** Write for 5 minutes—no more, no less—on this question: What single moment in your freshman experience thus far has been most (a) humorous, (b) promising, (c) vexing, (d) exasperating? Choose *one* and write.

> **C:** Select one page of notes from the presumably many you have taken in any of your classes. Reread the page and rewrite it, converting your first-pass notes into a well-organized study guide that would help you prepare for an exam. Devote 5 minutes to the effort.

Reflect on these exercises. Specifically, locate in your responses to each the points at which you believe your thinking took place. (Admittedly, this may be difficult, but give it a try.) Before completing Exercise A, you probably gave considerable thought to *where* you are or would like to be attending college. Examine your writing and reflect on your thinking: Were you in any way rethinking your choice of school as you wrote? Or were you explaining a decision you've already made—that is, reporting on *prior* thinking? Some combination? Now turn to your work for Exercise B, for which you wrote (most likely) on a new topic. Where did thinking occur here? *As* you wrote? Moments prior to your writing, as you selected the topic and focused your ideas? Last, consider Exercise C. Where did your thinking take place? How did revision change your first-draft notes? What makes your second draft a better study guide than your first draft? Finally, consider the differences in the relationship between writing and thinking *across* Exercises A, B, and C as you wrote on a topic you'd previously thought (but not written) about, on a new topic, and on a topic you've written about and are revising. Note the changing relationship between writing and thinking. Note especially how rewriting is related to rethinking.

In completing and reflecting on these exercises, you have glimpsed something of the marvelous complexity of writing. The job of this chapter is to help you develop some familiarity and comfort with a process that no one fully understands. It is a daunting task—and one for which you'll need to expect a certain amount of open-endedness. You will not learn to "solve" the process of writing as you learn to solve an equation. Your learning will be more circular and will never be definitive. Writers write for a lifetime without knowing, ultimately, where their words come from. This is not to say that writing is a mystical process; but neither is it mechanical or mastered absolutely. Twenty-year veterans work just as hard at their writing projects as do freshmen-level writers. Experts don't learn the process and then skip over it once they become proficient. It is more accurate to say that professional writers come to *trust the process* to lead them to desirable results. All writers, regardless of level, with every project, must begin somewhere. They must think and write, and—if they want to produce quality work—they must revise. There are no shortcuts.

If you apply yourself and learn the general approach to writing that we present in the pages that follow, you will improve. You will learn enough to write competently for most any occasion. The more you write, the more you will discover the particulars of your own writing process and the more comfortable you will become.

■ STAGES OF THE WRITING PROCESS

By breaking the process into stages, writers turn the sometimes overwhelming task of writing a paper into manageable pieces, each requiring different actions that, collectively, build to a final draft. Generally, the stages involve *understanding the task, gathering data, invention, drafting, revision*, and *editing*. You should realize at the outset of this discussion that no two writers work entirely alike, and over time (if you have not already done so) you will discover a process for writing that suits you uniquely. For the moment, we suggest that you regard the writing process in the broad stages that we outline here. Once you grow familiar with a general approach to sketching, writing, and refining your work, you will have a foundation on which to build your own approach.

Broadly speaking, the five stages of the writing process occur in the order we've listed. But writing is *recursive*; the process tends to loop back on itself. You will not typically begin at the beginning and follow a lock-step, straight-line path to the end. Writing is messier than that. For example, you might find a number of sources during the data-gathering stage of the process and, after reading and taking notes, you may feel ready to move on to the invention stage—perhaps listing your ideas about the subject. So far, so good. But

The Writing Process

- *Understanding the task:* Read—or create—the assignment. Understand scope and audience.
- *Gathering data:* Locate and review information—from sources and from your own experience—and formulate an approach.
- *Invention:* Use various techniques (e.g., listing, outlining, freewriting) to generate a definite approach to the assignment. Gather more data if needed. Aim for a working thesis, a tentative (but well-reasoned and well-informed) statement of the direction you intend to pursue.
- *Drafting:* Sketch the paper you intend to write and then write all sections necessary to support the working thesis. Stop if necessary to gather more data. Typically, you will both follow your plan and revise and invent a new (or slightly new) plan as you write. Expect to discover key parts of your paper as you write.
- *Revision:* Rewrite in order to make the draft coherent and unified.

  Revise at the *global* level, reshaping your thesis and adding to, rearranging, or deleting paragraphs in order to support the thesis. Gather more data as needed to flesh out paragraphs in support of the thesis.

  Revise at the *local* level of paragraphs, ensuring that each is well reasoned and supports the thesis.
- *Editing:* Revise at the *sentence* level for style and brevity. Revise for correctness: grammar, punctuation, usage, and spelling.

once you sketch your ideas, perhaps in outline form, you may see gaps in the information you've collected, requiring you to circle back and gather more data before proceeding to the next step of first-draft writing. The circling can happen at any point. Perhaps you are writing a draft and your ideas take you in an unexpected direction. You stop to consider: Do I want to follow this through? If so, you will need to rethink the overall organization of your work, which is an earlier stage. You get the point: You will move forward as you write, toward a finished product. But moving forward is seldom a straight-line process.

■ STAGE 1: UNDERSTANDING THE TASK

Papers in the Academic Disciplines

Although most of your previous experience with academic papers may have been in English classes, you should be prepared for instructors in other academic disciplines to assign papers with significant research components.

Here, for example, is a sampling of topics that have been assigned recently in a broad range of undergraduate courses:

Art History: *Discuss the main differences between Romanesque and Gothic sculpture, using the sculptures of Jeremiah (St. Pierre Cathedral) and St. Theodore (Chartres Cathedral) as major examples.*

Environmental Studies: *Choose a problem or issue of the physical environment at any level from local to global. Use both field and library work to explore the situation. Include coverage of the following: (1) the history of the issue or problem; (2) the various interest groups involved, taking note of conflicts among them; (3) critical facts and theories from environmental science necessary to understand and evaluate the issue or problem; (4) impact and significance of management measures already taken or proposed; (5) your recommendations for management of the solution.*

History: *Write a paper analyzing the history of a public policy (for example, the U.S. Supreme Court's role in undermining the civil rights of African Americans between 1870 and 1896), drawing your sources from the best, most current scholarly histories available.*

Physics: *Research and write a paper on solar cell technology, covering the following areas: basic physical theory, history and development, structure and materials, types and characteristics, practical uses, state of the art, and future prospects.*

Political Science: *Explain the contours of California's water policy in the past few decades and then, by focusing on one specific controversy, explain and analyze the way in which this policy was adapted and why. Consider such questions as these: Where does the water come from? How much is there? Who uses it? Who pays for it? How much does it cost? Should more water resources be developed?*

Religious Studies: *Select a particular religious group or movement present in the nation for at least 20 years and show how its belief or practice has changed since members of the group have been in America or, if the group began in America, since its first generation.*

Sociology: *Write on one of the following topics: (1) a critical comparison of two (or more) theories of deviance; (2) a field or library research study of those in a specific deviant career: thieves, drug addicts, prostitutes, corrupt politicians, university administrators; (3) portrayals of deviance in popular culture—e.g., television accounts of terrorism, incest, domestic violence; (4) old age as a form of deviance in the context of youth culture; (5) the relationship between homelessness and mental illness.*

Some of these papers allow students a considerable range of choice (within the general subject); others are highly specific in requiring students to address a particular issue. Most of these papers call for some library or online research; a few call for a combination of online, library, and field research; others may be based entirely on field research. As with all academic writing,

Important Word Meanings in Essay Assignments

Good answers to essay questions depend in part upon a clear understanding of the meanings of the important directive words. These are the words such as *explain, compare, contrast,* and *justify,* which indicate the way in which the material is to be presented. Background knowledge of the subject matter is essential. But mere evidence of this knowledge is not enough. If you are asked to *compare* the British and American secondary school systems, you will get little or no credit if you merely *describe them.* If you are asked to *criticize* the present electoral system, you are not answering the question if you merely *explain* how it operates. A paper is satisfactory only if it answers directly the question that was asked.

The words that follow are frequently used in essay examinations:

summarize: sum up; give the main points briefly. *Summarize the ways in which humans preserve food.*

evaluate: give the good points and the bad ones; appraise; give an opinion regarding the value of; talk over the advantages and limitations. *Evaluate the contributions of teaching machines.*

contrast: bring out the points of difference. *Contrast the novels of Jane Austen and William Makepeace Thackeray.*

explain: make clear; interpret; make plain; tell "how" to do; tell the meaning of. *Explain how humans can, at times, trigger a full-scale rainstorm.*

describe: give an account of; tell about; give a word picture of. *Describe the Pyramids of Giza.*

define: give the meaning of a word or concept; place it in the class to which it belongs and set it off from other items in the same class. *Define the term "archetype."*

compare: bring out points of similarity and points of difference. *Compare the legislative branches of the state government and the national government.*

discuss: talk over; consider from various points of view; present the different sides of. *Discuss the use of pesticides in controlling mosquitoes.*

criticize: state your opinion of the correctness or merits of an item or issue; criticism may approve or disapprove. *Criticize the increasing use of alcohol.*

justify: show good reason for; give your evidence; present facts to support your position. *Justify the American entry into World War II.*

trace: follow the course of; follow the trail of; give a description of progress. *Trace the development of television in school instruction.*

(continues)

> *interpret:* make plain; give the meaning of; give your thinking about; translate. *Interpret the poetic line, "The sound of a cobweb snapping is the noise of my life."*
>
> *prove:* establish the truth of something by giving factual evidence or logical reasons. *Prove that in a full-employment economy, a society can get more of one product only by giving up another product.*
>
> *illustrate:* use a word picture, a diagram, a chart, or a concrete example to clarify a point. *Illustrate the use of catapults in the amphibious warfare of Alexander.*
>
> Source: Andrew Moss and Carol Holder, *Improving Student Writing: A Guide for Faculty in All Disciplines* (Dubuque, IA: Kendall/Hunt, 1988) 17–18.

your first task is to make sure you understand the assignment. Remember to critically read and analyze the specific task(s) required of you in a paper assignment. One useful technique for doing so is to locate the assignment's key verb(s), which will stipulate exactly what is expected of you.

In addition to understanding the major task of the assignment, you should also note guidelines on expected length and documentation method. Length requirements help determine the extent of your data gathering and the scope of your thesis. What kinds of sources you use is also important information for proceeding at this stage. For later reference, you should clarify the documentation method you are asked to follow, such as standard MLA format, APA, CSE (formerly CBE), or some variant of these. In addition to documentation format, learn what kind of manuscript format your instructor prefers. Clarify these issues if they're not spelled out explicitly in the assignment, and be sure to attend to them before submitting your final draft.

Exercise 6.1

Analyze an Example Assignment

Read the assignments from across the disciplines, above, and complete the following for any *two*: (1) identify the key verb(s) in each; (2) list the type of print, interview, or graphical data you should gather to complete the assignment; and (3) reflect on your own experience to find some anecdote that might be appropriately included in a paper (or, absent that, a related experience that would provide a personal motivation for writing the paper).

Exercise 6.2

Analyze Your Own Assignment

Reread the instructions for a recent assignment from another course. Complete the three activities in Exercise 6.1 for this assignment.

■ STAGE 2: GATHERING DATA

When you begin a writing task, you will want to pose three questions:

1. What is the task?
2. What do I know about the subject?*
3. What do I need to know in order to begin writing?

These questions prompt you to reflect on the task and define what is expected. Taking stock of class notes, readings, and whatever resources are available, survey what you already know. Once you identify the gaps between what you know and what you need to know in order to write, you can begin to gather data—most likely in stages. You may gather enough, at first, to formulate initial ideas. You might begin to write and see new gaps and realize you need more data.

In an academic context, gathering data typically involves reading source materials and discovering among them the materials pertinent to your writing (also keeping careful track of sources so you can cite them accurately later and avoid any problems with plagiarism). But just as important, mine your own experience for material to include in your work or, less explicitly but perhaps more importantly, for a personal connection to the subject that will provide you with an enthusiasm for writing. In a sociology course you may be assigned a paper on the changes, over the past 50 years, in the living arrangements of seniors. Doubtless, you will be able to locate many (perhaps too many!) print sources on the subject. But you could also recall and gain powerful insights from personal experience. Perhaps you've seen a grandparent or elderly neighbor shuttled from one marginally satisfactory living arrangement to another. You are frustrated. Use that energy, informed by direct experience, to guide your research and to provide a motivation to write.

Think "large," therefore, when you focus on gathering data for your writing projects. Draw data from your life as well as from the library, and use both to inform your papers.

Types of Data

Data is a term used most often to refer to *quantitative* information, such as the frequencies or percentages of natural occurrences in the sciences or of social phenomena in the social sciences. But *data* also refers to *qualitative* information—the sort that is textual rather than numerical. For example, interviews or ethnographic field notes recorded by a social scientist, also considered to be *data*, are usually qualitative in nature, comprising in-depth interview responses or detailed observations of human behavior. In the humanities, the term *data* can refer to the qualitative observations one makes of a particular

Note: The terms subject *and* topic *are often used interchangeably. In this chapter, we use* subject *to mean a broad area of interest that, once narrowed to a* topic, *becomes the focus of a paper. Within a thesis (the major organizing sentence of the paper), we speak of* topic, *not* subject.

art object one is interpreting or evaluating. Generally, quantitative data encompasses issues of "how many," or "how often," whereas qualitative research accounts for such issues as "what kind?" and "why?"

Primary and Secondary Sources

When you collect either or both of these kinds of data, you are generating *primary* data—data that a researcher gathers directly by using the research methods appropriate to a particular field of study, such as experiments or observations in the sciences, surveys or interviews in the social sciences, and close reading and interpretation of unpublished documents and literary texts or works of art in the humanities. More commonly as an undergraduate, however, the types of data you will collect are *secondary* in nature: information and ideas collected or generated by others who have performed their own primary and/or secondary research. The data gathering for most undergraduate academic writing will consist of library research and, increasingly, research conducted online via Internet databases and resources; you will rely on secondary data more often than you will generate your own primary data.

Chapter 7 on research provides an in-depth discussion of locating and using secondary sources. Refer also to the material presented in Chapters 1 and 2 on summary, critical reading, and critique. The techniques of critical reading and assessment of sources will help you make the best use of your sources. And the material in Chapter 1 on avoiding plagiarism will help you conform to the highest ethical standards in your research and writing.

■ STAGE 3: INVENTION

Given an assignment and the fruits of preliminary data gathering, you are in a position to frame your writing project: to give it scope, to name your main idea, and to create conditions for productive writing. You must define what you are writing about, after all, and this you achieve—in a preliminary way—in the *invention* stage. This stage of the process can also be termed "brainstorming" or "predrafting." Regardless of the name, invention is an important part of the process that typically overlaps with data gathering. The preliminary data you gather on a topic will inform the choices you make in defining (that is, in "inventing" ideas for) your project. As you invent, you will often return to gather more data.

Writers sometimes skip over the invention stage, preferring to save time by launching directly from data gathering into writing a draft. But time spent narrowing your ideas to a manageable scope at the beginning of a project will pay dividends all through the writing process. Many, *many* efforts go wrong when writers choose too broad a topic, resulting in superficial treatment of subtopics, or when they choose too narrow a topic and then must "pad" their work to meet a length requirement.

The Myth of Inspiration

Some students believe that good writing comes primarily from a kind of magical—and unpredictable—formation of ideas as one sits down in front of blank paper or a blank computer screen. According to the myth, a writer must be inspired in order to write, as if given his or her ideas from some mystical source, such as a muse. While some element of inspiration may inform your writing, most of the time it is hard work—especially in the invention stage—that gets the job done. The old adage attributed to Thomas Edison, "Invention is one part inspiration and ninety-nine parts perspiration," applies here.

Choosing and Narrowing Your Subject

Suppose you have been assigned an open-ended, ten-page paper in an introductory course on environmental science. Not only do you have to choose a subject, but you also have to narrow it sufficiently and formulate your thesis. Where will you begin? We take the unusual case of an essentially directionless assignment to demonstrate how you can use invention strategies to identify topics of interest and narrow the scope of your paper. Typically, your assignments will provide more guidance than "write a ten-page paper." In that case, you can still apply the techniques discussed here, though you will have less work to do.

So, how to begin thinking about your paper in environmental science? First, you need to select broad subject matter from the course and become knowledgeable about its general features. What if no broad area of interest occurs to you?

- Work through the syllabus or your textbook(s). Identify topics that sparked your interest.
- Review course notes and pay especially close attention to lectures that held your interest.
- Scan recent headlines for news items that bear on your coursework.

Usually you can make use of material you've read in a text or heard in a lecture. The trick is to find a subject that is important to you, for whatever reason. For a paper in sociology, you might write on the subject of bullying because of your own experience with school bullies. For an economics seminar, you might explore the factors that threaten banks with collapse because your great-great-grandparents lost their life savings during the Great Depression. Whatever the academic discipline, try to discover a topic that you'll enjoy exploring; that way, you'll be writing for yourself as much as for your instructor.

Assume for your course in environmental science that you've settled on the broad subject of energy conservation. At this point, the goal of your research is to limit this subject to a manageable scope. A subject can be limited

The Myth of Talent

Many inexperienced writers believe that either you have writing talent or you don't, and if you don't, then you are doomed to go through life as a "bad writer." But again, hard work, rather than talent, is the norm. Yes, some people have more natural verbal ability than others—we all have our areas of strength and weakness. But in any endeavor, talent alone can't ensure success, and with hard work, writers who do not yet have much confidence can achieve great results. Not everyone can be a brilliant writer. But without question, everyone can be a competent writer.

in at least two ways. First, you can seek out a general article (perhaps an encyclopedia entry, though these are not typically accepted as sources in a college-level paper). A general article may do the work for you by breaking the larger topic down into smaller subtopics that you can explore and, perhaps, limit even further. Second, you can limit a subject by asking several questions about it:

Who?

Which aspects?

Where?

When?

How?

Why?

These questions will occur to you as you conduct your research and see the ways in which various authors have focused their discussions. Having read several sources on energy conservation and having decided that you'd like to use them, you might limit the subject by asking *which aspects*, and deciding to focus on energy conservation as it relates to motor vehicles.

Certainly, "energy-efficient vehicles" offers a more specific focus than does "energy conservation." Still, the revised focus is too broad for a ten-page paper. (One can easily imagine several book-length works on the subject.) So again you try to limit your subject by posing additional questions, from the same list. In this case, you might ask which aspects of energy-efficient vehicles are possible and desirable and how auto manufacturers can be encouraged to develop them. In response to these questions, you may jot down such preliminary notes. For example:

- Types of energy-efficient vehicles

  All-electric vehicles

  Hybrid (combination of gasoline and electric) vehicles

  Fuel-cell vehicles

- Government action to encourage development of energy-efficient vehicles

    Mandates to automakers to build minimum quantities of energy-efficient vehicles by certain deadlines

    Additional taxes imposed on high-mileage vehicles

    Subsidies to developers of energy-efficient vehicles

Focusing on any *one* of these aspects as an approach to encouraging use of energy-efficient vehicles could provide the focus of a ten-page paper, and you do yourself an important service by choosing just one. To choose more would obligate you to too broad a discussion that would frustrate you: Either the paper would have to be longer than ten pages, or, assuming you kept to the page limit, the paper would be superficial in its treatment. In both instances, the paper would fail, given the constraints of the assignment.

A certain level of judgment is involved in deciding whether a topic is too big or too small to generate the right number of pages. Judgment is a function of experience, of course, and in the absence of experience you will have to resort, at times, to trial and error. Still the strategies offered above (locate an article that identifies parts of a topic or pose multiple questions and identify parts) can guide you. Ultimately, you will be able to tell if you've selected an appropriate topic as you reread your work and answer this question: *Have I developed all key elements of the thesis in depth, fully?* If you have skimmed the surface, narrow the topic and/or the claim of your thesis and redraft the paper. If you have added filler to meet the assignment's page requirements, broaden the topic and/or claim and redraft the paper. In general, you will do well to spend ample time gathering data, brainstorming, gathering more data, and then brainstorming again in order to limit your subject before attempting to write about it. Let's take an example. Assume that you settle on the following as an appropriately defined topic for a ten-page paper:

Encouraging the development of fuel-cell vehicles

The process of choosing an initial subject (invention) depends heavily on the reading you do (data gathering). The more you read, the deeper your understanding. The deeper your understanding, the likelier it will be that you can divide a broad and complex subject into manageable—that is, researchable—topics. In the example above, your reading in the online and print literature may suggest that the development of fuel-cell technology is one of the most promising approaches to energy conservation on the highway. So reading allows you to narrow the subject "energy conservation" by answering the initial questions—those focusing on *which aspects* of the general subject. Once you narrow your focus to "energy-efficient vehicles," you may read further and quickly realize that this is a broad subject that also should be limited. In this way, reading stimulates you to identify an appropriate topic for your paper. Your process here is recursive—you move back and forth between Stages 1 and 2 of the process, each movement bringing you closer to establishing a clear focus *before* you attempt to write your paper.

Practice Narrowing Subjects

In groups of three or four classmates, choose one of the following subjects, and collaborate on a paragraph or two that explores the questions we listed above for narrowing subjects: Who? Which aspects? Where? When? How? See if you can narrow the subject.

- Downloading music off the Internet
- Internet chat rooms
- College sports
- School violence
- America's public school system

Invention Strategies

You may already be familiar with a variety of strategies for thinking through your ideas. Several such strategies are provided below.

Directed Freewriting

To freewrite is to let your mind go and write spontaneously, often for a set amount of time or set number of pages. The process of "just writing" can often free up thoughts and ideas about which we aren't even fully conscious, or that we haven't articulated to ourselves. In *directed freewriting*, you focus on a subject, and let what you think and know about the subject flow out of you in a focused stream of ideas. As a first step in the invention stage, you might sit down with an assignment and write continuously for 15 minutes. Such efforts might seem sluggish at first, but if you stick with it and try to let yourself write spontaneously, you'll be surprised at what comes out. You might generate questions whose answers lead to an argument, or logical connections between ideas that you hadn't noticed before. If you write for 15 minutes, and only one solid idea comes through, you've succeeded in using freewriting to help "free up" your thinking. As a second step, you might take that one idea and freewrite about it, shift to a different invention strategy to explore that one idea, or even begin to draft a thesis and subsequent rough draft, depending on the extent to which your idea is well formed.

Listing

Some writers find it helpful to make *lists* of their ideas, breaking significant ideas into sublists and seeing where they lead. Approach this strategy as a form of freewriting; let your mind go, and jot down words and phrases that are related. Create lists by pulling related ideas out of your notes or your course readings. A *caution:* The linear nature of lists can lead you to jump prematurely into planning your paper's structure before working out your ideas. Instead, list ideas as a way of brainstorming, and then generate another list that works out the best structure for your points in a draft.

Outlining

As a more structured version of a list, an *outline* groups ideas in hierarchical order, with main points broken into subordinate points, sometimes indicating evidence in support of these points. Use outlines as a first stage in generating ideas during your invention process, or use outlines as a second step in invention. After freewriting and/or listing, refine and build on your ideas by inserting them into an outline for a workable structure in which to discuss the ideas you've brainstormed.

Clustering and Branching

These two methods of invention are more visual, nonlinear versions of listing and outlining. With both clustering and branching, you start with an assignment's main topic, or with an idea generated by freewriting or thinking, and you brainstorm related ideas that flow from that main idea. *Clustering* involves writing an idea in the middle of a page and circling it. Then draw lines leading from that circle, or "bubble," to new bubbles in which you write subtopics of that central idea. Picking the subtopics that interest you most, draw lines leading to more bubbles wherein you note important aspects of the subtopics. (See the accompanying illustration.) *Branching* follows the same principle, but instead of placing ideas in bubbles, write them on lines that branch off to other lines that, in turn, contain the related subtopics of your larger topic.

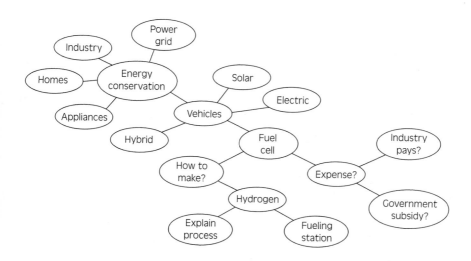

Clustering and branching are useful first steps in invention, for each helps isolate the topics about which you are most knowledgeable. As you branch off into the subtopics of a main paper topic, the number of ideas you generate in relation to these topics will help show where you have the most knowledge and/or interest.

Drafting

It is possible to discover your ideas *as* you write. Of course, this approach requires that you have some notion of what you want to write about. This method may be viewed as a highly focused and directed form of freewriting. You might start drafting your body paragraphs first, or begin with the introduction. Typically, what you write at first will need to be heavily revised (or even discarded) later. Your first paragraph or so serves as a kind of pump priming or throat clearing, but as you proceed you can warm up and start to generate more useful material.

You can modify and combine invention techniques in a number of ways. There is no one right way to generate ideas—or to write a paper—and every writer will want to try different methods to find those that work best. The point to remember is that time spent on invention, regardless of method, creates the conditions in which to write a productive first draft.

Exercise 6.4

Practice Invention Strategies

After completing the group exercise (Exercise 6.3, page 230), in which you narrowed a subject, work individually to brainstorm ideas about the subject your group chose. Use one of the invention strategies listed above—preferably one that you haven't used before. After brainstorming on your own, meet with your group again to compare the ideas you each generated.

■ STAGE 4: DRAFTING

It's usually best to begin drafting a paper after you've settled on at least a working or preliminary thesis. While consulting the fruits of your efforts during invention (notes, lists, outlines, and so on), you face a number of choices about how to proceed with drafting your paper. Let's look at some of these, including the crucial step of drafting the thesis.

Strategies for Writing the Paper

Some writers can sit down very early in the process and put their ideas into an orderly form as they write. This drafting method results in a completed *rough draft*. Good writers rarely, if ever, produce an adequate piece of writing in one draft. Most need to plan the structure of a paper before they can sit down to a first draft. Even if this initial structure proves to be little more than a sketch that changes markedly as the paper develops, some sort of scaffolding usually helps in taking the step from planning to writing a first draft.

Ultimately, *you* will decide how best to proceed. And don't be surprised if you begin different writing projects differently. Whether you jump in without a plan, whether you plan rigorously, or whether you commit yourself to the briefest preliminary sketch, ask yourself the following:

- On what main point do I intend to focus my paper?
- What subpoints do I need to address in order to develop my main point?
- In what order should my points be arranged? (Do certain subpoints lead naturally to others?)

At Stage 3, as you clarify the direction in which you believe your paper is heading, you ought to be able to formulate at least a *preliminary thesis* (see below). Your thesis can be very rough, but if you don't have a sense of your main point, writing the first draft will not be possible. In this case, you would have to consider what you've written a preliminary or a *discovery draft* (more of an invention strategy than an actual draft), a perfectly sensible way to proceed if you're having difficulty clarifying your thoughts. Even if you begin with what you regard as a clearly stated point, don't be surprised if by the end of the draft—just at the point where you are summing up—you discover that the paper you have in fact written differs from the paper you intended to write. However firmly your ideas may be when you begin, the act of writing a draft will usually clarify matters for you.

As you can see, the drafting and invention stages overlap. How much planning you do after working out your ideas and before drafting your paper is a matter of preference. Try different methods to see which work best for you, and keep in mind that different assignments may require new methods for invention and drafting.

Writing a Thesis

A thesis, as we have seen, is a one- or two-sentence summary of a paper's content. Whether it is explanatory, mildly argumentative, or strongly argumentative, the thesis is an assertion about that content—for instance, about what the content is, how it works, what it means, if it is valuable, if action should be taken, and so on. A thesis is similar, actually, to a paper's conclusion, but it lacks the conclusion's concern for broad implications and significance. The thesis is the product of your thinking; it therefore represents *your* conclusion about the topic on which you're writing, and therefore you have to have spent some time thinking (that is, in the invention stage) in order to arrive at the thesis that governs your paper.

For a writer in the drafting stages, the thesis establishes a focus, a basis on which to include or exclude information. For the reader of a finished product, the thesis anticipates the author's discussion. *A thesis, therefore, is an essential tool for both writers and readers of academic papers.*

This last sentence is our thesis for this section. Based on it, we, as authors, have limited the content of the section; and you, as the reader, will be able to form certain expectations about the discussion that follows. You can expect a definition of a thesis; an enumeration of the uses of a thesis; and a discussion focused on academic material. As writers, we will have met our obligations to you only if in subsequent paragraphs we satisfy these expectations.

The Components of a Thesis

Like any other sentence, a thesis includes a subject and a predicate, which consists of an assertion about the subject. In the sentence "Lee and Grant were different kinds of generals," "Lee and Grant" is the subject and "were different kinds of generals" is the predicate. What distinguishes a thesis from any other sentence with a subject and predicate is that *the thesis presents the controlling idea of the paper.* The subject of a thesis, and the assertion about it, must present the right balance between the general and the specific to allow for thorough discussion within the allotted length of the paper. The discussion might include definitions, details, comparisons, contrasts—whatever is needed to illuminate a subject and support the assertion. (If the sentence about Lee and Grant were a thesis, the reader would assume that the rest of the paper contained comparisons and contrasts between the two generals.)

Bear in mind when writing theses that the more general your subject and the more complex your assertion, the longer your paper will be. The broadest theses require book-length treatments, as in this case:

> Meaningful energy conservation requires a shrewd application of political, financial, and scientific will.

One could not write an effective ten-page paper based on this thesis. The topic alone would require pages merely to carefully define what is meant by "energy conservation" and then by "meaningful." Energy can be conserved in homes, vehicles, industries, appliances, and power plants, and each of these areas would need consideration. Having accomplished this task, the writer would then turn his or her attention to the claim, which entails a discussion of how politics, finance, and science individually and collectively influence energy conservation. Moreover, the thesis requires the writer to argue that "shrewd application" of politics, finance, and science is required. The thesis may very well be accurate and compelling. Yet it promises entirely too much for a ten-page paper.

To write an effective thesis and thus a controlled, effective paper, you need to limit your subject and your claims about it. We discussed narrowing your subject during the invention stage on pages 226–32; this narrowing process should help you arrive at a manageable topic for your paper. You will convert that topic to a thesis when you make an assertion about it—a *claim* that you will explain and support in the paper.

Making an Assertion

As noted in the previous section, thesis statements constitute an assertion or claim you wish to make *about* your paper's topic. If you have spent enough time reading and gathering information, and brainstorming ideas about the assignment, you will be knowledgeable enough to have something to say based on a combination of your own thinking and the thinking of your sources.

If you have trouble making an assertion, devote more time to invention strategies: Try writing your subject at the top of a page and then listing everything you now know and feel about it. Often from such a list you will discover an assertion that you then can use to fashion a working thesis. A good way to gauge the reasonableness of your claim is to see what other authors have asserted about the same topic. In fact, keep good notes on the views of others. These notes will prove a useful counterpoint to your own views as you write and think about your claim, and you may want to use them in your paper. Next, make several assertions about your topic, in order of increasing complexity, as in the following:

1. Fuel-cell technology has emerged as a promising approach to developing energy-efficient vehicles.

2. To reduce our dependence on nonrenewable fossil fuel, the federal government should encourage the development of fuel-cell vehicles.

3. The federal government should subsidize the development of fuel-cell vehicles as well as the hydrogen infrastructure needed to support them; otherwise, the United States will be increasingly vulnerable to recession and other economic dislocations resulting from our dependence on the continued flow of foreign oil.

Keep in mind that these are *working theses*. Because you haven't written a paper based on any of them, they remain *hypotheses* to be tested. You might choose one and use it to focus your initial draft. After completing a first draft, you would revise it by comparing the contents of the paper to the thesis and making adjustments as necessary for unity. The working thesis is an excellent tool for planning broad sections of the paper, but—again—don't let it prevent you from pursuing related discussions as they occur to you.

Starting with a Working Thesis

Professionals thoroughly familiar with a topic often begin writing with a clear thesis in mind—a happy state of affairs unfamiliar to most college students who are assigned papers. But professionals usually have an important advantage over students: experience. Because professionals know their material, are familiar with the ways of approaching it, are aware of the questions important to practitioners, and have devoted considerable time to study of the topic, they are naturally in a strong position to begin writing a paper. In addition, many professionals are practiced at invention; the time they spend listing or outlining their ideas helps them work out their thesis statements. Not only do professionals have experience in their fields, but also they have a clear purpose in writing; they know their audience and are comfortable with the format of their papers.

Experience counts—there's no way around it. As a student, you are not yet an expert and therefore don't generally have the luxury of beginning your writing tasks with a definite thesis in mind. But let's assume that you *do* have an area of expertise, that you are in your own right a professional (albeit not in academic matters). We'll assume that you understand some nonacademic subject—say, backpacking—and have been given a clear purpose for writing: to discuss the relative merits of backpack designs. Your job is to write a recommendation for the owner of a sporting-goods chain, suggesting which line of backpacks the chain should carry. Because you already know a good deal about backpacks, you may have some well-developed ideas on the subject before you start doing additional research.

Yet even as an expert in your field, you will find that crafting a thesis is challenging. After all, a thesis is a summary, and it is difficult to summarize a presentation yet to be written—especially if you plan to discover what you want to say during the process of writing. Even if you know your material well, the best you can do at the early stages is to formulate a working thesis—a hypothesis of sorts, a well-informed hunch about your topic and the claim to be made about it. Once you have completed a draft, you can evaluate the degree to which your working thesis accurately summarizes the content of your paper. If the match is a good one, the working thesis becomes the thesis. If, however, sections of the paper drift from the focus set out in the working thesis, you'll need to revise the thesis and the paper itself to ensure that the presentation is unified. (You'll know that the match between the content and thesis is a good one when every paragraph directly refers to and develops some element of the thesis.) Later in this chapter we'll discuss revision techniques that will be useful in establishing unity in your work.

This model works whether you are writing about a subject in your area of expertise—backpacking, for example—or one that is more in your professor's territory, such as government or medieval poetry. The difference is that when approaching subjects that are less familiar to you, you will have to spend more time gathering data and brainstorming. Such labor prepares you to make assertions about your subject.

Using the Thesis to Plan a Structure

A working thesis will help you sketch the structure of your paper, since structure flows directly from the thesis. Consider, for example, the third thesis (see p. 235) on fuel-cell technology:

> The federal government should subsidize the development of fuel-cell vehicles as well as the hydrogen infrastructure needed to support them; otherwise, the United States will be increasingly vulnerable to recession and other economic dislocations resulting from our dependence on the continued flow of foreign oil.

This thesis, compared to the mildly argumentative second statement and the explanatory first statement, is *strongly argumentative*, or *persuasive*. The economic catastrophes mentioned by the writer indicate a strong degree of urgency in the need for the solution recommended—federal subsidy of a national hydrogen infrastructure to support fuel-cell vehicles. If a paper based

> ## How Ambitious Should Your Thesis Be?
>
> Writing tasks vary according to the nature of the thesis.
>
> - The *explanatory thesis* is often developed in response to short-answer exam questions that call for information, not analysis (e.g., "How does James Barber categorize the main types of presidential personality?").
> - The *mildly argumentative thesis* is appropriate for organizing reports (even lengthy ones), as well as essay questions that call for some analysis (e.g., "Discuss the qualities of a good speech").
> - The *strongly argumentative thesis* is used to organize papers and exam questions that call for information, analysis, *and* the writer's forcefully stated point of view (e.g., "Evaluate the proposed reforms of health maintenance organizations").
>
> The strongly argumentative thesis, of course, is the riskiest of the three, since you must unequivocally state your position and make it appear reasonable—which requires that you offer evidence and defend against logical objections. But such intellectual risks pay dividends, and if you become involved enough in your work to make challenging assertions, you will provoke challenging responses that enliven classroom discussions and your own learning.

on this thesis is to be well developed, the writer must commit him- or herself to explaining (1) why fuel-cell vehicles are a preferred alternative to gasoline powered vehicles; (2) why fuel-cell vehicles require a hydrogen infrastructure (i.e., the writer must explain that fuel cells produce power by mixing hydrogen and oxygen, generating both electricity and water in the process); (3) why the government needs to subsidize industry in developing fuel-cell vehicles; and (4) how continued reliance on fossil fuel technology could make the country vulnerable to economic dislocations. This thesis therefore helps the writer plan the paper, which should include a section on each of these four topics. Assuming that the paper follows the organizational plan we've proposed, the working thesis would become the final thesis, on the basis of which a reader could anticipate sections of the paper to come. In a finished product, the thesis becomes an essential tool for guiding readers.

Note, however, that this thesis is still provisional. It may turn out, as you research or begin drafting, that the paper to which this thesis commits you will be too long and complex. You may therefore decide to drop the second clause of the thesis dealing with the country's vulnerability to economic dislocations and focus almost exclusively on the need for the government to subsidize the development of fuel-cell vehicles and of a hydrogen infrastructure, relegating the economic concerns to your conclusion (if at all). If you make this change, your final thesis would read as follows: "The federal government should subsidize the development of fuel-cell vehicles, as well as the hydrogen infrastructure needed to support them."

This revised thesis makes an assertive commitment to the subject, although the assertion is not as complex as the original. Still, it is more assertive than the second proposed thesis:

> To reduce our dependence on nonrenewable fossil fuel energy sources, the federal government should encourage the development of fuel-cell vehicles.

Here we have a *mildly argumentative* thesis (see p. 235) that enables the writer to express an opinion. We infer from the use of the words "should encourage" that the writer endorses the idea of the government promoting fuel-cell development. But a government that "encourages" development is making a lesser commitment than one that "subsidizes," which means that it allocates funds for a specific policy. So a writer who argues for mere encouragement takes a milder position than one who argues for subsidies. Note also the contrast between this second thesis and the first one, in which the writer is committed to no involvement in the debate and no government involvement whatsoever.

> Fuel-cell technology has emerged as a promising approach to developing energy-efficient vehicles.

This first of the three thesis statements is *explanatory*, or *informative*. In developing a paper based on this thesis, the writer is committed only to explaining how fuel-cell technology works and why it is a promising approach to energy-efficient vehicles. Based on this particular thesis, then, a reader would *not* expect to find the author strongly recommending, for instance, that fuel-cell engines replace internal combustion engines at some point in the near future. Neither does the thesis require the writer to defend a personal opinion; he or she need only justify the use of the relatively mild term "promising."

As you can see, for any topic you might explore in a paper, you can make any number of assertions—some relatively simple, some complex. It is on the basis of these assertions that you set yourself an agenda for your writing—and readers set for themselves expectations for reading. The more ambitious the thesis, the more complex will be the paper and the greater will be the readers' expectations.

To review: A thesis (a one-sentence summary of your paper) helps you organize your discussion, and it helps your reader anticipate it. Theses are distinguished by their carefully worded subjects and predicates, which should be just broad enough and complex enough to be developed within the length limitations of the assignment. Both novices and experts typically begin the initial draft of a paper with a working thesis—a statement that provides writers with structure enough to get started but with latitude enough to discover what they want to say as they write. Once you have completed a first draft, however, you test the "fit" of your thesis with the paper that follows. When you have a good fit, every element of the thesis is developed in the paper that follows. Discussions that drift from your thesis should be deleted, or the thesis changed to accommodate the new discussions. These concerns will be addressed more fully when we discuss the revision stage of the writing process.

Exercise 6.5

Drafting Thesis Statements

After completing the group exercise in which you narrowed a subject (Exercise 6.3, page 230), and the individual invention exercise (Exercise 6.4, page 232), work individually or in small groups to draft three possible theses in relation to your earlier ideas. Draft one explanatory thesis, one mildly argumentative thesis, and one strongly argumentative thesis.

Writing Introductions and Conclusions

All writers eventually face the task of writing their paper's introduction and conclusion. How to start? What's the best way to approach your topic? With a serious tone, a light touch, an anecdote? How to end? How best to make the connection from your work back to the reader's world?

Many writers avoid such decisions by putting them off—productively. Bypassing careful planning for the introduction and conclusion, they start by writing the body of the piece; only after they've finished the body do they go back to write the opening and closing paragraphs. There's a lot to be said for this approach. Because you have presumably spent more time thinking and writing about the topic itself than about how you're going to introduce or conclude it, you are in a better position to set out your ideas. And often, it's not until you've actually seen the piece on paper and read it over once or twice that a natural way of introducing or concluding it becomes apparent. You are generally in better psychological shape to write both the introduction and conclusion after the major task of writing is behind you and you know exactly what your major points are.

Introductions

The purpose of an introduction is to prepare the reader to enter the world of your paper. The introduction makes the connection between the more familiar world inhabited by the reader and the less familiar world of the writer's particular topic; it places a discussion in a context that the reader can understand. If you find yourself getting stuck on an introduction at the beginning of a first draft, skip over it for the moment. State your working thesis directly and move on to the body of the paper.

There are many strategies for opening a paper. We'll consider just a few of the most common.

Types of Introductions

- *Quotation* Offer a provocative or apt remark that sets the stage for discussion.
- *Historical Review* Provide background about what happened in the past to account for the present situation or phenomenon.
- *Review of a Controversy* Present in brief form the two (or more) opposing sides of a debate.
- *From the General to the Specific* Work logically from the big picture to the smaller one.
- *From the Specific to the General: Anecdote, Illustration* Present a particular case or story that illustrates the situation or problem to be discussed.
- *Question* Pose one or more questions that get to the heart of the situation or controversy.
- *Statement of Thesis* Begin with your main assertion about the subject.

Quotation   Here is an introduction to a paper on democracy:

> "Two cheers for democracy" was E. M. Forster's not-quite-wholehearted judgment. Most Americans would not agree. To them, our democracy is one of the glories of civilization. To one American in particular, E. B. White, democracy is "the hole in the stuffed shirt through which the sawdust slowly trickles . . . the dent in the high hat . . . the recurrent suspicion that more than half of the people are right more than half of the time" (915). American democracy is based on the oldest continuously operating written constitution in the world—a most impressive fact and a testament to the farsightedness of the founding fathers. But just how farsighted can mere humans be? In *Future Shock*, Alvin Toffler quotes economist Kenneth Boulding on the incredible acceleration of social change in our time: "The world of today . . . is as different from the world in which I was born as that world was from Julius Caesar's" (13). As we move into the twenty-first century, it seems legitimate to question the continued effectiveness of a governmental system that was devised in the eighteenth century; and it seems equally legitimate to consider alternatives.

The quotations by Forster and White help set the stage for the discussion of democracy by presenting the reader with provocative and well-phrased remarks. Later in the paragraph, the quotation by Boulding more specifically prepares us for the theme of change that will be central to the paper as a whole. Quoting the words of others offers you many points of departure for your paper. You can agree with the quotation. You can agree and expand. You can sharply disagree. You can use the quotation to set a context or tone.

Historical Review   In many cases, the reader will be unprepared to follow the issue you discuss unless you provide some historical background. Consider the following introduction to a paper on the film-rating system:

> Sex and violence on the screen are not new issues. In the Roaring Twenties there was increasing pressure from civic and religious groups to ban depictions of "immorality" from the screen. Faced with the threat of federal censorship, the film producers decided to clean their own house. In 1930, the Motion Picture Producers and Distributors of America established the Production Code. At first, adherence to the Code was voluntary; but in 1934 Joseph Breen, newly appointed head of the MPPDA, gave the Code teeth. Henceforth all newly produced films had to be submitted for approval to the Production Code Administration, which had the power to award or withhold the Code seal. Without a Code seal, it was virtually impossible for a film to be shown anywhere in the United States, since exhibitors would not accept it. At about the same time, the Catholic Legion of Decency was formed to advise the faithful which films were and were not objectionable. For several decades the Production Code Administration exercised powerful control over what was portrayed in American theatrical films. By the 1960s, however, changing standards of morality had considerably weakened the Code's grip. In 1968, the Production Code was replaced with a rating system designed to keep younger audiences away from films with high levels of sex or violence. Despite its imperfections, this rating system has proved more beneficial to American films than did the old censorship system.

The paper using the introduction above concerns the relative benefits of the rating system. By providing some historical background on the rating system, the writer helps readers understand his arguments. Notice the chronological development of details.

Review of a Controversy   A particular type of historical review provides the background on a controversy or debate. Consider the following introduction:

> The *American Heritage Dictionary*'s definition of civil disobedience is rather simple: "the refusal to obey civil laws that are regarded as unjust, usually by employing methods of passive resistance." However, despite such famous (and beloved) examples of civil disobedience as the movements of Mahatma Gandhi in India and the Reverend Martin Luther King, Jr., in the United States, the question of whether or not civil disobedience should be considered an asset to society is hardly clear cut. For instance, Hannah Arendt, in her article "Civil Disobedience," holds that "to think of disobedient minorities as rebels and truants is against the letter and spirit of a constitution whose framers were especially sensitive to the dangers of unbridled majority rule." On the other hand, a noted lawyer, Lewis Van Dusen, Jr., in his article "Civil Disobedience: Destroyer of Democracy," states that "civil disobedience, whatever the ethical rationalization, is still an assault on our democratic society, an affront to our legal order and an attack on our constitutional

government." These two views are clearly incompatible. I believe, though, that Van Dusen's is the more convincing. On balance, civil disobedience is dangerous to society.*

The negative aspects of civil disobedience, rather than Van Dusen's essay, are the topic of this paper. But to introduce this topic, the writer has provided quotations that represent opposing sides of the controversy over civil disobedience, as well as brief references to two controversial practitioners. By focusing at the outset on the particular rather than on the abstract qualities of the topic, the writer hoped to secure the attention of her readers and involve them in the controversy that forms the subject of her paper.

From the General to the Specific   Another way of providing a transition from the reader's world to the less familiar world of the paper is to work from a general subject to a specific one. The following introduction begins a paper on improving our air quality by inducing people to trade the use of their cars for public transportation.

> While generalizations are risky, it seems pretty safe to say that most human beings are selfish. Self-interest may be part of our nature, and probably aids the survival of our species, since self-interested pursuits increase the likelihood of individual survival and genetic reproduction. Ironically, however, our selfishness has caused us to abuse the natural environment upon which we depend. We have polluted, deforested, depleted, deformed, and endangered our earth, water, and air to such an extent that now our species' survival is gravely threatened. In America, air pollution is one of our most pressing environmental problems, and it is our selfish use of the automobile that poses the greatest threat to clean air, as well as the greatest challenge to efforts to stop air pollution. Very few of us seem willing to give up our cars, let alone use them less. We are spoiled by the individual freedom afforded us when we can hop into our gas-guzzling vehicles and go where we want, when we want. Somehow, we as a nation will have to wean ourselves from this addiction to the automobile, and we can do this by designing alternative forms of transportation that serve our selfish interests.†

From the Specific to the General: Anecdote, Illustration   The following paragraph quotes an anecdote in order to move from the specific to a general subject:

> In an article on the changing American family, Ron French tells the following story:
>
> > Six-year-old Sydney Papenheim has her future planned. "First I'm going to marry Jared," she told her mother. "Then I'm going to get

---

Michele Jacques, "Civil Disobedience: Van Dusen vs. Arendt," unpublished paper, 1993, 1. Used by permission.
†*Travis Knight, "Reducing Air Pollution with Alternative Transportation," unpublished paper, 1998, 1. Used by permission.*

divorced and marry Gabby." "No, honey," Lisa Boettcher says, "you don't plan it like that." That's news to Sydney. Her mother is divorced and remarried, as is her stepdad. Her grandparents are divorced and remarried, as are enough aunts and uncles to field a team for "Family Feud." She gets presents from her stepfather's ex-wife. Her stepfather's children sometimes play at the house of her father. "You never know what is going to happen from day to day," says Sydney's stepdad, Brian Boettcher. "It's an evolution." It's more like a revolution, from Norman Rockwell to Norman Lear.*†

> French continues on to report that by the year 2007, blended families such as the Boettcher's will outnumber traditional nuclear families. Yet most people continue to lament this change. We as a nation need to accept this new reality: the "till death do us part" version of marriage no longer works.**

The previous introduction went from the general (the statement that human beings are selfish) to the specific (how to decrease air pollution); this one goes from the specific (one little girl's understanding of marriage and divorce) to the general (the changing American family). The anecdote is one of the most effective means at your disposal for capturing and holding your reader's attention. For decades, speakers have begun their remarks with a funny, touching, or otherwise appropriate story; in fact, plenty of books are nothing but collections of such stories, arranged by subject.

Question   Frequently, you can provoke the reader's attention by posing a question or a series of questions:

> Are gender roles learned or inherited? Scientific research has established the existence of biological differences between the sexes, but the effect of biology's influence on gender roles cannot be distinguished from society's influence. According to Michael Lewis of the Institute for the Study of Exceptional Children, "As early as you can show me a sex difference, I can show you the culture at work." Social processes, as well as biological differences, are responsible for the separate roles of men and women.***

Opening your paper with a question can be provocative, since it places the reader in an active role: He or she begins by considering answers. *Are* gender roles learned? *Are* they inherited? In this active role, the reader is likely to continue reading with interest.

Statement of Thesis   Perhaps the most direct method of introduction is to begin immediately with the thesis:

---

*Ron French, "Family: The D-Word Loses Its Sting as Households Blend," Detroit News 1 Jan. 2000, 17 Aug. 2000 http://detnews.com/specialreports/2000/journey/family/family.htm.
†Norman Lear (b. 1922): American television writer and producer noted for developing groundbreaking depictions of the American family in the 1970s, such as "All in the Family," "Sanford and Son," and "Maude."
**Veronica Gonzalez, "New Family Formations," unpublished paper, 1999, 1. Used by permission.
***Tammy Smith, "Are Sex Roles Learned or Inherited?" unpublished paper, 1994, 1. Used by permission.

Every college generation is defined by the social events of its age. The momentous occurrences of an era—from war and economics to politics and inventions—give meaning to lives of the individuals who live through them. They also serve to knit those individuals together by creating a collective memory and a common historic or generational identity. In 1979, I went to 26 college and university campuses, selected to represent the diversity of American higher education, and asked students what social or political events most influenced their generation. I told them that the children who came of age in the decade after World War I might have answered the Great Depression. The bombing of Pearl Harbor, World War II, or perhaps the death of Franklin Roosevelt might have stood out for those born a few years later. For my generation, born after World War II, the key event was the assassination of John F. Kennedy. We remember where we were when we heard the news. The whole world seemingly changed in its aftermath.*

This selection begins with a general assertion—that large-scale social events shape generations of college students. Beginning like this immediately establishes the broader context. Stating your thesis in the first sentence of an introduction also works when you make a controversial argument. Stating a provocative point right away, such as "American democracy is dead," for a paper examining the problems plaguing representative government in current society, forces the reader to sit up and take notice—perhaps even to begin protesting. This "hooks" a reader, who is likely to want to find out how your paper will support its strong thesis. In the paragraph above, the thesis is followed by specific examples of social events, which prepares the reader to consider the experiences of students who were in college in 1979 and compare them to those of earlier generations.

One final note about our model introductions: They may be longer than introductions you have been accustomed to writing. Many writers (and readers) prefer a shorter, snappier introduction. The length of an introduction can depend on the length of the paper it introduces, and it is also largely a matter of personal or corporate style. There is no rule concerning the correct length of an introduction. If you feel that a short introduction is appropriate, use one. Or you may wish to break up what seems like a long introduction into two paragraphs.

Exercise 6.6

Drafting Introductions

Imagine that you are writing a paper using the topic, ideas, and thesis you developed in the exercises in this chapter. Conduct some preliminary research on the topic, using an Internet search engine such as Google or an article database available at your college. Choose one of the seven types of introductions we've discussed—preferably one you have never used before—and draft an introduction that would work to open a paper on your topic. Use our examples as models to help you draft your practice introduction.

---

*Arthur Levine, "The Making of a Generation," Change Sept.–Oct. 1993, 8.

Conclusions

One way to view the conclusion of your paper is as an introduction in reverse, a bridge from the world of your paper back to the world of your reader. A conclusion is the part of your paper in which you restate and (if necessary) expand on your thesis. Essential to many conclusions is the summary, which is not merely a repetition of the thesis but a restatement that takes advantage of the material you've presented. *The simplest conclusion is a summary of the paper, but you may want more than this.* Depending on your needs, you might offer a summary and then build onto it a discussion of the paper's significance or its implications for future study, for choices that individuals might make, for policy, and so on. You might also want to urge readers to change an attitude or modify behavior. Certainly, you are under no obligation to discuss the broader significance of your work (and a summary, alone, will satisfy the formal requirement that your paper have an ending); but the conclusions of better papers often reveal authors who are "thinking large" and want to connect their concerns with the broader concerns of society.

Two words of advice, however. First, no matter how clever or beautifully executed, a conclusion cannot salvage a poorly written paper. Second, by virtue of its placement, the conclusion carries rhetorical weight. It is the last statement a reader will encounter before turning from your work. Realizing this, writers who expand on the basic summary conclusion often wish to give their final words a dramatic flourish, a heightened level of diction. Soaring rhetoric and drama in a conclusion are fine as long as they do not unbalance the paper and call attention to themselves. Having labored long

Types of Conclusions

- *Statement of the Subject's Significance* Summarize why this subject is important, why people should care about it.
- *Call for Further Research* Explain how we can't come to firm conclusions, or suggest reasonable solutions to the situation or problem until we know more about it.
- *Solution/Recommendation* Based on what your discussion has revealed, suggest a solution to the problem or offer one or more recommendations.
- *Anecdote* Conclude with a story or illustration that sheds additional light on the subject.
- *Quotation* Conclude with a quotation that sums up the situation or sheds additional light on the subject.
- *Question* Pose one or more questions that invite the reader to provide or search for answers.
- *Speculation* Reflect upon what may happen in the future: how the situation may evolve if practical solutions are or are not found or if present trends are or are not changed.

hours over your paper, you may be inclined at this point to wax eloquent. But keep a sense of proportion and timing. Make your points quickly and end crisply.

Statement of the Subject's Significance   One of the more effective ways to conclude a paper is to discuss the larger significance of what you have written, providing readers with one more reason to regard your work as a serious effort. When using this strategy, you move from the specific concern of your paper to the broader concerns of the reader's world. Often, you will need to choose among a range of significances: A paper on the Wright brothers might end with a discussion of air travel as it affects economies, politics, or families; a paper on contraception might end with a discussion of its effect on sexual mores, population, or the church. But don't overwhelm your reader with the importance of your remarks. Keep your discussion well focused.

The following paragraphs conclude an article on George H. Shull, a pioneer in the inbreeding and crossbreeding of corn:

> . . . Thus, the hybrids developed and described by Shull 75 years ago have finally dominated U.S. corn production.
>
> The adoption of hybrid corn was steady and dramatic in the Corn Belt. From 1930 through 1979 the average yields of corn in the U.S. increased from 21.9 to 95.1 bushels per acre, and the additional value to the farmer is now several billion dollars per year.
>
> The success of hybrid corn has also stimulated the breeding of other crops, such as sorghum hybrids, a major feed grain crop in arid parts of the world. Sorghum yields have increased 300 percent since 1930. Approximately 20 percent of the land devoted to rice production in China is planted with hybrid seed, which is reported to yield 20 percent more than the best varieties. And many superior varieties of tomatoes, cucumbers, spinach, and other vegetables are hybrids. Today virtually all corn produced in the developed countries is from hybrid seed. From those blue bloods of the plant kingdom has come a model for feeding the world.*

The first sentence of this conclusion is a summary, and from it the reader can infer that the paper included a discussion of Shull's techniques for the hybrid breeding of corn. The summary is followed by a two-paragraph discussion on the significance of Shull's research for feeding the world.

Call for Further Research   In the scientific and social scientific communities, papers often end with a review of what has been presented (as, for instance, in an experiment) and the ways in which the subject under consideration needs to be further explored. *A word of caution:* If you raise questions that you call on others to answer, make sure you know that the research you are calling for hasn't already been conducted.

---

*William L. Brown, "Hybrid Vim and Vigor," Science Nov. 1984: 77–78.

The following conclusion comes from a sociological report on the placement of elderly men and women in nursing homes.

> Thus, our study shows a correlation between the placement of elderly citizens in nursing facilities and the significant decline of their motor and intellectual skills over the ten months following placement. What the research has not made clear is the extent to which this marked decline is due to physical as opposed to emotional causes. The elderly are referred to homes at that point in their lives when they grow less able to care for themselves—which suggests that the drop-off in skills may be due to physical causes. But the emotional stress of being placed in a home, away from family and in an environment that confirms the patient's view of himself as decrepit, may exacerbate—if not itself be a primary cause of—the patient's rapid loss of abilities. Further research is needed to clarify the relationship between depression and particular physical ailments as these affect the skills of the elderly in nursing facilities. There is little doubt that information yielded by such studies can enable health care professionals to deliver more effective services.*

Notice how this call for further study locates the author in a larger community of researchers on whom he depends for assistance in answering the questions that have come out of his own work. The author summarizes his findings (in the first sentence of the paragraph), states what his work has not shown, and then extends his invitation.

Solution/Recommendation   The purpose of your paper might be to review a problem or controversy and to discuss contributing factors. In such a case, it would be appropriate, after summarizing your discussion, to offer a solution based on the knowledge you've gained while conducting research, as the writer of the following conclusion does. If your solution is to be taken seriously, however, your knowledge must be amply demonstrated in the body of the paper.

> . . . The major problem in college sports today is not commercialism—it is the exploitation of athletes and the proliferation of illicit practices which dilute educational standards.
>
> Many universities are currently deriving substantial benefits from sports programs that depend on the labor of athletes drawn from the poorest sections of America's population. It is the responsibility of educators, civil rights leaders, and concerned citizens to see that these young people get a fair return for their labor both in terms of direct remuneration and in terms of career preparation for a life outside sports.
>
> Minimally, scholarships in revenue-producing sports should be designed to extend until graduation, rather than covering only four years of athletic eligibility, and should include guarantees of tutoring, counseling, and proper medical care. At institutions where the profits

---

*Adam Price, "The Crisis in Nursing Home Care," unpublished paper, 2001, 10. Used by permission.

are particularly large (such as Texas A & M, which can afford to pay its football coach $280,000 a year), scholarships should also provide salaries that extend beyond room, board, and tuition. The important thing is that the athlete be remunerated fairly and have the opportunity to gain skills from a university environment without undue competition from a physically and psychologically demanding full-time job. This may well require that scholarships be extended over five or six years, including summers.

Such a proposal, I suspect, will not be easy to implement. The current amateur system, despite its moral and educational flaws, enables universities to hire their athletic labor at minimal cost. But solving the fiscal crisis of the universities on the backs of America's poor and minorities is not, in the long run, a tenable solution. With the support of concerned educators, parents, and civil rights leaders, and with the help from organized labor, the college athlete, truly a sleeping giant, will someday speak out and demand what is rightly his—and hers—a fair share of the revenue created by their hard work.*

In this conclusion, the author summarizes his article in one sentence: "The major problem in college sports today is not commercialism—it is the exploitation of athletes and the proliferation of illicit practices which dilute educational standards." In paragraph 2, he continues with an analysis of the problem just stated and follows with a general recommendation—that "educators, civil rights leaders, and concerned citizens" be responsible for the welfare of college athletes. In paragraph 3, he makes a specific proposal, and in the final paragraph, he anticipates resistance to the proposal. He concludes by discounting this resistance and returning to the general point, that college athletes should receive a fair deal.

Anecdote   As you learned in the context of introductions, an anecdote is a briefly told story or joke, the point of which in a conclusion is to shed light on your subject. The anecdote is more direct than an allusion. With an allusion, you merely refer to a story ("Too many people today live in Plato's cave. . ."); with the anecdote, you actually retell the story. The anecdote allows readers to discover for themselves the significance of a reference to another source—an effort most readers enjoy because they get to exercise their creativity.

The following anecdote concludes a political-philosophical essay. First, the author includes a paragraph summing up her argument, and she follows that with a brief story.

Ironically, our economy is fueled by the very thing that degrades our value system. But when politicians call for a return to "traditional family values," they seldom criticize the business interests that promote and benefit from our coarsened values. Consumer capitalism values things over people; it thrives on discontent and unhappiness

---

since discontented people make excellent consumers, buying vast numbers of things that may somehow "fix" their inadequacies. We buy more than we need, the economy chugs along, but such materialism is the real culprit behind our warped value systems. Anthony de Mello tells the following story:

> Socrates believed that the wise person would instinctively lead a frugal life, and he even went so far as to refuse to wear shoes. Yet he constantly fell under the spell of the marketplace and would go there often to look at the great variety and magnificence of the wares on display.
>
> A friend once asked him why he was so intrigued with the allures of the market. "I love to go there," Socrates replied, "to discover how many things I am perfectly happy without." (27)*

The writer chose to conclude the article with this anecdote. She could have developed an interpretation, but this would have spoiled the dramatic value for the reader. The purpose of using an anecdote is to make your point with subtlety, so resist the temptation to interpret. When selecting an anecdote, keep in mind four guidelines: the anecdote should fit your content; it should be prepared for (readers should have all the information they need to understand it), it should provoke the reader's interest, and it should not be so obscure as to be unintelligible.

Quotation   A favorite concluding device is the quotation—the words of a famous person or an authority in the field on which you are writing. The purpose of quoting another is to link your work to theirs, thereby gaining for your work authority and credibility. The first criterion for selecting a quotation is its suitability to your thesis. But carefully consider what your choice of sources says about you. Suppose you are writing a paper on the American work ethic. If you could use a line by comedian Jay Leno or one by the current secretary of labor to make the final point of your conclusion, which would you choose and why? One source may not be inherently more effective than the other, but the choice certainly sets a tone for the paper. The following two paragraphs conclude an essay examining the popularity of vulgar and insulting humor in television shows, movies, and other popular culture:

> But studies on the influence of popular culture suggest that cruel humor serves as more than a release in modern society. The ubiquitous media pick up on our baser nature, exaggerate it to entertain, and, by spitting it back at us, encourage us to push the boundaries even further. As a result, says Johns Hopkins' Miller, "We're gradually eroding the kinds of social forms and inhibitions that kept [aggressive] compulsions contained."
>
> Before the cycle escalates further, we might do well to consider the advice of Roman statesman and orator Cicero, who wrote at the peak of the Roman empire: "If we are forced, at every hour, to watch

---

*Frances Wageneck, "Family Values in the Marketplace ," unpublished paper, 2000, 6. Used by permission.

> or listen to horrible events, this constant stream of ghastly impressions will deprive even the most delicate among us of all respect for humanity."*

The two quotations used here serve different but equally effective ends. The first idea provides one additional expert's viewpoint, then leads nicely into the cautionary note the writer introduces by quoting Cicero. The Roman's words, and the implied parallel drawn between Rome and contemporary culture, are strong enough that the author ends there, without stepping in and making any statements of her own. In other cases, quotations can be used to set up one last statement by the author of a paper.

Using quotations poses one potential problem: If you end with the words of another, you may leave the impression that someone else can make your case more eloquently than you. The language of the quotation will put your own prose into relief. If your prose suffers by comparison—if the quotations are the best part of your paper—spend some time revising. Avoid this kind of problem by making your own presentation strong.

Question Questions are useful for opening papers, and they are just as useful for closing them. Opening and closing questions function in different ways, however. The introductory question promises to be addressed in the article that follows. But the concluding question leaves issues unresolved, calling on the readers to assume an active role by offering their own answers. Consider the following two paragraphs, written to conclude an article on genetically modified (GM) food:

> Are GM foods any more of a risk than other agricultural innovations that have taken place over the years, like selective breeding? Do the existing and potential future benefits of GM foods outweigh any risks that do exist? And what standard should governments use when assessing the safety of transgenic crops? The "frankenfood" frenzy has given life to a policy-making standard known as the "precautionary principle," which has been long advocated by environmental groups. That principle essentially calls for governments to prohibit any activity that raises concerns about human health or the environment, even if some cause-and-effect relationships are not fully established scientifically. As Liberal Democrat MP [Member of Parliament] Norman Baker told the BBC: "We must always apply the precautionary principle. That says that unless you're sure of adequate control, unless you're sure the risk is minimal, unless you're sure nothing horrible can go wrong, you don't do it."

> But can any innovation ever meet such a standard of certainty—especially given the proliferation of "experts" that are motivated as much by politics as they are by science? And what about those millions of malnourished people whose lives could be saved by transgenic foods?**

---

*Nina J. Easton, "The Meaning of America," Los Angeles Times Magazine 7 Feb. 1993, 21.
**"Frankenfoods Frenzy," Reason 13 Jan. 2000, 17 Aug. 2000 <http://reason.com/bi/bi-gmf.html>.

Rather than ending with a question, you may choose to *raise* a question in your conclusion and then answer it, based on the material you've provided in the paper. The answered question challenges a reader to agree or disagree with you and thus also places the reader in an active role. The following brief conclusion ends a student paper entitled "Is Feminism Dead?"

> So the answer to the question "Is the feminist movement dead?" is no, it's not. Even if most young women today don't consciously identify themselves as "feminists"—due to the ways in which the term has become loaded with negative associations—the principles of gender equality that lie at feminism's core are enthusiastically embraced by the vast number of young women, and even a large percentage of young men.

Speculation   When you speculate, you ask about and explore what has happened or what might happen. Speculation involves a spinning out of possibilities. It stimulates readers by immersing them in your discussion of the unknown, implicitly challenging them to agree or disagree. The following paragraph concludes "The New Generation Gap" by Neil Howe and William Strauss. In this article, Howe and Strauss discuss the differences among Americans of various ages, including the "GI Generation" (born between 1901 and 1924), the "Boomers"(born 1943–1961), the "Thirteeners" (born 1961–1981), and the "Millennials" (born 1981–2000):

> If, slowly but surely, Millennials receive the kind of family protection and public generosity that GIs enjoyed as children, then they could come of age early in the next century as a group much like the GIs of the 1920s and 1930s—as a stellar (if bland) generation of rationalists, team players, and can-do civic builders. Two decades from now Boomers entering old age may well see in their grown Millennial children an effective instrument for saving the world, while Thirteeners entering midlife will shower kindness on a younger generation that is getting a better deal out of life (though maybe a bit less fun) than they ever got at a like age. Study after story after column will laud these "best damn kids in the world" as heralding a resurgent American greatness. And, for a while at least, no one will talk about a generation gap.*

Thus, Howe and Strauss conclude an article concerned largely with the apparently unbridgeable gaps of understanding between parents and children with a hopeful speculation that generational relationships will improve considerably in the next two decades.

Exercise 6.7

Drafting Conclusions

Imagine that you have written a paper using the topic, ideas, and thesis you developed in the earlier exercises in this chapter. Conduct some preliminary research on the topic, using an Internet search engine such as Google or an article database available at your college. Choose one of the seven types of

---

Neil Howe and William Strauss, "The New Generation Gap," Atlantic Monthly Dec. 1992, 65.

conclusions we've discussed—preferably one you have never used before—and draft a conclusion that would work to end your paper. Use our examples as models to help you draft your practice conclusion.

■ STAGE 5: REVISION

Perhaps it's stating the obvious to say that rough drafts need revision, but as we've noted, too often students skimp on this phase of the writing process. The word *revision* can be used to describe all modifications one makes to a written document. However, it's useful to distinguish among three kinds of revision.

Global revisions focus on the thesis, the type and pattern of evidence employed, the overall organization, the match between thesis and content, and the tone. A global revision may also emerge from a change in purpose.

Local revisions focus on paragraphs: topic and transitional sentences; the type of evidence presented within a paragraph; evidence added, modified, or dropped within a paragraph; and logical connections from one sentence (or set of sentences) within a paragraph to another.

Surface revisions deal with sentence style and construction as well as word choice. Sentence editing involves correcting errors of grammar, mechanics, spelling, and citation form.

Global and local revisions fall within Stage 5 of the writing process, while surface revisions are covered in Stage 6, editing.

We advise separating large-scale (global and local) revision from later (sentence-editing) revisions as a way of keeping priorities in order. Different tasks require different cognitive functions. For example, when you are working on revising the structure and content of a paragraph within a paper, getting caught up in rewording an awkward sentence can distract you from the larger task at hand—a task that may prompt you to delete the very sentence you find awkward. Get the large pieces in place first: *content* (your ideas), *structure* (the arrangement of your paragraphs), and *paragraph structure* (the arrangement of ideas within your paragraphs). Then tend to the smaller elements, much as you would in building a house. You wouldn't lay the carpet before setting the floor joists.

Think of revision as re-vision, meaning "seeing anew." In order to re-see, it's often useful to set your paper aside for a time and come back later to view your rough draft with a fresh eye, from a new perspective. Doing so will better allow you to determine whether your work exhibits the characteristics of a good paper.

Characteristics of Good Papers

Apply the principles of *unity, coherence,* and *development* to the revision process. Let's start with unity, which we've already discussed somewhat in the context of the thesis.

Unity

A paper is unified when focused on a main point. The chief tool for achieving paper unity is the thesis, as we've already noted: It's hard to achieve unity in a paper when a central point remains unstated. Unity, however, doesn't stop at the thesis; the body paragraphs that follow must clearly support and explain that thesis. Thus, the steps for determining unity are to first examine your introduction and make sure you have a clear, identifiable thesis. Next, check your paper's interior paragraphs to make sure your points all relate to that thesis. Ask yourself how your conclusion provides closure to your overall discussion.

Coherence

Coherence means "logical interconnectedness." When things cohere, separate elements hold together and make a whole. As applied to paper writing, coherence is very closely related to unity: Good papers cohere. They hold together logically and stay focused on a main point. All subordinate points addressed in the body of the paper clearly relate to the main point expressed in the thesis. Moreover, all those subpoints, examples, and supporting quotations are presented in a logical order so that connections between them are clear. You could write a highly unified paper, but if your points are discussed in a haphazard order, the reader will have a hard time following your argument or staying focused on your point. Lead readers along with your writing. Show them not only how subpoints relate to a main point, but also how they relate to one another.

Development

Good papers are also well developed, meaning that their points are fully explained and supported. Readers do not live inside your head. They will not fully understand your points unless you adequately explain them. A reader also may not be persuaded that your paper's main point is valid unless you provide sufficient support for your arguments by using examples, the opinions of authorities on the subject, and your own sound logic to hold all together.

Use the three principles of unity, coherence, and development to analyze what you have written and make necessary revisions. Does your paper stay focused on the main point? Do your paper's points clearly relate to each other? Do you need better transitions between some paragraphs to help the ideas flow more logically and smoothly? Have you fully explained and given adequate support for all your points?

These three principles for good papers also apply to the composition of good paragraphs. Paragraphs are "minipapers": they should stick to a main point (the topic sentence) and fully develop that point in an orderly fashion. Transitional words or phrases such as *however, thus, on the other hand,* and *for example* help make clear to a reader how the sentences within individual paragraphs are related.

The Reverse Outline

The *reverse outline* is a useful technique for refining a working thesis and for establishing unity between your thesis statement and the body of your paper. When you outline a paper you intend to write, you do so *prospectively*— that is, before the fact of writing. In a reverse outline you outline the paper *retrospectively*—after the fact. The reverse outline is useful for spotting gaps in logic or development as well as problems with unity or coherence. Follow these steps to generate a reverse outline:

1. On a fresh sheet of paper (or electronic document), restate your thesis, making certain that the thesis you began with is the thesis that in fact governs the logic of the paper. (Look for a competing thesis in your conclusion. In summing up, you may have clarified for yourself what your *actual* governing idea is as opposed to the idea you thought would organize the paper.)

2. In the margin of your draft, summarize *each* paragraph in a phrase. If you have trouble writing a summary, place an asterisk by the paragraph as a reminder to clarify it later.

3. Beneath your thesis, write your paragraph-summary phrases, one to a line, in outline format.

4. Review the outline you have just created. Is the paper divided into readily identifiable major points in support of the thesis? Have you supported each major point sufficiently? Do the sections of the outline lead logically from one to the next? Do all sections develop the thesis?

5. Watch especially for uneven development. Add or delete material as needed to ensure a balanced presentation.

■ STAGE 6: EDITING

After revising a paper's large-scale elements—its unity, coherence, and development of its content; its overall structure; and its paragraph structure—you are ready to polish your paper by editing its sentences for style and correctness. At this stage you may be tired, and the temptation to merely correct a few glaring mistakes here and there may be strong. Resist that impulse: A paper with excellent ideas and structure can be ruined by mechanical, sentence-level errors. After all your work, you don't want readers to get distracted by sentence or punctuation errors.

Editing for Style

Developing an engaging writing style takes long practice. It's beyond the scope of this book to teach you the nuances of writing style, and you can consult many fine books for help. (See, for example, William Zinsser's *On Writing Well*.) Here we'll focus on just one common stylistic problem: short, choppy sentences.

Perhaps out of fear of making sentence errors such as run-ons or comma splices, some writers avoid varying their sentence types, preferring strings of simple sentences. The result is usually unsatisfying. Compare, for instance, two versions of the same paragraph on study of the human genome:

> Scientists have finally succeeded in decoding the human genome. This accomplishment opens up a whole new field of study. Researchers now have new ways to understand human biological functioning. We may also be able to learn new perspectives on human behavior. For centuries people have wondered about how much we are shaped by genetics. They have also wondered how much environment shapes us. The age-old questions about nature vs. nurture may now be answered. Each individual's genetic heritage as well as his or her genetic future will be visible to geneticists. All of these discoveries may help us to improve and extend human life. Many diseases will be detectable. New treatments will be developed. These new discoveries open up a new area of ethical debate. Scientists and the public are going to have to decide how far to take this new genetic technology.

This paragraph illustrates the problems with choppy, repetitive sentences. First, the writer hasn't connected ideas, and sentences don't smoothly flow one to the next. Second, the same sentence structure (the simple sentence) appears repeatedly, each following the simple subject-verb-predicate form. The resulting repetition, while grammatically correct, taxes the reader's patience. Compare the preceding version to this revision (which represents just one way the paragraph could be rewritten):

> Scientists have opened a whole new field of study following their recent decoding of the human genome. Armed with new ways of understanding human biological and behavioral functioning, researchers may someday sort out the extent to which we are shaped by our genes and by our environment. When geneticists can examine an individual's genetic past and future, they may also be able to alter these things, with the goal of improving and extending human life through early disease detection and the development of new treatments. However, such promise is not without its pitfalls: genetic research must be scrutinized from an ethical standpoint, and scientists and the public will have to decide the uses and the limits of this new technology.

Not only is the edited version of this paragraph more pleasant to read, it's also more concise and clear, as well as more coherent. Sentences with related content have been combined. Brief sentences have been converted to clauses or phrases and incorporated into the structure of other sentences to form more complex units of meaning.

Guard against strings of short, choppy sentences in your own writing. Learn strategies for sentence-level revision by learning how different sentence structures work. You can link related ideas with subordinating conjunctions (*because, since, while, although,* etc.), commas and coordinating conjunctions (*for, and, nor, but, or, yet, so*), and semicolons and coordinating adverbs (*however, thus, therefore,* etc.).

Editing for Correctness

On matters of sentence style, there is no "correct" approach, per se. Each writer will have a different idea about what sentence structures, sentence lengths, and word choices sound best and best convey meaning. Often, personal style and taste influence sentence construction. Grammar and punctuation, on the other hand, follow more widely accepted, objective standards. Of these we (and your instructors) can speak in terms of "correctness"—of agreed-upon conventions, or rules, that people working in academic, professional, and business environments adopt as a standard of communication. You can find the rules (for comma placement, say, or the use of "amount" versus "number" or "affect" versus "effect") in up-to-date writing handbooks. Review this list of common sentence-level errors, and eliminate such errors from your papers before submitting them.

The Final Draft

When you have worked on a paper for days (or weeks), writing and revising multiple drafts, you may have trouble knowing when you're finished. With respect to poetry, the Pulitzer Prize–winning poet Henry Taylor once remarked that a writer is done when revisions begin to move the project laterally, instead of vertically. We think the same distinction applies to academic

Common Sentence-Level Errors

ERRORS IN GRAMMAR

Sentence fragments—incomplete sentences missing a subject or predicate

Run-on sentences—two independent clauses joined together without the proper conjunctions (connecting words) or punctuation

Comma splices—two independent clauses joined with only a comma when they need stronger separation such as coordinating conjunctions, conjunctive adverbs, semicolons, or periods

Subject-verb agreement errors—the verb form doesn't match the plural or singular nature of the subject

Pronoun usage—pronoun reference errors, lack of clarity in pronoun reference, and errors of pronoun-antecedent agreement

ERRORS IN PUNCTUATION

Misplaced commas, missing commas, improper use of semicolons or colons, missing apostrophes, and the like

ERRORS IN SPELLING

Misspelled words

writing. Assuming you have revised at the sentence level for grammar and punctuation, when you get the impression that your changes *do not actively advance* the main point with new facts or arguments or illustrations or supporting quotations, you are probably done. Stop writing and prepare a clean draft. Set it aside for a day or two (if you have that luxury), and read it one last time to catch remaining sentence-level errors.

Most difficult will be deciding when the paper is done stylistically, especially for the papers you care most deeply about. With respect to style, one could revise endlessly—and many writers do because there is no one correct way (stylistically speaking) to write a sentence. As long as a sentence is grammatical, you can write it numerous ways. Still, if a given sentence is dull, you will want to improve it, for an excessively dull style will bore the reader and defeat the paper as surely as a flawed argument or a host of grammatical errors. But having devoted time to polishing your sentences (for instance, to eliminating strings of short, choppy sentences—see p. 255), you will at some point need to pronounce yourself finished. Eventually, the time you invest will have diminishing returns. When your changes make your work merely different, not better, stop.

Your instructor will (likely) return the paper with comments and suggestions. Read these carefully. If you or the instructor feels that a revision is appropriate, think through the options for recasting the paper. Instructors generally respond well when you go into a conference with an action plan.

At some point, instructor's comments or no, the paper will be done and graded. Read it through one last time, and learn from it. Once you have determined what you did well and what you could improve for the next effort, it is time to move on.

WRITING ASSIGNMENT: PROCESS

Choose either of the following writing assignments.

1. Write a paper following the process outlined in this chapter. As a guide, you may want to complete Exercises 6.1–7, which will serve as prompts. As you write, keep a log in which you record brief observations about each stage of the writing process. Share the log with your classmates and discuss the writing process with them.

2. In this chapter you have learned to approach writing as a task separated into stages that blend together and loop back on one another: data gathering, invention, drafting, revision, and editing. Write a one- or two-page statement in which you compare your writing process *prior* to taking a composition course to the process you've learned from this text and from your instructor. What are the salient differences? similarities? At the end of your statement, you may want to speculate on the ways you might eventually alter this process to better suit you.

7 Locating, Mining, and Citing Sources

■ SOURCE-BASED PAPERS

Summaries, critiques, and analyses are generally based on only one or two sources. Syntheses, by contrast (and by definition), are based on multiple sources. But whatever you call the final product, the quality of your paper will be directly related to your success in locating and using a sufficient quantity of relevant, significant, reliable, and up-to-date sources.

Research involves many of the skills we have been discussing in this book. It requires you to (1) locate and take notes on relevant sources; (2) organize your findings; (3) summarize, paraphrase, or quote these sources accurately and ethically; (4) critically evaluate them for their value and relevance to your subject; (5) synthesize information and ideas from several sources that best support your own critical viewpoint; and (6) analyze subjects for meaning and significance.

The model argument synthesis in Chapter 4, "Keeping Volunteering Voluntary" (pp. 156–65), is an example of a research paper that fulfills these requirements.

Where Do We Find Written Research?

Here are just a few types of writing that involve research:

ACADEMIC WRITING

- **Research papers.** Research an issue and write a paper incorporating the results of that research.
- **Literature reviews.** Research and review relevant studies and approaches to a particular science or social-science topic.
- **Experimental reports.** Research previous studies in order to refine—or show need for—your current approach; conduct primary research.
- **Case studies.** Conduct both primary and secondary research.
- **Position papers.** Research approaches to an issue in order to formulate your own approach.

WORKPLACE WRITING

- **Reports** in business, science, engineering, social services, medicine

---

- **Market analyses**
- **Business plans**
- **Environmental impact reports**
- **Legal research:** memorandum of points and authorities

Writing the Research Paper

Here is an overview of the main steps involved in writing research papers. Keep in mind that, as with other writing projects, writing such papers is a recursive process. For instance, you will gather data at various stages of your writing, as the list below illustrates.

DEVELOPING THE RESEARCH QUESTION

- *Find a subject.* Decide what subject you are going to research and write about.
- *Develop a research question.* Formulate an important question that you would like to answer through your research.

LOCATING SOURCES

- *Conduct preliminary research.* Consult knowledgeable people, general and specialized encyclopedias, overviews and bibliographies in recent books, the *Bibliographic Index*, and subject heading guides.
- *Refine your research question.* Based on your preliminary research, brainstorm about your topic and ways to answer your research question. Sharpen your focus, refining your question and planning the sources you'll need to consult.
- *Conduct focused research.* Consult books, electronic databases, general and specialized periodicals, biographical indexes, general and specialized dictionaries, government publications, and other appropriate sources. Conduct interviews and surveys, as necessary.

MINING SOURCES

- *Develop a working thesis.* Based on your initial research, formulate a working thesis that attempts to respond to your research question.
- *Develop a working bibliography.* Keep track of your sources, either on paper or electronically, including both bibliographic information and key points about each source. Make this bibliography easy to sort and rearrange.
- *Evaluate sources.* Attempt to determine the veracity and reliability of your sources; use your critical reading skills; check *Book Review Digest*; look up biographies of authors.

(continues)

- *Take notes from sources.* Paraphrase and summarize important information and ideas from your sources. Copy down important quotations. Note page numbers from sources of this quoted and summarized material.
- *Develop a working outline and arrange your notes according to your outline.*

DRAFTING; CITING SOURCES

- *Write your draft.* Write the preliminary draft of your paper, working from your notes, according to your outline.
- *Avoid plagiarism.* Take care to cite all quoted, paraphrased, and summarized source material, making sure that your own wording and sentence structure differ from those of your sources.
- *Cite sources.* Use in-text citations and a Works Cited or References list, according to the conventions of the discipline (e.g., MLA, APA, CSE).

REVISING (GLOBAL AND LOCAL CHANGES)

- *Revise your draft.* Consider global, local, surface revisions. Check that your thesis still fits with your paper's focus. Review topic sentences and paragraph development and logic. Use transitional words and phrases to ensure coherence. Make sure that the research paper reads smoothly and clearly from beginning to end.

EDITING (SURFACE CHANGES)

- *Edit your draft.* Check for style, combining short, choppy sentences and ensuring variety in your sentence structures. Check for grammatical correctness, punctuation, and spelling.

■ THE RESEARCH QUESTION

Research handbooks generally advise students to narrow their subjects as much as possible, as we discussed in Chapter 6. A ten-page paper on the modern feminist movement would be unmanageable. You would have to do an enormous quantity of research (a preliminary computer search of this subject would yield several thousand items), and you couldn't hope to produce anything other than a superficial treatment of such a broad subject. You could, however, write a paper on the contemporary feminist response to a particular social issue, or the relative power of current feminist political organizations. It's difficult to say, however, how narrow is narrow enough. (A literary critic once produced a 20-page article analyzing the first paragraph of Henry James's *The Ambassadors*.)

Perhaps more helpful as a guideline on focusing your research is to seek to answer a particular question, a *research question*. For example, how did the Clinton administration respond to criticisms of bilingual education? To what extent is America perceived by social critics to be in decline? What factors led to the WorldCom collapse? How has the debate over genetic engineering evolved during the past decade? To what extent do contemporary cigarette ads perpetuate sexist attitudes? Or how do contemporary cigarette ads differ in message and tone from cigarette ads in the 1950s? Focusing on questions such as these and approaching your research as a way of answering such questions is probably the best way to narrow your subject and ensure focus in your paper. The essential answer to this research question eventually becomes your *thesis,* which we discussed in Chapter 6; in the paper, you present evidence that systematically supports your thesis.

Narrowing the Subject via Research

If you need help narrowing a broad subject, try one or more of the following:

- Search by subject in an electronic database to see how the subject breaks down into components.
- Search the subject heading in an electronic periodical catalog, such as *InfoTrac*®, or in a print catalog such as the *Readers' Guide to Periodical Literature.*
- Search the *Library of Congress Subject Headings* catalog (see Subject-Heading Guides, page 266 for details).

Exercise 7.1

Constructing Research Questions

Moving from a broad topic or idea to formulation of precise research questions can be challenging. Practice this skill by working with small groups of your classmates to construct research questions about the following topics (or come up with some topics of your own). Write at least one research question for each topic listed, then discuss these topics and questions with the other groups in class.

Racial or gender stereotypes in television shows

Drug addiction in the U.S. adult population

Global environmental policies

Employment trends in high-technology industries

U.S. energy policy

■ LOCATING SOURCES ■

Once you have a research question, you want to see what references are available. You'll begin with what we call "preliminary research," in which you familiarize yourself quickly with the basic issues and generate a preliminary list of sources. This effort will help you refine your research question and conduct efficient research once you move into the stage that we call "focused research."

■ **Types of Research Data** *(see also Chapter 6, pp. 225–26)*

PRIMARY SOURCES

- Data gathered using research methods appropriate to a particular field

    sciences: experiments, observations

    social sciences: experiments, surveys, interviews

    humanities: diaries, letters, and other unpublished documents; close reading/observation and interpretation

SECONDARY SOURCES

- Information and ideas collected or generated by others who have performed their own primary and/or secondary research

    library research: books, periodicals, etc.

    online research

■ PRELIMINARY RESEARCH

You can go about finding preliminary sources in many ways; some of the more effective ones are listed in the box on the next page. We'll consider a few of these suggestions in more detail.

Consulting Knowledgeable People

When you think of research, you may immediately think of libraries and print material. But don't neglect a key reference—other people. Your *instructor* probably can suggest fruitful areas of research and some useful sources. Try to see your instructor during office hours, however, rather than immediately before or after class, so that you'll have enough time for a productive discussion.

Once you get to the library, ask a *reference librarian* which reference sources (e.g., bibliographies, specialized encyclopedias, periodical indexes, statistical almanacs) you need for your particular area of research. Librarians won't do

Locating Preliminary Sources

- Ask your instructor to recommend sources on the subject.
- Scan the "Suggestions for Further Reading" sections of your textbooks. Ask your college librarian for useful reference tools in your subject area.
- Read an encyclopedia article on the subject and use the bibliography following the article to identify other sources.
- Read the introduction to a recent book on the subject and review that book's bibliography to identify more sources.
- Consult the annual *Bibliographic Index* (see page 266 for details).
- Use an Internet search engine to explore your topic. Type in different keyword or search term combinations and browse the sites you find for ideas and references to sources you can look up later (see the box on pages 268–69 for details).

your research for you, but they'll be glad to show you how to research efficiently and systematically.

You can also obtain vital primary information from people when you interview them, ask them to fill out questionnaires or surveys, or have them participate in experiments. We'll cover this aspect of research in more detail below.

Encyclopedias

Reading an encyclopedia entry about your subject will give you a basic understanding of the most significant facts and issues. Whether the subject is American politics or the mechanics of genetic engineering, the encyclopedia article—written by a specialist in the field—offers a broad overview that may serve as a launching point to more specialized research in a particular area. The article may illuminate areas or raise questions that you feel motivated to pursue further. Equally important, the encyclopedia article frequently concludes with an *annotated bibliography* describing important books and articles on the subject.

Encyclopedias have certain limitations, however. First, most professors don't accept encyclopedia articles as legitimate sources for academic papers. You should use encyclopedias primarily to familiarize yourself with (and to select a particular aspect of) the subject area and as a springboard for further research. Also, because new editions of encyclopedias appear only once every five or ten years, the information they contain—including bibliographies—may not be current. Current editions of the *Encyclopaedia Britannica* and the *Encyclopedia Americana*, for instance, may not include information about the most recent developments in biotechnology. Some encyclopedias are now also available online—*Britannica Online*, for example—and this may mean, but not guarantee, that information is up-to-date.

Some of the most useful general encyclopedias include the following:

Academic American Encyclopedia

Encyclopedia Americana

New Encyclopaedia Britannica (or *Britannica Online*)

Wikipedia (online)*

Keep in mind that the library also contains a variety of more *specialized encyclopedias*. These encyclopedias restrict themselves to a particular disciplinary area, such as chemistry, law, or film, and are considerably more detailed in their treatment of a subject than are general encyclopedias. Here are examples of specialized encyclopedias:

Social Sciences

Encyclopedia of Education

Encyclopedia of Psychology

West's Encyclopedia of American Law

International Encyclopedia of the Social & Behavioral Sciences

Humanities

Encyclopedia of American History

Dictionary of Art

Encyclopedia of Religion and Ethics

Film Encyclopedia

The New Grove Encyclopedia of Music

Science and Technology

Encyclopedia of Life Sciences

Encyclopedia of Electronics

Encyclopedia of Artificial Intelligence

Encyclopedia of Physics

McGraw-Hill Encyclopedia of Environmental Science

Van Nostrand's Scientific Encyclopedia

While users may find numerous Wikipedia articles informative and useful (particularly in the sciences), there are also—as the site itself admits—"many articles . . . which are amateurish, unauthoritative, and even incorrect, making it difficult for a reader unfamiliar with the subject matter to know which articles are correct and which are not."

Business

Encyclopedia of Banking and Finance
International Encyclopedia of Economics

Exploring Specialized Encyclopedias

Go to the Reference section of your campus library and locate several specialized encyclopedias within your major or area of interest. Look through the encyclopedias, noting their organization, and read entries on topics that interest you. Jot down some notes describing the kinds of information you find. You might also use this opportunity to look around at the other materials available in the Reference section of the library, including the *Bibliographic Index* and the *Book Review Digest*.

Overviews and Bibliographies in Recent Books

If your professor or a bibliographic source directs you to an important recent book on your subject, skim the introductory (and possibly the concluding) material to the book, along with the table of contents, for an overview of key issues. Look also for a bibliography, Works Cited, and/or References list. These lists are extremely valuable resources for locating material for research. For example, Robert Dallek's 2003 book *An Unfinished Life: John Fitzgerald Kennedy, 1917–1963* includes a seven-page bibliography of reference sources on President Kennedy's life and times.

Keep in mind that authors are not necessarily objective about their subjects, and some have particularly biased viewpoints that you may unwittingly carry over to your paper, treating them as objective truth.* However, you may still be able to get some useful information out of such sources. Alert yourself to authorial biases by looking up the reviews of your book in the *Book Review Digest* (described on the next page). Additionally, look up biographical information on the author (see Biographical Indexes, p. 278), whose previous writings or professional associations may suggest a predictable set of attitudes on the subject of your book.

Bias is not necessarily bad. Authors, like all other people, have certain preferences and predilections that influence the way they view the world and the kinds of arguments they make. As long as they inform you of their biases, or as long as you are aware of them and take them into account, you can still use these sources judiciously. (You might gather valuable information from a book about the Watergate scandal, even if it were written by former president Richard Nixon or one of his top aides, as long as you make proper allowance for their understandable biases.) Bias becomes a potential problem only when it masquerades as objective truth or is accepted as such by the reader. For suggestions on identifying and assessing authorial bias, see the material in Chapter 2 on persuasive writing (pp. 55–65) and evaluating assumptions (pp. 66–68).

Bibliographic Index

The *Bibliographic Index* is a series of annual volumes that enables you to locate bibliographies on a particular subject. The bibliographies referred to in
the Index generally appear at the end of book chapters or periodical articles,
or they may themselves be book or pamphlet length. Browsing through the
Bibliographic Index in a general subject area may give you ideas for further research in particular aspects of the subject, along with particular references.

Subject-Heading Guides

Seeing how a general subject (e.g., education) is broken down in other
sources also could stimulate research in a particular area (e.g., bilingual primary education in California). In the subsequent sources, general subjects
are analyzed into secondary subject headings, as chapter titles in a book's
table of contents represent subcomponents of a general subject (indicated in
the book title). To locate such sets of secondary subject headings, consult:

An electronic database

An electronic or print periodical catalog (e.g., *InfoTrac, Readers' Guide,*
Social Science Index)

The Library of Congress Subject Headings catalog

The *Propaedia* volume of the *Encyclopaedia Britannica* (2007)

Once you've used these kinds of tools to narrow your scope to a particular
subject and research question (or set of research questions), you're ready to
undertake more focused research.

■ FOCUSED RESEARCH

Your objective now is to learn as much as you can about your particular subject. Only in this way will you be qualified to make an informed response to
your research question. This means you'll have to become something of an
expert on the subject—or, if that's not possible, given time constraints, you
can at least become someone whose critical viewpoint is based solidly on the
available evidence. In the following pages we'll suggest how to find sources
for this kind of focused research. In most cases, your research will be
secondary in nature, based on (1) books; (2) electronic databases; (3) articles;
and (4) specialized reference sources. In certain cases, you may gather your
own *primary* research, using (5) interviews, surveys, structured observation,
diaries, letters, and other unpublished sources, or content/textual analysis
of literary or other artistic texts.

Electronic Databases

Much of the information that is available in print—and a good deal that is
not—is also available in electronic form. Almost certainly, your library card

catalog has been computerized, allowing you to conduct searches much faster and more easily than in the past. Increasingly, researchers access magazine, newspaper, and journal articles and reports, abstracts, and other forms of information through *online databases* (many of them on the Internet) and through databases on *CD-ROMs*. One great advantage of using databases (as opposed to print indexes) is that you can search several years' worth of different periodicals at the same time.

Online databases—that is, those that originate outside your computer—are available through international, national, or local (e.g., campus) networks. The largest such database is DIALOG, which provides access to more than 300 million records in more than 400 databases, ranging from sociology to business to chemical engineering. Another large database is LEXIS-NEXIS (like DIALOG, available only through online subscription). *LEXIS-NEXIS Academic* provides access to numerous legal, medical, business, and news sources. In addition to being efficient and comprehensive, online databases are generally far more up-to-date than print sources. If you have an Internet connection from your own computer, you can access many of these databases—including those available through commercial online services such as CompuServe and America Online—without leaving your room.

Access to online databases often requires an account and a password, which you may be able to obtain by virtue of your student status. In some cases, you will have to pay a fee to the local provider of the database, based on how long you are online. But many databases will be available to you free of charge. For example, your library's computers may offer access to magazine and newspaper databases, such as *Expanded Academic ASAP*, *InfoTrac*, *EbscoHost*, and *National Newspaper Index*, as well as to the Internet itself.

The *World Wide Web* offers graphics, multimedia, and hyperlinks to related material in numerous sources. To access these sources, you can either browse (i.e., follow your choice of paths or links wherever they lead) or type in a site's address.

To search for Web information on a particular topic, try using one of the more popular search engines:

Google: http://www.google.com

Yahoo: http://www.yahoo.com

Alta Vista: http://altavista.com

WebCrawler: http://webcrawler.com

SearchCom: http://www.search.com

Lycos: http://www.lycos.com

Review the "Help" and "Advanced Search" sections of search engines to achieve the best results. See the box on pages 268–69 for some general tips on searching online.

Many databases and periodical indexes are available online. Among them: the *Readers' Guide to Periodical Literature* [index only], *The New York Times* [available full-text online], *Film Index International* [index only], *PAIS International* [index only], and *America: History and Life* [index only], as are other standard reference sources, such as *Statistical Abstract of the U.S* [full text], *The Encyclopaedia Britannica* [full text—called *Britannica Online*], *Bibliography of Native North Americans* [index only], *Environment Reporter* [full text], and *National Criminal Justice Reference Service* [index with some links to full text]. Of particular interest is *InfoTrac*, which (if you are in a participating library or have a password) provides access to more than 1,000 general interest, business, government, and technological periodicals. In recent years, CD-ROM (compact disk-read only memory) indexes and databases have given way to online versions.

Keep in mind, however, that while electronic sources make it far easier to access information than do their print counterparts, they often do not go back more than 15 years. For earlier information (e.g., the original reactions to the Milgram experiments of the 1960s), therefore, you would have to rely on print indexes.

Using Keywords and Boolean Logic to Refine Online Searches

You will find more—and more relevant—sources on Internet search engines and library databases if you carefully plan your search strategies. *Note:* Some search engines and online databases have their own systems for searching, so review the "Help" section of each search engine, and use "Advanced Search" options where available. The following tips are general guidelines, and their applicability in different search engines may vary somewhat.

1. *Identify multiple keywords:*

   Write down your topic and/or your research question, then brainstorm synonyms and related terms for the words in that topic/question.

   Sample topic: Political activism on college campuses

   Sample research question: What kinds of political activism are college students involved in today?

   Keywords: Political activism; college students

   Synonyms and related terms: politics; voting; political organizations; protests; political issues; universities; colleges; campus politics

2. *Conduct searches using different combinations of synonyms and related terms.*

3. *Find new terms in the sources you locate and search with these.*

4. *Use quotation marks around terms you want linked: "political activism"*

5. *Use "Boolean operators" to link keywords:*

The words AND, OR, and NOT are used in "Boolean logic" to combine search terms and get more precise results than using keywords alone.

AND: Connecting keywords with AND narrows a search by retrieving only sources that contain *both* keywords:

political activism AND college students

OR: Connecting keywords with OR broadens a search by retrieving all sources that contain at least one of the search terms. This operator is useful when you have a topic/keyword for which there are a number of synonyms. Linking synonyms with OR will lead you to the widest array of sources:

political activism OR protests OR political organizing OR voting OR campus politics

college OR university OR campus OR students

AND and OR: You can use these terms in combination, by putting the OR phrase in parentheses:

(political activism OR protests) AND (college OR university)

NOT: Connecting keywords with NOT (or, in some cases, AND NOT) narrows a search by excluding certain terms. If you want to focus upon a very specific topic, NOT can be used to limit what the search engine retrieves; however, this operator should be used carefully as it can cause you to miss sources that may actually be relevant:

college students NOT high school

political activism NOT voting

Exercise 7.3

Exploring Electronic Sources

Use your library's Internet connection (or your home computer if you have Internet access) to access a search engine or academic/professional database. Select a topic/research question of interest to you, review the box Using Keywords and Boolean Logic to Refine Online Searches (pp. 268–69) and try different combinations of keywords and Boolean operators to see what sources you can find for your topic. Jot down notes describing the kinds of sources you find and which terms seem to yield the best results. Effective searching on the Internet takes practice; you'll save time when conducting research if you have a good sense of how to use these search strategies.

The Benefits and Pitfalls of the World Wide Web

In the past few years, the Web has become not just a research tool, but a cultural phenomenon. The pop artist Andy Warhol once said that in the future everyone would be famous for 15 minutes. He might have added that everyone would also have a personal Web site. People use the Web not just to look up information, but also to shop, to make contact with long-lost friends and relatives, to grind their personal or corporate axes, and to advertise themselves and their accomplishments.

The Web makes it possible for people sitting at home, work, or school to gain access to the resources of large libraries and explore corporate and government databases. In her informative book *The Research Paper and the World Wide Web*, Dawn Rodrigues quotes Bruce Dobler and Harry Bloomberg on the essential role of the Web in modern research:

> It isn't a matter anymore of using computer searches to locate existing documents buried in some far-off library or archive. The Web is providing documents and resources that simply would be too expensive to publish on paper or CD-ROM.
>
> Right now—and not in some distant future—doing research without looking for resources on the Internet is, in most cases, not really looking hard enough. . . . A thorough researcher cannot totally avoid the Internet and the Web.*

Indeed, Web sites are increasingly showing up as sources in both student and professional papers. But like any other rapidly growing and highly visible cultural phenomenon, the Web has created its own backlash. First, as anyone who has tried it knows, for many subjects, systematic research on the Web is rarely possible. For all the information that is on the Internet, a great deal more is not and never will be converted to digital format. One library director has estimated that only about 4,000 of 150,000 published scholarly journals are available online, and many of these provide only partial texts of relatively recent articles in the paper editions. *The New York Times* is available on the Web, but the online edition includes only a fraction of the content of the print edition, and online versions of the articles generally are abridged and often must be paid for. If you are researching the rise of McCarthyism in America during the early 1950s or trying to determine who else, since Stanley Milgram, has conducted psychological experiments on obedience, you are unlikely to find much useful information for your purpose on the Web.

Moreover, locating what *is* available is not always easy, since there's no standardized method—like the Library of Congress subheading and call number system—of cataloging and cross-referencing online information. The tens of thousands of Web sites and millions of Web pages, together with

---

Dawn Rodrigues, The Research Paper and the World Wide Web *(Upper Saddle River, NJ: Prentice-Hall, 1997).*

the relative crudity of search engines such as Yahoo, Google, AltaVista, and WebCrawler, have made navigating an ever-expanding cyberspace an often daunting and frustrating procedure.

Second, it is not a given that people who do research on the Web will produce better papers as a result. David Rothenberg, a professor of philosophy at New Jersey Institute of Technology, believes that "his students' papers had declined in quality since they began using the Web for research."* Neil Gabler, a cultural critic, writes:

> The Internet is such a huge receptacle of rumor, half-truth, misinformation and disinformation that the very idea of objective truth perishes in the avalanche. All you need to create a "fact" in the web world is a bulletin board or chat room. Gullible cybernauts do the rest.**

Another critic is even blunter: "Much of what purports to be serious information is simply junk—neither current, objective, nor trustworthy. It may be impressive to the uninitiated, but it is clearly not of great use to scholars."*** The accuracy and reliability of articles on the popular—and vast—online encyclopedia *Wikipedia* has been called into question because anyone with an Internet connection can write or edit most articles.

Of course, print sources are not necessarily objective or reliable either, and in Chapter 2, Critical Reading and Critique, we discussed some criteria by which readers may evaluate the quality and reliability of information and ideas in *any* source (pages 54–65). Web sources, however—particularly self-published Web pages—present a special problem. In most cases, material destined for print has to go through one or more editors and fact checkers before being published, since most authors don't have the resources to publish and distribute their own writing. But anyone with a computer and a modem can "publish" on the Web; furthermore, those with a good Web authoring program and graphics software can create sites that, outwardly at least, look just as professional and authoritative as those of the top academic, government, and business sites. These personal sites will appear in search-engine listings—generated through keyword matches rather than through independent assessments of quality or relevance—and uncritical researchers who use their information as a factual basis for the claims they make in their papers do so at their peril.

The Internet has also led to increased problems with plagiarism. Many college professors complain these days about receiving work copied directly from Web sites. Such copying runs the gamut from inadvertent plagiarism of passages copied and pasted off the Web into notes and then transferred

---

*Steven R. Knowlton, "Students Lost in Cyberspace," Chronicle of Higher Education 2 Nov. 1997: 21.
**Neil Gabler, "Why Let Truth Get in the Way of a Good Story?" Los Angeles Times "Opinion," 26 Oct. 1997: 1.
***William Miller, "Troubling Myths About On-Line Information," Chronicle of Higher Education 1 Aug. 1997: A44.

verbatim to papers, to intentional theft of others' work, pasted together into a document and claimed as the student's own. In one recent case, an instructor reports that she received a student paper characterized by a more professional writing style than usual for that student. The instructor typed a few keywords from the paper into an Internet search engine, and one of the first sources retrieved turned out to be a professional journal article from which the student had copied whole passages and pasted them together to create a "report." This student received an "F" in the course and was referred to a university disciplinary committee for further action.

The Internet sometimes proves a very tempting source from which to lift materials. But not only is such activity ethically wrong, it is also likely to result in serious punishment, such as permanent notations on your academic transcript or expulsion from school. One thing all students should know is that while cheating is now made easier by the Internet, the converse is also true: Instructors can often track down the sources for material plagiarized from the Internet just as easily as the student found them in the first place. (Easier, in fact, because now instructors can scan papers into software or Internet programs that will search the Web for matching text.) For more on plagiarism, see the section devoted to this subject in Chapter 1, pages 48–50.

We certainly don't mean to discourage Web research. Thousands of excellent sites—and numerous invaluable databases—exist in cyberspace. The reference department of most college and university libraries will provide lists of such sites, and the most useful sites also are listed in the research sections of many handbooks. Most people locate Web sites, however, by using search engines and by "surfing" the hyperlinks. And for Web sources, more than print sources, the warning *caveat emptor*—let the buyer beware—applies.

Evaluating Web Sources

In their useful site "Evaluating Web Resources" <www.widener.edu/Tools_Resources/Libraries/Wolfgram_Memorial_Library/Evaluate_Web_Pages/659/>, reference librarians Jan Alexander and Marsha Tate offer important guidelines for assessing Web sources. First, they point out, it's important to determine what *type* of Web page you are dealing with. Web pages generally fall into one of six types, each with a different purpose: (1) entertainment, (2) business/marketing, (3) reference/information, (4) news, (5) advocacy of a particular point of view or program, (6) personal page. The purpose of the page—informing, selling, persuading, entertaining—has a direct bearing on the objectivity and reliability of the information presented.

Second, when evaluating a Web page, one should apply the same general criteria as are applied to print sources: (1) accuracy, (2) authority, (3) objectivity, (4) currency, (5) coverage. As we've noted, when assessing the *accuracy* of a Web page, it's important to consider the likelihood that its information has been checked by anyone other than the author. When assessing the *authority* of the page, one considers the author's qualifications to write on the subject and the reputability of the publisher. In many cases on the Web, it's difficult to determine not just the qualifications, but the very identity of the author. When assessing the *objectivity* of a Web page, one considers the bias on the part of the author or authors and the extent to which they are trying to sway their reader's opinion. Many Web pages passing themselves off as informational are in fact little more than "infomercials." When assessing the *currency* of a Web page, one asks whether the content is up-to-date and whether the publication date is clearly labeled. Many Web pages lack clearly indicated dates. And even if a date is provided, it may be difficult to tell whether the date indicates when the page was written, when it was placed on the Web, or when it was last revised. Finally, when assessing the *coverage* of a Web page, one considers which topics are included (and not included) in the work and whether the topics are covered in depth. Depth of coverage has generally not been a hallmark of Web information.

Other pitfalls of Web sites: Reliable sites may include links to other sites that are inaccurate or outdated, so users cannot rely on the link as a substitute for evaluating the five criteria just outlined. Web pages also are notoriously unstable, frequently changing or even disappearing without notice.

Perhaps most serious, the ease with which it's possible to surf the Net can encourage intellectual laziness and make researchers too dependent on Web resources. Professors are increasingly seeing papers largely or even entirely based on information in Web sites. While Web sources are indeed an important new source of otherwise unavailable information, there's usually no substitute for library or primary research, such as interviews or field study. The vast majority of printed material in even a small college library—much of it essential to informed research—does not appear on the Web, nor is it likely to in the immediate future. Much of the material you will research in the next few years remains bound within covers. You may well learn of its existence in electronic databases, but at some point you'll have to walk over to a library shelf, pull out a book, and turn printed pages.

Above all, remember that you must apply the critical reading skills you've been practicing throughout this textbook to all your sources—no matter what types they are or where you found them (see Chapter 2 for coverage of critical reading).

Exercise 7.4

Practice Evaluating Web Sources

To practice applying the evaluation criteria discussed in the section above on Web sources, go to an Internet search engine and look for sources addressing a topic of interest to you (perhaps following completion of Exercise 7.3, page 269). Try to locate one source representing each of the six types of Web pages (entertainment, business/marketing, reference/information, news, advocacy, and personal). Print out the main page of each of these sources and bring the copies to class. In small groups of your classmates look over the sites each student found and make notes on each example's (1) accuracy, (2) authority, (3) objectivity, (4) currency, and (5) coverage.

Periodicals: General

Because many more periodical articles than books are published every year, you are likely (depending on the subject) to find more information in periodicals than in books. By general periodicals, we mean the magazines and newspapers that are generally found on newsstands, such as the *New York Times, Newsweek,* or *The New Yorker*. By their nature, general periodical articles tend to be more current than books. The best way, for example, to find out about the federal government's current policy on Social Security reform is to look for articles in periodicals and newspapers. However, periodical articles may have less critical distance than books, and like books, they may become dated, to be superseded by more recent articles. Let's first look at the use of magazines from a research perspective.

Magazines

General periodicals (such as *Time, The New Republic,* and *The Nation*) are intended for nonspecialists. Their articles, which tend to be highly readable, may be written by staff writers, freelancers, or specialists. But usually they do not provide citations or other indications of sources, and so are of limited usefulness for scholarly research.

The most well-known general index to this kind of material is the *Readers' Guide to Periodical Literature,* an index of articles that have appeared in several hundred general-interest magazines and a few more specialized magazines such as *Business Week* and *Science Digest*. Articles in the *Readers' Guide* are indexed by author, title, and subject.

Another general reference for articles is the *Essay and General Literature Index,* which indexes essays (sometimes called book articles) contained in anthologies.

Increasingly, texts and abstracts of articles are available on online databases. These texts may be downloaded to your computer or emailed to you.

Newspapers

News stories, feature stories, and editorials (even letters to the editor) may be important sources of information. Your library certainly will have the *New York Times* index, and it may have indexes to other important newspapers, such as the *Washington Post,* the *Los Angeles Times,* the *Chicago Tribune,* the *Wall Street Journal,* and the *Christian Science Monitor*. Newspaper holdings will be on microfilm, CD-ROM, or online. You will need a micro-printer/viewer to get hard copies if you are using microfilm.

Note: Because of its method of cross-referencing, the *New York Times* index may at first be confusing. Suppose that you want to find stories on bilingual education during a given year. When you locate the "Bilingual education" entry, you won't find citations but rather a *"See also* Education" reference that directs you to seven dates (August 14, 15, and 17; September 11; October 20, 29, and 30) under the heading of "Education." Under this major heading, references to stories on education are arranged in chronological order from January to December. When you look up the dates you were directed to, you'll see brief descriptions of these stories on bilingual education.

Periodicals: Specialized

Many professors will expect at least some of your research to be based on articles in specialized periodicals or "scholarly journals." So instead of (or in addition to) relying on an article from *Psychology Today* (which would be considered a general periodical even though its subject is somewhat specialized) for an account of the effects of crack cocaine on mental functioning, you might also rely on an article from the *Journal of Abnormal Psychology*. If you are writing a paper on the satirist Jonathan Swift, in addition to a recent reference that may have appeared in the *New Yorker*, you may need to locate a relevant article in *Eighteenth-Century Studies*. Articles in such journals normally are written by specialists and professionals in the field, rather than by staff writers or freelancers, and the authors will assume that their readers already understand the basic facts and issues concerning the subject. Other characteristics of scholarly journals: they tend to be heavily researched, as indicated by numerous footnotes/endnotes and references; they are generally published by university presses; most of the authors represented are university professors; the articles, which have a serious, formal, and scholarly tone, are generally peer reviewed by other scholars in the field.

To find articles in specialized periodicals, you'll use specialized indexes—that is, indexes for particular disciplines. You also may find it helpful to refer to *abstracts*. Like specialized indexes, abstracts list articles published in a particular discipline over a given period, but they also provide summaries of the articles listed. Abstracts tend to be more selective than indexes, since they consume more space (and involve considerably more work to compile); but, because they also describe the contents of the articles covered, they can save you a lot of time in determining which articles you should read and which ones you can safely skip. Don't treat abstracts alone as sources for research; if you find useful material in an abstract, you need to locate the article to which it applies and use that as your source of information.

Here are some of the more commonly used specialized periodical indexes and abstracts in the various disciplines.

Note: The format (print, online, or CD-ROM) of these databases will vary by library. Online databases (as opposed to their print counterparts) are enhanced by more flexible search capability and, in some cases, by links to the full text.

Social Science

Anthropological Index

Education Index

Index to Legal Periodicals

Psychological Abstracts (online as *PsycInfo)*
Public Affairs Information Service (PAIS)
Social Science Index
Sociological Abstracts
Women's Studies Abstracts
ERIC (Educational Resources Information Center)
Social SciSearch
Worldwide Political Science Abstracts

Humanities

America: History and Life
Art Index
Essay and General Literature Index
Film/Literature Index
Historical Abstracts
Humanities Index
International Index of Film Periodicals
MLA International Bibliography of Books and Articles on Modern Languages and Literature
Music Index
Religion Index
Year's Work in English Studies
Arts and Humanities Citation Index
MLA Bibliography
Philosophers' Index
Historical Abstracts

Science and Technology Indexes

Applied Science and Technology Index
Biological Abstracts
Chemical Abstracts
Engineering Index
General Science Index
Index to Scientific and Technical Proceedings (ceased publication in 1999)

Science and Technology

Aerospace & High Technology Database
Agricola (agriculture)
Biosis Previews (biology, botany)

Chemical Abstracts (chemistry)

Compendex (engineering)

Environment Abstracts

INSPEC (engineering)

MathSciNetPubMed (medical)

ScienceCitation Index

SciSearch

Business Indexes

Business Index

Business Periodicals Index

Economic Titles/Abstracts

Wall Street Journal *Index*

Business Databases

ABI/INFORM (index with access to some full text)

EconLit (index only)

STAT-USA (full text)

Standard & Poor's News (full text)

Law Databases

LEXIS-NEXIS (full text)

Westlaw (full text)

Exercise 7.5

Exploring Specialized Periodicals

Visit your campus library and locate the specialized periodical indexes for your major or area of interest (ask a reference librarian to help you). Note the call numbers for specialized periodicals (also called academic journals) in your field, and visit the periodical room or section of the library, where recent editions of academic journals are usually housed. Locate the call numbers you've noted, and spend some time looking through the specialized periodicals in your field. The articles you find in these journals represent some of the most recent scholarship in your field—the kind of scholarship many of your professors are busy conducting. Write half a page or so describing some of the articles you find interesting, and why.

Books

Books are useful in providing both breadth and depth of coverage of a subject. Because they generally are published at least a year or two after the events treated, they also tend to provide the critical distance that is sometimes missing from articles. Conversely, this delay in coverage also means that the information you find in books will not be as current as information you find in journals. And, of course, books also may be shallow, inaccurate, outdated, or hopelessly biased; for help in making such determinations, see *Book Review Digest*, discussed below. You can locate relevant books through the electronic or card catalog. When using this catalog, you may search in four ways: (1) by *author*, (2) by *title*, (3) by *subject*, and (4) by *keyword*. Entries include the call number, publication information, and frequently, a summary of the book's contents. Larger libraries use the Library of Congress cataloging system for call numbers (e.g., E111/C6); smaller ones use the Dewey Decimal System (e.g., 970.015/C726).

Book Review Digest

Perhaps the best way to determine the reliability and credibility of a book you may want to use is to look it up in the *Book Review Digest* (also available online and issued monthly and cumulated annually). These volumes list (alphabetically by author) the most significant books published during the year, supply a brief description of each, and most important, provide excerpts from (and references to) reviews. If a book receives bad reviews, you don't necessarily have to avoid it (the book still may have something useful to offer, and the review itself may be unreliable). But you should take any negative reaction into account when using that book as a source.

Biographical Indexes

To look up information on particular people, you can use not only encyclopedias but an array of biographical sources. You can also use these biographical sources to alert yourself to potential biases on the part of your source authors, as such biases may be revealed by other work these authors have done and details of their backgrounds. A brief selection of biographical indexes follows.

Living Persons

Contemporary Authors: A Biographical Guide to Current Authors and Their Works

Current Biography

International Who's Who

Who's Who in America

Persons No Longer Living

Dictionary of American Biography

Dictionary of National Biography (Great Britain)

Dictionary of Scientific Biography

Who Was Who

Persons Living or Dead

Biography Almanac
McGraw-Hill Encyclopedia of World Biography
Webster's Biographical Dictionary

Dictionaries

Use dictionaries to look up the meaning of general or specialized terms. Here are some of the most useful dictionaries:

General

Oxford English Dictionary
Webster's New Collegiate Dictionary
Webster's Third New International Dictionary of the English Language

Social Sciences

Black's Law Dictionary
Dictionary of the Social Sciences
McGraw-Hill Dictionary of Modern Economics

Humanities

Dictionary of American History
Dictionary of Films
Dictionary of Philosophy
Harvard Dictionary of Music
McGraw-Hill Dictionary of Art

Science and Technology

Computer Dictionary and Handbook
Condensed Chemical Dictionary
Dictionary of Biology
Dorland's Medical Dictionary

Business

Dictionary of Advertising Terms
Dictionary of Business and Economics
Mathematical Dictionary for Economics and Business Administration
McGraw-Hill Dictionary of Modern Economics: A Handbook of Terms and Organizations

Other Sources/Government Publications

Besides those already listed, you have many other options and potential sources for research. For statistical and other basic reference information on a subject, consult a *handbook* (such as *Statistical Abstracts of the United States*). For current information on a subject as of a given year, consult an *almanac* (such as *World Almanac*). For annual updates of information, consult a *yearbook* (such as *The Statesman's Yearbook*). For maps and other geographic information, consult an *atlas* (such as *New York Times Atlas of the World*). Often, simply browsing through the reference shelves for data on your general subject—such as biography, public affairs, psychology—will reveal valuable sources of information. And of course, much reference information is available on government sites on the Web.

In addition to all their other holdings, many libraries keep pamphlets in a *vertical file* (i.e., a file cabinet). For example, a pamphlet on global warming might be found in the vertical file rather than in the library stacks. Such material is accessible through the *Vertical File Index* (a monthly subject-and-title index to pamphlet material).

Finally, note that the U.S. government regularly publishes large quantities of useful information. Some indexes to government publications include the following:

American Statistics Index
Congressional Information Service

Interviews and Surveys

Depending on the subject of your paper, some or all of your research may be conducted outside the library. In conducting such primary research, you may perform experiments in science labs or make observations or gather data in courthouses, city government files, shopping malls (if you are observing, say, patterns of consumer behavior), the quad in front of the humanities building, or in front of TV screens (if you are analyzing, say, situation comedies or commercials, or if you are drawing on documentaries or interviews—in which cases you should try to obtain transcripts or tape the programs).

You may also want to *interview* your professors, your fellow students, or other individuals knowledgeable about your subject. Additionally, or alternatively, you may wish to conduct *surveys* via *questionnaires* (see box, p. 281). When well prepared and insightfully interpreted, such tools can produce valuable information about the ideas or preferences of a group of people.

Guidelines for Conducting Interviews

- Become knowledgeable about the subject before the interview so that you can ask intelligent questions. Prepare most of your questions beforehand.
- Ask "open-ended" questions designed to elicit meaningful responses, rather than "forced choice" questions that can be answered with a word or two, or "leading questions" that presume a particular answer. For example, instead of asking "Do you think that male managers should be more sensitive to women's concerns for equal pay in the workplace?" ask, "To what extent do you see evidence that male managers are insufficiently sensitive to women's concerns for equal pay in the workplace?"
- Ask follow-up questions to elicit additional insights or details.
- If you record the interview (in addition to or instead of taking notes), get your subject's permission, preferably in writing.

Guidelines for Conducting Surveys and Designing Questionnaires

- Determine your *purpose* in conducting the survey: what kind of *information* you seek, and *whom* (i.e., what subgroup of the population) you intend to survey.
- Decide whether you want to collect information on the spot or have people send their responses back to you. (You will get fewer responses if they are sent back to you, but those you do get will likely be more complete than surveys conducted on the spot.)
- Devise and word questions carefully so that they (1) are understandable and (2) don't reflect your own biases. For example, if, for a survey on attitudes toward capital punishment, you ask, "Do you believe that the state should endorse legalized murder?" you've loaded the question to influence people to answer in the negative.
- Devise short answer or multiple-choice questions; open-ended questions encourage responses that are difficult to quantify. (You may want to leave space, however, for "additional comments.") Conversely, "yes" or "no" responses or rankings on a 5-point scale are easy to quantify.
- It may be useful to break out the responses by as many meaningful categories as possible—for example, gender, age, ethnicity, religion, education, geographic locality, profession, and income.

■ MINING SOURCES ■

Having located your sources (or at least having begun the process), you'll proceed to "mining" them—that is, extracting from them information and ideas that you can use in your paper. To keep track of these sources, you'll need to compile a working bibliography so that you know what information you have and how it relates to your research question. Of course, you'll need to take notes on your sources and evaluate them for reliability and relevance. And you should develop some kind of *outline*—formal or informal—that allows you to see how you are going to subdivide and organize your discussion and, thus, at what points you'll be drawing on relevant sources. In doing this you are engaging in a process that has identifiable stages. For an extended discussion of this writing process, see Chapter 6.

Critical Reading for Research

- *Use all the critical reading tips we've suggested thus far.* The tips contained in the boxes Critical Reading for Summary on page 7, Critical Reading for Critique on page 78, Critical Reading for Synthesis on page 126, and Critical Reading for Analysis on pages 200–01 are all useful for the kinds of reading used in conducting research.
- *Read for relationships to your research question.* How does the source help you formulate and clarify your research question?
- *Read for relationships between sources.* How does each source illustrate, support, expand upon, contradict, or offer an alternative perspective to those of your other sources?
- *Consider the relationship between your source's form and content.* How does the form of the source—specialized encyclopedia, book, article in a popular magazine, article in a professional journal—affect its content, the manner in which that content is presented, and its relationship to other sources?
- *Pay special attention to the legitimacy of Internet sources.* Consider how the content and validity of the information on the Web page may be affected by the purpose of the site. Assess Web-based information for its (1) accuracy, (2) authority, (3) objectivity, (4) currency, and (5) coverage (see pages 272–73).

■ THE WORKING BIBLIOGRAPHY

As you conduct your research, keep a *working bibliography*—that is, a compilation of bibliographic information on all the sources you're likely to use in preparing the paper. Note *full* bibliographic information on each source you consider. If you're meticulous about this during the research process, you'll be spared the frustration of having to go back to retrieve information—such as the publisher or the date—just as you're typing your final draft.

Now that library catalogs and databases are available online, it's easy to copy and paste your sources' (or potential sources') bibliographic information into a document, or to email citations to yourself for cutting and pasting later. A more traditional but still very efficient way to compile bibliographic information is on 3" x 5" cards. (Note, also, that certain software programs allow you to create sortable electronic records.) Using any of these methods, you can easily add, delete, and rearrange individual bibliographic records as your research progresses. Whether you keep bibliographic information on 3" x 5" cards or in a document, be sure to record the following:

- The author or editor (last name first) and, if relevant, the translator
- The title (and subtitle) of the book or article
- The publisher and place of publication (if a book) or the title of the periodical
- The date and/or year of publication; if periodical, volume and issue number
- The edition number (if a book beyond its first edition)
- The inclusive page numbers (if article)
- The specific page number of a quote or other special material you might paraphrase

You also may want to include:

- A brief description of the source (to help you recall it later in the research process)
- The library call number (to help you relocate the source if you haven't checked it out)
- A code number, which you can use as a shorthand reference to the source in your notes (see example note card on p. 285)

Your final bibliography, known as "Works Cited" in Modern Language Association (MLA) format and "References" in American Psychological Association (APA) format, consists of the sources you have actually summarized, paraphrased, or quoted in your paper. When you compile the bibliography, arrange your sources alphabetically by authors' last names.

Here is an example of a working bibliography notation or record for a book used in the example argument paper in Chapter 4:

> Gorham, Eric B. National Service, Political Socialization, and Political Education. Albany: SUNY P, 1992.
>
> Argues that the language government uses to promote national service programs betrays an effort to "reproduce a postindustrial, capitalist economy in the name of good citizenship." Chap. 1 provides a historical survey of national service.

Here is an example of a working bibliography record for an article:

> Gergen, David. "A Time to Heed the Call." <u>U.S. News & World Report</u> 24 Dec. 2001: 60-61.
>
> Argues that in the wake of the surge of patriotism that followed the September 11 terrorist attacks, the government should encourage citizens to participate in community and national service. Supports the McCain-Bayh bill.

Here is an example of a working bibliography record for an online source:

> Bureau of Labor Statistics. Table 1: Volunteers by Selected Characteristics, September 2002 and 2003. 18 Dec. 2003. Accessed 17 Jan. 2004. <http://www.bls.gov/news.release/volun.t01.htm>.
>
> Provides statistical data on volunteerism in the U.S.

Some instructors may ask you to prepare—either in addition to or instead of a research paper—an *annotated bibliography*. This is a list of relevant works on a subject, with the contents of each briefly described or assessed. The sample bibliography records shown could become the basis for three entries in an annotated bibliography on national service. Annotations differ from *abstracts* in that annotations do not claim to be comprehensive summaries; they indicate, rather, how the items may be useful to the researcher.

Note-Taking

People have their favorite ways of note-taking. Some use use legal pads or spiral notebooks; others type notes into a laptop computer, perhaps using a database program. Some prefer 4" x 6" cards for note-taking. Such cards have some of the same advantages as 4" x 6" cards for working bibliographies: They can easily be added to, subtracted from, and rearranged to accommodate changing organizational plans. Also, discrete pieces of information from the same source can easily be arranged (and rearranged) into subtopics—a difficult task if you have taken three pages of notes on an article without breaking the notes down into subtopics.

Whatever your preferred approach, we recommend including, along with the note itself,

- a topic or subtopic label, corresponding to your outline (see below)
- a code number, corresponding to the number assigned the source in the working bibliography;
- a page reference at end of note.

Here is a sample note record for the table "Volunteers by Selected Characteristics, September 2002 and 2003" by the Bureau of Labor Statistics (bibliographic record above):

Pervasiveness of Volunteerism (I)   7

Shows that 28.8 percent of Americans age 16 and older, 63.8 million in all, devote time to community service.

Here is a note record for the periodical article by Gergen (see bibliography note on page 284):

Beneficial paid volunteer programs (II)   12

Both the community and the individual benefit from voluntary service programs. Cites Teach for America, Alumni of City Year, Peace Corps as programs in which participants receive small stipends and important benefits (60). "Voluntary service when young often changes people for life. They learn to give their fair share." (60)

Both note records are headed by a topic label followed by the tentative location in the paper outline where the information may be used. The number in the upper right corner corresponds to the bibliography note. The note itself in the first record uses *summary*. The note in the second record uses *summary* (sentence 1), *paraphrase* (sentence 2), and *quotation* (sentence 3). Summary is used to condense important ideas treated in several paragraphs in the sources; paraphrase (with relevant page number), for the important detail on specific programs; quotation (again with relevant page number), for particularly incisive language by the source authors. For general hints on when to use each of these three forms, see Chapter 1, page 46.

At this point we must stress the importance of using quotation marks around quoted language *in your notes.* Making sure to note the difference between your own and quoted language will help you avoid unintentionally using someone else's words or ideas without crediting them properly. Such use, whether intentional or unintentional, constitutes plagiarism—a serious academic offense—something that professors don't take lightly; you don't want to invite suspicion of your work, even unintentionally. See the discussion of plagiarism on pages 48–50 for more details.

Evaluating Sources

Sifting through what seems a formidable mountain of material, you'll need to work quickly and efficiently; you'll also need to do some selecting. This means, primarily, distinguishing the more important from the less important (and the unimportant) material. Draw on your critical reading skills to help you determine the reliability and relevance of a source. See the box Critical Reading for Research on page 282, and review Chapter 2, Critical Reading and Critique, particularly the sections Evaluating Informative Writing (pp. 55–57) and Evaluating Persuasive Writing (pp. 58–65). The hints in the box on the next page may also simplify the task.

> ### Guidelines for Evaluating Sources
>
> * *Skim the source.* With a book, look over the table of contents, the introduction and conclusion, and the index; zero in on passages that your initial survey suggests are important. With an article, skim the introduction and the headings.
> * *Be alert for references* in your sources to other important sources, particularly to sources that several authors treat as important.
> * Other things being equal, the more *recent* the source, the better. Recent work usually incorporates or refers to important earlier work.
> * If you're considering making multiple references to a book, *look up the reviews* in the *Book Review Digest* or the *Book Review Index.* Also, check the author's credentials in a source such as *Contemporary Authors* or *Current Biography.*

■ ARRANGING YOUR NOTES: THE OUTLINE

Using your original working thesis (see Chapter 6 on theses)—or a new thesis that you have developed during the course of data-gathering and invention—you can begin constructing a *preliminary outline.* This outline indicates the order in which you plan to support your thesis.

Some people prefer not to develop an outline until they have more or less completed their research. At that point they will look over their note records, consider the relationships among the various pieces of evidence, possibly arrange notes or cards into separate piles, then develop an outline based on their perceptions and insights about the material. Subsequently, they rearrange and code the note records to conform to their outline—an informal outline indicating just the main sections of the paper and possibly one level below that. Thus, the model paper on national service (see Chapter 4) could be informally outlined as follows:

> Intro: Pervasiveness of volunteerism in America;
> Thesis: We should not turn the success of volunteerism in
>   America into an argument for compulsory national service.
> Intellectual history of public service: James, Plato
> Can government compel citizens to public service?
>   Military service: yes, in time of war
>   Civilian service: no—logical, legal, moral reasons
> Conclusion: Government should expand opportunities for
>   public service, but should not compel such service.

Such an outline will help you organize your research and should not be unduly restrictive as a guide to writing.

The *formal outline* is a multileveled plan with Roman and Arabic numerals, capital and small lettered subheadings that can provide a useful blueprint for composition as well as a guide to revision.

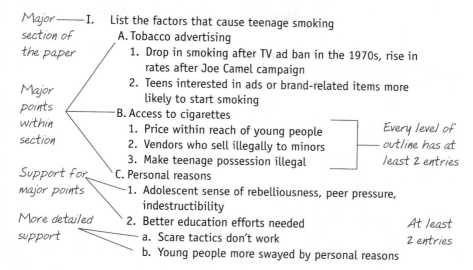

Major —— I. List the factors that cause teenage smoking
section of　　A. Tobacco advertising
the paper　　　1. Drop in smoking after TV ad ban in the 1970s, rise in rates after Joe Camel campaign
Major　　　　2. Teens interested in ads or brand-related items more likely to start smoking
points
within —— B. Access to cigarettes
section　　　1. Price within reach of young people　　　*Every level of*
　　　　　　　2. Vendors who sell illegally to minors　—— *outline has at*
　　　　　　　3. Make teenage possession illegal　　　*least 2 entries*
Support for　C. Personal reasons
major points　　1. Adolescent sense of rebelliousness, peer pressure, indestructibility
More detailed　2. Better education efforts needed　　　　*At least*
support　　　　　a. Scare tactics don't work　　　　　*2 entries*
　　　　　　　　　b. Young people more swayed by personal reasons

After you have written your draft, outlining it may help you discern structural problems: illogical sequences of material, confusing relationships between ideas, poor unity or coherence, and sections that are too abstract or underdeveloped. (See the discussion of *reverse outlines* in Chapter 6, page 254.) Many instructors also require that formal outlines accompany the finished research paper.

The formal outline should indicate the logical relationships in the evidence you present. But it also may reflect the general conventions of a particular academic field. Thus, after an *abstract* and an *introduction*, papers in the social sciences often proceed with a description of the *methods* of collecting information, continue with a description of the *results* of the investigation, and end with a *discussion* and a *conclusion*. Papers in the sciences often follow a similar pattern. Papers in the humanities generally are less standardized in form. In devising a logical organization for your paper, ask yourself how your reader might best be introduced to the subject, be guided through a discussion of the main issues, and be persuaded that your viewpoint is a sound one.

Formal outlines are generally of two types: *topic outlines* and *sentence outlines*. In the topic outline, headings and subheadings are indicated by words or phrases—as in the informal outline above. In the sentence outline, each heading and subheading is indicated in a complete sentence. Both topic and sentence outlines generally are preceded by the thesis.

For the complete formal topic outline of the national service paper in Chapter 4, see pages 154–55.

■ CITING SOURCES ■

When you refer to or quote the work of another, you are obligated to credit or cite your source properly. There are two types of citations—*in-text citations* and *full citations* (Works Cited or References) at the end of a paper—and they work in tandem.

If you are writing a paper in the humanities, you probably will be expected to use the Modern Language Association (MLA) format for citation. This format is fully described in the *MLA Handbook for Writers of Research Papers*, 6th ed. (New York: Modern Language Association of America, 2003). A paper in the social sciences will probably use the American Psychological Association (APA) format. This format is fully described in the *Publication Manual of the American Psychological Association*, 5th ed. (Washington, D.C.: American Psychological Association, 2001).

In the following section, we will focus on MLA and APA styles, the ones you are most likely to use in your academic work. Keep in mind, however, that instructors often have their own preferences. Some require the documentation style specified in the *Chicago Manual of Style*, 15th ed. (Chicago: University of Chicago Press, 2003). This style is similar to the American Psychological Association style, except that publication dates are not placed within parentheses. Instructors in the sciences often follow the Council of Science Editors (CSE) format (formerly Council of Biology Editors). Or they may prefer a number format: Each source listed on the bibliography page is assigned a number, and all text references to the source are followed by the appropriate number within parentheses. Some instructors like the old MLA style, which calls for footnotes and endnotes. Check with your instructor for the preferred documentation format if this is not specified in the assignment.

Types of Citations

- Citations that indicate the source of quotations, paraphrases, and summarized information and ideas. These citations, generally limited to author's last name, relevant page number, and publication date of source, appear *in the text*, within parentheses.
- Citations that appear in an alphabetical list of "Works Cited" or "References" *at the end of the paper* usually starting on a new page (check with your instructor). These citations provide full bibliographical information on the source.

■ IN-TEXT CITATION

The general rule for in-text citation is to include only enough information to alert the reader to the source of the reference and to the location within that source (Behrens and Rosen 288). Normally, this information includes the author's last name and the page number (plus the year of publication, if using APA guidelines). But if you have already named the author in the preceding text, the page number is sufficient.

Content Notes

Occasionally, you may want to provide a footnote or an endnote as a *content note*—one that provides additional information bearing on or illuminating, but not directly related to, the discussion at hand. For example

> ¹ Equally well-known is Forster's distinction between story and plot: In the former, the emphasis is on sequence ("the king died and then the queen died"); in the latter, the emphasis is on causality ("the king died and then the queen died of grief").

Notice the format: The first line is indented five spaces or one-half inch and the note number is raised one-half line in MLA or APA style. A single space from there, the note begins. Subsequent lines of the note are flush with the left margin. If the note is at the bottom of the page (a footnote), it is placed four lines below the text of the page, and the note itself is single-spaced. APA has a section of Footnotes after the References. Double spaces are used between notes. Content notes are numbered consecutively throughout the paper; do not begin renumbering on each page. Most word-processing programs have functions for inserting consecutive footnotes, formatting them, and placing them in the appropriate position on your pages.

■ FULL CITATIONS

In MLA format, your complete list of sources, with all information necessary for a reader to locate a source, is called "Works Cited" (and should begin on a new page). In APA format, the list of sources is called "References." Entries in such listings should be double-spaced, with second and subsequent lines of each entry indented (a "hanging indent")—five spaces or one-half inch. In both styles, a single space follows the period. For comparison of MLA and APA citation styles, here are two samples of journal citations. Citation of books and other sources follow slightly different guidelines.

The main differences between MLA and APA styles are these: (1) In MLA style, the date of the publication follows the name of the publication; in APA style, the date is placed within parentheses following the author's name. (2) In APA style, only the initial of the author's first name is given, and only the first word (and any proper noun) of the book or article title is capitalized. The first letter of the subtitle (after a colon in a title) is also capitalized. In MLA style, the author's full name is given, and all words following the first word of the title (except articles and prepositions) are capitalized. (3) In APA style (unlike MLA style), quotation marks are not used around journal/magazine article titles. (4) APA style (unlike MLA style) requires the use of "p." and "pp." in in-text citations to indicate page numbers of periodical articles. (5) In APA format, titles of books *and* journals are italicized, as are the punctuation that follows and the volume (but not issue) numbers; MLA requires underlining for book and journal titles (ending periods are *not* underlined). (6) When citing books, both MLA and APA rules dictate that publishers' names should be shortened; thus, "Random House" becomes "Random"; "William Morrow" becomes "Morrow." However, MLA style uses a more extensive system of abbreviations for publishers' names.

Note: The hanging indent (second and subsequent lines indented) is the recommended format for both MLA and APA style references.

Sample MLA Full Citation (for a journal article)

Haan, Sarah C. "The 'Persuasion Route' of the Law: Advertising and Legal

Persuasion." Columbia Law Review 100 (2000): 1281-1326.

Sample APA Full Citation (for a journal article)

Haan, S. C. (2000). The "persuasion route" of the law: Advertising and legal

persuasion. *Columbia Law Review, 100,* 1281–1326.

Provided below are some of the most commonly used citations in MLA and APA formats. For a more complete listing, consult the MLA *Handbook,* the APA's *Publication Manual,* or whichever style guide your instructor has specified. Please note that achieving conformance to either citation system requires precision and attention to detail, down to every keystroke and punctuation mark.

■ MLA STYLE

In-Text Citation

Here are sample in-text citations using the MLA system:

> From the beginning, the AIDS antibody test has been "mired in controversy" (Bayer 101).

Notice that in the MLA system no date and no punctuation come between the author's name and the page number within the parentheses. Notice also that the parenthetical reference is placed *before* the final punctuation of the sentence, because it is considered part of the sentence.

If you have already mentioned the author's name in the text—in a *signal phrase* (e.g., "According to . . .")—it is not necessary to repeat it in the citation:

> According to Bayer, from the beginning, the AIDS antibody test has been "mired in controversy" (101).

In MLA format, you must supply page numbers for summaries and para-phrases of print sources, as well as for quotations:

> According to Bayer, the AIDS antibody test has been controversial
> from the outset (101).

Use a block, or indented form, for quotations of five lines or more. Introduce the block quotation with a full sentence followed by a colon. Indent one inch or ten spaces (that is, double the normal paragraph indentation). Place the parenthetical citation *after* the final period:

> Robert Flaherty's refusal to portray primitive people's contact with
> civilization arose from an inner conflict:
>
>> He had originally plunged with all his heart into the role of
>> explorer and prospector; before Nanook, his own father was
>> his hero. Yet as he entered the Eskimo world, he knew he
>> did so as the advance guard of industrial civilization, the
>> world of United States Steel and Sir William Mackenzie and
>> railroad and mining empires. The mixed feeling this gave
>> him left his mark on all his films. (Barnouw 45)

Again, were Barnouw's name mentioned in the sentence leading into the quotation, the parenthetical reference would be simply (45).

Usually parenthetical citations appear at the end of your sentences; however, if the reference applies only to the first part of the sentence, the parenthetical information is inserted at the appropriate points *within* the sentence:

> While Baumrind argues that "the laboratory is not the place to study
> degree of obedience" (421), Milgram asserts that such arguments are
> groundless.

At times, you must modify the basic author/page number reference. Depending on the nature of your source(s), you may need to use one of the following citation formats:

Quoted Material Appearing in Another Source

> (qtd. in Garber 211)

An Anonymous Work

> ("Obedience" 32)

Two Authors

> (Bernstein and Politi 208)

A Particular Work by an Author, When You List Two or More Works by That Author in the List of Works Cited

> (Toffler, Wave 96-97)

Two or More Sources as the Basis of Your Statement

(Butler 109; Carey 57)

The Location of a Passage in a Literary Text

for example, Hardy's The Return of the Native (224; ch. 7)

[Page 224 in the edition used by the writer; the chapter number, 7, is provided for the convenience of those referring to another edition.]

A Multivolume Work

(3: 7-12)

[volume number: page numbers; note the space between the colon and the page numbers]

The Location of a Passage in a Play

(1.2.308-22) [act.scene.line number(s)]

The Bible

(John 3.16)

(Col. 3.14) [book. chapter.verse]

In-Text Citation of Electronic Sources (MLA)

Web sites, CD-ROM data, and e-mail generally do not have numbered pages. Different browsers may display and printers may produce differing numbers of pages for any particular site. You should therefore omit both page numbers and paragraph numbers from in-text citations to electronic sources, unless these page or paragraph numbers are provided within the source itself. For in-text citations of electronic sources, MLA prefers that you cite the author's name in the sentence rather than in a parenthetical, where possible. In APA style, use parentheses for citation of author's name and the year of publication as you would when citing print material.

Examples of MLA Citations in Works Cited List

Electronic Sources (MLA)

According to guidelines in the 2003 *MLA Handbook for Writers of Research Papers*, the following information should be included when crediting electronic sources:

1. *Name of the author, editor, compiler, or translator* (if given)
2. *Title* of the work, with quotation marks if something other than a book; underlined if it is a book
3. Information, if any, about *print publication*
4. Information about electronic publication, including title of the Internet site or name of any organization or institution sponsoring the site

5. *Access information,* including
   a. the date of electronic publication or latest update, if available
   b. the researcher's date of access
   c. the URL

If the URL of the exact document is extremely long and complex, making transcription errors possible, instead give the URL of the relevant search page or home page. From there, using other publication facts given in the citation, readers should be able to locate the cited document. URLs should include the access-mode identifier—*http* or *www.* Enclose URLs in angle brackets (< >) followed by a period. When a URL continues from one line to the next, *break it only after a slash.* Do not add a hyphen.

Because few standards currently exist for those who post publications on the Internet, you may not necessarily be able to find or supply all the desired information. Thus, you may simply settle for what is available while aiming for comprehensiveness. Formatting conventions are illustrated by the following models:

An Entire Internet Site for an Online Scholarly Project or Database

The Piers Plowman Electronic Archive. Ed. Robert Adams et al. 2003. Society for

   Early English and Norse Electronic Texts, University of Virginia Institute for

   Advanced Technology in the Humanities. 15 July 2003 <http://

   www.iath.virginia.edu/seenet/piers/piersmain.html>.

Note: information presented is (1) title of site, project, or database; (2) name of the editor of project or site; (3) electronic publication information, including date of electronic publication or latest update and name of sponsoring institution; and (4) date of access and URL.

A Short Work within a Scholarly Project

Dugan, Hoyt N. "The Nature of the Problem." The Piers Plowman Electronic

   Archive. Ed. Robert Adams et al. 2003. Society for Early English and Norse

   Electronic Texts, University of Virginia Institute for Advanced Technology

   in the Humanities. 15 July 2003 <http://www.iath.virginia.edu/seenet/

   piers/pagearchivegoals1994body.html#natureofproblem>.

A Personal Home Page or Professional Site

Winter, Mick. How to Talk New Age. 28 July 2003 <http://www.well.com/user/

   mick/newagept.html>.

Note: In addition to date of access (shown here), the citation should include the date of last update, if given (as in the next example):

An Online Book

Smith, Adam. <u>The Wealth of Nations</u>. Oxford: Oxford UP, 1985. <u>The Adam Smith Institute</u>. 2001. 15 July 2003 <http://www.adamsmith.org/smith/won-intro.htm>.

A Part of an Online Book

Smith, Adam. "Of the Division of Labour." <u>The Wealth of Nations</u>. Oxford: Oxford UP, 1985. <u>The Adam Smith Institute</u>. 2001. 15 July 2003 <http://www.adamsmith.org/smith/won-b1-c1.htm>.

An Article in a Scholarly Journal

Epstein, Paul. "The Imitation of Athena in the Lysistrata of Aristophanes." <u>Animus</u> 7 (2002). 16 July 2003 <http://www.swgc.mun.ca/animus/current/epstein7.htm>.

An Unsigned Article in a Newspaper or on a Newswire

"Verizon to Rehire 1,100 Laid-off Workers." <u>AP Online</u> 16 July 2003. 18 July 2003 <http://www.nytimes.com/aponline/technology/AP-Verizon-Jobs.html>.

A Signed Article in a Newspaper or on a Newswire

Vartabedian, Ralph. "Columbia's Crew Lived after Radio Calls Ended." <u>Chicago Tribune</u> 16 July 2003. 20 July 2003 <http://www.chicagotribune.com/technology/la-na-shuttle16jul16,1,1997210.story?coll=chi-news-hed>.

An Article in a Magazine

Kim, Jimin. "When Cell Phones Meet Camcorders." <u>Forbes</u> 16 July 2003. 12 Aug. 2003 <http://www.forbes.com/home/2003/07/16/cx_jk_0716tentech.html>.

A Review

Vaneechoutte, Mario. Rev. of <u>The Theory and Practice of Institutional Transplantation</u>, ed. M. De Jong et al. <u>Journal of Mimetics</u> 7.2 (2003). 13 Jan. 2004 <http://jom-emit.cfpm.org/2003/vol7/vaneechoutte_m.html>.

An Editorial or Letter to the Editor

Park, Charlie. "The Matrix Is Everywhere." Letter. <u>Wired</u> 11.7 (July 2003). 13 Jan. 2004 <http://www.wired.com/wired/archive/11.07/rants.html>.

An Abstract

Arden, Heather. "The Harry Potter Stories and French Arthurian Romance."
    Arthuriana 13.2 (2003): 54-68. Abstract. 16 July 2003
    <http://www.smu.edu/arthuriana/>. Path: Abstracts; A-F.

Electronic Copy of a Periodical Article Retrieved from a Database

Murphy, Cullen. "The Utmost Measures: A Word in Behalf of Subjectivity.
    (Innocent Bystander)." The Atlantic Monthly 290.3 (Oct.
    2002): 18(2). Expanded Academic ASAP. Thomson Gale. UC Santa Barbara
    (CDL). 26 January 2006 <http://find.galegroup.com>.

Material from a Periodically Published Database on CD-ROM

Ellis, Richard. "Whale Killing Begins Anew." Audubon 94.6 (1992): 20-22.
    General Periodicals Ondisc-Magazine Express. CD-ROM UMI-Proquest. 1992.

A Nonperiodical Source on CD-ROM, Diskette, or Magnetic Tape

Clements, John. "War of 1812." Chronology of the United States. CD-ROM.
    Dallas: Political Research, 1997.

An E-Mail Communication

Mendez, Michael R. "Re: Solar power." E-mail to Edgar V. Atamian. 11 Sept.
    2003.

Armstrong, David J. E-mail to the author. 30 Aug. 2003.

An Online Posting For online postings, discussion groups, or synchronous
communications, cite a version stored as a Web file, if one exists, so that your
readers can more easily find your sources. Label sources as needed (e.g., Online posting, Online defense of dissertation, etc., with neither underlining
nor quotation marks). Several models follow.

Flanders, Julia. "Mentoring in Humanities Computing." Online posting.
    8 May 2003. Humanist Discussion Group. 16 July 2003 <http://
    lists.village.virginia.edu/lists_archive/Humanist/v17/0001.html>.

Synchronous Communication

Mendez, Michael R. Online debate. "Solar Power Versus Fossil Fuel Power." 3 Apr.
    2000. CollegeTownMOO. 3 Apr. 2000 <telnet://next.cs.bvc.edu.7777>.

Downloaded Computer Software

Quicktime. Vers. 6.3. 16 July 2003 <http://www.apple.com/
    quicktime/download/>.

Periodicals (MLA)

Continuous Pagination throughout Annual Cycle

Binder, Sarah. "The Dynamics of Legislative Gridlock, 1947-1996." American Political Science Review 93 (1999): 519-31.

> [Note style of page ranges and use of hyphen.]

Separate Pagination Each Issue

> O'Mealy, Joseph H. "Royal Family Values: The Americanization of Alan Bennett's The Madness of King George III." Literature/Film Quarterly 27.2 (1999): 90-97.

Monthly Periodical

> Davison, Peter. "Girl, Seeming to Disappear." Atlantic Monthly May 2000: 108-11.

Signed Article in Weekly Periodical

> Gladwell, Malcolm. "The New-Boy Network." New Yorker 29 May 2000: 68-86.

Unsigned Article in Weekly Periodical

> "GOP Speaker Admits 'Exaggerations.'" New Republic 14 Aug. 2000: 10-11.

Signed Article in Daily Newspaper

> Vise, David A. "FBI Report Gauges School Violence Indicators." Washington Post 6 Sept. 2000: B1+.

Unsigned Article in Daily Newspaper

> "The World's Meeting Place." New York Times 6 Sept. 2000: A11.

Review

> Barber, Benjamin R. "The Crack in the Picture Window." Rev. of Bowling Alone: The Collapse and Revival of American Community, by Robert D. Putnam. Nation 7 Aug. 2000: 29-34.

Books (MLA)

One Author

> Fahs, Alice. The Imagined Civil War: Popular Literature of the North and South, 1861-1865. Chapel Hill: U of North Carolina P, 2003.

Note: MLA convention dictates abbreviating the names of university presses (e.g., Oxford UP for Oxford University Press or the above for University of North Carolina Press). Commercial publishing companies are also shortened by dropping such endings as "Co.," or "Inc." The *MLA Handbook* includes a list of abbreviations for publishers' names.

Two or More Books by the Same Author

Gubar, Susan. Critical Condition: Feminism at the Turn of the Century. New York: Columbia UP, 2000.

---. Racechanges: White Skin, Black Face in American Culture. New York: Oxford UP, 1997.

Note: For MLA style, references to works by the same author are listed in alphabetical order of title.

Two Authors

Gerson, Allan, and Jerry Adler. The Price of Terror. New York: Harper, 2003.

Three Authors

Booth, Wayne C., Gregory G. Colomb, and Joseph M. Williams. The Craft of Research. 2nd ed. Chicago: U of Chicago P, 2003.

More than Three Authors

Burawoy, Michael, et al. Global Ethnography: Forces, Connections, and Imaginations in a Postmodern World. Berkeley: U of California P, 2000.

Book with an Editor and No Author

Dean, Bartholomew, and Jerome M. Levi, eds. At the Risk of Being Heard: Identity, Indigenous Rights, and Postcolonial States. Ann Arbor: U of Michigan P, 2003.

Later Edition

Whitten, Phillip. Anthropology: Contemporary Perspectives. 8th ed. Boston: Allyn, 2001.

Republished Book

Dreiser, Theodore. An American Tragedy. 1925. Cambridge, UK: Bentley, 1978.

A Multivolume Work

Slovenko, Ralph. Psychiatry in Law/Law in Psychiatry. 2 vols. New York: Brunner-Routledge, 2002.

Translation

Saramago, Jose. All the Names. Trans. Margaret Jull Kosta. New York: Harcourt, 1999.

Selection from an Anthology

Hardy, Melissa. "The Heifer." The Best American Short Stories. Ed. Sue Miller. Boston: Houghton, 2002. 97-115.

Government Publication

National Institute of Child Health and Human Development. Closing the Gap: A
National Blueprint to Improve the Health of Persons with Mental
Retardation. Washington: GPO, 2002.

United States. Cong. House. Committee on Government Reform. Interim Report
of the Activities of the House Committee on Government Reform. 107th
Cong. 1st sess. Washington: GPO, 2001.

The Bible

The New English Bible. New York: Oxford UP, 1972.

Signed Encyclopedia Article

Kunzle, David M. "Caricature, Cartoon, and Comic Strip." The New Encyclopaedia
Britannica: Macropaedia. 15th ed. 2002.

Unsigned Encyclopedia Article

"Tidal Wave." Encyclopedia Americana. 2nd ed. 2001.

Other Sources (MLA)

Interview Conducted by the Researcher

Emerson, Robert. Personal interview. 10 Oct. 2002.

Dissertation (Abstracted in Dissertation Abstracts International)

Sheahan, Mary Theresa. "Living on the Edge: Ecology and Economy in Willa
Cather's 'Wild Land': Webster County Nebraska, 1870-1900." Diss. Northern
Illinois U, 1999. DAI 60 (1999): 1298A.

Note: If the dissertation is published on microfilm by University Microfilms,
give the order number at the conclusion of the reference. Example, in MLA
format: Ann Arbor: UMI, 1999. AAT 9316566.

Lecture

Osborne, Michael. "The Great Man Theory: Caesar." Lecture. History 401.
University of California, Santa Barbara, 5 Nov. 2003.

Paper Delivered at a Professional Conference

Brodkey, Linda. "The Rhetoric of Race in Practice." Conf. on Coll. Composition
and Communication. Palmer House, Chicago. 20 Mar. 2003.

Film

The Pianist. Dir. Roman Polanski. Perf. Adrien Brody. Focus Features and
Universal, 2002.

Recording of a TV Program or Film

Legacy of the Hollywood Blacklist. Dir. Judy Chaikin. Videocassette. One Step
    Productions and Public Affairs TV, 1987.

Audio Recording

Raman, Susheela. "Song to the Siren." Salt Rain. Narada, 2001.

Schumann, Robert. Symphonies no. 1 and 4. Cond. George Szell. Cleveland
    Orchestra. Columbia, 1978.

Or, to emphasize the conductor rather than the composer:

Szell, George, cond. Symphonies no. 1 and 4. By Robert Schumann. Cleveland
    Orchestra. Columbia, 1978.

■ APA STYLE

In-Text Citation

Here are sample in-text citations using the APA system:

> A good deal of research shows that rather than inducing any lasting
> changes in a child's behavior, punishment "promotes only momentary
> compliance"(Berk, 2002, p. 383).

Notice that in the APA system, there is a comma between the author's name, the date, and the page number, and the number itself is preceded by "p." or "pp." Notice also that the parenthetical reference is placed *before* the final punctuation of the sentence.

If you have already mentioned the author's name in the text, it is not necessary to repeat it in the citation:

> According to Berk (2002), a good deal of research shows that rather
> than inducing any lasting changes in a child's behavior, punishment
> "promotes only momentary compliance"(p. 383).

OR:

> According to Berk, a good deal of research shows that rather than
> inducing any lasting changes in a child's behavior, punishment
> "promotes only momentary compliance"(2002, p. 383).

When using the APA system, provide page numbers only for direct quotations, not for summaries or paraphrases. If you do not refer to a specific page, simply indicate the date:

> Berk (2002) asserted that many research findings view punishment as
> a quick fix rather than a long-term solution to behavior problems in
> children.

For quotations of 40 words or more, use block (indented) quotations. In these cases, place the parenthetical citation *after* the period:

> Various strategies exist for reducing children's tendency to view the world in a gender-biased fashion:
>
> > Once children notice the vast array of gender stereotypes in their society, parents and teachers can point out exceptions. For example, they can arrange for children to see men and women pursuing nontraditional careers. And they can reason with children, explaining that interests and skills, not sex, should determine a person's occupation and activities. (Berk, 2002, p. 395)

Again, were Berk's name mentioned in the sentence leading into the quotation, the parenthetical reference would be simply (2002, p. 395) for APA style.

If the reference applies only to the first part of a sentence, the parenthetical reference is inserted at the appropriate points *within* the sentence:

> Shapiro (2002) emphasizes the idea that law firms are "continually in flux" (p. 32), while Sikes focuses on their stability as institutions.

At times you must modify the basic author/page number reference. Depending on the nature of your source(s), you may need to use one of the following citation formats:

Quoted Material Appearing in Another Source

> (as cited in Garber, 2000, p. 211)

An Anonymous Work

> ("Obedience," 2003, p. 32)

Two Authors

> (Striano & Rochat, 2000, p. 257)
>
> [Note use of ampersand.]

Two or More Sources as the Basis of Your Statement (Arrange Entries in Alphabetic Order of Surname)

> (Ehrenreich 2001, p. 68; Hitchens, 2001, p. 140)

A Multivolume Work

> (Brown, 2003, vol. 2, p. 88)

In-Text Citation of Electronic Sources (APA)

As noted earlier, Web sites, CD-ROM data, and e-mail generally do not have numbered pages (unless they are PDF reproductions of print material). If paragraph numbers are visible in the source, you can use them instead of page numbers for in-text citations. If the document has headings but no page or paragraph numbers, cite the heading and the number of the paragraph following it.

Citation to an Electronic Source with Headings

(Kishlansky, 2002, Conclusion section, ¶2)

Examples of APA Citations in References List

Electronic Sources (APA)

The basic information needed to cite electronic sources using APA documentation style includes

1. *Name of the author* (if given)
2. *Date* of publication, update, or retrieval
3. *Document title, description,* and/or *source*
4. The *URL,* or Internet address (the most crucial element)

The *APA Publications Manual* recommends that writers check the URLs regularly, while drafting a paper and before submission, as the location of documents sometimes changes. As with MLA citations, include as much pertinent information as is available to help your reader find the source, such as volume and issue numbers if available.

The general APA format for online periodical sources is as follows:

Author, I. (date). Title of article. *Name of Periodical. Volume* and issue number

(if available). Retrieved month, day, year, from source

For online sources, do not add periods or other punctuation immediately following URLs. Also, if you need to continue a URL across lines, break the URL after a slash or before a period. Do not use a hyphen. An extra hyphen or period may prevent a reader from accessing the source. Note APA's use of italics.

An Article in an Internet-Only Scholarly Journal

Sheehan, K. B., & Hoy, M. G. (1999). Using e-mail to survey Internet users in

the United States: Methodology and assessment. *Journal of Computer-*

Mediated Communication, 4(3). Retrieved August 14, 2001, from

http://www.ascusc.org/jcmc/vol4/issue3/sheehan.html

Note: The APA guidelines distinguish between Internet articles that are based on a print source, and those that appear in Internet-only journals. When an Internet article is reproduced from a print source, simply follow the usual journal article reference format, and include the phrase "Electronic version" in brackets following the title of the article. In such a case, you don't need to include the URL or date retrieved from the Internet.

Stand-alone Document with Author and Date

Winter, M. (2003). *How to talk new age.* Retrieved July 25, 2003, from

http://www.well.com/user/mick/newagept.html

Note: When no date of publication is given, indicate this with n.d. for "no date" in parentheses where the date usually would appear. If no author is identified, begin the reference with the document title.

An Unsigned Article in a Newspaper or on a Newswire

Verizon to rehire 1,100 laid-off workers. (2003, 16 July). *AP Online*. Retrieved

July 18, 2003, from http://www.nytimes.com/aponline/technology/

AP-Verizon-Jobs.html

A Signed Article in a Newspaper or on a Newswire

Vartabedian, R. (2003, 16 July). Columbia's crew lived after radio calls ended.

Chicago Tribune. Retrieved July 20, 2003, from

http://www.chicagotribune.com/technology/

la-na-shuttle16jul16,1,1997210.story?coll=chi-news-hed

An Article in a Magazine

Kim, J. (2003, July 16). When cell phones meet camcorders. *Forbes*. Retrieved

August 12, 2003, from http://www.forbes.com/home/

2003/07/16/cx_jk_0716tentech.html

An Abstract

Eliaphson, N., & Lichterman, P. (2003). Culture in interaction. *American Journal*

of Sociology. Abstract retrieved October 25, 2003, from http://

www.journals.uchicago.edu/AJS/journal/issues/v108n4/040241/brief/

040241.abstract.html

Electronic Copy of a Periodical Article Retrieved from a Database

Bergeron, L. R. (2002). Family preservation: An unidentified approach in elder

abuse protection. *Families in Society, 83*, 547–556. Retrieved July 28,

2003, from XanEdu Research Engine, ProQuest.

[Note style of page ranges: full numbers separated by a hyphen.]

For online postings or synchronous communications, the APA recommends referencing only those sources that are maintained in archived form. However, archived discussions or postings are rarely peer reviewed, are not generally regarded as having scholarly content, and are not archived for very long, so APA advises that you cite them with care in formal works. APA also advises against using nonarchived postings, as they are not retrievable by your readers. If you do choose to include sources that are not archived—and this includes e-mail communications between individuals—the APA suggests citing them as personal communications in the text of your work, but leaving them out of the References list. For archived sources, follow these models as appropriate.

Message Posted to an Electronic Mailing List

Hammond, T. (2002, July 19). A bootstrapping mechanism for DOI. Message posted to General DOI Discussion Forum, archived at http://www.doi.org/mail-archive/discuss-doi/msg00440.html

Message Posted to an Online Forum or Discussion Group

Pagdin, F. (2001, July 3). New medium for therapy [Msg 498]. Message posted to http://www.groups.yahoo.com/group/cybersociology/message/498

Computer Software

Gamma UniType for Windows 1.5 (Version 1.1) [Computer software]. (1997). San Diego, CA: Gamma Productions.

Note: Reference entries are needed for specialized or limited-distribution software only. If an individual has proprietary rights to the software, name that person as the author.

Periodicals (APA)

Continuous Pagination Throughout Annual Cycle

Tomlins, C. L. (2003). In a wilderness of tigers: Violence, the discourse of English colonizing, and the refusals of American history. *Theoretical Inquiries in Law, 4,* 505–543.

Separate Pagination Each Issue

O'Mealy, J. H. (1999). Royal family values: The Americanization of Alan Bennett's *The Madness of King George III. Literature/Film Quarterly, 27*(2), 90–97.

Monthly Periodical

Davison, P. (2000, May). Girl, seeming to disappear. *Atlantic Monthly, 285,* 108–111.

Signed Article in Weekly Periodical

Gladwell, M. (2000, May 29). The new-boy network. *The New Yorker,* 68–86.

Unsigned Article in Weekly Periodical

Spain and the Basques: Dangerous stalemate. (2003, July 5). *The Economist, 368,* 44–45.

Signed Article in Daily Newspaper, Discontinuous Pages

Vise, D. A. (2000, September 6). FBI report gauges school violence indicators. *The Washington Post,* pp. B1, B6.

Unsigned Article in Daily Newspaper

The world's meeting place. (2000, September 6). *The New York Times,* p. A11.

Review

Barber, B. R. (2000, August 7). The crack in the picture window. [Review of the book *Bowling alone: The collapse and revival of American community*]. *The Nation,* 29–34.

Note: Some weekly magazines do not have volume numbers, in which case, include only the date and page numbers in your reference.

Books (APA)
One Author

Fahs, Alice. (2003). *The imagined civil war: Popular literature of the north and south, 1861–1865.* Chapel Hill: University of North Carolina Press.

Two or More Books by the Same Author

Gubar, S. (1997). *Racechanges: White skin, black face in American culture.* New York: Oxford University Press.

Gubar, S. (2000). *Critical condition: Feminism at the turn of the century.* New York: Columbia University Press.

Note: For APA style, references to works by the same author are listed in chronological order of publication, earliest first. Use the author's name in all entries.

Two Authors

Gerson, A., & Adler, J. (2003). *The price of terror.* New York: Harper.

Three Authors

Booth, W. C., Colomb, G. C., & Williams, J. M. (2003). *The craft of research* (2nd ed.). Chicago: University of Chicago Press.

More than Three Authors

Burawoy, M., Blum, J. A., George, S., Gille, Z., Gowan, T., Haney, L., et al. (2000). *Global ethnography: Forces, connections, and imaginations in a postmodern world.* Berkeley: University of California Press.

Note: If more than six, list only the first six, followed by *et al.*

Book with an Editor and No Author

Dean, B., & Levi, J. M. (Eds.). (2003). *At the risk of being heard: Identity, indigenous rights, and postcolonial states.* Ann Arbor: University of Michigan Press.

Later Edition

Whitten, P. (2001). *Anthropology: Contemporary perspectives* (8th ed.). Boston: Allyn & Bacon.

Republished Book

Dreiser, T. (1978). *An American tragedy*. Cambridge, MA: R. Bentley. (Original work published 1925)

A Multivolume Work

Slovenko, R. (2002). *Psychiatry in law/law in psychiatry*. (Vols. 1–2). New York: Brunner-Routledge.

Translation

Saramago, J. (1999). *All the names*. (M. J. Kosta, Trans.). New York: Harcourt.

Selection from an Anthology

Halberstam, D. (2002). Who we are. In S. J. Gould (Ed.), *The best American essays 2002* (pp. 124–136). New York: Houghton Mifflin.

Government Publication

Caring for children act of 2003: Report of the Senate Committee on Health, Education, Labor, and Pensions, S. Rep. No. 108-37 (2003).

National Institute of Child Health and Human Development. (2002). *Closing the gap: A national blueprint to improve the health of persons with mental retardation*. Washington, DC: U.S. Government Printing Office.

Signed Encyclopedia Article

Kunzle, D. M. (2002). Caricature, cartoon, and comic strip. In *The new encyclopaedia Britannica*. (Vol. 15, pp. 539–552). Chicago: Encyclopaedia Britannica.

Unsigned Encyclopedia Article

Tidal wave. (2001). In *The encyclopedia Americana*. (Vol. 26, p. 730). Danbury, CT: Grolier.

Other Sources (APA)

Dissertation (Abstracted in Dissertation Abstracts International)

Sheahan, M. T. (1999). Living on the edge: Ecology and economy in Willa Cather's "Wild Land": Webster County, Nebraska, 1870–1900 (Doctoral dissertation, Northern Illinois University, 1999). *Dissertation Abstracts International, 60,* 1298A.

Note: If the dissertation is obtained from University Microfilms, give the UMI number in parentheses at the conclusion of the reference, after the DAI number: (UMI No. AAD9315947).

Lecture

> Baldwin, J. (1999, January 11). *The self in social interactions.* Sociology 2 lecture, University of California, Santa Barbara.

Paper Delivered at a Professional Conference

> Hollon, S. D. (2003, August). Treatment and prevention of depression with drugs and psychotherapy. Paper presented at the annual convention of the American Psychological Association, Toronto, Ontario.

Film

> Polanski, R. (Director). (2002). *The pianist* [Motion picture]. United States: Focus Features and Universal.

TV Series

> Chase, D. (Producer). (2001). *The Sopranos* [Television series]. New York: HBO.

Music Recording

> Raman, S. (2001). Song to the siren. On *Salt Rain* [CD]. Milwaukee, WI: Narada.

WRITING ASSIGNMENT: SOURCE-BASED PAPER

Using the methods we have outlined in this chapter—and incorporating the skills covered in this textbook as a whole—conduct your own research on a topic and research question that falls within your major or your area of interest. Your research process should culminate in a 1500- to 1700-word paper in which you use your sources to present an answer to your research question.

Part Three ▪ *Applications*

A Case Study in 8
Academic Writing

We turn now to an example of academic writing, an assignment from a general humanities course and the paper that resulted. You will find here the sources that writer Ryan Cheever used in his response to the assignment, an outline, and his source-based paper in MLA format (including a partial earlier draft). The creativity Cheever demonstrates in this paper, the clear thinking, the straightforward structure, and the ample development of content are typical of successful college-level writing. Obviously, the specifics of particular assignments and papers will change as you move from class to class; but each will require of you a similarly informed, thoughtful response.

The assignment and Cheever's paper are typical in another way: both assume a *blending* or a *combination* of the common structures of academic writing discussed in previous chapters. In "Death in War: A Comparative Analysis of John Singer Sargent's *Death and Victory* and Erich Maria Remarque's *All Quiet on the Western Front*," Ryan Cheever interweaves summary, quotation, analysis, and synthesis in order to respond effectively to the assignment.

The structures discussed earlier—summary, critique, synthesis (both argument and explanatory), and analysis—are presented separately for clarity of instruction only. In actual academic writing, you'll probably use a variety of these structures in a single assignment. Arguments may consist, partly, of explanations and/or critiques. Your critiques and analyses will build from summaries. Your explanations will almost certainly require you to evaluate sources for reliability and may even shade toward argument in your conclusions. Most of your academic writing will be source-based, like Ryan Cheever's; and you may therefore need to conduct additional research to discover the sources you will subsequently use (and cite) in your papers.

Follow the development of Cheever's work, from assignment to final draft. You won't be able to use this one paper as a template, exactly, for your own writing, since assignments (and the writing that follows from them) will differ. Nonetheless, you can use Cheever's approach and high standards as effective models. Learn the component parts of academic writing: summary, critique, synthesis, and analysis. Then sequence or blend them according to your purpose.

■ THE ASSIGNMENT:
A COMPARATIVE ANALYSIS

Here is the assignment that led Ryan Cheever to writing his paper:

COMPARATIVE ANALYSIS

Good writers paint with words. They use word choice, sentence patterns, and various other techniques to convey tone and theme to readers and to construct a mental picture. Visual artists also communicate to an audience, but they do so with color, line, and images, rather than with words. It is important to recognize how a piece of visual art can convey the same, or different, themes as a written work.

In this assignment, select a work of visual art concerning World War I to compare to *All Quiet on the Western Front*. Analyze the visual art as you would a passage in a play or novel—with the goal of seeing more clearly into the artwork and understanding it more deeply. Carefully consider the following:

- What is the artist "saying"—about the moment you see before you, about war on a larger scale?

- How does the artist say this? What techniques are used—what colors, what materials, symbols, etc.?

- What tone and emotions do these techniques convey?

- What is the overall theme of the art work?

Recommended structure:

Opening paragraph:

- *Set a context.*

- Write a thesis that answers the "so what" question. Your thesis should make a definite point about the comparative analysis to follow.

Body paragraphs:

- Devote at least three paragraphs of analysis to *All Quiet on the Western Front*. Devote another three (or more) paragraphs of analysis to your choice of visual art. Conduct both analyses by referring to *specific* elements.

- Be sure that each paragraph of analysis ties the artistic device you are discussing (whether in the novel or in the visual art) to a theme developed in the artwork. For each technique, you might think of many themes or a single theme.

- Write a transitional paragraph between your discussion of the visual art and the novel.

Conclusion:

Compare/contrast the visual art with *All Quiet on the Western Front*.

- How are the works similar? How do they differ?

- What does each artist have to say about war, and how does each say it?

- Show; don't tell.

■ THE SOURCES

The assignment calls for the student to develop a comparative analysis: to analyze patterns of meaning in a novel, *All Quiet on the Western Front*; to analyze a work of *visual* art that also concerns World War I; and in comparing them to develop a deeper understanding of each.

To locate sources, Ryan Cheever turned both to print sources and the World Wide Web. For the work of art he would compare to Erich Maria Remarque's *All Quiet on the Western Front*, Cheever chose the mural *Death in Victory* by the American portraitist John Singer Sargent (1856–1925).

We include here all the sources on which Ryan Cheever drew to write his analysis comparing the painting and novel. We begin with an excerpt from the novel, follow with a reproduction of Sargent's mural, which hangs in a stairwell at Harvard's Widener Memorial Library, and continue with several sources that explain symbolism common to cemetery settings. Notice Cheever's margin notes on each source—his earliest indications of how he might selectively use his sources to develop parts of his paper.

FROM ALL QUIET ON THE WESTERN FRONT
Erich Maria Remarque

Along with Siegfried Sassoon, Wilfred Owen, and Robert Graves, Erich Maria Remarque (pen name for Erich Paul Remark, 1898–1970) is among the best-known writers to emerge from the horrors of World War I. At 18, Remarque was sent to the front lines to fight for his native Germany. There he witnessed first-hand the war's devastation and survived multiple wounds. In 1929, he published his antiwar classic All Quiet on the Western Front. *An instant success (1.2 million copies sold the first year), Remarque's bitter denunciation of the war and its pointlessness marked him politically. Within five years the Nazis would ban the novel, burning it in public and accusing its author of "pacifism." Remarque later emigrated to the United States and became a naturalized citizen. His other novels include* The Way Back *(1931),* Three Comrades *(1937),* Arch of Triumph *(1946),* A Time to Love and a Time to Die *(1954), and* Shadows in Paradise *(1971).*

This excerpt from the end of the novel follows the protagonist and narrator Paul Bäumer as he carries his good friend Kat, who has been wounded, to an aid station.

I raise him up, he stands on the uninjured leg and supports himself against a tree. I take up the wounded leg carefully, then he gives a jump and I take the knee of the sound leg also under my arm.

The going is more difficult. Often a shell whistles across. I go as quickly as I can, for the blood from Kat's wound drips to the ground. We cannot shelter ourselves properly from the explosions; before we can take cover the danger is all over.

We lie down in a small hole to wait till the shelling is over. I give Kat some tea from my water bottle. We smoke a cigarette. "Well, Kat," I say gloomily, "We are going to be separated at last."

He is silent and looks at me.

5 "Do you remember, Kat, how we commandeered the goose? And how you brought me out of the barrage when I was still a young recruit and was wounded for the first time? I cried then. Kat, that is almost three years ago."

He nods.

The anguish of solitude rises up in me. When Kat is taken away I will not have one friend left.

"Kat, in any case we must see one another again, if it is peace-time before you come back."

"Do you think that I will be marked A1 again with this leg?" he asks bitterly.

10 "With rest it will get better. The joint is quite sound. It may get all right again."

"Give me another cigarette," he says.

"Perhaps we could do something together later on, Kat." I am very miserable, it is impossible that Kat—Kat my friend, Kat with the drooping shoulders and the poor, thin moustache, Kat, whom I know as I know no other man, Kat with whom I have shared these years—it is impossible that perhaps I shall not see Kat again.

"In any case give me your address at home, Kat. And here is mine, I will write it down for you."

I write his address in my pocket book. How forlorn I am already, though he still sits here beside me. Couldn't I shoot myself quickly in the foot so as to be able to go with him.

15 Suddenly Kat gurgles and turns green and yellow, "Let us go on," he stammers.

I jump up, eager to help him, I take him up and start off at a run, a slow, steady pace, so as not to jolt his leg too much.

My throat is parched; everything dances red and black before my eyes, I stagger on doggedly and pitilessly and at last reach the dressing station.

There I drop down on my knees, but have still enough strength to fall on to the side where Kat's sound leg is. After a few minutes I straighten myself up again. My legs and my hands tremble. I have trouble in finding my water bottle, to take a pull. My lips tremble as I try to think. But I smile—Kat is saved.

After a while I begin to sort out the confusion of voices that falls on my ears.

20 "You might have spared yourself that," says an orderly.

I look at him without comprehending.

He points to Kat. "He is stone dead."

I do not understand him. "He has been hit in the shin," I say.

The orderly stands still. "That as well."

25 I turn round. My eyes are still dulled, the sweat breaks out on me again, it runs over my eyelids. I wipe it away and peer at Kat. He lies still. "Fainted," I say quickly.

The orderly whistles softly. "I know better than that. He is dead. I'll lay any money on that."

I shake my head: "Not possible. Only ten minutes ago I was talking to him. He has fainted."

Kat's hands are warm, I pass my hand under his shoulders in order to rub his temples with some tea. I feel my fingers become moist. As I draw them away from behind his head, they are bloody. "You see——" The orderly whistles once more through his teeth.

On the way without my having noticed it, Kat has caught a splinter in the head. There is just one little hole, it must have been a very tiny, stray splinter. But it has sufficed. Kat is dead.

30 Slowly I get up.

"Would you like to take his paybook and his things?" the lance-corporal asks me.

I nod and he gives them to me.

The orderly is mystified. "You are not related, are you?"

No, we are not related. No, we are not related.

35   Do I walk? Have I feet still? I raise my eyes, I let them move round, and turn myself with them, one circle, one circle, and I stand in the midst. All is as usual. Only
the Militiaman Stanislaus Katczinsky has died.

Then I know nothing more.

DEATH IN VICTORY
John Singer Sargent

The famous American painter John Singer Sargent (1856–1925) was born in Florence, Italy, to American parents. Singer studied in Europe and quickly established himself as a portraitist in society circles both in Europe and America. A prolific artist (he painted more than five hundred portraits and over a thousand landscapes and watercolors), Singer turned at the end of his career to a series of murals for the Boston Public Library and Harvard's Widener Memorial Library, where Death and Victory *hangs opposite* Entering the War *in the library's main stairwell.*

palm branch

Victory: wings + nurturing breast

Soldier grabbing Death *and* Victory

2 angels w/trumpets here

See color—light where Victory is, dark + shadowy assoc. w/ Death

Earth colors here

JOHN SINGER SARGENT'S MURALS
Mary Crawford Volk

Art historian and author Mary Crawford Volk wrote brief explanations to accompany a Web site on John Singer Sargent's murals. Her explanations of Sargent's Death and Victory *appear below. See <http://www.sargentmurals.bpl.org/site/sargent/03_hvd.html> for Volk's complete article on Sargent.*

Death and Victory

The mural . . . *Death and Victory* glorifies the grim price that this war exacted. A lone Harvard soldier, gripped closely by the partly shrouded figure of Death, embraces the form of beautiful, luminous Victory, with her palm branch held high. Beneath his feet lies a fallen German, amid blood, barbed wire, and ammunition—the mortal enemy defined. The jingoistic, collective fervor of *Entering the War* [the second of Sargent's Harvard murals] becomes here an altarpiece for a youthful martyr.

Sargent's Harvard Murals

In the fall of 1920, Harvard University commissioned Sargent to produce two paintings for the main stairwell at Widener Library as part of the University's enduring tribute to its World War I dead. Six years later the University published plans for a Memorial Church to face Widener across the Yard and permanently display the Honor Roll, listing the names of the nearly 400 Harvard men who perished in the war. This programmatic ensemble, located at the physical center of the University, forms the most elaborate World War I memorial in the Boston area.

CEMETERY SYMBOLISM
Pam Reid

Pam Reid's article on cemetery symbolism first appeared in Ancestry Magazine, *September/ October 2000. See <http://www.ancestrylibrary.com/learn/library/article.aspx?article=2977>. Reid is a genealogical researcher.*

As more and more researchers venture into cemeteries to seek out ancestral graves, questions arise about the meanings of the artwork and symbols found on the tombstones. The researcher wants to know what a symbol might mean and if the meaning of the symbol might provide more clues about this ancestor and his life, ideals, associations, etc. . . .

[Selected symbols found in cemeteries]

Mortality

Arrow—mortality

Broken column—decay, loss of family head

Broken ring—severed family circle

Candle being snuffed—loss of life

Coffin—mortality

Figure with dart—mortality

Grim reaper—death personified

Hourglass—time has run out

Scythe—death cuts us down

Skull, crossed bones—death

Spade, crossed spade and shovel—death

Religion

Angels—spirituality and tomb guarding

Holy books—Christianity

Chalice—sacraments

Cherub—angelic innocence

Crescent—Islam

Crown—glory of life after death

Cross—faith . . .

Heart (sacred)—suffering of Christ

Menorah—Judaism

Star of David—Judaism

Resurrection, Eternal Life, Immortality

Angel, flying or trumpeting—rebirth, resurrection

Bird (dove) or bird flying—eternal life, resurrection

Cross—resurrection

Flame, light, lamp, torch—immortality of the spirit, resurrection

Garland or wreath—saintliness, glory, victory in death

Horns—resurrection

Ivy—immortality

Rooster—awakening, resurrection

Star—death could not overpower the light

Sun—light, warmth, renewed life, life everlasting

Trumpeters—harbingers of the resurrection

Urn—immortality (The storing of the vital organs was of extreme importance to the ancient Egyptians who believed that life would be restored through the vital organs placed in the urn.)

CEMETERY SYMBOLS: THE PALM
Richard O. Reisem

Richard O. Reisem's pamphlet "A Field Guide to Forest Lawn Cemetery" (Buffalo, NY) includes a section on symbolism commonly found in cemetery architecture and artwork, including tombstones and mausoleums. You can find his complete discussion at <http://ah.bfn.org/a/forestL/symbols/index.html>. Reisem is a writer and student of architecture and history.

Palm

Signifies Victory and rejoicing. The palm has a variety of sacred and secular associations. In the Cabbala, it symbolizes the righteous man (tzaddik) and was an emblem of Judea after the Exodus. One of the four plants paraded on the Sukkot to celebrate God's bounty, it represents the Jew who studies the Torah but does not obey the commandments. Other interpretations include the spine that bends before God, and God. In Christianity, it signifies righteousness, resurrection, and martyrdom based on Christ's entry into Jerusalem where palm branches were laid in his path. In the Middle Ages, a palm leaf was a badge of pilgrimage to the Holy Land and people wearing it were called 'palmers.' Because of its height and radiating leaves, it was an early fertility and sun symbol. The Babylonians considered it a divine tree because of its association with the sun. In many early Middle Eastern civilizations the palm was a Tree of Life; the Phoenician god Baal-Tamar was the lord of the palm and the palm was the emblem of the goddesses Astarte and Ishtar. In ancient Rome, victors were presented with palm branches and the palm took on victory as its meaning in ancient Rome, Egypt and Greece. The palm has also signified fame and peace. In contemporary, secular culture it represents tropical delights.

■ THE OUTLINE

Consider Ryan Cheever's initial thesis for his comparative analysis:

> There are considerable differences between Erich Maria Remarque's view of war, as expressed in <u>All Quiet on the Western Front</u>, and John Singer Sargent's view, as expressed in his painting <u>Death and Victory</u>.

In conference with his instructor, Cheever realized that his thesis was unfocused. The statement makes no commitment about the *nature* of the differences between the novel and the painting—precisely the kind of information readers need in order to anticipate what is to come. A vague thesis not only jeopardizes readers' interest in a paper, it also undermines the writing of a first draft by denying the writer specific points around which to organize paragraphs. This assignment calls for Cheever to reach some definite conclusion about the works of art he is analyzing and comparing. (Recall that the assignment asks for a thesis that answers the "so what?" question.) His initial thesis does not satisfy this requirement, but his revised thesis does. The revised thesis both expresses a definite opinion and at the same time suggests an outline for the paper to follow, giving Cheever a direction for his argument:

Introduction:	Introduce Sargent's mural and Remarque's novel.
Thesis:	The glories of death for a valiant cause in Sargent's painting Death and Victory could not differ more with Remarque's bitter view of death in All Quiet on the Western Front.
Analysis #1:	Death and Victory 1. Sargent uses gender as symbol. 2. He uses a palm branch, a wreath, and a trumpet as symbols. 3. He uses lighting to suggest rebirth.
Transition:	Introduce Erich Maria Remarque's novel and state the contrast: There is no glory in death in this artistic work.
Analysis #2:	All Quiet on the Western Front 1. Descriptions of pain suggest no glory. 2. Description of Kat's death suggests no glory. 3. Description of Paul's anonymous death suggests no glory.
Conclusion:	Compare and contrast the two works of art.

■ THE PAPER

Before you read the final draft of Ryan Cheever's paper and wonder if you could produce an equally polished final product, consider several paragraphs from his first draft, accompanied by his own revisions and his instructor's remarks. We include a section of Cheever's early draft so that you will not be intimidated by the clear structure and careful word choice of the final version or fooled into imagining that these were products of a first draft. Cheever's early efforts were, in turns, awkward, haphazardly developed, and lacking in coherence, unity, and sentence-level clarity and correctness. Through three revisions—one that focused primarily on global matters (unity and coherence in the whole paper), another on paragraphs, and a third on word choice, punctuation, and grammar—Cheever markedly improved his effort. The revision that follows shows the instructor's comments in blue and Ryan's revisions in black.

An Example of Revision

He points to Kat. "He is stone dead."

I do not understand him. "He has been hit in the shin," I say.

The orderly stands still. "That as well."

I turn around. My eyes are still dulled, the sweat breaks out on me again, it runs over my eyelids. I wipe it away and peer at Kat. He lies still. "Fainted," I say quickly.

Cut

The orderly whistles softly. "I know better than that. He is dead. I'll lay any money on that."

Keep this

I shake my head: "Not possible. Only ten minutes ago I was talking to him. He has fainted."

Kat's hands are warm, I pass my hand under his shoulders in oder to rub his temples with some tea. I feel my fingers become moist. As I draw them away from behind his head, they are bloody. ["You see--" The orderly whistles once more through his teeth. (290)]

~~In this passage, Paul is informed of Kat's death. The orderly tells him that he is dead, but at first Paul doesn't understand or believe it. Only after feeling Kat's blood on his hands does he realize what has happened.~~ In this passage, the

who receives and examines Kat

orderly displays an utter lack of emotion and caring

The orderly

as he tells Paul the bad news. ~~He~~ "whistles softly,"

and says, "He is dead. I'll lay any money on that."

Paragraph Revision

You likely do not need to quote this entire passage. Quote selectively and run key phrases in with your sentences.

The orderly

He speaks as if Kat's death is some sort of game, something to bet on. He sees this dead man in front of him and continues as if nothing has happened at all. After Paul has confirmed the orderly's claim, the orderly says, "You see--," and then "whistles once more through his teeth." ~~The orderly views Kat's~~ [The orderly (290).]

~~death as nothing more than a common occurrence.~~ *So many young men died in the war that an orderly,*
~~It seems that the orderly would rather be right~~ *whose job it is to deliver care, couldn't feel*
~~about Kat's death than to have him still be alive.~~ *emotion. To the orderly, Kat's death makes no*
~~This is not glory or victory; it is painful, brutal~~ *difference. Kat dies without glory or victory.*
~~death. Even more evidence of this is found shortly~~ *Remarque offers no angels raising him to heaven.*

afterward when Paul thinks to himself, "All is usual. Only the Militiaman Stanislaus Katczinsky has died" (291). He says, "All is usual," as if to imply nothing out of the ordinary has happened. War has hardened him to view death as an everyday occurrence, as nothing new. Unlike Sargent's painting, the is no glory or victory in Kat's death; he goes unnoticed and unrecognized to the grave.

~~A final example of when Remarque portrays~~

~~death as not containing glory or victory is when the~~

~~fair-headed recruit is killed.~~ *For example, after one* After the firefight in

~~the~~ *a* graveyard, Paul and Kat tend to a wounded

soldier ~~that is discovered~~ *who turns out* to be the "fair-haired

~~recruit. They realize it is the fair-haired recruit~~ *", a new soldier in the company. Paul and Kat recognize the wounded man, which*

because he is wearing no underwear. ~~He took off his~~

~~underwear~~ after he soiled himself out of terror during his first bombardment. As they are dressing his wound, Paul thinks to himself:

> The youngster will hardly survive the
> carrying, and at most he will only last a few

Paragraph Revision
Ryan, you are merely repeating information from the passage above, not advancing it with analysis. Make a point —and <u>develop</u> it.

Paragraph Revision
If you want to discuss Paul's reaction to Kat's death, begin a new paragraph. The present paragraph belongs to the "orderly"—to what happens when Paul brings Kat to the dressing station and to what this means.

Sentence-level Revision
"of when/is when": Awkward construction. Avoid.

Move this section up

days. What he has gone through so far is nothing to what he's in for till he dies. Now he is numb and feels nothing. In an hour he will become one screaming bundle of intolerable pain. Every day that he can live will be a howling torture. (72)

Paul ~~has just thought about how much pain and suffering this young boy will endure on his way to death. He~~ realizes that ~~he~~ *the recruit* will ~~be in~~ *endure* relentless agony as his life slowly ends. This is no way to die.

It is not glorious, and the fair-headed recruit *The description "howling torture" and "one screaming* certainly feels no victory in his death. ~~All he feels~~ *bundle of intolerable pain" are vivid images of suffering,* ~~is unrelenting agony, pain, and suffering.~~ In *not glory. This one death is symbolic of a generation of* ~~extreme~~ contrast to Sargent's painting, the fair- *"fair-haired recruits" who went to war expecting* headed recruit dies miserably and seemingly *something glorious and found, instead, brutal death.* without purpose.

> **Global revision:**
> Ryan—arrange your references to and discussion of All Quiet on the Western Front in chronological order. The "young recruit" scene takes place well before Kat's death.

> **Paragraph revision:**
> Make a more specific point in the paragraph with direct references to the passage you have quoted. This paragraph is vague.

THE FINAL PAPER

Cheever 1

Ryan Cheever

Professor Sedlak

Humanities 106

6 November 2005

Death in War: A Comparative Analysis of John Singer Sargent's Death and Victory
and Erich Maria Remarque's All Quiet on the Western Front

(1)   In 1920, Harvard University commissioned John Singer Sargent to paint Death and Victory (see Fig. 1) to commemorate the fallen soldiers of World War I who had attended Harvard (Volk). In the painting, a Harvard soldier has died and his body is being pulled by both the figures of Death and Victory. Death, represented by a shrouded figure, grasps the soldier and pulls him downward.

Figure 1   John Singer Sargent's Death and Victory. Widener Memorial Library. Harvard University. Cambridge, MA. 1922.

Victory, represented by a winged angel, pulls the soldier up toward heaven. This painting glorifies death in war. It shows a soldier being uprooted from his resting place on the field of battle and thrust into the light of heaven. By contrast, another famous work of art on World War I, All Quiet on the Western Front, portrays war as a terrible, vicious, and empty endeavor that results only in death. In this novel, Erich Maria Remarque shows men dying without glory and without patriotism, romance, or beauty. For Remarque, there is only death in war. He writes from the standpoint of someone who has witnessed death in its utmost ruthlessness. The glories of death for a valiant cause in Sargent's painting could not differ more with Remarque's bitter view of death in <u>All Quiet on the Western Front</u>.

In <u>Death and Victory</u>, two main elements contribute to the feeling of glory in death: Sargent's use of symbolism and his use of lighting. Two main types of symbolism dominate the painting. The first involves gender. Sargent links death and glory in the portion of the painting where the soldier is being pulled from the battlefield by both Death and Victory simultaneously. The soldier clutches the shrouded figure of Death while grasping equally for the winged angel of Victory. This image suggests that both death and victory can be achieved at once. Also, in this painting, Sargent depicts Victory as a woman with her breasts exposed to the soldier, and he depicts Death as a shroud-covered man. As a woman, Victory shows the nurturing side of life generally not seen in war. With her bare breasts, Victory is a life-giving entity who represents nurturing and health, while the shrouded figure of Death represents the opposite. The figure of Death emphasizes men's role in war: to kill.

Sargent also attaches symbolism suggesting glory in death in his use of a palm branch, a wreath, and a trumpet. The winged angel of Victory carries a palm branch and wreath. These objects are symbols that strengthen the image of victory. The palm branch is an ancient Judeo-Christian symbol representing "victory and rejoicing" and, in the case of Christianity, "righteousness, resurrection, and martyrdom" (Reisem). Righteousness, resurrection, and martyrdom suggest that this soldier has died for a just cause he believes in and that, in return for his sacrifice, he will be resurrected in heaven. The symbol of the wreath reasserts this notion of victory. The winner of a race receives a wreath to acknowledge his victory, and it is commonplace to see wreaths on graves because they signify "victory [even] in death" (Reid). Sargent provides another example of symbolism close to the soldier in the sky above: the two angels playing trumpets serve as "harbingers of the resurrection" (Reid) and remind us of death's defeat.

Finally, Sargent's use of lighting encourages the notion of glory in death. Light colors draw the viewer's eyes upward and away from the death on the battlefield. Sargent draws the viewer's line of vision to the center and upper regions of the painting to show the dead soldier being pulled toward heaven. The eye is drawn to the "luminous" (Volk) portions of the painting first. Sargent uses yellow and white in this part of the painting so that the viewer will at first see victory and glory rather than the destruction and pain on the battlefield below. Sargent places two angels above the figure of Victory. The coloration of these angels is bright and nearly glowing. By contrast, the images of death and destruction painted around the soldier are dark earth tones, bland and monotonous. This use of color emphasizes the pull of the viewer's vision towards the center and upper regions of the painting, the part that strongly affirms the soldier's glory and victory, even in death.

In contrast to Sargent's use of symbolism and light to glorify death in war, Remarque also uses artistic techniques in All Quiet on the Western Front--but to make a very different point. All Quiet on the Western Front is one of the great anti-war novels. Remarque tells the story of Paul Bäumer as he goes off to fight in World War I. We follow Paul, the narrator, through battles and watch many people die and suffer. In no part of the novel does Remarque provide an example of a battlefield death that is glorious.

For example, after one firefight in a graveyard, Paul and his friend Kat tend to a wounded soldier who turns out to be the "fair-haired recruit," a new soldier in the company. Paul and Kat recognize the wounded man because he is wearing no underwear, which he took off after he soiled himself out of terror during his first bombardment. As they are dressing his wound, Paul thinks to himself:

> The youngster will hardly survive the carrying, and at most he
> will only last a few days. What he has gone through so far is

> nothing to what he's in for till he dies. Now he is numb and
> feels nothing. In an hour he will become one screaming bundle
> of intolerable pain. Every day that he can live will be a howling
> torture. (72)

Paul realizes that the recruit will endure relentless agony as his life slowly ends. This is no way to die. It is not glorious, and the fair-haired recruit certainly feels no victory in this death. The description "howling torture" and "one screaming bundle of intolerable pain" are vivid images of suffering, not glory. This one death is symbolic of a generation of "fair-haired recruits" who went to war expecting something glorious and found, instead, brutal death. In extreme contrast to Sargent's painting, the fair-headed recruit dies miserably and seemingly without purpose.

⑦ Another example of Remarque's dismissal of death without even the slightest hint of glory or victory comes when Paul's friend Kat dies. Kat's leg is wounded in battle, and Paul carries him a long way back to a dressing station to have his shin bandaged. What Paul does not realize is that, en route, Kat took shrapnel to the head and died. In this passage, the orderly who receives and examines Kat displays an utter lack of caring as he tells Paul the bad news. The orderly "whistles softly" and says, "'He is dead. I'll lay any money on that.'" The orderly speaks as if Kat's death is some sort of game, something to bet on. He sees this dead man in front of him and continues as if nothing happened at all. After Paul confirms the orderly's claim, the orderly says, "'You see--'" and "The orderly whistles once more through his teeth" (290). So many young men died in the war that an orderly, whose job it is to deliver care, couldn't feel emotion. To the orderly, Kat's death makes no difference. Kat simply is another body—one of the 22 million sacrificed during the war. Remarque offers no angels raising him to heaven.

⑧ At the end of the novel, Paul dies as well. At this point, Remarque introduces a new narrator who reports that "He fell in October 1918" (296). Paul has just died, but no one has given his body or his soul any recognition. He is a true hero, and the only notice he gets is a short description of his face and the bullet that killed him: "Turning him over one saw that he could not have suffered long; his face had an expression of calm, as though almost glad the end had come"(296). Paul carries no victory with him in death; Remarque does not mention heaven or resurrection. Paul's death came on a day that was characterized as "so quiet and still on the whole front, that the army report confined itself to the single sentence: All quiet on the Western Front" (296). These lines imply that Paul's own army, the force he has been fighting for and has given his life to, doesn't recognize his death as significant or even worthy of record. Paul tastes no Victory in his death; he isn't pulled into glory by a winged angel: he is thrown into death, alone and anonymous, just like everyone else who fights in the war.

⑨   John Singer Sargent's <u>Death and Victory</u> and Erich Maria Remarque's <u>All Quiet on the Western Front</u> offer opposing views of war. Sargent's painting shows that in war, death comes with glory and victory, but Remarque's novel tells a completely different story. Remarque dramatizes the fact that, in war, death is a terrible, unrelenting abyss into which many fall. For Remarque, there is no glory or victory in death, just painful suffering. It is not by chance that these works embodied the views that they do. Sargent and Remarque had different backgrounds and different motives for creating their works. Sargent was an American painter who had never fought in a war; he was commissioned by Harvard to paint an inspiring and uplifting scene commemorating Harvard soldiers who had died. Remarque was a soldier <u>in</u> the war who witnessed death and destruction first hand. Also, he wrote his novel of his own accord. <u>Death and Victory</u> and <u>All Quiet on the Western Front</u> show insight into two very different people: John Singer Sargent, an American painter who thought he knew of war, and Erich Maria Remarque, a German writer who knew all too much of war.

Cheever 7

Works Cited

Reid, Pam. "Cemetery Symbolism." <u>Ancestry Magazine</u> 18.5 (2000).
    20 Oct. 2005 <http://www.ancestrylibrary.com/learn/library/
    article.aspx?article=2977>.

Reisem, Richard O. "A Field Guide to Forest Lawn Cemetery." Forest Lawn
    Heritage Foundation, Buffalo. 2002. 22 Oct. 2005
    <http://ah.bfn.org/a/forestL/symbols/index.html>.

Remarque, Erich Maria. <u>All Quiet on the Western Front</u>. 1929. Trans. A.W.
    Wheen. New York: Fawcett, 1991.

Sargent, John Singer. <u>Death and Victory</u> [oil on canvas]. Widener Memorial
    Library. Harvard University. Cambridge, MA. 1922. 17 Oct. 2005
    <http://www.kingsgalleries.com/1024x768/galleries/sargent/expanded/
    picture-26.htm>.

Volk, Mary Crawford. "Death and Victory"; "Sargent's Harvard Murals." 2003. 17
    Oct. 2005 <http://www.sargentmurals.bpl.org/site/sargent/03_hvd.html>.

■ DISCUSSION

In response to his assignment, Cheever analyzed *two* separate objects—a novel and a painting—and then compared them. He has written both an *analysis* and, because he is also *comparing and contrasting*, a *synthesis*. Because he makes a definite interpretive point with his synthesis, we can classify the paper as an *argument*. In addition, Cheever must *summarize* elements of Sargent's painting and Remarque's novel as the first part of his analyses. Consider this passage from the paper:

> The soldier clutches the shrouded figure of Death while grasping
> equally for the winged angel of Victory. This image suggests that both
> death and victory can be achieved at once.

The first sentence *summarizes* one aspect of the painting. The second sentence conducts an *analysis*. Cheever repeats this pattern throughout. The ability to analyze assumes the ability to summarize. So both on the scale of the paper itself (which is *an analysis and an argument* arranged as a *comparison and contrast synthesis*), and on the scale of individual parts of the paper, Cheever combines the forms of academic writing presented in Part I of this book. And so will you in your papers.

In Chapter 5 you learned that in an analysis the writer uses a definition or principle as a lens to examine an object under study. That use of definition can be formal—in which case the writer will quote and cite the source of the definition or principle (a technique illustrated in the model paper in Chapter 5, pp. 187–91). The use of definition can also be informal, without citation—which is Cheever's technique, above. In that example, the "principle" Cheever works with could be stated this way: "A fallen soldier who grasps equally at two supports (Death and Victory) relies on both. Both of them are meaningful, and the soldier links them." That is an implied principle, and its logic is clear enough that Cheever can use it without needing to find some external source to cite as an authority.

In other parts of the paper, Cheever turns to outside authorities and cites his sources:

> Sargent also attaches symbolism suggesting glory in death in his use of a palm branch, a wreath, and a trumpet. The winged angel of Victory carries a palm branch and wreath. These objects are symbols that strengthen the image of victory. The palm branch is an ancient Judeo-Christian symbol representing "victory and rejoicing" and, in the case of Christianity, "righteousness, resurrection, and martyrdom" (Reisem). Righteousness, resurrection, and martyrdom suggest that this soldier has died for a just cause he believes in and that, in return for his sacrifice, he will be resurrected in heaven. The symbol of the wreath also ensures this notion of victory. The winner of a race receives a wreath to acknowledge his victory, and it is commonplace to see wreaths on graves because they signify "victory [even] in death" (Reid). Sargent provides another example of symbolism close to the soldier in the sky above: the two angels playing trumpets serve as "harbingers of the resurrection" (Reid) and remind us that death has not won.

Whether he formally cites a source for his analytical principle or generates and then applies his own principle, Cheever repeats this pattern of analytical writing throughout the two main sections of the paper: the analysis of Sargent's painting and the analysis of Remarque's novel.

Notice, also, the focus and careful development of the paragraph above. Cheever begins with a clear topic sentence that promises a three-part paragraph. He follows through, first with a sentence that focuses us on two of the three symbols we can use to see more deeply into the painting: the palm branch and the wreath held by the winged angel of victory. He devotes five sentences to developing this part of the analysis. He concludes with the third and final section of analysis by exploring the meaning of trumpets in the painting. Every sentence of the paragraph is on point: it is unified. And every sentence leads logically, one to the next: the paragraph is coherent. Regardless of paragraph topic, you find this same careful development throughout Cheever's paper.

Finally, consider this paper as a comparison and contrast synthesis. The paper follows the structure suggested in the assignment, with Cheever careful to relate each part of his analysis (the three paragraphs analyzing the painting, and the three analyzing the novel) to a clear theme in each work. That theme in Sargent's panting is the possibility of linking death in war to everlasting glory; in Remarque's novel, the theme is the meaninglessness of death in war. Cheever organizes his comparison/contrast synthesis by source, first analyzing the painting and then the novel. He concludes by discussing both works in light of one another.

Remember that the clear, well-developed paper you have read started as an unevenly written draft that Ryan Cheever revised several times. Through revision, he clarified his thinking—both for himself and for his readers.

Practicing ■ 9
Academic Writing

■ MERIT VS. PRIVILEGE IN COLLEGE ADMISSIONS

This chapter will give you the chance to apply the skills you have learned in summary, critique, synthesis, and analysis. You will read 10 brief selections on the competing roles of merit (hard work and talent) versus privilege (birth and connections) in personal advancement. You will then write several responses, drawing on the source materials provided.

The specific issue for your writing is "legacy" admissions: the controversial policy of giving special consideration to the sons and daughters of alumni during the admissions process at certain colleges. Through legacy programs, alumni children are sometimes admitted to a freshman class over applicants with higher test scores and higher grades. Is this fair? Is it necessary, from the school's point of view? Whether or not you attend a college with a legacy program, the broader questions involved are central to your present and future success.

Here's why: Americans are a people who regard merit—that is, talent—as the fundamental measure of a person's worth. (At least this is what we're taught in school.) In a meritocracy, hard work and talent supposedly trump the privileges of family name, money, and connections. Privileging family over merit was the old, European way of doing business. Americans broke with that tradition when we founded a republic.

For most students, especially those who may be the first of their families to attend college, the conviction that one rises through merit, not birth, is the foundation upon which all dreams of the future rest. Why else would anyone work two jobs while attending school or study until 3 A.M. to get an A on an exam? The assumption, the bargain we make, is that hard work pays off. You put in the effort, get the grades, and gain access to all America offers: a good job or a first-rate education if you have truly shined in your studies.

What you will discover in the following readings is a more complicated reality. College admissions staffs routinely allow privilege to trump merit in selecting candidates for a freshman class. You will read about this issue and will explore it through writing. As you do so, remember that the question at hand is broader than college admissions. Imagine for a moment that on completing your degree you apply for a job and lose out because the company decides instead to hire the son or daughter of an existing employee—someone clearly less qualified than you. How would you feel? Most likely, angry and betrayed, as if someone had changed the rules mid-game. The issues with legacy admissions are identical.

Your main assignment in this practice chapter will be to write an argument that synthesizes what various authors have written on the topic with your own insights. To prepare, you will complete several briefer assignments that require you to work closely with your sources. In this progression of assignments, you will write a combination of summaries, paraphrases, critiques, and explanations that will prepare you for—and that will actually produce sections of—your more ambitious argument synthesis. In this respect, the assignment at hand is typical of other writing you will do in college: While, at times, you will be called on to write a stand-alone critique or a purely explanatory paper, you will also write papers that blend the basic forms of college writing that you have studied in this text.

The set of readings on legacy admissions amounts to controlled research. We have provided the topic; and through a search of books, journals, magazines, and newspapers, we have gathered selections that can provide the basis of an informed discussion that you will present as an academic paper. When an instructor asks you to write a research paper, the end point of your research will be exactly what you will encounter below: a series of readings that await your synthesis.

■ THE ASSIGNMENTS

Summary

Summary Assignment #1: Summarizing Text

Summarize the *USA Today* editorial that supports the practice of legacy admissions (pp. 351–52) and the article by DeKoven (pp. 342–44), which opposes the practice. Make careful notes on the selections as you prepare your summary. Follow the guidelines covered in Chapter 1, particularly the Guidelines for Writing Summaries box on pages 8–9. Also, consult the advice on note taking (pp. 284–85).

As for the selections you are *not* summarizing, read carefully and highlight the text *as if* you were preparing to write a summary.

Summary Assignment #2: Summarizing Tables

Study the two tables (p. 348, p. 349) in Mark Megalli's article "So Your Dad Went to Harvard." In a paragraph summarize the key information contained in these tables.

Paraphrase

Write a paraphrase of the second paragraph in Howell and Turner's article, "The History of Legacy Admissions" (pp. 344–46). Read the paragraph with care, using a dictionary as necessary, to understand difficult passages. Then follow the suggestions for writing a paraphrase on pages 32–37.

Critique

Choose the *USA Today* editorial favoring legacy admissions (pp. 351–52) or the DeKoven article (p. 342–44), which opposes the practice, and write a critique. If you want to save yourself some work later when writing your argument synthesis, critique the selection that *opposes* the position you will be taking in your argument. (In an academic argument, you raise and then respond to objections to your own position. Thus, if in this assignment you critique the article that opposes your position, you will be able to use your work in the larger argument.) To select which of the passages to critique, read the Argument assignment (pp. 332–33), read the selections, and then choose a position.

Since the writing you do for this assignment will be incorporated into a larger argument with its own introduction and conclusion, you need not write an introduction or conclusion for this critique. Instead, write an *abbreviated* critique, consisting of the following parts:

1. a summary of the selection (your response to Summary assignment #1);

2. an evaluation of the presentation for accuracy, clarity, logic, and/or fairness; and

3. a statement of your agreement and/or disagreement with the author.

For parts 2 and 3, be sure to support your evaluation with reasons. Refer to the selection, summarizing, or quoting key elements, as needed. See pages 68–70 for advice on writing critiques, particularly, the Guidelines for Writing Critiques box on page 70, along with the hints on incorporating quoted material into your own writing, pages 42–48.

Explanatory Synthesis

Based on the reading selections in this chapter, write three explanations that might follow one another in a larger paper. The explanations should each be one or two well-developed paragraphs. The topics are as follows: (1) Explain the practice of legacy admissions, making sure to explain how widespread the practice is, why it exists, and whom it affects. (2) Explain the arguments *in favor* of legacy admissions. (3) Explain the arguments *opposing* legacy admissions.

Key requirements for each explanation:

- Each paragraph of explanation should begin with a clear topic sentence.

- Each paragraph of explanation should refer to *at least two* different sources. Be sure to set up the reference (which can be a summary, paraphrase, or quotation) with care. Use appropriate citation format, likely MLA (see pp. 290–92).

- To help you explain, use facts, examples, statistics, and expert opinions from your sources, as needed.

Argument Synthesis

Develop an argument in which you adopt *one* of four positions regarding the controversy over legacy admissions in college. You will complete your chosen claim by providing reasons to be developed in your paper:

1. Giving legacy applicants preferred treatment in the admissions process is a defensible practice because . . .

2. Giving legacy applicants preferred treatment in the admissions process is an indefensible practice because . . .

3. Admissions Offices should keep private their policies concerning legacy applicants because . . .

4. Admissions Offices should openly discuss their policies concerning legacy applicants because . . .

In developing reasons to support your claim, draw on the sources that follow. You don't have to use *all* of the passages; as you plan your synthesis, you may want to research additional sources (for instance, the legacy policies of your own school or a school that rejected you). Your response to this assignment, like many of the arguments you will write in college, will combine elements of summary, evaluation, and explanation. Specifically, you will be using your responses to the earlier writing assignments, above, in preparing your argument synthesis. Your paper should consist of these parts:

- An introductory paragraph that sets a context for the topic and presents the claim you are going to support in the argument that follows. Your claim (your thesis) may appear at the end of this paragraph (or introductory section).

- A paragraph defining the practice and extent of legacy admissions. See the Explanation assignment and the second Summary assignment.

- A paragraph that paraphrases the history of legacy admissions. See the Paraphrase assignment.

- A paragraph or two explaining the objections to legacy admissions. See the Explanation assignment and the first Summary assignment.

- A paragraph or two explaining the support for legacy admissions. See the Explanation assignment and the first Summary assignment.

- Reasons for supporting or rejecting legacy admissions, if you choose to write on claim #1 or #2; OR reasons for supporting or rejecting the current, largely hidden, practice in considering legacy admissions, if you choose to write on claims #3 or #4. *This is the main section of the argument.* It should consist of several paragraphs—at least three or four, each focused on a specific reason to support your claim. Use source materials to help present these reasons.

- Counterargument: A paragraph explaining the merits of the argument opposing yours. See the Summary assignment. (Use your summary of the reading selection that *opposes* the position you take in this argument.)

- Rebuttal to counterargument: A paragraph or two evaluating and ultimately rejecting the argument opposing yours. See the Critique assignment. (If you chose to critique a reading that opposes your position in this argument, use that critique here.)

- A conclusion.

Where you place the various elements of this argument synthesis will be your decision, as writer. Which sources to use and what logic to present in defense of your claim are also yours to decide. See pages 168–72 for help in thinking about structuring and supporting your argument.

A Note on Incorporating Quotations   Identify the sources you intend to use for your synthesis. Working with a phrase, sentence, or brief passage from each, use a variety of the techniques discussed in the section Incorporating Quotations into Your Sentences (pp. 42–48) to write sentences that you can use to advance your argument. Some of these sentences should demonstrate the use of ellipsis marks and brackets. See pages 44–48 in Chapter 1.

Analysis

As an alternative to the argument synthesis assignment above, complete *one* of the following analysis assignments:

Analysis Assignment #1

In preparation for writing an analysis, read "Making Ethical Decisions" by Gerald F. Cavanagh (pp. 354–56). In this piece you will find three principles for analysis—*utilitarianism, justice,* and *individual rights*—that you can use to answer the following question: Is the college admissions practice of giving legacy applicants preferential treatment ethical?

To answer this question, select one—or, if you are feeling ambitious, more than one—principle from Cavanagh's article and use it as a lens to analyze the controversy over legacy admissions. In using different principles for analysis, you may reach different conclusions, an outcome consistent with what you read at the outset of the discussion of analysis in Chapter 5. Cavanagh himself suggests a process for using all three principles in reaching an ethical decision. But you may choose to use one or two principles. As you write, be sure to focus on answering the question posed above. Your answer will be an argument, guided by one of two claims:

1. The college admissions practice of giving legacy applicants preferential treatment is ethical because . . .

2. The college admissions practice of giving legacy applicants preferential treatment is unethical because . . .

Complete your chosen claim by providing reasons to be developed through your analysis.

In writing your analysis, follow the Guidelines on pp. 192–93, in Chapter 5. Use the fruits of your earlier assignments involving summary, paraphrase, and explanation. Certainly, before you analyze a phenomenon, you must define or explain it, and your earlier work should help you to do this. Consider using the following structure for your analysis:

- A paragraph of introduction that sets a context for the topic and presents the claim you are going to support in the analysis that follows. Your claim (your thesis) may appear at the end of this paragraph (or introductory section).

- A paragraph defining the practice and extent of legacy admissions. See the Explanatory assignment and the second Summary assignment.

- A paragraph that paraphrases the history of legacy admissions. See the Paraphrase assignment.

- A paragraph or two explaining the objections to legacy admissions. See the Explanatory assignment and the first Summary assignment.

- A paragraph or two explaining the support for legacy admissions. See the Explanatory assignment and the first Summary assignment.

- An analysis of legacy admissions using one (or more) of Cavanagh's principles for reaching ethical decisions. *This is the key part of your paper.* If you use one of Cavanagh's principles, your analysis should be three or four paragraphs. If you use more than one of Cavanagh's principles, limit yourself to two paragraphs of development for each. Remember that your analysis provides your reasons for judging the practice of legacy admissions to be ethical or unethical.

- A conclusion in which you argue that, based on the insights gained through your analysis, the practice of legacy admissions is ethical or unethical.

Analysis Assignment #2

Write an analysis of the legacy admission phenomenon. Follow the advice presented in Chapter 5. See especially the Guidelines for Writing Analyses box on pp. 192–93. In preparing your paper, use, as needed, the fruits of your earlier assignments involving summary, paraphrase, and explanation. Certainly before you analyze a phenomenon you must define or explain it, and your earlier work should help you to do this.

You might follow the suggestions above, in Analysis Assignment #1, for structuring your analysis. However, instead of basing your analysis on a principle from Cavanagh's article, use one of the following statements—or another of your own choosing—drawn from the sources that follow. Plan to write three or four well-developed paragraphs of analysis, based on the principle you select:

The more you look at modern America, the more you are struck by how frequently it departs from the meritocratic ideal.

—The Economist, "The Curse of Nepotism"

While people may argue that everyone should be treated exactly the same, the truth is that we all favor some sorts of criteria. The ethical trick is to make those criteria morally relevant.

—Miriam Schulman, "May the Best Man or Woman Win"

[T]here is no defense—moral, practical, or financial—for [elite colleges'] hereditary spoils system.

—Jesse Shapiro, "A Second Look: Attacking Legacy Preference"

Simply put, legacy admissions are defensible and, in any event, affect such a tiny portion of the nation's college applicants as to be negligible.

—Debra Thomas and Terry Shepard, "Legacy Admissions are Defensible Because the Process Can't Be 'Fair'"

Elite schools, like any luxury brand, are an aesthetic experience—an exquisitely constructed fantasy of what it means to belong to an elite—and they have always been mindful of what must be done to maintain that experience.

—Malcolm Gladwell, "Getting In: The Social Logic of College Admissions"

[T]he legacy preferential system perpetuates elitism by conferring considerable advantage upon privileged white children and, as a result, disfavoring blacks and others whose parents were less likely to have gone to college.

—Mark Megalli, "So Your Dad Went to Harvard"

At the end of the day, this isn't about money. It's about right and wrong.

—John Edwards, "End Special Privilege"

Choosing a diverse student body that contributes to a stimulating campus environment is a freedom worth preserving.

—USA Today, "Preserve Universities' Right to Shape Student Community"

■ THE READINGS

Read the following passages, then complete the writing assignments, above. In summarizing, quoting, paraphrasing, evaluating, analyzing, and synthesizing these sources, you practice the skills fundamental to all college-level writing.

A cautionary note: When writing syntheses, it is all-too-easy to become careless in properly crediting your sources. Before drafting your paper, please review the section on Avoiding Plagiarism in Chapter 1 (pp. 48–50) as well as the relevant sections on Citing Sources in Chapter 7 (pp. 288–306).

THE CURSE OF NEPOTISM

The Economist

Nepotism *is the favoring of friends, family, or others closely associated with decision makers. The term suggests a lack of fairness and, at its worst, corruption. This piece first appeared in* The Economist *(January 10, 2004).*

America likes to think of itself as the very embodiment of the spirit of meritocracy: a country where all people are judged on their individual abilities rather than their family connections. The American Revolution swept away the flummery of feudal titles. Thomas Jefferson dreamed of creating a "natural aristocracy." Benjamin Franklin sniped that "a man who makes boast of his ancestors doth but advertise his own insignificance."

The Founding Fathers had a rather narrow view of who should be admitted to their meritocratic republic, to be sure. But today most Americans believe that their country has done a reasonable job of getting rid of the most blatant forms of discrimination towards blacks and women and building a ladder of educational opportunity. Americans are far more confident than Europeans that people deserve what they get in life.

But are they right? The more you look at modern America, the more you are struck by how frequently it departs from the meritocratic ideal. George Bush's Washington is a study in family influence: look at the Powells, the Chao/McConnells, the Scalias and the Cheneys, not to mention the Shrub himself.*

The biggest insult to meritocracy, however, is found in the country's top universities. These institutions, which control access to the country's most impressive jobs, consider themselves far above Washington and its grubby spoils system. Yet they continue to operate a system of "legacy preferences"—affirmative action for the children of alumni.

5   These preferences are surprisingly widespread. In most Ivy League institutions, "legacies" make up between 10% and 15% of every freshman class. At Notre Dame they make up 23%. They are also common in good public universities such as the University of Virginia. Legatees are two to four times more likely to be admitted to the best universities than non-legatees.

---

*President George W. Bush

America's universities are probably the most politically correct places on the planet. So what are they doing pandering to the (overwhelmingly white) children of the overclass? University administrators offer two justifications. The first may be crudely characterised as fund-raising. Universities are always asking their alumni for a helping hand and for money. The least the alumni can expect in return is that the universities will take a careful look at their college-age offspring.

But is it reasonable for universities to use their admissions systems as tools of alumni management—let alone fund-raising? Universities are supposed to be guardians of objective standards. They are also the recipients of huge amounts of public money as well as private donations. In short, there is no need to.

The second justification is that alumni preferences aren't really preferences at all. William Fitzsimmons, dean of admissions at Harvard College, considers them simply an "ever so slight tip." He admits that 40% of the children of alumni get into Harvard compared with only 11% of ordinary applicants, but says that is mainly because of self-selection. Successful legatees have almost the same test scores as successful non-legatees.

Given the secrecy of the admissions process, this argument is hard to verify. It is worrying that a Department of Education report in 1990 concluded that the average Harvard legacy student is "significantly less qualified" than the average non-legacy student in every area except sports. But even if you give Harvard the benefit of the doubt, the system is still a disgrace. This is a university that has to turn down more than 2,000 high-school valedictorians every year. If you are going to offer a "slight tip" to anyone, why offer it to people who are already on the inside track—who not only come from privileged homes, but also have an insider's knowledge of how the admissions system works?

MAY THE BEST MAN OR WOMAN WIN
Miriam Schulman

According to Miriam Schulman, those who pin their hopes on meritocracy for a "fair" outcome in college admissions might find, on closer examination, that "[e]qual is not necessarily fair." Shulman is Director of Communications at the Markkula Center for Applied Ethics (Santa Clara University). The center publishes Issues in Ethics, *in which this selection first appeared (Fall 1996).*

An old teacher of mine used to claim he graded our papers by throwing them all up the stairs and giving A's to the ones that landed on the top step. Now, there was a case of someone treating every student equally.

Although this example is obvious *reductio ad absurdum*, it serves to demonstrate an important point: Equal is not necessarily fair. That principle is worth reiterating in any discussion of affirmative action in college admissions, which often boils down to a controversy over fairness. While people may argue that everyone should be treated exactly the same, the truth is that we all favor some sorts of criteria. The ethical trick is to make those criteria morally relevant.

If you think this is an easy matter, consider legacy admissions: young people who get into a school because their parents are alums. According to a report from U.C.-Berkeley's Institute for the Study of Social Change issued in 1991, more legacy students were admitted to 10 of the country's most elite institutions than the combined number of all African Americans and Chicanos admitted under affirmative action programs.

Many people defend legacy admissions as acceptable because they help to ensure the financial continuity of the institution, without which no one would be able to enter the university. But such a rationale can be a slippery slope. Indeed, the hypocrisy tweakers had a field day recently when the *Los Angeles Times* reported that several of the U.C. regents who had voted to abolish affirmative action had themselves pulled strings to get relatives, friends, and the children of business associates into UCLA.

Morally Relevant Criteria

5   My point here is not so much to challenge the moral relevance of this particular preference, but to point out that race is only one among many possible attributes we might take into account in admission decisions. If, ultimately, we want to disallow it as a basis for preference, we should be prepared to justify why it is any less worthy than other characteristics we do consider.

One justifiable criterion might be ability: May the best man or woman win. While there may be general agreement on the relevance of this determinant, there is much less agreement on a fair way to measure it. On the surface, it might seem logical that the people with the best grades and scores should get the college slots. Indeed, this argument is at the heart of several cases, such as *Bakke vs. Regents of the University of California*, which have challenged affirmative action in the courts.

Although we might conclude that grades and scores are the most objective criteria we can come up with to assess ability, there are more than a few reasons to question our moral certainty about the justice of this system. First, standards of grading vary enormously from school to school; an A from one might be a C from another. Such variability was behind the creation of standardized tests like the SATs, which were supposed to provide a single measure for students across the country.

But these tests have been accused repeatedly of bias against minorities. In 1990, a national commission sponsored by the Ford Foundation found that the differences in test scores between minority and majority test takers were typically larger than the differences in their grades or job ratings. "We must stop pretending that any single standard test can illuminate equally well the talents and help promote the learning of people from dramatically different backgrounds," their report concluded.

Flutists and Football Players

While academic ability is hard to measure fairly, most people still want to include that factor in college admissions. But it is not, by far, the only characteristic that might be considered. A long-established criterion has been diversity. By this, I don't mean only the relatively new argument that student bodies should reflect the multiethnic society from which they are drawn; I mean the old practice of creating a freshman class that has a much-needed linebacker, a new first flute for the university orchestra, and a high-school senior-class president who may go on to a leadership position in college student government.

10   Athletic prowess, musical talent, and unusual community service have all been defended as morally acceptable considerations for college admissions because they add to the well-roundedness of the student body. If these attributes can be considered relevant to admissions, why not race?

Of course, there is nothing inherently edifying about attending school with people who have different physical attributes. Introducing more redheads into a student population would bring about no discernible benefit. But, in this country, having a different skin color means having a different life experience. Bringing that difference into the mix at our universities can greatly enhance the quality of the dialogue that goes on there.

On the larger stage, our society is enriched by the many different backgrounds and traditions of its members. For example, as a woman, I know I benefit from the increasing numbers of female health practitioners, who have brought women's health issues such as breast cancer to the fore-front of national consciousness. It does not surprise or even anger me that male doctors did not pursue these issues more forcefully—they lie outside men's personal experience—but I do want my experience to be represented.

Similarly, I have to confront the needs and perspectives of other members of my community, which I might ignore, however unwittingly, were they not represented in our universities and in the larger public discussion.

LEGACY ADMISSIONS ARE DEFENSIBLE BECAUSE THE PROCESS CAN'T BE 'FAIR'

Debra Thomas and Terry Shepard

In an article that generated heated reader feedback, Debra Thomas and Terry Shepard defend the practice of legacy admissions. Thomas is a public relations director at Rice University. Shepard is vice president for public affairs at Rice. This selection first appeared in The Chronicle of Higher Education *(March 14, 2003).*

It was inevitable that the U.S. Supreme Court's decision to hear two lawsuits involving affirmative action in admissions at the University of Michigan would prompt discussion of other types of admissions preferences. The policies of most colleges to grant preference to children of alumni—so-called legacies—have suddenly become a hot topic.

Meanwhile, who is discussing issues with far greater impact and importance—like the sorry state of government support for elementary and secondary education? In his book *Savage Inequalities* (Crown, 1991), Jonathan Kozol described the horrors of districts so poor that they could do no more than cover gaping holes in roofs with canvas; schools with no working restrooms; and a classroom consisting of an abandoned swimming pool. That was a decade ago, and, if anything, support for public schools in areas outside prosperous suburbs has deteriorated.

But instead of focusing on that crucial issue, politicians like Senator John Edwards, a Democrat from North Carolina, along with newspapers and magazines like *The Wall Street Journal, The New York Times,* and *Time,* are talking about how legacy admissions should be impermissible. State universities in Georgia and California already have eliminated legacy consideration in the face of such challenges.

Let's clear the smoke screen that obscures the real issues. Simply put, legacy admissions are defensible and, in any event, affect such a tiny portion of the nation's college applicants as to be negligible.

5   That view results from our decades of collective experience at many different kinds of institutions—including a large public university and four highly selective private colleges—and our evaluations, as outside consultants, of the admissions programs of more than 20 other institutions. We have seen firsthand numerous admissions staffs agonize over choosing from an excess of highly qualified applicants.

What we have learned is that objective merit and fairness are attractive concepts with no basis in reality. Admissions decisions cannot be "fair" when there are fewer spots in a class than qualified applicants. Moreover, there exists no single standard of "merit" that can be objectively applied. Rather, admission to any institution that has more qualified applicants than it has spaces is based on an array of attributes that lead an institution to prefer the students it selects.

It may be useful, therefore, to ask: Is there a preference that most people would agree is permissible?

Should a state university give preference to in-state students? We would suggest yes, since the taxes paid by state residents support the institution. If one agrees, then that establishes that preference is permissible for those who financially support the university—especially if their support contributes to a better education for all of the students enrolled.

Alumni support their colleges and universities, public and private alike, in many ways, including financially. In 2001, alumni provided 28 percent of the private donations to higher education, or almost $7 billion. The major donors contribute far more than the cost of their children's education. Thus, having agreed that state universities may give preference to students whose families support them through their tax dollars, should we not agree that institutions also may give preference to those whose families voluntarily support them and all other students as well? (And it is all other students: Since even full tuition at most private institutions pays for only about 60 percent of the cost of an undergraduate education, the only reason any student gets a high-quality education is the generosity of donors.)

10   Moreover, any development professional will testify that a family's financial commitment is likely to grow with additional members' and generations' common affiliation. Witness the multimillion-dollar gifts that the Packard family has given Stanford.

In the most practical terms, honoring alumni commitment is a way to maintain quality. If states fully supported their public universities, they would have at least some justification to consider barring any preference for the children of alumni or, indeed, anyone from out of state. However, many "state" universities receive far less than half the support they need from their state—and the portion is declining. With inadequate government support, public universities face a choice: Allow the quality of education to drop to the level of support; raise tuition to levels that the public would reject; or cultivate supporters among their alumni. Which makes the most sense?

Because the tuition at private institutions, too, covers only a portion of the cost of instruction, they face a similar choice: Drop the quality of education to the level that net tuition income can support; virtually double tuition and cut back on financial aid; or cultivate alumni support. Again, which makes the most sense for all of the students of an institution?

Apart from those logical rationales, legacy preference is simply not the major issue that the news media, through dominant play and dire tone, suggest. Let's review a few facts:

- Legacy preference is a nonissue for the vast majority of college applicants. At no more than 100 of the nation's 3,500 colleges and universities are admissions competitive enough for such a status to matter. At that handful of institutions, legacies are only a small fraction of the applicants. And only a portion of those legacy applicants are admitted. Many of those admitted are top students who would have been accepted in any event. (For example, *The New York Times* reported in February that the average SAT of 30 legacies in the current freshman class at Middlebury College was 1389—33 points higher than that of the class as a whole.) Thus, the legacy issue involves a fraction of a portion of a fraction of applicants at 3 percent of all institutions.

- Legacy status does not guarantee admission. Many legacies are turned down. There is one universally relevant standard for admission: Does the student have the ability to complete the course of study at the institution? A college would be foolish to admit a legacy who could not meet that standard, for the student would fail and the family would be alienated.

- Upward mobility does not depend on admission to the handful of institutions where admission is competitive enough for legacy status to matter. On the contrary, a study of Fortune 500 CEO's showed a vast array of alma maters— liberal-arts colleges and nonflagship state universities greatly outnumbering Ivy League institutions or big-name publics. One can get a top education, and a great start in life, at hundreds of institutions. Alas, that seemed better understood when high-school counselors, a good education, and a good fit—not status and magazine rankings—guided college decisions.

- Legacy preference will increasingly include minority students. It was only one generation ago that most colleges began enrolling and graduating significant numbers of minority students. In coming years, those graduates' children will increasingly show up as second-generation applicants.

Those who call for admissions to be based only on "merit" have yet to provide a rational definition. Which shows more merit—an A in an easy course or a B in a much tougher course? Does a brilliant student who suffers from test anxiety have less merit than a student with a natural aptitude for multiple-choice questions? Besides grades and test scores, are other attributes nonmeritorious? A university with a school of music lacks a bassoon in its student orchestra. Who has more merit for admission: a talented bassoonist or a nonmusician with slightly higher grades and test scores?

We have been led to believe that merit can be defined and measured, and that prospective students can be ranked by it. All an institution must do is start at the top of such a list and work its way down. But can the value and potential of human beings be strictly ranked? Could any of us rank our friends by merit? Yes, our best friends might be fairly easy to name; likewise, admissions offices have little trouble identifying the students they most desire. But how would we distinguish between our No. 7 friend and our No. 8 friend? How do we compare their different kinds of merit—one is more thoughtful, another has a better sense of humor, a third is particularly generous, a fourth a great conversationalist? And how could one possibly, as some expect of an admissions office, distinguish between the 649th and 650th friends, or the 5,296th and 5,297th?

15   Colleges and universities have done themselves a disservice by trying to portray their admissions decisions as "fair." Those decisions, like most other conclusions about the potential of human beings, involve experience, judgment, perception, and intuition. In other words, they are an art. And "fair" has no meaning in art.

We should strive to describe our admissions processes as what they are: not fair, but rational. Rational because they seek a rounded class of students who can learn from each other. Rational because they contribute to our institutions' specific and clearly stated goals and missions. Rational because they exercise the First Amendment rights that Justice Felix Frankfurter referred to as the "four essential freedoms" of a university to determine for itself, on academic grounds, who may teach, what may be taught, how it shall be taught, and who may be admitted to study.

Let us be rational in another way. Let us not allow the negligible matter of legacies to obscure issues that have vastly greater impact on vastly greater numbers of students. Let's start with the need for government support of primary and secondary public education, especially in poor school districts. Let's see some headlines about preparing all of America's children for access to, and success in, college.

TIME TO BURY THE LEGACY

Robert DeKoven

The following article opposing legacy admissions first appeared in the San Diego Union-Tribune *on February 12, 2003. Robert DeKoven teaches at California Western School of Law.*

As the Supreme Court considers admissions standards in college admissions, perhaps the court should review how college admissions treat not just the disadvantaged, but also the advantaged, a group that public and private college officials have long recruited and favored over the less affluent.

Parents and students are not aware that many students on college campuses today are not there based entirely upon merit, but because a parent attended the university, or the family contributed money in the past or made a pledge to the school.

Private universities depend upon tuition and endowment income. So it's no secret that, in achieving a "diverse" student body, some schools accept students whose entering credentials are less than glowing.

One practice that benefits the affluent is preferring legacies, or children of alumni, almost always contributors.

5   At Notre Dame, for example, 57 percent of students admitted were children of alumni, with 23 percent of these students actually enrolled at the university.

Overall, 10 percent to 15 percent of students at many Ivy League schools are children of graduates and are also admitted in much higher rates than other students. It's not as if the legacies have to meet the same standards as other prospective students.

In 1964, George W. Bush applied to Yale University with a C average from high school and a 566 SAT verbal score. However, George W. was a legacy—a third-generation legacy—and Yale University accepted him and rejected others with far more impressive credentials.

Private schools defend the legacy practice because it builds school loyalty and generates alumni contributions. Prospective students have an incentive to apply and attend, knowing that their kids will have an edge when they apply.

Public colleges, which receive most of their support from public tax dollars, also prefer legacies. According to *The Badger Herald,* while a "minor" factor, the University of Wisconsin considers "being the child of an alumni" a "plus factor," among many indicators.

10   But other elite public schools, such as the University of Virginia and University of Pennsylvania, also prefer legacies. Penn admitted 41 percent of legacies and enrolled 14 percent of them.*

Giving an edge based upon being a legacy is, in reality, an advantage based largely upon race. Keep in mind that many private universities routinely discriminated against persons of color (and women) in admissions. Even public universities engaged in segregation until 1954.

The reality is that getting that playing field even for persons of color and women wasn't even started until passage of federal laws in the 1960s and 1970s denying funds (and tax-exempt status) to schools engaged in race or gender bias.

Even so, under-represented minorities, in addition to other obstacles, have had to contend with the legacy factor as they tried to get admitted into schools based upon merit, while others, like George W., have had lesser credentials, but benefited from the legacy factor.

Legacies are a form of positive bias based upon one's lineage. It's bad when done privately, but antithetical to the Constitution and our notions of fairness when the state gives credit for being born to affluent parents. It's a mark of achievement to overcome poverty and adversity, it's luck of the gene pool to be the son of George H.W. and Barbara Bush.

Union-Tribune Editors: the University of Pennsylvania is [not] a public institution. In fact, it is private, although it is chartered by the state of Pennsylvania and the governor is president of the Board of Trustees. [February 14, 2003.]

15   For a state university to give weight for having been born into a home of college-educated folks violates the Equal Protection Clause of the Constitution. Another practice that is even more controversial is the practice of preferring students whose parents are major donors to the university or who have made a pledge.

The practice received attention in "The Sopranos," where Tony Soprano, whose trade is extortion, discovered that he could really improve his daughter's chances of getting admitted to a prestigious school if he simply pledged money for a building fund. Though he didn't like the shakedown, he realized it was a cost of doing business, and he did it.

Data about this practice are difficult to get, especially from private colleges, which can claim student privacy to defeat access to data to show how pledges and admissions correlate.

One case from Illinois, involving the admission of 83 entering medical students in the 1970s, showed that 64 had pledges made in their behalf, totaling $2 million. Apparently the medical school seats went from between $3,000 to $100,000, presumably based upon the applicant's entering credentials.

How widespread the practice continues to be is difficult to know. It's not like university admissions files are audited to see that the data that schools present in their reports to college guides is truly accurate.

20   If we learned anything from last summer's episode involving admissions officers at one Ivy League school getting caught tampering with the computer files of students at another Ivy League school, some schools are not above unethical behavior and espionage.

California law prohibits the use of race as a factor in admissions for public colleges. But the law should extend to legacies and admissions based on whether the applicant or his or her family has donated or pledged funds to secure admission.

Affirmative action for the affluent is a practice that shouldn't need a Supreme Court edict to end this inequality.

The History of Legacy Admissions

Cameron Howell and Sarah E. Turner

You may be surprised to learn that the history of legacy admissions in America is tied to an unpleasant history of race and ethnicity. The brief overview that follows first appeared in Research in Higher Education (June 2004). Cameron Howell wrote his doctoral dissertation on legacy admissions, with a focus on that practice at the University of Virginia. Sarah Turner works at the National Bureau of Economic Research, also at the University of Virginia. (Note: For the sake of brevity, the authors' list of references has been deleted.)

leg_a_cy (lĕg'E-sē) *n., pl.* **–cies.** 1. Money or property bequeathed to someone by will. 2. Something handed on from those who have come before. [< Lat. *legare*, to bequeath as a legacy.]

—*American Heritage Dictionary,* Second College Edition

In the world of college and university admissions, the word "legacy" has a peculiar definition that cannot be found in most standard dictionaries. It means "the son or daughter of an alumnus or alumna," but the practical application of the word, in the admissions community, reveals how it has been derived from its original meaning of inheritance. Graduates of many of America's most elite institutions of higher education bequeath to their sons and daughters a sizable advantage in the admissions process. Known as legacies, these children are admitted at twice the rate of other applicants at some universities (Bowen and Bok, 1998; Lamb, 1993), and average SAT scores for legacies are, in some cases, lower than the average scores of their peers (U.S. Department of Education's Office for Civil Rights, 1990). On the surface, these facts raise serious questions for the admissions enterprise, which heralds the ideals of merit and equity.

• • •

Institutions of higher education have promoted intergenerational attachments since the earliest days of Harvard College. Henry Adams (1907), who graduated from Harvard in 1858, described the familial ties among Harvard alumni in his autobiography:

> For generation after generation, Adamses and Brookses and Boylstons and Gorhams had gone to Harvard College, and although none of them, as far as known, had ever done any good there, or thought himself the better for it, custom, social ties, convenience, and, above all, economy, kept each generation in the track. (1907, p. 55)

In the era before increased competition in college admissions, "all alumni children who could demonstrate a minimum level of ability were admitted" to U.S. institutions of higher education (Duffy and Goldberg, 1998, p. 47). This policy attracted no attention until it was threatened. The threat materialized early in the twentieth century, when a series of dynamics increased the quantity and quality of applicants vying for admission to elite colleges. Among these applicants were a growing number of highly qualified Jewish students. In the 1920s, Ivy League institutions such as Harvard, Yale, and Princeton formalized their admissions policies that favored children of alumni in order to appease graduate fathers and in order to limit the number of Jewish matriculants (Lamb, 1993; Synnott, 1979).

Later in the twentieth century, a boom in the number of college-age students coincided with improved access to institutions of higher education. Increasingly, students began to apply to and attend colleges and universities outside of their home states (Hoxby, 2002). Geographic integration of selective institutions began in earnest after World War II, when a combination of factors including reduced transportation costs and increased reliance on standardized testing enabled the recruitment of highly talented students from across the nation. Then, beginning in the late 1960s, many institutions entered the era of coeducation, admitting women to undergraduate degree programs. (Coeducation at selective institutions had the dual effects of increasing the number of qualified applicants while also increasing the size of the legacy pool.) During the same decade, colleges and universities responded to the Civil Rights movement by actively seeking to increase minority enrollment. In some Southern states, this era brought an end to segregation in higher education. These changes in the gender, race, and geographic representation of applicants increased the overall level of competition for admission to these institutions, thereby infringing on the traditional advantages of legacy applicants while also making legacy preferences more valuable to their potential recipients. Alumni fathers feared that more and better applicants would surely displace their children in the admissions process.

These fears became especially frenzied at Yale University, when R. Inslee Clark was named the Dean of Admissions in 1965 (Lemann, 1999). The share of alumni sons admitted to the university plummeted from 20% to 12% in Clark's first year as dean, and "open warfare" commenced (p. 149). "An apocrypha of Clark horror stories" circulated among the alumni, who felt insulted and threatened (p. 150). William F. Buckley Jr. lobbied for a position on the Yale Corporation, the university's overseeing board, on the premise that Yale's favoritism of alumni sons should be restored. Kingman Brewster Jr., the President of Yale, managed to ease tensions among the alumni after he published an apologetic piece in the university's alumni magazine and leaked an internal letter stating that "[t]he only preference by inheritance which seems to deserve recognition is the Yale son" (p. 151).

5   To this day, a preference by inheritance persists at Yale and other selective colleges. Three national surveys—conducted by the American Association of Collegiate Registrars and Admissions Officers, American College Testing, the College Board, Educational Testing Service, and the National Association of College Admission Counselors—track the use of legacy policies among college and universities across time (Breland et al., 1995). The survey results show that both public and private institutions of higher education commonly provide some preference for children of alumni.

The prevalence of legacy admissions preferences at selective colleges and universities is also evident in the share of legacies that comprise some undergraduate student bodies. At Notre Dame, 23% of enrolled students are children of alumni (Golden, 2003). The percentage of legacies among enrolled students reaches 14% at the University of Pennsylvania, 13% at Harvard, 11% at Princeton, and 11% at the University of Virginia. Thus, at many institutions, the share of legacies enrolled is far from trivial and often exceeds the percentage of black students within the student body.

GETTING IN: THE SOCIAL LOGIC OF IVY LEAGUE ADMISSIONS

Malcolm Gladwell

The following selection is excerpted from the final section of a review of Jerome Karabel's The Chosen: The Hidden History of Exclusion at Harvard, Yale, and Princeton *(2005), which first appeared in* The New Yorker *on October 10, 2005. Malcolm Gladwell, a staff writer at* The New Yorker, *earned rave reviews for* The Tipping Point *(2000), an exploration of how ideas and products "tip" from relative obscurity to becoming cultural phenomena. He is the author most recently of* Blink *(2005), an exploration of instinct-based decision making.*

I once had a conversation with someone who worked for an advertising agency that represented one of the big luxury automobile brands. He said that he was worried that his client's new lower-priced line was being bought disproportionately by black women. He insisted that he did not mean this in a racist way. It was just a fact, he said. Black women would destroy the brand's cachet. It was his job to protect his client from the attentions of the socially undesirable.

This is, in no small part, what Ivy League admissions directors do. They are in the luxury-brand-management business, and [Jerome Karabel's] *The Chosen*, in the end, is a testament to just how well the brand managers in Cambridge, New Haven, and Princeton have done their job in the past seventy-five years. In the nineteen twenties, when Harvard tried to figure out how many Jews they had on campus, the admissions office scoured student records and assigned each suspected Jew the designation j1 (for someone who was "conclusively Jewish"), j2 (where the "preponderance of evidence" pointed to Jewishness), or j3 (where Jewishness was a "possibility"). In the branding world, this is called customer segmentation. In the Second World War, as Yale faced plummeting enrollment and revenues, it continued to turn down qualified Jewish applicants. As Karabel writes, "In the language of sociology, Yale judged its symbolic capital to be even more precious than its economic capital." No good brand manager would sacrifice reputation for short-term gain. The admissions directors at Harvard have always, similarly, been diligent about rewarding the children of graduates, or, as they are quaintly called, "legacies." In the 1985-92 period, for instance, Harvard admitted children of alumni at a rate more than twice that of non-athlete, non-legacy applicants, despite the fact that, on virtually every one of the school's magical ratings scales, legacies significantly lagged behind their peers. Karabel calls the practice "unmeritocratic at best and profoundly corrupt at worst," but rewarding customer loyalty is what luxury brands do. Harvard wants good graduates, and part of their definition of a good graduate is someone who is a generous and loyal alumnus. And if you want generous and loyal alumni you have to reward them. Aren't the tremendous resources provided to Harvard by its alumni part of the reason so many people want to go to Harvard in the first place? The endless battle over admissions in the United States proceeds on the assumption that some great moral principle is at stake in the matter of whom schools like Harvard choose to let in—that those who are denied admission by the whims of the admissions office have somehow been harmed. If you are sick and a hospital shuts its doors to you, you are harmed. But a selective school is not a hospital, and those it turns away are not sick. Elite schools, like any luxury brand, are an aesthetic experience—an exquisitely constructed fantasy of what it means to belong to an elite—and they have always been mindful of what must be done to maintain that experience.

SO YOUR DAD WENT TO HARVARD
Mark Megalli

In the following selection, Mark Megalli examines the pro-white racial bias inherent in legacy admissions. He argues that conservatives who criticize affirmative action, an admissions practice favoring candidates of color, should be willing in the name of consistency to criticize legacy programs. Both programs "subvert meritocracy," he claims. This article first appeared in the Journal of Blacks in Higher Education (Spring, 1995).

Legacy preference is limited neither to the Ivy League nor to the elite northeastern higher education establishment. According to data provided by The College Board, well over 600 universities and colleges across the nation use or accept the "common application form" (CAF) in the admissions process. The CAF, meant to cut down on the sheer volume of paperwork that must be completed by applicants to several schools, asks the "legacy question" and thus ensures that legacy preference at least will be made possible, if not actually put into practice, at the hundreds of schools that use the form. Colleges that use the form, besides Harvard, include Wesleyan, Johns Hopkins, Williams, New York University, Duke, Swarthmore, Rice, and Vassar. Of course, many schools, including Yale, Princeton, Stanford, and Amherst, that do not use the CAF in the application process still ask on their own forms where an applicant's parents were educated.

The U.S. Department of Education's Office for Civil Rights (OCR) report on Harvard found that preference for legacies disproportionately helps white applicants—hardly shocking, because 96 percent of all living Ivy League alumni are white. However, the commission did not charge Harvard with violating Title VI of the Civil Rights Act of 1964, which states in part, "No person in the United States shall on the ground of race, color, or national origin be excluded from participation in, be denied the benefits of, or be otherwise subjected to discrimination under any program to which this part applies." Instead, OCR held that Harvard's preferences for children of alumni is a "legitimate institutional goal" necessary to "1) encourage alumni volunteer services; 2) encourage alumni financial contributions; and, 3) maintain community relations."

At Many of the Nation's Most Prestigious Universities, Legacy Applicants Are Accepted Far More Frequently Than Applicants in General

Institution	% of All Applicants Accepted	% of Legacy Applicants Accepted
Harvard	16%	35%
Yale	22	45
Princeton	15	43
Dartmouth	27	57
Columbia	32	51
Univ. of Penn.	40	66
Cornell	37	43
MIT	30	55

Sources: The Washington Monthly, *June 1991, p. 10; Lamb, pp. 503 and 505;* Daily Princetonian, *November 19, 1993; and JBHE telephone interviews conducted in February 1994 and April 1995.*

Critics have faulted OCR for applying a rational basis test rather than a disparate impact analysis in exculpating Harvard from charges of discrimination against its minority applicants. In other words, some say OCR should have found the legacy policy at Harvard to be discriminatory against minorities because the actual effect is that minorities are disproportionately disadvantaged by such a policy. Instead

OCR dismissed such charges due to a lack of de jure discrimination. Simply put, OCR bought Harvard's "economics" argument.

But many do not accept the idea that in order to maintain their financial strength, elite universities must open the floodgates to the often less-qualified children of alumni. According to the OCR report, alumni in 1989 gave $36 million to the Harvard College Fund, "much of which is used to provide financial aid and scholarship to needy students." Let us conservatively assume "much" to mean "all," and let us further consider that based on the fact that there were 63,088 living Harvard College alumni that year, the average alumni contribution to the Harvard College Fund was $571. If legacies were admitted at the rate of nonlegacies, as estimated above, there would be about 200 fewer accepted legacy applicants in a given year. Assuming the alumni parents of every one of these rejected candidates for admission never gave another penny to Harvard, the total lost by the institution per year would be expected to amount to $114,200 based on the average $571 alumni contribution. Even under these extremely conservative conditions, this sum is indeed paltry considering the fact that Harvard *earns* an equivalent sum on its $6.2 billion endowment in a little over two hours.* The calculation does not include added revenue from donations given by the families of nonlegacy students who would end up taking the places of the 200 rejected legacies in this scenario. So we see that, even by this incredibly conservative estimate, the "financial necessity" argument holds little water.

Alumni Children Have Lower SAT Scores

Mean Scores of Admitted Students at Harvard University on Selected Admissions Criteria 1983 to 1992

	Children of Alumni	Nonalumni/Nonathlete
SAT math	695.0	717.7
SAT verbal	674.1	686.7
Athletic rating	3.08	3.11
Academic rating	2.40	2.19
Extracurricular rating	2.52	2.43
Personal rating	2.53	2.44
Teacher rating	2.32	2.08
Counselor rating	2.34	2.14
Alumni rating	2.25	2.06
Class rank	92.47	96.73

Note: SAT scores range from 200 to 800. For other ratings, lower numbers indicate superior performance. Class rank ranges from 0 (worst) to 100 (best).

5   Furthermore, one might wonder why applicants of wealthy families in general are not given preference based on the financial-needs argument. Certainly Harvard

---

*Assuming an 8 percent annual return on Harvard's endowment, the university earns $496 million per year or $56,621 per hour. [Editors: As of 2005, Harvard's endowment was $25.5 billion.]

would be able to raise more money if its entire student body consisted of million-aires, yet few would give credence to a policy that based admission primarily on family wealth. The practice of legacy preferences amounts to a toned-down version of this absurd scenario.

Conservatives who are quick to point out the unfairness of preferential admissions for racial minorities on the grounds that these preferences "subvert meritocracy" would do well to reexamine their views on the legacy systems currently in place at the nation's leading universities. In addition to the racial impact, the legacy preferential system perpetuates elitism by conferring considerable advantage upon privileged white children and, as a result, disfavoring blacks and others whose parents were less likely to have gone to college.

Preserve Universities' Right to Shape Student Community

USA Today

USA Today's editorial page editors argue against interfering in a university's admissions policies. The editors hold that universities should be free to shape their freshman class as they see fit—a prerogative that extends to legacy admissions. This editorial ran on January 26, 2004, in tandem with an editorial opposing legacy admissions by Senator John Edwards, the Democratic candidate for Vice President in 2004.

Each year, Dickinson College admits about half of the students who apply to the Pennsylvania liberal arts school. But if applicants' parents or siblings graduated from Dickinson, their chance of admission shoots up to 75%. Overall, 12% of Dickinson's incoming freshmen have family connections that give them a leg up over other applicants that has nothing to do with grades or SAT scores.

Universities long have favored legacy admissions as a way to boost support from alumni, who are more likely to stay active and make donations if their children are enrolled. But now the practice is coming under fire. Critics claim legacy preference programs are most likely to give affluent white students a boost. That's particularly unfair, they say, now that minorities increasingly are being excluded from admission preference plans because some colleges are dropping their affirmative action programs.

Sen. John Edwards of North Carolina, who is seeking the Democratic presidential nomination, says legacies undermine the principle that college admissions should be based on a student's academic accomplishments. Sen. Ted Kennedy, D-Mass., himself a Harvard legacy, is pushing legislation that would require colleges to disclose how many legacy students they accept.

Critics rightly point out that legacy applicants get at least a degree of special treatment that isn't based on academics. But they aren't unique. To attract students with a range of talents and interests, colleges commonly show preferences for attributes that go beyond academics. Hence, special provisions are made to attract gifted athletes, ensure broad geographic diversity or even maintain a renowned a capella group. While any preference program can be taken too far, such admissions acknowledge that a vibrant college is more than the sum of students' grades and standardized test scores.

5   By pressuring colleges to drop legacy admissions, the federal government would interfere with the right of universities to manage their own affairs as long as they aren't violating anti-discrimination laws.

Some universities are ending legacy admissions on their own. Texas A&M stopped the practice last month in the face of criticism that it kept legacy preferences even after dropping affirmative action.

Pressuring all universities to follow Texas A&M's example, however, sends the federal government down a slippery slope. Using the same logic, the government could question colleges' freedom to:

- Reflect their unique character. The University of Notre Dame's freshman class is 85% Roman Catholic. Federal attempts to dictate admissions policies could infringe on a college's ability to shape its student body.

- Control their financing. Many colleges rely on private giving, often from alumni. At Dickinson, alumni provide 25% of its budget, allowing the school to keep tuition to $28,380 and offer aid to families that can't afford the cost. College officials say eliminating legacy admissions would reduce donations and drive up tuition.

Donations aren't the sole reason colleges have legacy policies. Many say students of alumni fortify school traditions and have more active parents. They also say legacy students have stronger academic records on average than other students admitted.

Critics say admissions should be based solely on merit. But that argument assumes an objective standard can assess merit across the nation's wide range of college-bound students. In the subjective world of admissions, pure merit does not exist. Nor should it.

10   Choosing a diverse student body that contributes to a stimulating campus environment is a freedom worth preserving.

ADMISSIONS CONFIDENTIAL: AN INSIDER'S ACCOUNT OF THE ELITE COLLEGE SELECTION PROCESS

Rachel Toor

Rachel Toor spent three years as an admissions officer at Duke University. In this passage, excerpted from her book Admissions Confidential: An Insider's Account of the Elite College Selection Process *(2001), she describes the manner in which children of Duke alumni and of major donors to the university ("development" applicants) are treated during the stages (rounds) of the admission process. During this process, admissions officers assign applicants numerical points for their scores in such areas as GPA, College Board tests, and AP classes. The Admissions Office sets threshold scores. Anyone exceeding the threshold is automatically admitted; anyone below the threshold is automatically denied admission—unless special numerical codes assigned for other, non-academic qualifications are added to the score during subsequent rounds of the admissions process.*

Then there was the preparation for alum and development rounds. . . . The director [of admissions] never wanted to admit these kids and had to fight to be able to keep them out. He usually lost. He wanted to make sure that the admissions officer gave him as much ammunition as possible to use against them. He'd make sure we looked for midterm grades and new testing. He was not much interested in our personal opinions of the applicant and didn't give an opportunity to express them. That rarely stopped us.

Alum and development rounds consisted of the director, the head of the university's development [fundraising] office, and the Alumni liaison to admissions. Alumni were coded as either A or B. An A meant that they had been active and involved with the school since graduation; often this meant that they had a history of consistent giving, but also rewarded were the good soldiers who showed up for reunions and were involved in their local alumni clubs. The alum B category got less of a boost—it simply meant that these people kept their records and whereabouts up-to-date with the alumni office. And then there were the alum Xs. The alumni office had lost track of them, so even if a kid had written on her application that her parent had gone to Duke, it didn't help. Development codes were high, for those who had not only the potential to give loads of money, but who had a history of giving it to Duke; medium, those who also had loads of money, had never given it to Duke but had given to similar kinds of places; and low, which could mean that the family was rich but not philanthropic, or that someone somewhere (usually fairly high up, could be a trustee, could be the basketball coach) had some kind of personal interest in the application. These kids were always discussed, but the director often triumphed in keeping them out.

Alum and development rounds were usually an all-day affair. We were allowed to sit in and speak only if spoken to. It was hard to remain silent and sometimes I failed. But the process gave a good overview of long-term institutional goals and the directions of the university, a big picture focus that we the foot soldiers in admissions were rarely privy to. Here we would learn about plans for a new Center for Jewish Life, a Genomics Institute, an addition to the gym. These planning goals were being made possible by large gifts, and although there was never a quid pro quo for donors with children applying, the development office wanted to be sure that everything possible was done for them. So they arranged special tours and VIP interviews for these applicants (didn't help them, but it made them feel special), and then they came into rounds to plead their case.

The kids who went to these special rounds had already been denied, either as auto denies [automatic denials, based on numerical codes corresponding to applicants' academic qualifications] or in committee. They were, without a doubt, the weakest portion of our applicant pool. Sitting in on the rounds could be highly amusing—the director of development was a smart, very funny man. It could also be tense. The director had to reserve a number of places in the class for these kids, places that could easily have been filled by regular kids whom we then had to deny in rounds. Our target numbers for our regions were deflated; even though I was only able to admit forty kids from Massachusetts, once you took into account the athletes and the alum and development admits, the final number would be much greater.

5 　 Most admissions officers hated to see these kids get in. I know I did. Occasionally you'd find a kid you liked whom you knew wasn't going to make it on her own. Those you hoped might be coded [provided additional points for non-academic reasons]. That happened rarely. More often they were arrogant, entitled, or just plain not smart enough for you to want to have them admitted and take a place from a more deserving kid. The biggest problem with admitting so many of these truly mediocre kids—they made the BWRK's [bright, well-rounded kids] look like fascinating geniuses—was that when they were admitted they usually matriculated. Though the top tier of our applicant pool generally turned us down for other schools, the alum and development kids were lucky to get in and came. The Duke student body was disproportionately heavy with them.

For Analysis Assignment #1 only:

MAKING ETHICAL DECISIONS
Gerald F. Cavanagh

Gerald Cavanagh is professor of management, associate dean, and director of Graduate Programs in the University of Detroit's College of Business Administration. Cavanagh holds degrees in engineering, philosophy, theology, and management. He was ordained as a Jesuit priest in 1964. This selection appeared originally in his book American Business Values *(1990).*

The basic method of making ethical judgments involves just three steps: (1) gathering relevant factual information, (2) determining the moral norm that is most applicable, and (3) making the ethical judgment on the rightness or wrongness of the act or policy.

　 Nevertheless, ethical judgments are not always easy to make. The facts of the case are often not clear-cut, and the ethical criteria or principles to be used are not always agreed on, even by the experts themselves.

• • •

Ethical Norms for . . . [Decision Making]

Ethical criteria and ethical models have been the subject of much reflection over the centuries. Of all ethical theories, utilitarianism is the one businesspeople feel most at home with. This is not surprising, as the theory traces its origins to Adam Smith, the father of modern economics. The main proponents of utilitarianism, however, were Jeremy Bentham and John Stuart Mill, both of whom helped to formulate the theory more precisely. Utilitarianism evaluates actions in terms of their consequences. In any given situation, the one action which would result in the greatest net gain for all concerned parties is considered to be the right, or morally obligatory, action. The theory of rights focuses on the entitlements of individual persons. Immanuel Kant (personal rights) and John Locke (property rights) were the first to fully develop the theory of rights. The theory of justice has a longer tradition, going back to Plato and Aristotle in the fourth century B.C. . . .

The Norm of Utilitarianism

Utilitarianism judges that an action is right if it produces the greatest utility, "the greatest good for the greatest number." The decision process is very much like a cost-benefit analysis applied to all parties who would be touched by the decision. That action is right which produces the greatest net benefit when all the costs and benefits to all the affected parties are taken into account. Although it would be convenient if these costs and benefits could be measured in some comparable unit, this is rarely possible. Many important values (e.g., human life and liberty) cannot be quantified. Thus, the best that can be done is to enumerate the effects and the magnitude of their costs and benefits as clearly and accurately as possible.

5   The utilitarian principle says that the right action is that which produces the greatest net benefit over any other possible action. This does not mean that the right action produces the greatest good for the person performing the action. Rather, it is the action that produces the greatest net good for all those who are affected by the action. Utilitarianism can handle some ethical cases quite well, especially those that are complex and affect many parties. Although the model and the methodology are clear in theory, carrying out the calculations is often difficult. Taking into account so many affected parties, along with the extent to which the action touches them, can be a tallying nightmare.

Hence several shortcuts have been proposed that can reduce the complexity of utilitarian calculations. Each shortcut involves a sacrifice of accuracy for ease of calculation. Among these shortcuts are (1) adherence to a simplified rule (e.g., the Golden Rule, "Do unto others as you would have them do unto you"); (2) calculation of costs and benefits in dollar terms for ease of comparison; (3) restriction of consideration to those directly affected by the action, putting aside indirect effects. In using these shortcuts, an individual should be aware that they result in simplification and that some interests may not be sufficiently taken into consideration.

In the popular mind, the term *utilitarianism* sometimes suggests selfishness and exploitation. For our purposes, the term should be considered not to have these connotations. However, a noteworthy weakness of utilitarianism as an ethical norm is that it can advocate, for example, abridging an individual's right to a job or even life for the sake of the greater good of a larger number of people. . . . One additional caution in using utilitarian rules is in order: It is considered unethical to opt for narrower benefits (e.g., personal goals, career, or money) at the expense of the good of a larger number, such as a nation or a society. Utilitarian norms emphasize the good of the group; it is a large-scale ethical model. As a result, an individual and what is due that individual may be overlooked. The theory of rights has been developed to emphasize the individual and the standing of that individual with peers and within society.

The Norm of Individual Rights

A right is a person's entitlement to something. Rights may flow from the legal system, such as our constitutional rights of freedom of conscience or freedom of speech. The U.S. Bill of Rights and the United Nations Universal Declaration of Human Rights are examples of documents that spell out individual rights in detail. Legal rights, as well as others which may not be written into law, stem from the human dignity of persons. Moral rights have these characteristics: (1) They enable individuals to pursue their own interests, and (2) they impose correlative prohibitions or requirements on others.

Hence, every right has a corresponding duty. My right to freedom of conscience is supported by the prohibition of other individuals from unnecessarily limiting that freedom of conscience. From another perspective, my right to be paid for my work corresponds to a duty of mine to perform "a fair day's work for a fair day's pay." In the latter case, both the right and duty stem from the right to private property, which is a traditional pillar of American life and law. However, the right to private property is not absolute. A factory owner may be forced by law, as well as by morality, to spend money on pollution control or safety equipment. . . .

10   People also have the right not to be lied to or deceived, especially on matters which they have a right to know about. A supervisor has the duty to be truthful in giving feedback on work performance even if it is difficult for the supervisor to do so. Each of us has the right not to be lied to by salespeople or advertisements. Perjury under oath is a serious crime; lying on matters where another has a right to accurate information is also seriously unethical. Truthfulness and honesty are basic ethical norms.

• • •

The Norm of Justice

Justice requires all persons, and thus managers too, to be guided by fairness, equity, and impartiality. Justice calls for evenhanded treatment of groups and individuals (1) in the distribution of the benefits and burdens of society, (2) in the administration of laws and regulations, and (3) in the imposition of sanctions and the rewarding of compensation for wrongs suffered. An action or policy is just if it is comparable to the treatment accorded to others.

Standards of justice are generally considered to be more important than the utilitarian consideration of consequences. If a society is unjust to a minority group (e.g., apartheid treatment of blacks in South Africa), we generally consider that society to be unjust and we condemn it, even if the results of the injustices bring about greater economic productivity. On the other hand, we seem willing to trade off some equity if the results will bring about greater benefits for all. For example, income and wealth differences are justified only if they bring greater benefits for all.

Standards of justice are not as often in conflict with individual rights as are utilitarian norms. This is not surprising, since justice is largely based on the moral rights of individuals. The moral right to be treated as a free and equal person, for example, undergirds the notion that benefits and burdens should be distributed equitably. . . .

CHAPTER 1

Chatwin: From *In Patagonia* by Bruce Chatwin. Reprinted with permission of Simon & Schuster Adult Publishing Group, Inc. Copyright © 1977 by Bruce Chatwin.

Feldman: "The (Un)Acceptability of Betrayal: A Study of College Students' Evaluations of Sexual Betrayal by a Romantic Partner and Betrayal of a Friend's Confidence" by S. Shirley Feldman, et al. Fig. 1, page 511, *Journal of Youth and Adolescence*, 2000, 29:4, pages 498–523. Reprinted by permission of Plenum Publishing.

Goodwin: From *Team of Rivals: The Political Genius of Abraham Lincoln* by Doris Kearns Goodwin. Reprinted with the permission of Simon & Schuster Adult Publishing Group. Copyright © 2005 by Blithedale Productions, Inc. All rights reserved.

Graham: "The Future of Love" by Barbara Graham, *Utne Reader*, January/February 1997, pages 20–23.

CHAPTER 2

Flowers: "With No Boys to Ogle, We Had Time to Learn" by Christine Flowers, *Newsweek*, Oct. 24, 2005, page 26. © 2005 *Newsweek*, Inc. All rights reserved. Reprinted by permission.

Ralston: "Critique of 'We Are Not Created Equal in Every Way' by Joan Ryan" by Eric Ralston. Reprinted by permission.

Ryan: "We Are Not Created Equal in Every Way" by Joan Ryan, *San Francisco Chronicle* (1865–). Copyright 2000 by *San Francisco Chronicle*. Reproduced with permission of *San Francisco Chronicle* in the format Textbook via Copyright Clearance Center.

CHAPTER 3

Bayon: "The Fuel Subsidy We Need" by Ricardo Bayon, *Atlantic Monthly*, January/February 2003, pages 117–118. Ricardo Bayon is currently director of Ecosystem Marketplace (www.ecosystemmarketplace.com). Used by permission of the author.

Boston Globe: "Military Abuse," Editorial, *Boston Globe*, Sept. 28, 2005. Reprinted by permission of *The Boston Globe*.

CHAPTER 4

Kikuchi: "Keeping Volunteerism Voluntary" by Michael Kikuchi. Reprinted by permission.

Landrum: Excerpt from "Call for National Service," from *National Service: Social, Economic, and Military Impacts* by Roger Landrum, Donald J. Eberly, and Michael W. Sherraden. Reprinted by permission of the editors and Roger Landrum, one of the first Peace Corps volunteers and a leader in building the foundation for the National and Community Service Acts of 1990 and 1993.

McCain: "A New Start for National Service" by John McCain and Evan Bayh, *New York Times*, November 6, 2001. Copyright © 2001 The New York Times Co. Reprinted by permission.

Rhem: "Rumsfeld: No Need for Draft; 'Disadvantages Notable'" by Kathleen T. Rhem, *American Forces Information Service*, January 7, 2003. www.dod.gov/news/Jan2003/n01072003_200301074.html.

Chapter 5

Cohen: Excerpt from "Elements of an Effective Layout," from *Advertising* by Dorothy Cohen. © 1988. Reprinted by permission of Pearson Education, Inc., Upper Saddle River, NJ.

Collins: Excerpt from *Sociological Insight: An Introduction to Non-Obvious Sociology* by Randall Collins, 2nd Edition, 1992, page 74.

Marchand: Excerpt from "The Appeal of the Democracy of Goods," from *Advertising the American Dream: Making Way for Modernity 1920–1940* by Roland Marchand. © 1985 The Regents of the University of California. Reprinted by permission.

Maslow: "A Theory of Human Motivation" by Abraham Maslow, *Psychological Review*, 50:4, 1943, pages 370–396.

Peselman: "The Coming Apart of Dorm Society" by Edward Peselman. Reprinted by permission.

Winn: "Television and Addiction," from "Cookies or Heroin?" in *The Plug-In Drug, Revised and Updated 25th Anniversary Edition* by Marie Winn. Copyright © 1977, 1985, 2002 by Marie Winn Miller. Used by permission of Viking Penguin, a division of Penguin Group (USA) Inc.

Chapter 6

Examples: Example introductions and conclusions by Michele Jacques, Travis Knight, Veronica Gonzalez, Tammy Smith, Adam Price, Frances Wageneck. Reprinted by permission.

Moss: "Important Word Meanings in Essay Assignments," from *Improving Student Writing: A Guide for Faculty in All Disciplines* by Andrew Moss and Carol Holder, 1988, University of California, Los Angeles. Reprinted by permission of UCLA Department of History.

Naison: Excerpt from "Scenario for Scandal" by Mark Naison, *Commonweal*, 109:16, 1982. © 1982 Commonweal, reprinted by permission.

CHAPTER 8

Cheever: "Death in War: A Comparative Analysis of John Singer Sargent's *Death in Victory* and Erich Maria Remarque's *All Quiet on the Western Front*." Reprinted by permission.

LaChiusa: "Palm" from http://ah.bfn.org/a/forestL/symbols/index.html. Reprinted by permission of Chuck LaChiusa.

Reid: Pam Reid. "Cemetery Symbolism." *Ancestry Magazine* 18.5 (2000). Copyright © 2000, MyFamily.com, Inc. All rights reserved. Used with permission.

Remarque: *All Quiet On The Western Front* by Erich Maria Remarque. "Im Westen Nichts Neus," copyright 1928/by Ullstein A.G.; Copyright renewed © 1956 by Erich Maria Remarque. "All Quiet On The Western Front", copyright 1929, 1930 by Little, Brown and Company; Copyright renewed © 1957, 1958 by Erich Maria Remarque. All rights reserved.

Sedlak: "Comparative Analysis Assignment." Peter Sedlak. 2006. Used by permission.

Volk: Mary Crawford Volk, Description of "Death and Victory"; "Sargent's Harvard Murals." The Sargent Murals at the Boston Public Library: History, Interpretation, Restoration, 2003.

CHAPTER 9

Cavanagh: "Ethics in Business," from *American Business Values*, 3rd Edition, by Gerald Cavanagh, © 1990. Reprinted by permission of Pearson Education, Inc., Upper Saddle River, NJ.

DeKoven: "Time to Bury the Legacy" by Robert DeKoven, *The San Diego Union-Tribune*, February 12, 2003. Reprinted by permission of the author.

The Economist: "The Curse of Nepotism," from *The Economist*, January 10, 2004. © 2004 The Economist Newspaper Ltd. All rights reserved. Reprinted with permission. Further reproduction prohibited. www.economist.com.

Gladwell: "The Social Logic of Ivy League Admissions" by Malcolm Gladwell, *The New Yorker*, October 10, 2005. Used by permission.

Howell: "The History of Legacy Admissions" by Cameron Howell and Sarah E. Turner, *Research in High Education,* June 2004, with kind permission of Springer Science and Business Media.

Megalli: "So Your Dad Went to Harvard" by Mark Megalli, *Journal of Blacks in Higher Education,* Spring 1995, pages 72–73 and two tables on pages 72, 73. Reprinted by permission of *The Journal of Blacks in Higher Education.*

Schulman: "May the Best Man or Woman Win" by Miriam Schulman, *Issues in Ethics,* Fall 1996. Published by the Markkula Center for Applied Ethics, Santa Clara University.

Thomas: "Legacy Admissions Are Defensible Because the Process Can't Be 'Fair'" by Debra Thomas and Terry Shepard, *The Chronicle of Higher Education,* March 14, 2003. Copyright Debra J. Thomas and Terry Shepard, who have a combined 54 years in higher education administration at such institutions as Bryn Mawr College, the University of Illinois, Stanford University, and Rice University. Used by permission.

Toor: "Admissions Confidential: An Insider's Account of the Elite College Selection Process," excerpt from *Admissions Confidential* by Rachel Toor. Copyright © 2001 by the author and reprinted by permission of St. Martin's Press, LLC.

USA Today: "Preserve Universities' Right to Shape Student Community," Editorial, *USA Today,* January 26, 2004.

PHOTO CREDITS

Page 207: http://www.fancyfeast.com.

Page 208: Courtesy of IKEA.

Page 209: Courtesy of GE.

Page 313: Harvard University Portrait Collection.

Page 316: Buffalo Architecture and History, http://ah.bfn.org.

Page 321: Harvard University Portrait Collection.